High Speed Computer and Algorithm Organization

ACADEMIC PRESS RAPID MANUSCRIPT REPRODUCTION

Proceedings of the symposium on High Speed Computer and Algorithm Organization, held at the University of Illinois, April 13–15, 1977

High Speed Computer and Algorithm Organization

EDITED BY

DAVID J. KUCK
DUNCAN H. LAWRIE
AHMED H. SAMEH

Department of Computer Science
University of Illinois
Urbana, Illinois

ACADEMIC PRESS, INC.   New York   San Francisco   London   1977
A Subsidiary of Harcourt Brace Jovanovich, Publishers

The material was prepared with the support of National Science Foundation Grant No. MCS 76-10823. However, any opinions, findings, conclusions, or recommendations expressed herein are those of the author(s) and do not necessarily reflect the views of NSF.

COPYRIGHT © 1977, BY UNIVERSITY OF ILLINOIS
ALL RIGHTS RESERVED.
NO PART OF THIS PUBLICATION MAY BE REPRODUCED OR TRANSMITTED IN ANY FORM OR BY ANY MEANS, ELECTRONIC OR MECHANICAL, INCLUDING PHOTOCOPY, RECORDING, OR ANY INFORMATION STORAGE AND RETRIEVAL SYSTEM, WITHOUT PERMISSION IN WRITING FROM THE PUBLISHER.

ACADEMIC PRESS, INC.
111 Fifth Avenue, New York, New York 10003

United Kingdom Edition published by
ACADEMIC PRESS, INC. (LONDON) LTD.
24/28 Oval Road, London NW1

Library of Congress Cataloging in Publication Data

Symposium on High Speed Computer and Algorithm
    Organization, University of Illinois, 1977.
    High speed computer and algorithm organization.

        1.   Electronic digital computers—Congresses.
2. Algorithms—Congresses.   I.   Kuck, D. J.
II. Lawrie, Duncan Hamish, Date   III. Sameh, Ahmed.
IV. Title.

QA76.5.S95 1977   001.64'4   77-14236
ISBN 0-12-427750-0

PRINTED IN THE UNITED STATES OF AMERICA

Contents

Contributors   viii
Preface   xi

I. COMPUTER SYSTEM DESIGN AND THEORY   1

1. It's Really Not as Much Fun Building a Supercomputer as It Is Simply Inventing One (invited)
   N. R. Lincoln   3
2. Component Progress: Its Effect on High Speed Computer Architecture and Machine Organization (invited)
   E. Bloch and D. J. Galage   13
3. The Interpretive Interface: Resources and Program Representation in Computer Organization (invited)
   Michael J. Flynn   41
4. An Evaluation of the CRAY-1 Computer (invited)
   Forest Baskett and Tom W. Keller   71
5. Burroughs Scientific Processor (invited)
   Richard A. Stokes   85
6. Networks and Interconnection Schemes (invited)
   James E. Thornton   91
7. A Discourse on a New Super Computer, PEPE
   Hiram G. Martin   101
8. Efficient High Speed Computing with the Distributed Array Processor
   P. M. Flanders, D. J. Hunt, S. F. Reddaway, and D. Parkinson   113
9. A Complexity Result on a Pipeline Processor Design Problem
   Michael Schlansker and D. E. Atkins   129
10. Application of Data Flow Computation to the Weather Problem
    Jack B. Dennis and Ken K.-S. Weng   143
11. An Investigation of Fault-Tolerant Architectures for Large-Scale Numerical Computing
    Algirdas Avižienis, Miloš Ercegovac, Tomás Lang, Pierre Sylvain, and Alexander Thomasian   159
12. Fault-Tolerance and Longevity: Goals for High-Speed Computers of the Future
    Algirdas Avižienis   173
13. Semigroups of Recurrences
    Daniel D. Gajski   179
14. Array Processors and Their Application
    T. E. Rudy   185
15. The Use of Ladders for the Execution of APL
    Charles R. Minter   189
16. Distributed Signal Processing as Implemented in the L-2000 Remote Radar Tracking Station
    Frank P. Hiner III   191
17. A Family of Special-Purpose Processors for Distributed Dedicated Computer Systems
    Maniel Vineberg   195

18. The Parallel Processing of Large Applications
    Harvey S. Koch ... 199
19. Processor Interconnection Networks, Some New Results
    David Stevenson and Gary Feierbach ... 201
20. A Massively Parallel Processing Computer
    Lai-wo Fung ... 203

II. NUMERICAL ALGORITHMS ... 205

1. Numerical Parallel Algorithms—A Survey (invited)
   Ahmed H. Sameh ... 207
2. The Influence of Vector Computer Architecture on Numerical Algorithms (invited)
   Robert G. Voigt ... 229
3. Algorithms for Solving Two-Point Boundary Value Problems (invited)
   Victor Pereyra ... 245
4. Vectorization for the CRAY-1 of Some Methods for Solving Elliptic Difference Equations (invited)
   B. L. Buzbee, G. H. Golub, and J. A. Howell ... 255
5. Minimal Storage Band Elimination
   S. C. Eisenstat, M. H. Schultz, and A. H. Sherman ... 273
6. A Large Mathematical Model Implementation on the STAR-100 Computers
   E. Dick Giroux ... 287
7. An Analysis of the Recursive Doubling Algorithm
   P. Dubois and G. Rodrigue ... 299
8. Algorithm Design for Digital Image Correlation on a Parallel Processor
   David L. Ackerman ... 307
9. Iterative Methods for Asynchronous Multiprocessors
   Gérard M. Baudet ... 309
10. Experience with a Vectorized General Circulation Climate Model on STAR-100
    David B. Soll, Nadim R. Habra, and Gary L. Russell ... 311
11. Some Linear Algebraic Algorithms and Their Performance on CRAY-1
    T. L. Jordan and Kirby Fong ... 313
12. Nonlinear Recurrences and Parallel Computation
    D. Stott Parker, Jr. ... 317
13. Minimal Parallelism for Computations under Time Constraints
    Don Heller ... 321
14. Effectiveness of Multi-Microprocessor Networks for Solving the Nonlinear Poisson Equation
    Gerard G. L. Meyer ... 323

III. SYSTEM, SOFTWARE, AND ALGORITHM PERFORMANCE ... 327

1. Analysis of Applications Programs and Software Requirements for High Speed Computers (invited)
   John M. Gary ... 329
2. Algorithms and Architecture (invited)
   Paul Budnik, Jr., and Joseph Oliger ... 355
3. The Costs of Processing Power: The Process, the Programmer, and the Processor
   David W. Hogan, John C. Jensen, and Merrill Cornish ... 371

4.	Matching Machines and Problems *J. E. Wirsching and T. Kishi*	379
5.	To Vectorize or to "Vectorize": That Is the Question *R. N. Remund and K. A. Taggart*	399
6.	The Effect of Computer Architecture on Algorithm Decomposition and Performance *Robert W. Hon and D. Raj Reddy*	411
7.	A Software Technique for Reducing the Routing Time on a Parallel Computer with a Fixed Interconnection Network *H. T. Kung and D. Stevenson*	423
8.	Prepaging and Applications to the STAR-100 Computer *Kishor S. Trivedi*	435
9.	Application of the Vectorizer for Effective Use of High-Speed Computers *John M. Levesque*	447
10.	The Impact of Scalar Performance on Vector and Parallel Processors *L. Rudsinski and J. Worlton*	451
11.	Performance Bounds in Parallel Processor Organizations *Ruby Bei-Loh Lee*	453
12.	Automatic Error Analysis for Serial and Parallel Algorithms *John Larson*	457
13.	Some Numerical Effects of a FORTRAN Vectorizing Compiler on a Texas Instruments Advanced Scientific Computer *Myron Ginsberg*	461
14.	Computers in Chemistry: The American Chemical Society and the National Resource for Computation in Chemistry *Peter Lykos*	463

List of Referees   *468*

Contributors

ACKERMAN, DAVID L.   Topographic Division, U. S. Geological Survey, Reston, Virginia 22092

ATKINS, D. E.   Systems Engineering Laboratory, Department of Electrical and Computer Engineering, The University of Michigan, Ann Arbor, Michigan 48104

AVIŽIENIS, ALGIRDAS   Computer Science Department, University of California, Los Angeles, Los Angeles, California 90024

BASKETT, FOREST   Los Alamos Scientific Laboratory, University of California, Los Alamos, New Mexico 87545

BAUDET, GÉRARD M.   Department of Computer Science, Carnegie-Mellon University, Pittsburgh, Pennsylvania 15213

BLOCH, E.   IBM Corporation, Hopewell Junction, New York 12533

BUDNIK, PAUL, JR.   Systems Control, Inc., Palo Alto, California 94304

BUZBEE, B. L.   Los Alamos Scientific Laboratory, University of California, Los Alamos, New Mexico 87545

CORNISH, MERRILL   Texas Instruments, Inc., Austin, Texas 78769

DENNIS, JACK B.   MIT Laboratory for Computer Science, Cambridge, Massachusetts 02139

DUBOIS, P.   Numerical Mathematics, Lawrence Livermore Laboratory, University of California, Livermore, California 94550

EISENSTAT, S. C.   Department of Computer Science, Yale University, New Haven, Connecticut 06520

ERCEGOVAC, MILOŠ   Computer Science Department, University of California, Los Angeles, Los Angeles, California 90024

FEIERBACH, GARY   Institute for Advanced Computation, Sunnyvale, California 94086

FLANDERS, P. M.   Research and Advanced Development Centre, International Computers, Ltd., Stevenage, England

FLYNN, MICHAEL J.   Digital Systems Laboratory, Stanford University, Stanford, California 94305

FONG, KIRBY   Los Alamos Scientific Laboratory, University of California, Los Alamos, New Mexico 87545

FUNG, LAI-WO   Image Systems Section, NASA/Goddard Space Flight Center, Greenbelt, Maryland 20771

GAJSKI, DANIEL D.   Department of Computer Science, University of Illinois, Urbana, Illinois 61801

GALAGE, D. J.   IBM Corporation, Hopewell Junction, New York 12533

GARY, JOHN M.   Department of Computer Science, University of Colorado, Boulder, Colorado 80309

GINSBERG, MYRON   Department of Computer Science, Southern Methodist University, Dallas, Texas 75275

GIROUX, E. DICK   Lawrence Livermore Laboratory, University of California, Livermore, California 94550

GOLUB, G. H.   Computer Science Department, Stanford University, Stanford, California 94305

HABRA, NADIM R.   GTE Information Systems, Inc., Goddard Institute for Space Studies, New York, New York 10025

HELLER, DON   Computer Science Department, The Pennsylvania State University, University Park, Pennsylvania 16802

HINER, FRANK P., III   Data Systems Division, Litton Data Systems, Van Nuys, California 91409

HOGAN, DAVID W.   Texas Instruments, Inc., Austin, Texas 78769

HON, ROBERT W.   Department of Computer Science, Carnegie-Mellon University, Pittsburgh, Pennsylvania 15213

HOWELL, J. A.   Los Alamos Scientific Laboratory, University of California, Los Alamos, New Mexico 87545
HUNT, D. J.   Research and Advanced Development Centre, International Computers, Ltd., Stevenage, England
JENSEN, JOHN C.   Texas Instruments, Inc., Austin, Texas 78769
JOHNSON, R.   Burroughs Corporation, Detroit, Michigan 48232
JORDAN, T. L.   Los Alamos Scientific Laboratory, University of California, Los Alamos, New Mexico 87545
KELLER, TOM W.   Los Alamos Scientific Laboratory, University of California, Los Alamos, New Mexico 87545
KISHI, T.   Technical Information Department, Lawrence Livermore Laboratory, University of California, Livermore, California 94550
KOCH, HARVEY S.   Department of Computer and Information Science, The Ohio State University, Columbus, Ohio 43210
KUNG, H. T.   Department of Computer Science, Carnegie-Mellon University, Pittsburgh, Pennsylvania 15213
LANG, TOMÁS   Computer Science Department, University of California, Los Angeles, Los Angeles, California 90024
LARSON, JOHN   Department of Computer Science, University of Illinois, Urbana, Illinois 61801
LEE, RUBY BEI-LOH   Digital Systems Laboratory, Stanford University, Stanford, California 94305
LEVESQUE, JOHN M.   R & D Associates, Marina del Rey, California 90291
LINCOLN, N. R.   Control Data Corporation, Research and Advanced Design Laboratory, St. Paul, Minnesota 55112
LYKOS, PETER   Illinois Institute of Technology, Chicago, Illinois 60616
MARTIN, HIRAM G.   System Development Corporation, Huntsville, Alabama 35805
MEYER, GERARD G. L.   Department of Electrical Engineering, North Carolina State University, Raleigh, North Carolina 27607
MINTER, CHARLES R.   Department of Computer Science, Yale University, New Haven, Connecticut 06520
OLIGER, JOSEPH   Computer Science Department, Stanford University, Stanford, California 94305
PARKER, D. STOTT, JR.   Department of Computer Science, University of Illinois, Urbana, Illinois 61801
PARKINSON, D.   International Computers, Ltd., London, England
PEREYRA, VICTOR   Department of Applied Mathematics, California Institute of Technology, Pasadena, California 91100
REDDAWAY, S. F.   Research and Advanced Development Centre, International Computers, Ltd., Stevenage, England
REDDY, D. RAJ   Department of Computer Science, Carnegie-Mellon University, Pittsburgh, Pennsylvania 15213
REMUND, R. N.   Los Alamos Scientific Laboratory, University of California, Los Alamos, New Mexico 87545
RODRIGUE, G.   Numerical Mathematics, Lawrence Livermore Laboratory, University of California, Livermore, California 94550
RUDSINSKI, L.   Argonne National Laboratory, Argonne, Illinois 60439
RUDY, T. E.   Lawrence Livermore Laboratory, University of California, Livermore, California 94550
RUSSELL, GARY L.   GTE Information Systems, Inc., Goddard Institute for Space Studies, New York, New York 10025
SAMEH, AHMED H.   Department of Computer Science, University of Illinois, Urbana, Illinois 61801

SCHLANSKER, MICHAEL   Systems Engineering Laboratory, Department of Electrical and Computer Engineering, The University of Michigan, Ann Arbor, Michigan 48104

SCHULTZ, M. H.   Department of Computer Science, Yale University, New Haven, Connecticut 06520

SHERMAN, A. H.   Department of Computer Sciences, University of Texas at Austin, Austin, Texas 78712

SOLL, DAVID B.   GTE Information Systems, Inc., Goddard Institute for Space Studies, New York, New York 10025

STEVENSON, DAVID   Institute for Advanced Computation, Sunnyvale, California 94086

STOKES, RICHARD A.   Burroughs Corporation, Paoli, Pennsylvania 19301

SYLVAIN, PIERRE   Computer Science Department, University of California, Los Angeles, Los Angeles, California 90024

TAGGART, K. A.   Los Alamos Scientific Laboratory, University of California, Los Alamos, New Mexico 87545

THOMASIAN, ALEXANDER   Computer Science Department, University of California, Los Angeles, Los Angeles, California 90024

THORNTON, JAMES E.   Network Systems Corporation, Brooklyn Center, Minnesota 55430

TRIVEDI, KISHOR S.   Department of Computer Science, Duke University, Durham, North Carolina 27706

VINEBERG, MANIEL   Naval Electronics Laboratory Center (NELC), San Diego, California 92152

VOIGT, ROBERT G.   ICASE, NASA Langley Research Center, Hampton, Virginia 23665

WENG, KEN K.-S.   MIT Laboratory for Computer Science, Cambridge, Massachusetts 02139

WIRSCHING, J. E.   Technical Information Department, Lawrence Livermore Laboratory, University of California, Livermore, California 94550

WORLTON, J.   Los Alamos Scientific Laboratory, University of California, Los Alamos, New Mexico 87545

Preface

The Symposium on High Speed Computer and Algorithm Organization was held on April 13-15, 1977, in Champaign, Illinois. It was sponsored by the University of Illinois, Department of Computer Science, in cooperation with the IEEE Computer Society and the ACM, SIGARCH, and SIGNUM, with support from the National Science Foundation. About 50 papers were presented covering high speed computer design, high speed algorithms, the software, and the performance of such systems. With the exception of the paper presented by Robert Johnson, which is not available for publication, the present volume contains long or short versions of all the papers presented at the symposium.

Our original motivations for proposing such a symposium were to attempt to capture the state of the world of supercomputers and their performance in the 1970s. It has been twenty years since the design of the IBM STRETCH, ILLIAC II, UNIVAC LARC, ATLAS, etc.; fifteen years since the design of the CDC 6600; and ten years since the design of the CDC STAR, Burroughs ILLIAC IV, and TI ASC. What are the present trends and what might the future hold?

The recently announced CRAY-1, Burroughs BSP, and the redesigned CDC STAR all indicate that supercomputer developments will continue. The availability of large-scale integrated circuits including microprocessors, large semiconductor memory chips, etc., indicates that there may be some new and interesting tradeoffs in the design of such systems. On the other hand, the programming and development of software for large systems is always a problem, as is the understanding of algorithms that fit well with new machine organizations.

Our hope was that this symposium would bring together workers from the hardware, software, and algorithm areas (a fairly rare event) and lead to a proceedings volume that would reflect these three aspects of high speed computation. Since all three aspects are crucial for the success of a computer system, we felt that such a volume would be useful for practitioners as well as students of high speed computer system design and use. We invited 13 papers and selected the remaining ones from a much larger number of submitted papers.

The papers can be partitioned under three headings:
    (1) computer system design and theory,
    (2) numerical algorithms, and
    (3) system, software, and algorithm performance.

This book is divided into these three sections and within each section the papers are organized as follows. First, the invited papers are presented, followed by long contributed and then short contributed papers. Within each of these categories, we tried to arrange the topics from general to specific discussions or from simple machines to more complex, although in a number of cases a somewhat arbitrary ordering was used.

The success of the symposium and the final form of this book has been shaped by a number of people to whom we are indebted. First, the program committee consisted of S. Fernbach, M. J. Flynn, J. Gary, C. W. Gear, and J. Ortega. John Lehmann of the NSF provided much help as did the publisher. Ed Kalb of the Office of Continuing Education at the University of Illinois carried out much of the symposium planning. A list of referees appears at the end of the book; we are much indebted to all of them for their insightful and prompt work. We are grateful to J. N. Snyder for his welcoming remarks, and the session chairmen: R. M. Brown, E. W. Davis, Jr., E. Davidson, J. B. Dennis, F. Dorr, M. J. Flynn, M. Franklin, D. Gajski, D. Heller, J. Lehmann, C. L. Liu, D. McIntyre, D. Mickunas, J. Robertson, and D. Slotnick. Most importantly, the final form of the book was shaped by Mrs. Vivian Alsip; we are very grateful to her for her careful and devoted help.

I
Computer System Design and Theory

IT'S REALLY NOT AS MUCH FUN BUILDING A SUPERCOMPUTER
AS IT IS SIMPLY INVENTING ONE

N. R. Lincoln
Control Data Corporation

At least one segment of the computer milieu seems to be awash with creative genius these days. The advent of "cheap", "dense", "high-speed" circuit technology has made it possible for just about everyone in the business to become a "supercomputer" architect. Readers of "trade journals" are constantly titillated by the potential of "a mass of minis", or "a melange of micros". The range of application of new LSI parts seems limitless when employed in building a super processor of the 100-1000 megaflop (millions of floating point operations per second) category. For those who have been privileged (or cursed) to participate in the genesis, production and delivery of what are loosely called super-computers, the current rage of optimism and naivete about such projects is disconcerting.

Perhaps it might be useful to provide the prospective producers and consumers of this "new wave" of supercomputer horsepower with some of the insights gained over the past fifteen-plus years of large scale machine developments. The point to be made by this is that not only is there a great gap in time, money and resources between the "inventing" and the "doing", but there are many risks to be assumed by manufacturer and customer alike when dealing with advanced technologies and architectures.

PREMISES

1. There will be a continuing need for computers of the "supercomputer" class (1000-5000 "megaflops" in 1985).

2. The realization of such computers will be governed by the same economic and engineering considerations that have dominated past efforts.

3. Parallelism in data handling, control and computation will be needed to achieve the supercomputer goals.

4. Reliability, maintainability and system integrity must meet standards exceeding those commonly met by 1977 standard product medium-scale computer systems.

5. Programmability (the ability to quickly and efficiently map an algorithm onto a given machine) of any new supercomputer will be a preeminent concern of almost all users.

LESSONS LEARNED

The history of supercomputer developments (from the manufacturers' point of view) has taught us a few things about:

1. The effects of technology,
2. Software interaction,
3. The human element.

1. Technology

The design of the CDC 6600 began originally in 1960 and ended abruptly in the summer of 1961. Technology wasn't yet ready to match the vision of the chief architect. Not only did major features such as large memory (131K), long word (60 bits), and an ensemble of peripheral processors (PPU's) dominate the direction of the project, but the performance goal for an interregister transfer to be completed in 200 nanoseconds was an absolute requirement. With a hardheaded and singleminded engineer/architect in charge this meant that the semiconductor art of that time would have to be stretched until circuit technology yielded a device capable of meeting the performance goals. The first such effort, requiring a symphysis of circuit design and transistor technology, failed. Thus resulted a hiatus in the summer of 1961 as the chief designer awaited a new birth at "silicon valley" to give him the tools to meet a 100 nanosecond clock speed.

The fact that a new circuit was successful with a second attempt in a few short months indicates the incredibly dynamic environment at the silicon vendor's plant at that time, and more significantly, the chief architect's ability to assess the probable state-of-the-art and match it to his concept for a supercomputer.

Lesson I

Most supercomputers are conceived around a set of compromises between what is desired and what is possible, with the final specification usually requiring some extension of the extant technology beyond its comfortable limits. At the moment of their conception, few supercomputers were built with standard off-the-shelf parts, since speed requirements generally demanded aggressive developments in circuit performance (with little regard to cost and power dissipation), packaging and circuit interconnect. What is needed at such a time is a modicum of ESP and the ability to make judicious choices in selecting the technologies to be employed. Among the considerations that affect such choices are:

a. The state of development and maturity of a given technology at project inception versus the expected state of that technology at the time the computer is being mass produced and delivered. (What we have here is a restatement of the "learning curve", wherein we want to guess the best possible time and the best possible version to grab and run with to build a supercomputer);

b. The vendor ability or willingness to build the technology for us. (Low volumes, high start-up costs and high manufacturing skill requirements are characteristic of this breed of technology);

c. The probability that the technology will achieve high volume usage by other customers, thus ensuring alternate vendors long-term product availability, reduced costs and greater reliability due to the ability to select from larger volumes of devices.

Having conquered the circuit speed problem, it was still necessary to deal with the packaging of the devices. Two major objectives had to be achieved:

a. Reduction of the delay between circuits;

b. Increased density to permit the packing together of multiple functional elements. (Increased density also reduces the transit time across chassis of logic.)

The creation of the "cordwood" package provided the needed system with resistors providing the connective tissue between opposed circuit boards. Higher circuit density not only meant higher speeds however, but also higher power densities. The problem of evacuating 3 watts of power from a collection of logic in about 8 cubic inches was not inconsequential. Freon cooling, once established as the means for removing this heat, challenged the mechanical design team of the 6600 as much as the manufacturability of the tightly knit "cordwood" package.

Lesson II

Circuit design and system architecture are only pieces in a large puzzle called "Supercomputer CPU." A major limitation on the feasibility of a given supercomputer project could well be the mechanical, power, packaging and cooling requirements of the overall electronic design. The physical space necessary to surround high performance circuits with heavy bus bars and cooling coils or air plenums may, in fact, be so great as to make the computer physically too large to install in any installation short of the Grand Canyon, or to power or to cool short of submergence in the waters of Hoover Dam.

Once it became clear that several copies of the CDC 6600 were going to be sold, consideration for long-term manufacturability and maintenance became highly important. Reducing circuit interconnect delays works against freely accessible logic (for maintenance and construction purposes). Certain tradeoffs have to be made, of course, but in the long run, supercomputers have emphasized performance over the manufacturing processes. It is alleged that many of the present supercomputer proposals, while highly ingenious and efficient, may in fact be unmanufacturable with processes commonly used in the 1970's.

Early installation experience with any breed of supercomputers has, almost as a matter of tradition, yielded discomfitting degrees of reliability and stability. To a degree, in the past such behavior has been acceptable for the "first-of-its-kind" computers. Since many states-of-the-art are usually being stretched along the way, customers have to contend with "first batch" parts, and not-quite-mature technology. Although this risk has always been present in any initial super procurements, the actual effects have not been realistically assessed in some instances.

Lesson III

"State-of-the-art" developments have usually required some forbearance, a great deal of patience and a grotesque sense of humor on the part of the end-user. The fact is that the first-ever-in-the-world model of a super mainframe manages to mainly prove feasibility and viability. It then usually takes a massive engineering effort to improve the operational characteristics of the computer, as well as a sufficient passage of time to allow the critical technologies to mature. To meet the computational demands of the customers, however, it has been normal for the "first-ever" machine to be shipped to a site and then jackhammered into production.

Not only is this method of operation intolerable, it is truly unacceptable in the computing world of 1977. Further, it is becoming unnecessary as sophisticated computer aided design tools are available for supercomputer production and as photo-lithographic systems are developed to produce most of the circuits and interconnect systems automatically.

Lesson IV

The time to deliver a useful, working supercomputer to a customer once design of the machine has begun is always twice as long as the most pessimistic estimates. It seems an immutable law of computer science that to achieve a new generation of supercomputing it is necessary to make radical departures in architecture, circuitry and design. As always, the major machine features are readily implemented but the "end cases" cause the project schedule to slip unceasingly and unmercilessly. Each new architectural innovation is certain to introduce unforeseen, niggling design "kinks" which absorb key talent and time. If a new architecture must be implemented, both the developer and user can expect to encounter major delivery delays, even in the most well-managed project.

It has been born out on the CDC 6600, the CDC 7600 and the CDC STAR-100 projects that technology, architecture and design must be merged properly to yield a useful supercomputer. The selection of the right point at the right time in the development of the circuit packaging system must be matched by the careful setting of performance goals that meet computational needs and can result in a computer that is buildable and maintainable.

2. Software

As the technology considerations have demanded patience on the part of developer and user, so too has software production for these super-beasts required some perseverance. The CDC 6600 computer was created at a time when it was well matched to the speed requirements of existing computations. On the other hand, it became operational at a time when the "software world" was undergoing an upheaval which, when added to the architectural newness of the CDC 6600, caused veritable chaos in operating system development for that machine. The situation in 1964 was thus:

1. The expectations of consumers for operating system features such as file management, scheduling and such were expanding at a rate greater than software developers could meet demands. The announced plans for IBM 360 OS made such expectations appear to be the norm for even large scale computing environments.

2. The precipitate exploitation of time-sharing and multiprogramming imposed new requirements for job security, integrity and recovery which caused massive convolutions in operating system and program structure.

3. The CDC 6600 presented software folk with a new challenge in the form of the multiprocessing PPU/CPU structure and the multiprogrammable main CPU. The somewhat asynchronous behavior of the multiple processors provided ample opportunity for software design missteps, and occasionally, almost impossible-to-trace operating system bugs.

The result was that early software developments for these new architectures were beset with performance and stability difficulties as designers learned to cope with radically new hardware. At one point in time, system throughput was reduced to one-third of its original capacity when extensive file and tape labeling procedures were first injected into the cooperative PPU environment.

Lesson V

Total usable performance of the system is governed not only by the hardware technology but by the software through which the hardware is accessed. Software features must be traded off against reliability and producability as do their hardware counterparts.

Lesson VI

The resource and development time requirements for essentially simple software systems can exceed estimates by astronomical amounts when a radically new architecture is at hand.

The FORTRAN compiler suffered much the same fate as the operating system and thus Lessons V and VI apply to it. There was, in 1964, no great body of theoretical work to guide compiler developers in dealing with the multiplicity of CDC 6600 functional units, and its many, asymetrical registers. After nearly <u>ten years</u>, a truly optimum match between language features, compiler, object code reliability and machine organization was finally achieved. To expect less of an effort for similar results with new supercomputer schemes is fatuous.

One way in which software development risks can be substantially reduced is to couple the high performance CPU to an existing (and thus stable and well supplied with software) mainframe. This approach can thus insulate the user from dramatic changes in the computational CPU architecture while preserving his ability to use "super power" when it is needed. To be effective, however, this "coupling" must have sufficient flexibility and bandwidth to be usable for all problems and data bases to be submitted to the high speed processor.

3. <u>The Human Element</u>

Nowhere is the effect of personalities and human foibles more evident in the computer development business than in the highly visible, high cost, high risk, supercomputer segment.

The success and failure of high risk computer developments can quite often be traced to a single individual. It is not accidental that unique persons such as Gene Amdahl, Seymour Cray, Fred Brooks and Bob Barton have become recognized leaders in the computer architecture and design field. Their reputations did not arise from a happy coincidence of

being associated with a successful project; rather, they
stand out because of their ability to generate a system-wide
concept, determine a course of action to get it implemented,
make the necessary tradeoffs and finally drive through all
obstacles to ensure completion of their vision.

Lesson VII

Committee design of supercomputers is never as successful as reliance on a single, highly opinionated, forceful individual. Even though the individual may make mistakes along the way, the singleness of purpose and vision that one person has is more important in the long run.

The negative aspect of invoking strong personalities into hardware and software development is the inevitable clash of wills, philosophies and differing perceptions about the project. Critical design decisions are often made on the basis of "gut feel" and emotion based on previous experience. The injection of volatile interpersonal relationships makes rational "gut feel" decisions harder to make and justify.

Lesson VIII

Human emotions and interactions can have more dramatic effects on project success than the most ingenious design ideas or the stupid blunders in the manufacturing process.

Although this is a truism for any project, the intense pressure witnessed on the CDC 6600, 7600 and STAR projects, involving both hardware and software, seemed to aggravate the interpersonal and human problems. At one point on an experimental STAR project, the designer of the Floating Point unit was shot and killed by a deranged ex-employee. For months after the incident, work in the Floating Point design areas was halted because the managers of the experiment, although mature, rational people, were unable to cope with the individual's death and thus were unable to deal with the work he had left behind.

Lesson IX

The success or failure of any new supercomputer development is finally going to rest on the ability and willingness of users to adapt to the strange world of parallel processing, and the consequent need to restructure algorithms, if not total processes.

The degree to which existing parallel architectures have not been exploited has been related to customers' unwillingness to abandon the familiar arena of FORTRAN programming and structures, and their vain hope that technological breakthroughs in circuit speeds would make it unnecessary to change their mode of thinking and programming. For a supercomputer development to be successful, more than the hardware must be running. The entire system must be applied to <u>all</u> of the problems where it is needed and must be efficiently utilized to achieve performance objectives. There is no doubt that this will require major changes in our thought patterns regarding computation. Such changes are going to create technical and emotional upheaval on the part of the designers, implementors, programmers and even computer science curricula. The technological tools to achieve dramatic increases in performance seem to be available. The question: Is the human element ready?...The moment of truth is at hand...

COMPONENT PROGRESS:
ITS EFFECT ON HIGH SPEED COMPUTER
ARCHITECTURE AND MACHINE ORGANIZATION

E. Bloch and D. J. Galage
International Business Machines Corp.

I. INTRODUCTION

During the past 25 years, there has been an almost unparalleled growth in two industries -- namely, the data processing industry and the semiconductor components industry. From a fresh start in the early 1950's the data processing industry in 1976 had yearly sales of $20 billion and the components industry sales of $3 billion. The growth of the two industries is the result of symbiotic interaction between the capabilities of one and the requirements of the other. This relationship, and the interacting stimulus between their capabilities and requirements, was -- and will be in the future -- a major point in propelling their respective developments forward at a rapid rate.

Any conference that is concerned with understanding the past, present, and future of high-speed computing must of necessity focus on progress in the components field, and formulate searching questions about the outlook and future of that technology, and how it affects progress in high-speed computer development.

Reviewing the developments in these two industries and their respective technologies leads to a number of major considerations that will inevitably reshape both industries:

a) One would like to understand the limit to the performance, cost, and reliability improvements in semiconductor components, as well as the rate of technological progress in the future as compared with the past.
b) One should understand, the dynamic driving forces behind progress in semiconductor components in order to influence the direction that these developments take.
c) New and increased capabilities in components can cause and create new approaches in systems architecture and machine design. It is important to consider the possible implications of this interaction.
d) The development of new and improved memory and storage hierarchies is, and will be more so in

the future, tied to developments in semiconductors and components. The potential results are important to understand in view of the capitalization, investment, and manpower requirements involved.

e) Finally, in the past, progress in semiconductor components was driven by the need for high-performance computing systems. Progress today is equally driven by the capability for creating complex packets of logic at low cost. This development, in its most interesting form, is the cause for a proliferation of microprocessor and low-cost memory devices. How the availability of these devices will affect the high-performance computer area is of paramount interest. Related to this development is the role of distributed processing.

The limits of space and time do not allow a comprehensive and exhaustive treatment of the issues raised above; it is hoped that the discussion in this paper will provide stimulus and background against which details of these issues, and many others, can be judged and answers developed. We will review, therefore, progress in component developments, systems progress, interactions of the two areas and their impacts, as well as future developments.

II. PROGRESS IN COMPONENT TECHNOLOGY

Over the last 25 years component technology has progressed from vacuum tubes to large-scale integration (LSI). The impetus for this progress has been the advances made in semiconductor technology as well as advances in circuit design and packaging-related areas.

A. Semiconductor Technology

Within semiconductor technology, increasingly sophisticated developments in materials, processes, and tooling have been major driving forces for substantial progress in component density and performance capabilities.

The predominant semiconductor material is silicon. Better understanding of this material, as well as exacting controls during the growth and processing of the wafer, has resulted in an increase in wafer size from 25 mm in the 1950's to 100-125 mm today and decreasing imperfections as shown in Fig. 1. This enables the design of ever smaller structures in ever denser arrays. It also allows increasing the chip size from 0.5 mm^2 in the early 1960's to 40 mm^2 today and to 150 mm^2 in a few years.

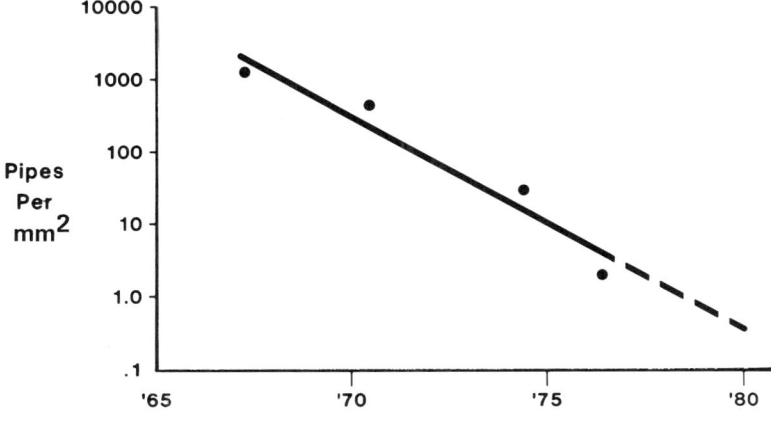

Fig. 1. Defect Density.

From a process viewpoint, improvements in materials have been matched with improvements in the fabrication processes themselves. Minimum line width (Fig. 2), which is a good indicator of cost and performance, has been significantly decreased through the use of projection optical systems and, of late, non-optical direct writing on the wafer by means of E-beams. This latest development has eliminated one of the main barriers to further improvements in performance and packaging densities, namely, the generation of smaller dimensions.

In the fabrication operations, the use of chemical processes for etching, and high-temperature thermal processes such as diffusion for determining the characteristics of semiconductor components, poses severe limitations on future developments. Therefore, dry etching (using plasmas and

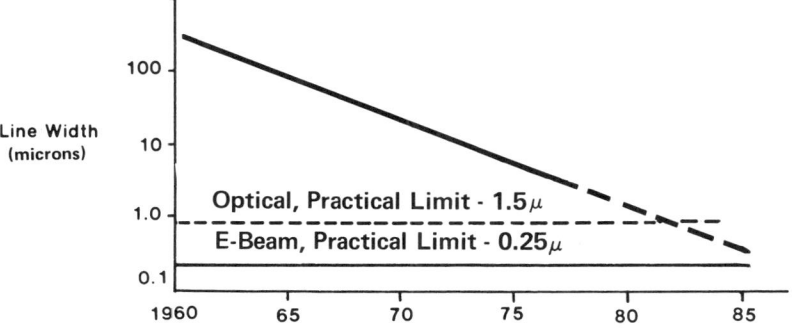

Fig. 2. Minimum Line Width.

sputtering techniques in place of chemical etching) and use of ion implantation (in place of thermal diffusions for more precise control of impurities and less undesirable side effects, such as distortion of the wafer), will be important contributors to driving the state of the art beyond current capabilities.

As line width decreases from 3 μ towards 1 μ, and defect densities improve by an order of magnitude, the circuit productivity at the wafer level as shown in Fig. 3 improves by an order of magnitude. Note that both defect density and line width should improve together, otherwise productivity will virtually remain on a plateau.

If, in addition to the foregoing, increasing wafer size is taken into account productivity is enhanced even further. The name of the game for cost and performance, therefore, is making devices smaller, wafers larger and understanding and designing materials and processes to minimize imperfections.

Putting all of these factors together, it is safe to predict that progress in productivity will be considerable. Productivity here is defined as good circuits per wafer which is closely related to cost and probably a better indicator than cost itself.

B. Packaged High-Performance Logic

The results of progress in materials and processes have led to significant enhancements in logic and memory components. This, together with new circuit techniques, has resulted in enhancement of computing capabilities in both performance and cost.

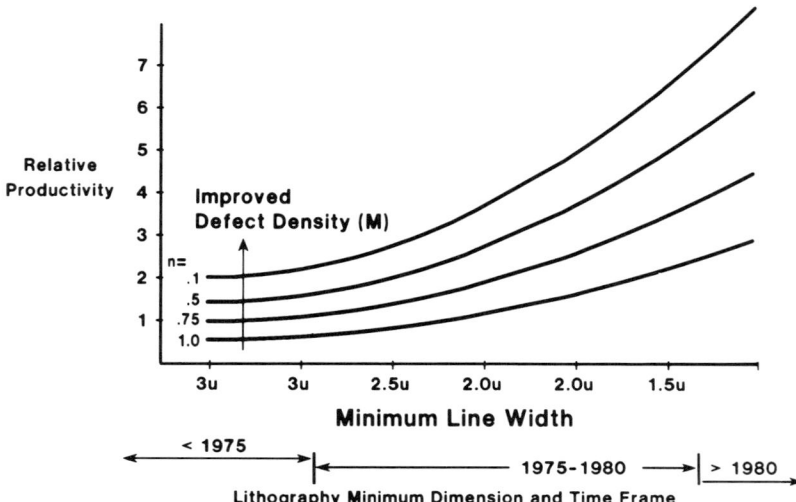

Fig. 3. Wafer Productivity.

Average performance of a circuit in a machine environment has significantly changed over time (Fig. 4) from a few hundred ns/stage delay in 1955 to 3 ns/stage delay in today's shipped machines. With progress in photolithography as discussed above, the 1 ns performance range will be reached by the late 70's or early 1980's.

This improvement is a function of many interrelated parameters, including the following.

1. Higher Integration

Chip densities are increasing at a fast rate from a few circuits a few years ago, to 50 - 100 circuits today, to 1,000 and more circuits by 1980. Progress in the low-performance FET area has been more pronounced in the past, but the bipolar technology is narrowing the gap as shown in Fig. 5.

2. Lower Power

Significant progress in reducing circuit power (Fig. 6) as circuit integration increases has been achieved through smaller geometries and circuit design advances. In addition, because of reduced circuit loading and shorter time of flight, for example, the increased circuit integration effectively reduces power requirements.

3. Packaging Advances

Improvements at the chip level have reduced the amount of higher-level packaging required (cards/boards) for a

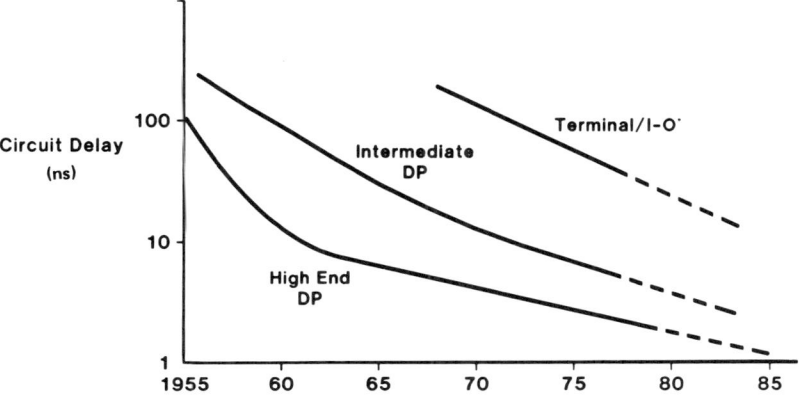

Fig. 4. Packaged Circuit Performance.

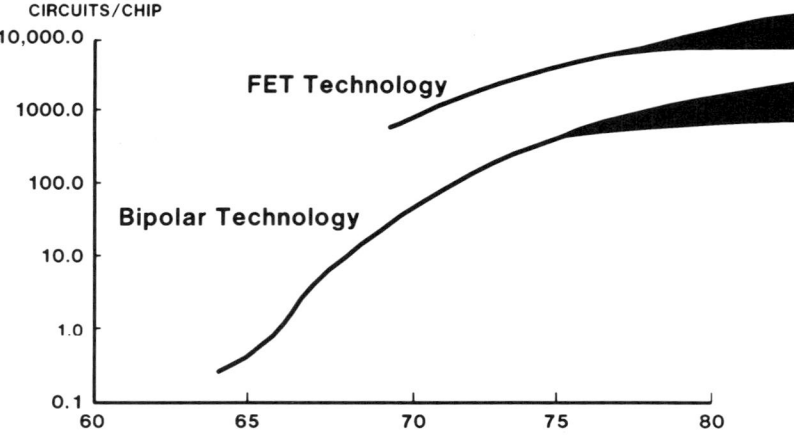

Fig. 5. Logic Circuits Integration Level.

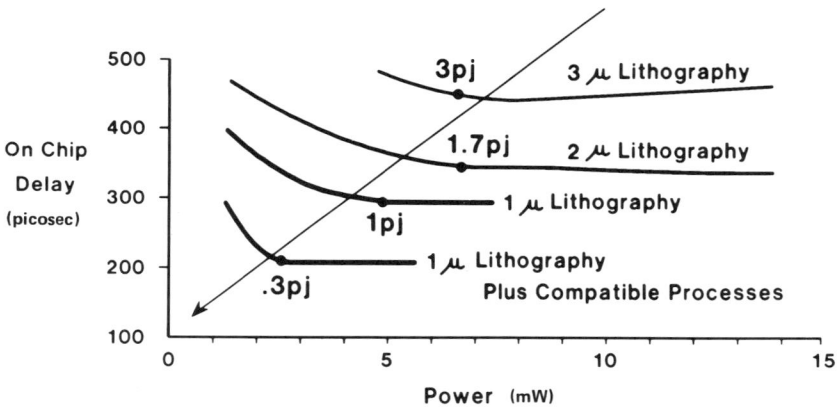

Fig. 6. Current Switch Speed-Power Curves.

particular systems design. These improvements, however, have also placed new demands on the packaging technologies for greater input-output connection densities, improved wirability, power distribution, and cooling.

4. Interconnection Aspects

As chips and higher-level packages contain more and more logic circuits, the ratio of numbers of circuits to the number of input/output connections improves. However, the rate of improvement in this ratio is not sufficient to avoid requiring the total number of communication lines to this group of circuits to increase. Historically derived relationships between connections required and the number of circuits for a package show that

$$P \simeq k \cdot C^b$$

where P = number of pins
C = number of circuits.
$0.5 \leq b \leq 0.7$

Machine design can be biased to minimize the total number of connections required through various design approaches such as encoding/decoding or multiplexing into and from the package of logic. Also, as the number of circuits on the package approaches a total function, the number of connections required is less than what the historical relationship would predict. For high-performance machine designs, the techniques to minimize connections by trading off against the circuit performance can only be partially utilized. To keep the increase in connections from enlarging the physical size of the package and increasing the time of flight between groups of circuits a demand for higher connection densities is imposed on the packaging technology. This increase, whether at the pads of the chip or at the connections to the next level package, puts a demand for improved wirability in the total package. Increased performance places demands on improved impedance control of interconnecting lines. In addition, stub length and loading must be carefully controlled if electrical reflections are to be minimized.

5. *Power and Related Factors*

As the technology progresses and enables smaller and lower power circuits, one option available is to increase the chip circuit density. This requires the packaging system to provide improved power distribution (electrical properties to cope with higher current densities and current changes) and to help remove the heat generated at the chip as well as the heat generated across the total package.

Advances in packaging have not occurred at the same rate as improvements at the chip level. As a result the circuit speed proper is the parameter that provides the largest percent improvement in total delay/stage. (See Fig. 7.) Package and loading delay, as well as the tolerance adders for design and process variations, are first-order factors to focus on in the future, as progress in high-performance logic continues.

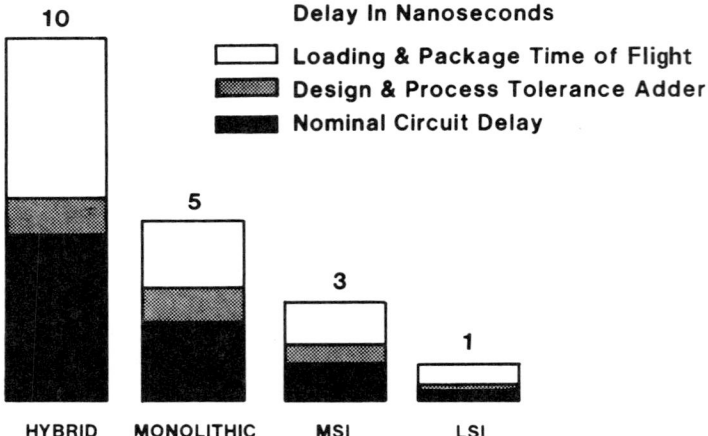

Fig. 7. *Logic Circuit Delay per Stage.*

6. Reliability Factors

Hand in hand with all the improvements discussed before will be the improvement in reliability of a circuit in a machine. In the evolution of almost every generation of technology, an order-of-magnitude improvement in reliability has been achieved. Reasons for the improvement are:

o Better process control.
o Fewer external physical connections per circuit or element.
o Increased circuit tolerance.
o Better protection of the chip surface from environmental contamination.

While LSI has resulted in increasing the density of the package (Figs. 8 and 9) as well as the total system, it causes other changes. For one, it causes a proliferation of part numbers (Fig. 10) at the chip level.

This is one of the big problems that designers and manufacturers will face. This problem will either demand a very flexible design and manufacturing system (allowing for fast turn-around times from design through the finished product) or it could very well mean that in a deliberate kind of way (by creating high levels of universal functional parts such as microprocessors) the exploitation of LSI will be sub-optimized. It could also be a mix of the two approaches -- namely, the use of a large number of part numbers, together with clever exploitation of multi-use high-level functions.

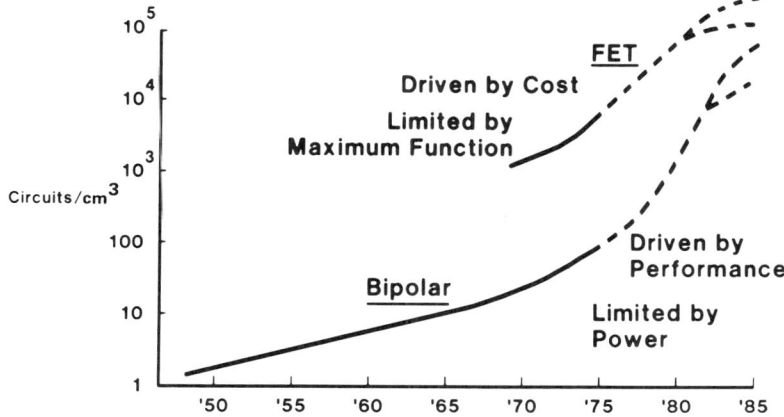

Fig. 8. Packaged Logic Circuits (Board Level).

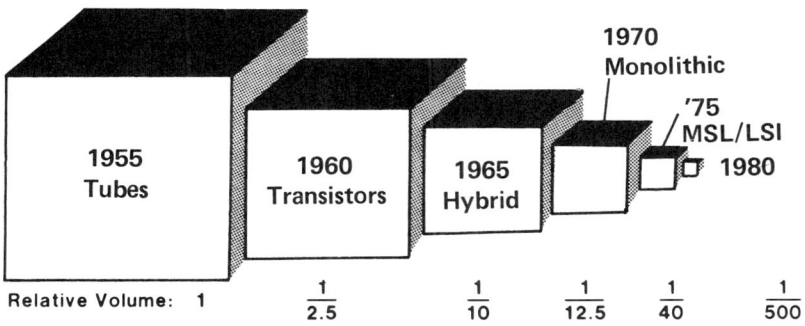

Fig. 9. Logic Circuits: Volumetric Evolution.

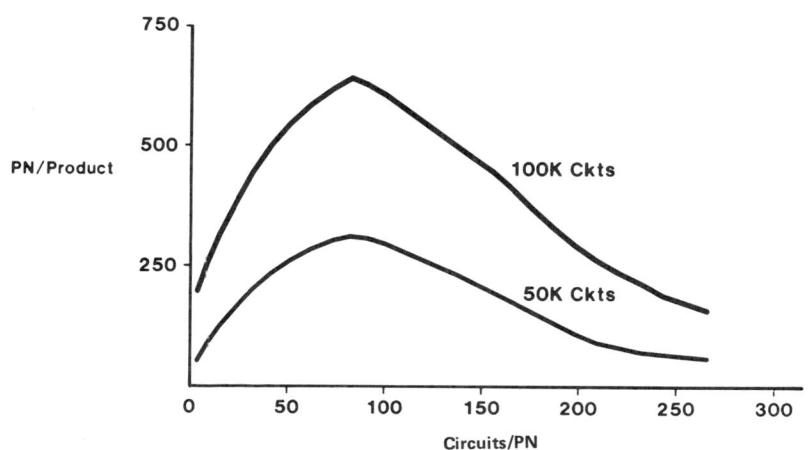

Fig. 10. Part Number Trend.

The part number dependency as a function of integration level is a well-known phenomenon. In the past it applied to pluggable cards; now it applies equally to semiconductor logic chips.

Despite this shortcoming of chip part number proliferation, LSI will spread to all products, including the high-performance area because of the speed and cost advantage it affords.

In summary, since 1960 to the present, the integration level in the high-performance logic area has increased by a factor of 1000 because of improvements in:

Chip area	40 times
Photolithography	6 times
Circuit factors	5 times

In the same time frame, performance of circuits has improved by an order of magnitude.

In the foreseeable future, significant improvements in density and performance are in store. In density, an order of magnitude or more with improvements in:

Chip area	4 times
Lithography	3 times
Circuit factors	3 times

In performance, at least a factor of 3 improvement will occur in bipolar high-performance technology.

FET technology is similarly affected by technical advances, and the improvement factors, while not identical, are comparable.

We are therefore in the middle of a decided growth period of semiconductor and logic capabilities, with significant improvements yet to come.

C. Memory

Progress similar to that in packaged logic is being experienced in the memory and storage area of computer technology. Progress in semiconductors in terms of density (Fig. 11), performance, and cost resulted in the displacement of cores as the major memory technology.

Within the field of semiconductor memories, both FET and bipolar versions have been used. It should be noted that an interesting trend is occurring. While densities in FETs, and consequently cost, have always been better than in bipolar, the bipolar trend in higher densities is improving at an accelerating rate. This has been primarily caused by the use of new circuit techniques, such as I^2L or merged-transistor logic (MTL).

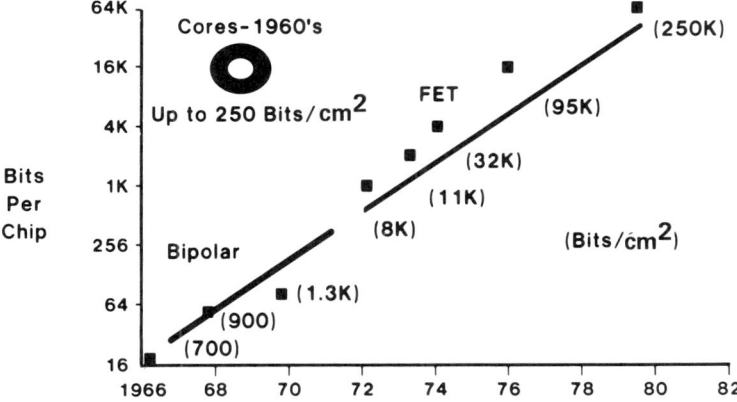

Fig. 11. Memory Technology Evolution.

1. Cache

The use of lower-performance FET memories in high-performance systems has been made possible by the use of the buffer or cache concept, thus giving major improvements in effective memory access time (Fig. 12). The cache acts, in an efficient way, as a speed-matching device between the high-performance logic circuits in a CPU and the lower-performance main memory. (See Section IV.) The cache uses a specially designed part number of a bipolar chip governed by the same technology used in the rest of the logic.

2. Density Factors

Improvements in memory density (Fig. 11) have been even more pronounced than in logic. The area density improvement since semiconductor memory came into being has been 300-fold. The cause for this increase has been:

o The same improvements in processes, materials, and photolithography as discussed previously.
o The regularity of interconnections so that wiring does not determine chip size as it does in logic.
o Substantial progress in memory cell design -- reducing the number of active components/cell from six to one and reducing the cell size (Fig. 13). This has had the added effect of reducing the average power considerably, thus making high integration levels feasible.

Developments in volumetric efficiency (Fig. 14) have been equally impressive, allowing for memory integration within the central processing unit and allowing the attachment of larger memories with a resultant systems performance improvement.

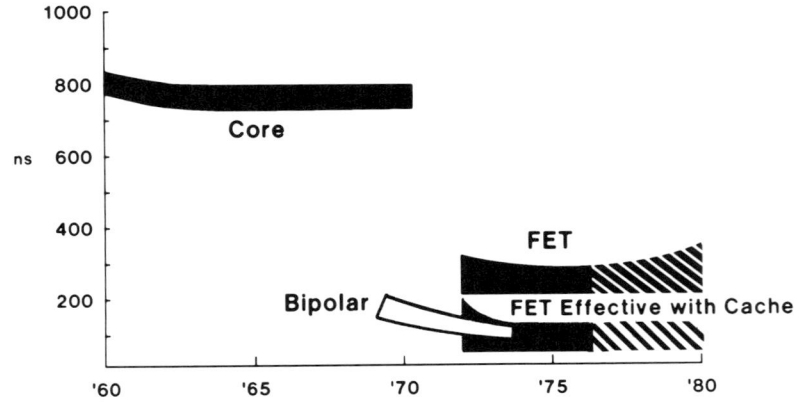

Fig. 12. Main Memory Access Time.

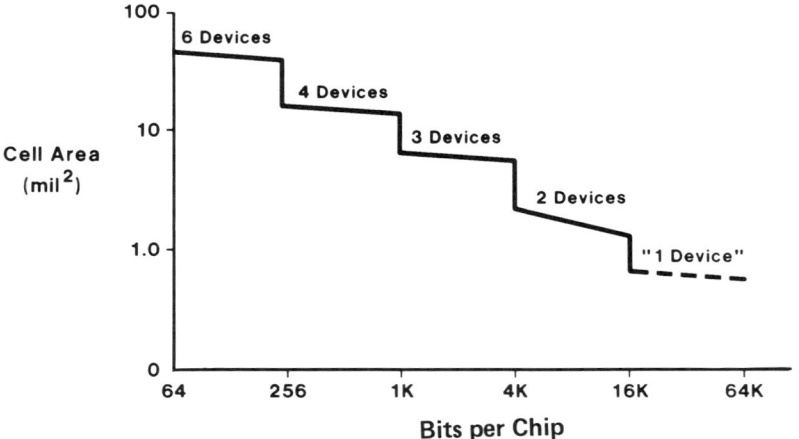

Fig. 13. Memory Cell Size Evolution.

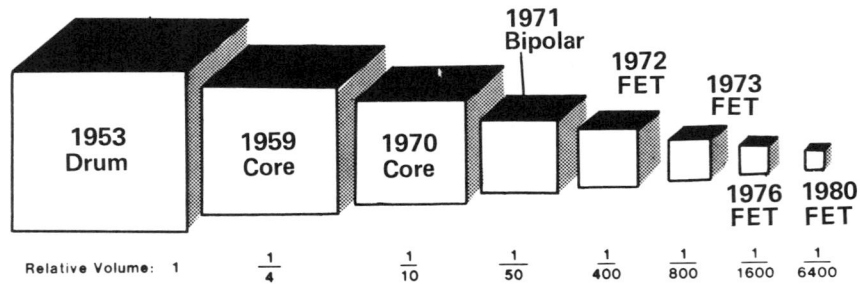

Fig. 14. Main Memory Trends - Physical Size Comparison.

III. SYSTEM PROGRESS

Advances in computer systems have resulted from order-of-magnitude improvements in many of the supporting system elements. Printers have increased speeds from 150 lines per minute to over 10,000 lines per minute. Disk access times and tape data rates have shown similar ratios of improvement. In software, we have seen a progression from assemblers through compilers to complex control programs including data management, queue handling, and other features.

These advances, along with new architecture and machine design techniques such as virtual machines and concurrency, have been combined with the component technology improvements discussed. In total, these produce higher-performance systems with improved reliability, reduced cost, and reduced space.

Such improvements (Fig. 15) have resulted in systems whose performance is measured in MIPS (millions of instructions per second) whereas in the early 1960's they were measured in KIPS (thousands of instructions per second). In scientific applications, even greater performance has been achieved. In those special application areas where parallel/array processors or multiple interconnected processors (Fig. 16) can be used, performance will approach the BIPS (billions of instructions per second) range.

A. Machine Organization

In machine organization techniques emphasis on high-performance system design focused in reducing the machine cycle time (Fig. 17), even while maintaining the ability to do complex functions within that cycle. In addition, designs

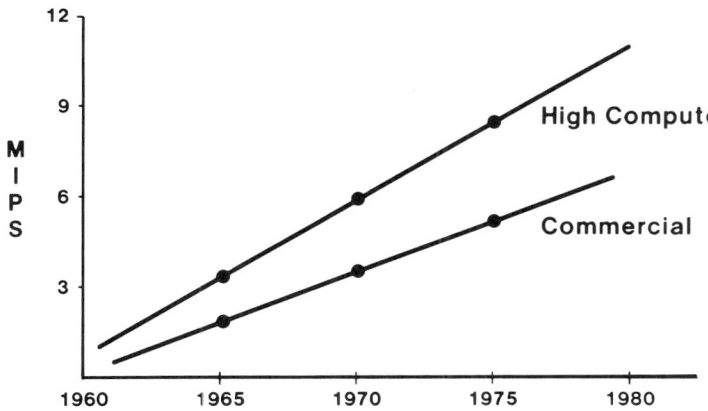

Fig. 15. Uniprocessor Performance (MIPS).

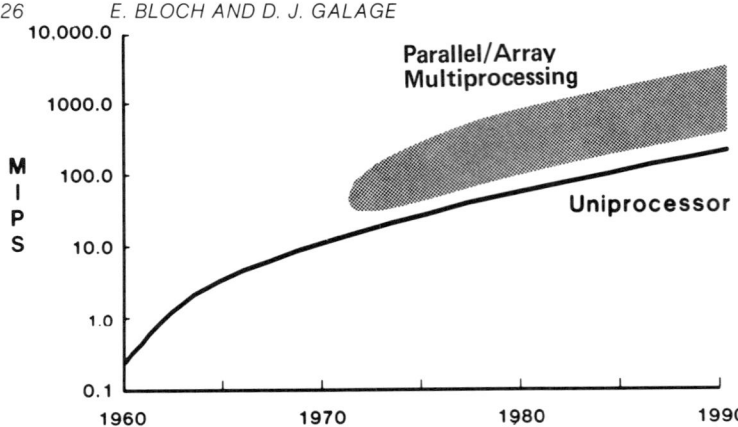

Fig. 16. Uniprocessor and Advanced Configuration Performance.

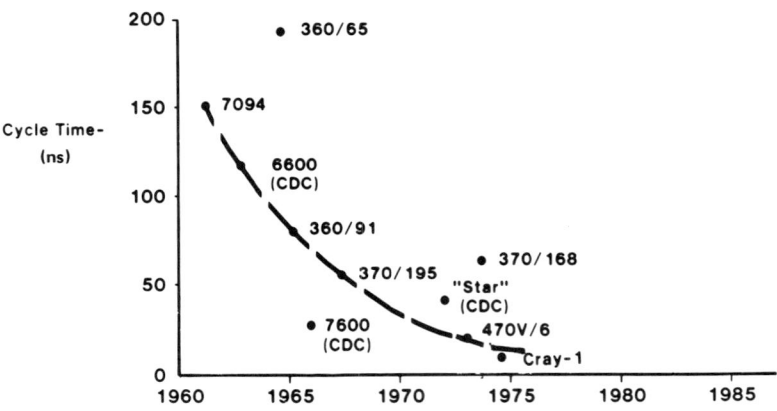

Fig. 17. Machine Cycle Time.

permit overlap of functions so that, where possible, independent strings of instruction can be operated on concurrently. This reduces the total time required to perform a given task.

Interaction between the system design techniques and advancements in the performance of the technology itself, along with its reliability, cost, and smaller size, encourages evaluation of new independent units such as Vector Units and units to allow specialization of other data processing functions.

Another well-known technique for using hardware concurrently is that of pipelining. Here a much used process, such as utilized in executing instructions, is subdivided into its key elements (I Fetch, Decode, Address Generation, Operand Fetch, and Execution). This provides a means by which a pipeline flow is established where each stage can be operating concurrently on a different instruction.

Thus, when working well, instructions will complete at a rate determined by the dedicated function design rather than the time required to execute a single instruction.

B. Operational Techniques

Additional techniques had to be developed to allow these concurrent approaches to operate efficiently, within the confines of the code being executed. Look-ahead and buffering techniques were established to isolate these mechanisms from the effects of a main memory request. An instruction stack with the appropriate mechanisms to keep it full provides an inventory of instructions, and a series of store buffers isolates operands from memory. Buffering units allow a queue of work to develop, thereby improving concurrency and smoothing overall work flow.

Disruptions to the flow in highly overlapped, pipelined machines can reduce the benefits possible from hardware design. Branching has the basic effect of disrupting the work queue for the decoder. Techniques for circumventing this type of problem have been developed. One such technique couples the use of a branch table with the means to conditionally issue operations from the decoder. The branch table maintains a history of the direction taken by previous branch instructions. Based on the prior history the probability of the next branch path is calculated.

Another disruptive situation affecting high-performance machine designs is the occurrence of an interrupt during the execution of an instruction which has long since been issued by the Instruction unit. Here, techniques have evolved for allowing recovery to take place even though concurrent, non-sequential operations are being performed.

C. Impact of Evolution

This evolution in machine design has enabled the utilization of more and more circuits to efficiently increase the internal performance of a general-purpose uniprocessor (Fig. 18). From the straightforward use of wider data paths to the sophisticated use of pipelining, concurrency, and branch table prediction, the designer is advancing the product performance range compared with what simpler designs can provide.

Over the past twenty years (Table 1) the developments in both components and systems have resulted in a greater than 100 times reduction in the processing time and cost of a given unit of work. This resulted in a 16,000-fold cost/performance improvement over this time period. Undoubtedly, this progress will continue in the future as the productivity improvements referred to previously become realized in new products.

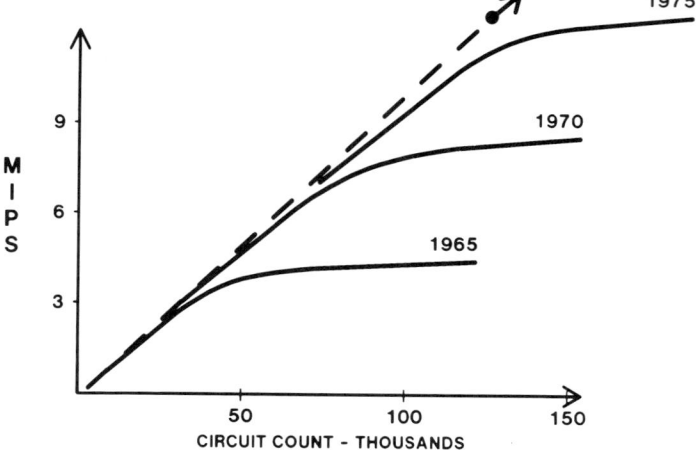

Fig. 18. Processor Circuit Growth.

TABLE I

System Cost Progress

Year	Technology	Processing Time* (Sec)	Cost		
			Total $*	Main Memory $/MB	Storage Unit $/MB
1955	Tubes Cores Disc	375	14.54	8.5M	6.7K
1960	Discrete Transistors	47	2.48	6M	2.3K
1965	Hybrid	37	.59	1.6M	697
1974	Monolithics	5	.28	150K	185
1976	LSI	3	.11	90K	78

* For Mix of 1700 Computer Operations

IV. INTERACTION BETWEEN COMPONENT AND SYSTEM TECHNOLOGIES

While we have discussed the progress and outlook in the components technologies as well as the progress in the high-compute systems area, a few observations on their interactions are in order.

High-performance machines depend on a fast cycle time
and a minimum number of machine cycles per instruction.
Here, the semiconductor advances (Fig. 19), driven by high-
performance system needs, have produced a steady reduction
in the time required to produce a logic decision. Analyzing
the growth of uniprocessor performance over time and comparing
this with technology performance advances provide the following
observations:

o *Commercial processing improvements have been mainly due
  to improvements in semiconductor component technology.*
o *High-compute processors have advanced by combining this
  same technology with advances in machine design previously
  mentioned.*

A. Memory Hardware Developments

High-performance machine design also requires faster
memory access and cycle times to minimize the effect of
instruction and operand fetching. These demands were first
met by improving core memory performance through the utilization
of smaller cores and 2D wiring configurations, and through
the use of techniques such as wider data paths, buffering,
and memory interleaving. All these techniques were designed
to improve the effective operation of the memory as seen by
the processor. As practical limits were reached by costs
and the machine techniques, semiconductor technology had
reached a stage where it could provide better performance,
cost, and growth capabilities.

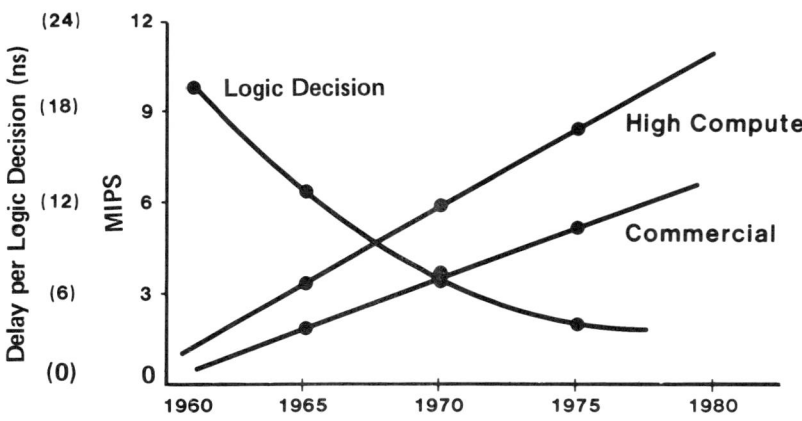

Fig. 19. Uniprocessor Performance.

B. Memory Organization Developments

Programming systems and application problems run on these high-performance machines required a greater data capacity of main memory while simultaneously demanding higher performance (Fig. 20). Fortunately, the technique of obtaining a fast effective access to data was evolved through a heuristically derived algorithm that capitalized on the statistics of how memory is used. This allowed separation of the contradictory requirements of "faster" and "bigger" demands on memory. As discussed in Sec. II. C.1, a small fast access/cycle memory, using the advantages of semiconductors, was used as a cache in conjunction with a larger-capacity, slower memory. Because of the use of the cache concept, the progress of packaged logic performance has been matched by effective memory performance.

V. IMPACT OF PROGRESS IN COMPONENT SYSTEMS TECHNOLOGIES

As has been reviewed in the previous section, during the past twenty years there has been an improvement in cost performance at the systems level as well as a reduction in the time to process a given unit of work, measured by several orders of magnitude.

It is common wisdom in the physical sciences and in engineering that, when improvements or changes occur by an order of magnitude, new avenues of use open up with a profound result on the user or those affected by the use of the new technology. With a three-to-four order-of-magnitude improvement in cost/performance, the effects on all areas that come in contact with computing and data processing have indeed been profound.

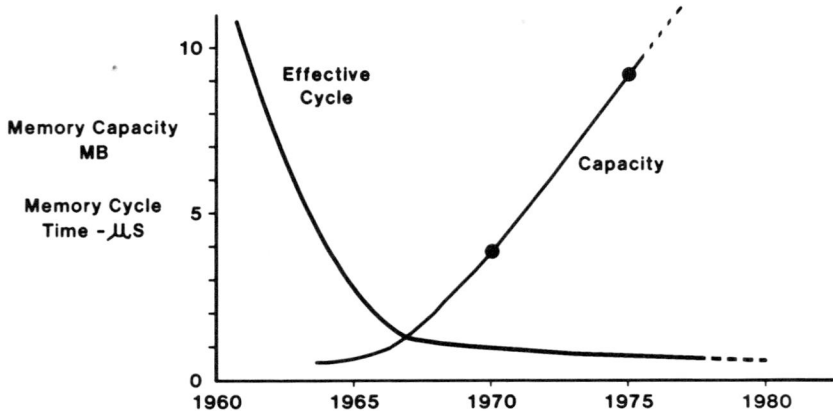

Fig. 20. Main Memory Cycle Time and Capacity.

A. Rate of Progress

The rate of progress in components, and therefore in compute capability, has been accelerating: From digital vacuum tube circuits to monolithics took 18 years of development; from monolithics to LSI, a much bigger step in use and application, took only 8 years. There are no signs that this accelerated process of development is diminishing, and, therefore, we can look forward to more developments of major significance such as the ones the industry has experienced in the past.

It should be noted that, despite some assertions about revolutionary progress in component technology, significant and major changes are the result of a steady evolution along a broad front of disciplines and techniques such as materials, tools, processes, design approaches, and, finally, the proper exploitation of all of these in a product application.

B. Migration of Concepts

In addition to the technology usage in other application areas, concepts of machine design and architecture first encountered in high-compute systems tend to migrate to new applications. To name just a few: Overlapped operations, cycle stealing, floating-point arithmetic, virtual memory, real-time driven interrupt mechanisms -- all these find use and applications in a trickle-down process to the smallest of computers, terminals, and industrial control mechanisms. This broadened and generalized use of capabilities stimulates the use of the technologies in turn, which enhances the capabilities and cost in the area of high-performance machines and systems. Even the procedures developed in machine-design techniques in the high end find usage in other less performance-oriented products. Examples are higher-level languages, design languages, compilers, and generalized software that are available today with microprocessors and across a broad spectrum of system performances.

With regard to one such development, namely microprocessors, it should be noted that their rapid progress will make application to high-end computing possible. While today the microprocessor is limited to relatively low performances, the use of bipolar technologies will significantly broaden its performance. Some proposals already have been made to use microprocessors as building blocks in complex high-performance systems. While it is too early to judge the extent of this development, it might turn out that the use of microprocessors in at least parts of high-performance systems could be expedient and efficient.

Within the other parts of the system, such as the communications area, the printing subsystem, and the terminal subsystem, the use of LSI in the form of microprocessors, as well as directly in memory and random logic, has given rise to increased capabilities which are replacing older electromechanical techniques.

VI. FUTURE DEVELOPMENTS

Looking forward to where changes in system architecture and component technologies might occur and to what new opportunities might present themselves is always speculative. We will view these aspects from past technology and system trends, along with what opportunities the advancing technologies will provide.

Technology will proceed in two directions -- low cost and high performance. These two approaches are not mutually exclusive. In fact, the same design parameters determining success in one area are fundamental in the evolution of the other.

To achieve lower cost, chip density must increase and therefore linear dimension must decrease. The same is true to achieve performance, but the design points are different for the two application areas, for example, power and circuit configurations.

The high-compute systems area will take advantage of the high-performance trend and productivity accomplishments to generate more powerful systems both in raw speed and in functional capability. Let's look at some of the possible results.

A. System Design Variables

As a first-order analysis, a high-compute system is governed by the following relationship:

$$\frac{1}{MIPS} = \frac{Cycles}{Instr} \times MC + BMR \times \frac{Ref}{Instr} \times MAT$$

where

MC = Machine cycle
BMR = Cache miss ratio (0.05 - 0.02)
MAT = Main memory access time
$\frac{Cycles}{Instr}$ = Rate of instructions, assuming an infinite cache (range 2-8)

It will be noted that for constant architecture and machine design, memory speed requirements will increase considerably as performance requirements of the system increase (Fig. 21)

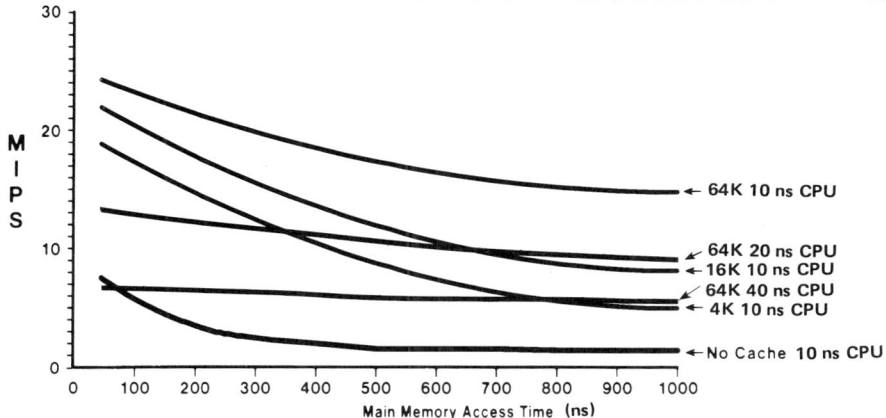

Fig. 21. *Performance of Pipelined Machine Design vs Memory Speed, Cycle Time, and Cache Size.*

An important variable is the machine cycle. It is determined primarily by technology parameters, for a given architecture and machine design, as follows:

$$\text{Machine Cycle} = L[PS_i + (1-P)S_e]$$

where
- L = Number of circuit stages in the critical path
- P = Fraction of circuit stages L, contained internal to the chips in the critical path.
- S_i, S_e = The delay for logic stages contained completely on chips (S_i) and contained between chips (S_e)

where
- Sx = Dx + (Wx · Vx)
- Dx = circuit delay
- Wx = wire length
- Vx = media speed

It should be realized that for minimum cycle time the critical path should be all on a single chip. Today's high-performance machines have about 20% of a critical path on a chip and the integration level must increase by 1 - 2 order of magnitude before this design criterion can be achieved.

B. Design Point Choices

Component optimization and selection for high-performance systems to meet fast cycle times is complex. Many factors will enter into this process. Some key ones will center on the semiconductor geometries being practiced, and the choice of how much power to use in each circuit, along with the preferred packaging and cooling approaches to follow (Fig. 22). Another key element will involve the design and manufacturing tools available to implement the manufacture of the product.

An example of this trade-off process can be illustrated by looking at the selection of a chip density for a high-performance application. The more power applied to a circuit the faster it can switch, and therefore the smaller the delay. Another way to obtain an equivalent circuit delay at lower power would be to reduce the physical size of the circuit by utilizing smaller geometries in the component design and manufacture.

These two selections having been made, the next step would involve the choice of how many circuits to put onto a chip. Before this can be done, however, it is necessary to view how the chips will be packaged in the design of the proposed product and how this packaging will affect the desired performance. High chip density with a fast circuit results in high power dissipation for that chip. When the packaging and cooling constraints are factored into such design, it may become evident that these chips must be spaced for cooling to the extent that the desired overall delay is exceeded. This may then require lowering the chip density in order to reduce the chip power dissipation which will allow closer spacing on the package, or to lower the circuit power while maintaining chip density to accomplish the same effect.

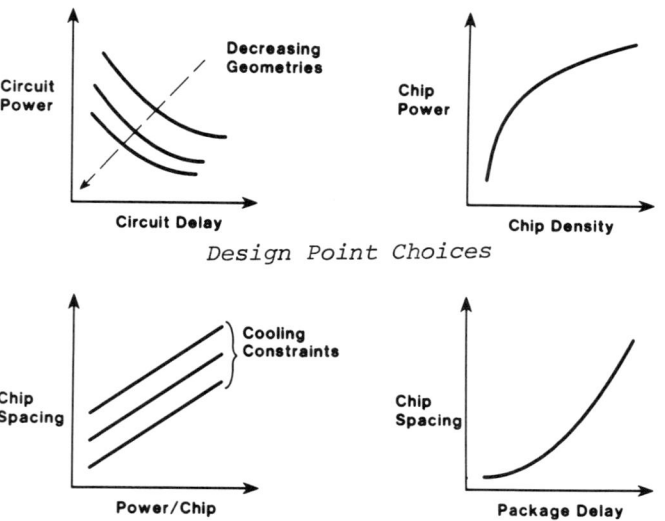

Fig. 22. Design Criteria.

One can envision bipolar logic technologies achieving machine cycle times in the few ns range, with commensurate memory and storage technologies and architectures supporting uniprocessors in the 25-100 MIPS range over the next 10 years.

C. Trends

As in the past, future product advances are most likely to occur in areas where an overlap of both technology and system improvements is beginning to take shape. In technology, substantial progress is being made in logic density, lower cost memory, and new-serial storage devices. High-performance system design techniques continue to evolve, and experience with operating array/vector and parallel processors has started.

A few words will be said about some of the more important possibilities.

1. Hardware Functions

Continued advances in denser, lower cost components make independent hardware functions more practical. The separate functions and the hardware to provide the buffering in these units so they may operate self-sufficiently will be more economical. This allows high-level macro-instructions to be implemented and greater pipelining and overlap to take place with and between these units.

2. Vector Instructions

Technology advances make array/vector hardware less expensive, and the design may benefit from high multiple usage of parts. These combined improvements may make this an economical feature, attachable to many processors. This approach is useful, not only for scientific and engineering applications, but also for vector-based languages, such as APL. This is finding widespread use in classical business applications where arrays of data must be manipulated.

3. Electronic Storage

Progress has been made in what is called the serial-storage technologies of CCD, magnetic bubbles, and in electron beam addressable memory (Fig. 23). Both CCD's and magnetic bubbles lean very heavily on the manufacturing base established for semiconductors. Therefore progress in the silicon component areas will directly affect progress in these technologies, and the cost improvement of logic and memory

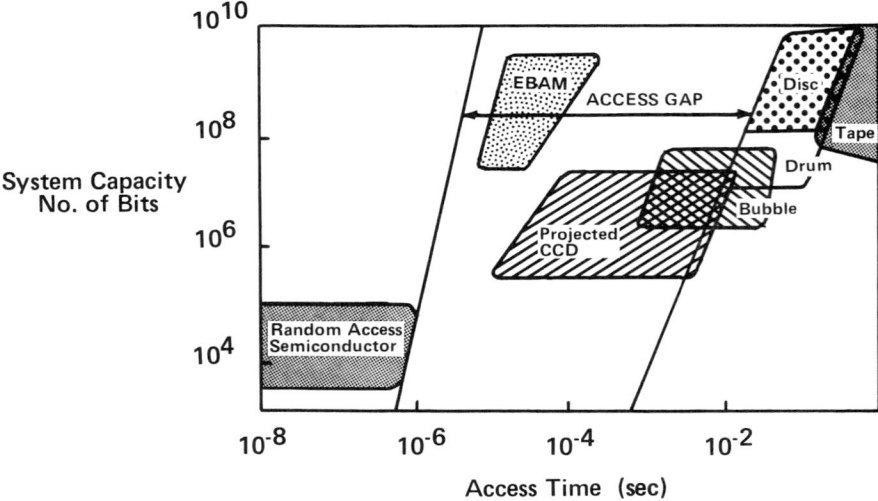

Fig. 23. Storage Technology Comparisons.

will carry over into CCD applications. Projections are being made that the cost per bit will decline rapidly and offer a cost advantage of 3 to 10 over semiconductor RAM. These new technologies may make different storage hierarchies more economical than the structures of today, and provide simpler approaches to managing overall storage.

Several options are possible, with the most obvious the substitution of one of these products for fixed head devices in the current usages. This is often referred to as an **electronic** drum. Other, more interesting options involve replacing this type of product in the storage hierarchy with software providing transparency to the user.

4. *Distributed Computing and Multiple Processors*

Centralized and distributed computing services will exist in the future. The technology advances will make large centralized data bases and localized computers more economical. High-compute systems must accommodate distributed processing and multiple processors at many levels:

- o *Within a uniprocessor -- multiple independent arithmetical and logical organs.*
- o *Within a computer system -- in the form of multiprocessing of a high order ($n > 2$), n = number of uniprocessors*
- o *Within a total data processing network -- in the form of front end processors, communication links, and local computing data processing.*

VII. SUMMARY

From those aspects of system organization and component technology which we have reviewed, we would like to draw these conclusions:

a) The interaction between high-speed compute requirements and component development has produced and will continue to produce capabilities that have far-reaching effects and provide higher-performance systems than those available today.
b) A dual trend for low cost and high performance is mutually supportive.
c) Improvements in performance and productivity will continue at a high rate.
d) The impact of LSI will require new and different design and manufacturing techniques. It will also permit different choices for system architecture, machine organization, and function.
e) There is a merging of logic, memory, and storage technologies resulting in improved system performance.
f) The trade-off between hardware and software as hardware becomes less expensive requires new analysis.
g) Second-order effects in technology such as packaging, cooling, and power distribution will assume greater importance than in the past.
h) New approaches and functions in machine architecture and organization will result because of improved technology capabilities and must be seriously considered in planning for the future.

All of these factors, interacting constructively in the fields of semiconductor technology and system design, will combine to provide new and wider user applications.

VIII. BIBLIOGRAPHY

The following bibliography lists pertinent papers arranged by major subject matter.

A. Technology and Logic

1. Anon., "Semiconductor forecast: steady technical growth," Circuits Manufacturing 17 (2), 8, 10 (1977).
2. Branscomb, L. M., "Promising areas of research in computer science and technology," Proceedings of the 2nd USA-Japan Computer Conference, AFIPS & IPST, pp. 1-7, 1975.

3. Haddad, J. A., "Implication of LSI," 1974 International Solid State Circuits Conference, Digest of the Technical Papers, pp. 50-51.
4. Henle, R. A., Ho, I. T., Johnson, W. S., Pricer, W. D., and Walsh, J. L., "The application of transistor technology to computers," IEEE Trans. Comp. C-25 (12), 1289-303 (1976).
5. Hodges, David A., "Trends in computer hardware technology," Computer Design, Vol. 15, No.2, pp. 77-85 (Feb. 1976).
6. Moore, G. E., "Progress in digital integrated electronics," 1975 International Electron Devices Meeting (Technical digest), Washington, D. C. USA, 1-3 Dec. 1975 (New York, USA: IEEE 1975), pp. 11-13.
7. Noyce, R. N., "Large Scale Integration: What is yet to come?" Science 195, 4283, pp. 1102-; March 18, 1977.
8. Keyes, Robert W., "Physical Limits in Digital Electronics," Proceedings of the IEEE 63 (5), pp. 740-767, May 1975.
9. Turn, R., "Computer systems technology forecast," Report P5344, Rand Corp., Santa Monica, Calif., 31 pp., USA (Jan. 1975).
10. Wallmark, J. T., "Fundamental physical limitations in integrated electronic circuits," Proceedings of the European Conference on Solid State Devices, 1974, pp. 133-67, EEA 78-24530.

B. Memory and Storage

11. Hodges, D. A., "A review and projection of semiconductor components for digital storage," Proceedings of IEEE 63, 1136-47 (1975), EEA78-28869.
12. Liptay, J. S., "The Model 85 Buffer Storage," IBM Systems Journal, Vol. 7, No. 1, 1968.
13. Markkula, A. C., Jr., "Semiconductor memory costs present and future," 1974 IEEE Intercon Technical Program Papers, No. 10-3.
14. Martin, R. R., "Electronic disks in the 1980's," Computer (USA) Vol. 8, No. 2, pp 24-30 (Feb. 1975).
15. Panigrahi, G., "Charge-coupled memories for computer systems," Computer 9 (4), 3342 (1976).
16. Rege, S.I., "Cost, performance, and size tradeoffs for different levels in a memory hierarchy," Computer (USA) Vol. 9, No. 4, pp. 43-51 (April 1976).

C. Systems Architecture and Design

17. Anon., "Cray-1 Computer," Report, Cray Research, Inc., 34 pp. May 20, 1975.
18. Batcher, K. E., "STARAN parallel processor system hardware," Proc. 1974 Nat. Computer Conference, 405-410.

19. Bouknight, W., Denenberg, S. A., McIntyre, D. E., Randall, J. M., Samch, A. H., and Slotnick, D. L, "The Illiac IV System," Proc. IEEE 60, April 1972, 369-388.
20. Hintz, R. G. and Tate, D. P., "Control Data STAR-100 processor design," Digest of Papers of the Sixth Annual IEEE Computer Society International Conference, San Francisco, Calif. USA, 12-14 Sept. 1972, pp. 1-4, (New York, USA-IEEE 1972).
21. Joseph, E. C., "Distributed function computer systems; Innovative trends," IEEE Computer Society International Conference, 8th COMPCON 1974 pp 71-73.
22. Papers on System/360 Model 91, IBM Journal of Research and Development, Vol. 11, No. 1, Jan. 1967.
23. Sayford, R. B., "The Amdahl 470 System," Proceedings of Share XLIV, Vol. 3, Los Angeles, Calif. pp 1564-1570, March 1975.
24. Thurber, K. J. and Wald, L. D., "Associative and parallel processors," Computing Surveys 7, pp. 215-255, December 1975.
25. Ware, W. H., "The ultimate computer," IEEE Spectrum 9 (3), 84-91 (1972).
26. Wirsching, J. E., "Computer of the 1980's - Is it a network of microcomputers?" IEEE Computer Society International Conference, pp. 23-26, COMPCON 1975.

THE INTERPRETIVE INTERFACE:
RESOURCES AND PROGRAM REPRESENTATION
IN COMPUTER ORGANIZATION*

Michael J. Flynn
Stanford University

ABSTRACT

Traditional machine architectures are based on premises of slow memory access and fixed, low-level instruction interpretation. Improved memory technology and machine understanding allow new, more efficient program representations.

A Canonic Interpretive Form (CIF) of higher level language programs is proposed to measure the "minimum" space to represent and time to interpret a given program. This "ideal" is a basis for a comparison with traditional machine languages which require ten times more program space than the CIF.

Synthesis of program forms (called Directly Executed Languages--DELs) which approach CIF measures is proposed as well as results of a recently completed FORTRAN DEL (DELTRAN).

I. INTRODUCTION

Much of the work I will report here is based upon continuing studies at the Stanford Emulation Laboratory [7] supported especially by my colleagues L. W. Hoevel and C. J. Neuhauser.

The inadequacies of present machine architectures both as program representations and as vehicles for machine interpretation is becoming increasingly obvious to many workers in the field, especially this author. The inadequacies are illustrated by program size, execution time, as well as many less obvious secondary effects which lead to Byzentine implementations of compilers, translators, operating systems and machine interlock mechanisms for detecting possible concurrency in instruction execution. Furthermore, implementation approaches

---

* The work described herein was supported in part by the U.S. Energy Research and Development Administration under Contract No. E(04-3)-326 P.A.39, and in part by the Army Research Office-Durham under Grant No. DAAG29-76-G-0001.

to the aforementioned system components tend to be ad hoc in that they adopt tacit assumptions about traditional machine instructions.

The purpose of this paper is to explore these tacit assumptions and investigate uniform and systematic methods of developing "ideal" program representations and expeditious execution of these program.

II. THE HIERARCHICAL MODEL [1]

Consider the following sentence: An algorithm specifies <u>tasks</u> composed of higher level language <u>statements</u> which are represented as <u>instruction units</u> which cause <u>state transitions in a host machine</u>. This sentence describes a five level hierarchical interpretation (see Fig. 1). Each level represents the same object (program) in a different way; i.e. the same state transitions and resources are required, yet the coding of the requests are different. The problem of efficient program interpretation begins at the upper most level. It is difficult, if not impossible, to recover from faulty representation at one level by interpretation at lower levels. At each level we would like to minimize space to represent the program and the time to interpret the program. The significance of uniform formal techniques to define ideal program representations and their interpretations for each level seems to be imperative. The focus of the remainder of this paper will be on the lowest three nodes of the hierarchy tree.

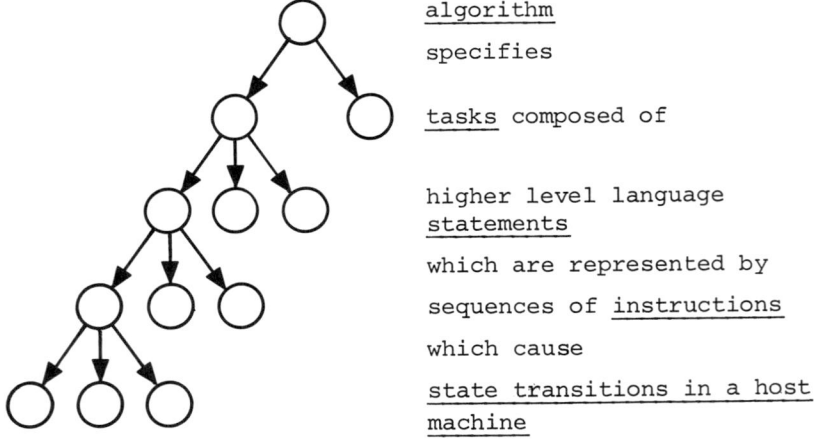

Fig. 1 Hierarchical Structure of a Problem

The remainder of the paper will include a review of traditional machine language problems, a discussion of ideal intermediate program representation at the instruction level, and a generalized discussion of synthesis of program structures for interpretation.

III. TRADITIONAL MACHINE LANGUAGE PROBLEMS AND SOME FUNDAMENTAL CONCEPTS

Traditional instruction sets have been designed within the following constraints:

(a) The instruction repertoire is static and cannot be dynamically modified. The introduction of new instructions is a difficult procedure at best.
(b) Instruction execution time is dominated by the time required to fetch an instruction and its operands from memory. As many as ten or twenty internal operations (cycles) comprise the interpretation of an instruction.
(c) Since most of the time is spent accessing memory, the instruction set is chosen to minimize the number of memory references at the expense of new and more complex instructions. This gives rise to the rich and powerful instruction sets of second and third generation architectures.

These constraints, while understandable in the context of slow memory technology, give rise to significant inefficiencies in program representation. Moreover, substantial improvements in memory technology have yet to be reflected in improvements in these representations. Some more notable inefficiencies include:

1. fixed name and space representations
2. rigid operational environments
3. limited format types

We review each of these areas as well as a preliminary evaluation of efficiency in the remainder of this section.

A. Name Space

A program consists of a set of action rules defined over a space of <u>object names</u>. A set of all object names that can be acted on directly by the programs defines the <u>name space</u> of the program. The key word here is directly. When a program accesses a file it cannot act directly on the data in that file. Rather we must first move it into the name space available to the program. The name space then consists of all locations visible to the action rules (or instruction set) of the program. Clearly, this includes the program location themselves, the register set and all possible data areas.

Some characteristics of the name space of a program include:

1. range and resolution
2. homogeneity
3. flexibility in interpreting object structures

1. Range and Resolution

The range and resolution refer to the constraints on the maximum number of objects that can be specified in a program space and the minimum size of an object in that space, respectively. The traditional instruction set arrangement has resolution to an 8 bit byte and range defined as large as one can comfortably accomodate within the bounds of a reasonable instruction size and, hence, program size. It is, on the other hand, no secret that the information contents of such an arrangement is very low, Hammerstrom [2] estimates less than 5% information content in a typical address sequence in instructions. In fact, the entire artifact of the use of cache in computer organizations is predicated on this low information content in the address field. The principal of locality in programs defines regions of current activity which can be captured in a small fast working storage. Since each region is of small size, it is clear that the actual entropy in the address information is far less than the total range of the program address.

2. The Homogeneity of the Name Space

The name space may be partitioned in many different ways for different purposed and at different levels. There may be a supervisor/problem state partition--leaving certain elements of the name space visible only to the processor control program (supervisor) and the remainder of the name space available to problem programs. Even within a process, partitioning of the space may be done for reasons of performance--for example, breaking the space into a set of named registers and "main memory". Thus, many familiar machines have their name space partitioned into a register space and memory space: System 360, PDP-11, etc. As the partitioning of the name space increases, its <u>homogeneity</u> decreases. As we shall see, available data does not support such partitions for performance improvement. In order to improve performance, the incidence of load and store instructions into registers from the memory space must be small enough to justify the partition. For example, consider the following accumulator oriented sequence:

    Load accumulator, A
    Add accumulator, B
    Store accumulator, C
compared to a three address instruction. The reason for the
accumulator in the designers eye, was to avoid unnecessary
data references to memory. The premise is that programs
could be partitioned into relatively long sequences of
arithmetic operations with a minimum of register initialization.
When the average incidence of load and store instructions
approach twice the incidence of functional operations,
this premise has vanished.

3. *Interpretation Flexibility*

Flexibility of interpretation of the object structure
refers to the number, variety and richness of the data
structures available to the operation vocabulary. Inflexible
object structures result in considerable program representation
manipulation to cause proper functional transformations.

4. *Examples of Name Space*

Some examples in traditional machine terminology might
be useful. System 360 has a range of 2^{24} elements with
resolution to the byte, has a nonhomogeneous name space consisting
of 16 general purpose registers, 8 floating point
registers and 2^{24} memory space elements. It may specify and
interpret such object structures as integers, character
strings, decimal and floating point numbers and logical
vectors. The PDP-11 has a memory space range of 2^{16} bytes,
its name space is split into 8 general purpose registers and
the memory space. It allows interpretation of integers,
bytes, logical vectors and floating point representations
(optional).

B. Operational Environments

Higher level language representation of programs presents
a serious mismatch between the functional operations in the
language and the actual operation vocabulary of the processor.
Thus, inconsistencies between arithmetic types as well as
procedural facilities in the instruction set program representation
and the higher level languages representation
creat additional instructions and, thus, require additional
interpretation time to fully execute the higher level
language statement.

Familiar examples include the IF statement--a three way
branch in FORTRAN which may require three machine language
instructions; the DO statement involves at least the same
number of machine instructions. Even a simple assignment

often requires both a load and a store instruction as a result of the previously mentioned splitting of the name space.

C. Format Limitations

Most familiar machines used for large computation are of the fixed format type. The size of the instruction may vary but not the interpretation or the transformation of the operands. Thus, A op B → A is the familiar System 360 transformation, where A, B may be either a register name or memory space name. It is generally impossible to do A op B → B if op is non-commutative. It is also not possible to implicitly specify a stack or accumulator.

This rigidity in type of transformation and incompleteness of classes of transformation represents another source of inefficiency in machine instruction program representation that will be discussed next.

D. Measuring the Efficiency of Machine Instruction Program Representation [3]

In this section we review some well known data describing instruction usage in the IBM 7090 computer series and System 360. This code usage data is examined as to the relationship of a computer architecture to its user environment. Different architectures exist because they presume to provide more efficient program representations and executions. That is, the static program size (amount of storage required to represent a program) as well as the dynamic program size (number of instructions required for program execution) have in some sense been minimized.

One measure of this "optimization" is to compare program statistics for a particular architecture against an ultimately simple, fully explicit architecture. In a simple architecture nothing is implied--no registers or counters are invisible to the problem state programmer. Each instruction contains an operation, the full generalized address specification (allowing, if necessary, multiple levels of indirection through tables, etc.) for both source operands, a result operand, and a test of the result which selects an address for the next instruction. Of course, familiar architectures achieve their compact instruction representation at the expense of additional "overhead" instructions to load and store registers, alter the in-line sequence of code (branch), etc.

We define three types of instructions[1]:

M-instructions are memory partition movement instruction; such as the LOAD and STORE instruction which move data items within a storage hierarchy.

P-instructions are procedural instructions which perform functions associated with instruction sequencing, i.e., TEST, BRANCH, COMPARE, etc., but perform no transformation on data.

F-instructions perform computational functions in that they operate on data. They include arithmetic operations of all types, as well as logical and shifting operations.

Instructions which merely rearrange data across partitions of a memory name space or which alter ordinary sequencing are "overhead" instructions. The ratio of these overhead instructions to functional instructions is indicative of the use of an architecture. An overhead instruction exists in the representation of a program so as to match the original program requirements to the requirements of the machine languages. The most common overhead instructions in program representation concern the range, resolution and homogeneity of the name space: e.g. load and store of registers, push and pop the stack, etc. Overhead instructions are clearly undesirable because they require additional units in the representation of the program as well as additional interpretation time of the execution of the program.

To quantify "overhead" we define three ratios:

1. M-ratio: ratio of M-instructions to F-instructions

2. P-ratio: ratio of P-instructions to F-instructions

3. NF-ratio: ratio of the sum of M and P instructions to F-instructions.

These ratios are tabulated in Table 3 for IBM 7090, System 360 and PDP-10 [4].

---

[1] The categorization of M, P and F type instructions is for the technical code presented only. Obviously for a SORT program a MOVE might be a F-type instruction: pointing up the more general problem of separating an architectural artifact from a true program function.

TABLE 1

Gibson Mix, 7090 based, General technical programs

Instruction Type	Frequency Per 100 Instructions	
Load/Store	31.2 }	49.2 M-type
Index	18	
Branch	16.6 }	20.4 P-type
Compare	3.8	
Fixed Point	6.9	
Floating Point	12.2 }	25.1 F-type
Shift/Boolean	6.0	
Other	5.3	5.3

TABLE 2

360 instruction frequencies

Instruction Type	Frequency Per 100 Instructions General Technical	
M-type: (includes)		
Storage - Register		
Register - Reg. and		
Storage - Storage		
(total)		45.1 M-type
P-type:		
Branching	27.5 }	
Compare	10.8	
(total)		38.3 P-type
F-type:		
Fixed Point	7.6	
Floating Point	3.2 }	
Boole/Shift	4.5	
(total)		15.3 F-type
Other:	1.3	

TABLE 3

Processor	"Ideal"	7090	360	PDP-10
M-ratio	0.0	2.0	2.9	1.5
P-ratio	0.0	0.8	2.5	1.1
NF-ratio	0.0	2.8	5.5	2.6

Note that the "ideal" machine would have a zero entry for all ratios. Also note that for these machines between 2.6 and 5.5 non-functional instructions are required for each functional instruction emplying that the size of programs could be reduced by this factor.

IV. TOWARDS AN IDEAL PROGRAM REPRESENTATION

What are the criteria which might define an "ideal" program representation? The measure must lie in some sort of space-time product; i.e., space to represent the program and the time to interpret it. Actually, the requirements are more general than this since they should also consider at least space to contain the compiler which will create the program representation as well as time for the compilation, and further the space requirements of the interpreter itself. However, for the moment let us focus on the issue of space to represent the program and the time to interpret it. Further, let us concentrate on the primary location of inefficiency in the program representation, the machine language level.

A. The Canonic Interpretive Form of Programs

The search for an "ideal" program representation is certainly an undecideable issue. Therefore, it is imperative to find a constructive measure for program space and interpretation time that one could then use as an exploration of alternate representations. This characterization or measure, while not necessarily achievable, should intuitively represent a clearly superior program representation and also be readily definable and easy to use.

We propose the following "Canonic Interpretive Form" of a program. This form has space measure in number of bits of program size; and time measure in number of memory references to a target name space. The rules for the measures of "Canonic Interpretive Form" of a program are given in Table 4.

We are assuming that the source program to which this measure is applied is in optimal form. The generation of the form is relatively straightforward. For each source statement ($n \leq 2$) in the original representation there is one instruction in the form. For the moment one might think that a traditional three address format would accomplish this. However, rule 2 requires that only unique variables be identified explicitly. The statement $X + X \rightarrow X$, has only one unique variable; thus by rules 1 and 2 this statement should be represented by a single instruction unit consisting of a single operation and single operand specification.

TABLE 4

CANONIC INTERPRETIVE FORM (CIF) OF A PROGRAM

1) <u>The 1:1 property</u>: for each Higher Level Language (HLL) statement with n ≤ 2 operations there is one instruction unit allowed in the CIF. For n > 2 operations there are n-1 instruction units.

2) <u>Instruction unit size</u>:
   (i) each instruction unit consists of a single operation container, OP, of size $\log_2$[number of HLL operations in a scope (or program environment)] bits

   (ii) a single operand container is allowed for each unique HLL statement variable

   (iii) the size of this operand container is: $\log_2$[number of HLL variables in a scope] bits

3) <u>Memory references</u>:
   (i) Each HLL procedural statement creates a single procedural instruction unit. Each such procedural instruction causes one reference.

   (ii) Each unique variable causes one reference.

What is an operation? The functional operations (+, -, *, ÷, SQRT, etc.) are clear; however, some allowance must be made for array operations. If the element of an array is identified, A(I,J), then that specification at the source level should be thought of an an operation in the canonic form. Thus, consider the previous example, A(I,J) + A(I,J) → A(I,J), requires two instruction units, the first to compute A(I,J), the second to compute the sum of the elements as before. Thus:

Example 1: X + X → X | + | X |

Example 2: A(I,J) + A(I,J) → A(I,J) | ARRAY | A | I | J | A(I,J) |

where array computes the address of | + | A(I,J) |
A(I,J)--this address is stores: i.e. completes the local identification of the name A(I,J). This then is used in the second instruction unit as before.

For purposes of this measure procedural operator such as IF or DO, each count as a single functional operator. The predicate expression of the IF statement must be evaluated independently by the above measures. Distinct labels are treated as distinct operands.

Example 3: IF (X-Y) A,B,C, might be represented as:

| - | X | Y |

| IF | A | B | C |

The third measure, memory reference activity, has two parts. A reference is allowed for each unique variable. In the statement X + X → X, one reference is allowed for X in the range and one is allowed for X the domain of the function + since they are not the same. Concerning instruction fetching, only a change to the reference pattern is accounted for since most instructions lie in line and referencing activity can be predicted.

The first measure evaluates both space and time of the program representation since fewer instructions occupy less space and require less time for interpretation. The second measure is a measure of space alone, since it requires conciseness only in identification of the number of variables and the size of each variable. The third measure is a measure of time alone.

The measures may be applied either statically or dynamically. It should be pointed out that a static measure of memory reference activity in the uninterpreted source is strictly a comparative measure and is of limited value.

Rules (1) and (2) represent a notion of <u>statement transformational completeness</u> in program representation. That is, that there exists a transformation for binary and lower order operations such that explicit temporary storage identification can always be avoided by using implied resources and variable formats. Since we have not made allowances for multiple formats, i.e. transformation types, programs representation techniques which attempt to realize a canonic measure will fall short by at least a few bits per instruction unit for format identifier.

B. An Example

The following FORTRAN subroutine body presents a simple example:

1.   I = I + 1
2.   J = (J-1)*I
3.   K = (J-1)*(K-I)

I, J and K are "full-word" integers whose initial values are in memory and whose final values must be stored in memory for output later in the program.

The canonic measures for this example can be readily computed

(1) Instruction units:
    Statement 1 - 1 i.u. (n=2)
    Statement 2 - 2 i.u. (n=3)
    Statement 3 - 3 i.u. (n=4)
        total   6 i.u.

(2) Size of Instruction units

$$\text{OP container} = \lceil \log_2 4 \rceil = 2 \text{ bits}$$

(operations are +, -, *, =)

$$\text{OPERAND container} = \lceil \log_2 4 \rceil = 2 \text{ bits}$$

(operands are 1, I, J, K)

number of operand containers:
    Statement 1 - 2 containers
    Statement 2 - 3 containers
    Statement 3 - 4 containers
        total   9 containers

(3) Number of memory references:
     1 for instruction run
     9 for operand fetches
     3 for operand stores
    13 total

(4) Total program size:
    6 i.u. x 2 bits = 12 bits for OP code
    9 container x 2 bits = 18 bits for operands
                               30 bits

Below is the listing produced for an IBM System 370 optimizing compiler (FORTRAN IV level H opt = 2)

```
1   L     10, 112( 0,13)
    L     11,  80( 0,13)
    LR    3,11
    A     3,   0( 0,10)
    ST    3,   0( 0,10)
2   L     7,   4( 0,10)
    SR    7,11
    MR    6, 3
    ST    7,   4( 0,10)
3   LR    4, 7
    SR    4, 3
    LCR   3, 3
    A     3,   8( 0,10)
    MR    2, 4
    ST    3,   8( 0,10)
```

The increased program size is a direct result of the 370 split name space, indirect memory name referencing (thru base registers) and restricted formats.

Table 5 compares this code to CIF measures:

TABLE 5

Comparison for the Example

		370 FORTRAN H opt	Extended non opt	CIF
(1)	number of instructions	15	19	6
(1.1)	M-type	9	13	0
(1.2)	F-type	6	6	6
(2)	M-ratio (=NF-ratio)	1.5	2.7	0.0
(3)	Program size	368 bits	604 bits	30 bits
(4)	Memory References	23	36	13

C. Synthesis of Canonic Program Representations

Before treating the synthesis problem the introduction of some additional concepts will be useful.

Target Machine: The semantics of a program representation at any hierarchical level J defines the target machine for

that representation. Traditional machine languages are
usually thought of as target machines for emulation while
newer concepts in environmentally oriented program representations are referred to as directly executed languages (DELs).

Directly Executed Language (DEL): We define the DEL as
the target machine which corresponds to a simple one step
mapping of a higher level language program representation.
The DEL, being a target machine, consists of
1. a name space
2. operation vocabulary
3. sequence rules.

Host Machine and DEL Interpreter: A host machine,
together with a particular DEL interpreter, is the agent that
responds to DEL rules and causes correct transitions in the
DEL name space. The host machine is actually a target machine
at level J-1. In turn, it may be interpreted by a J-1 interpreter together with a J-2 host machine. While not important
in our context, the level 0 machine is the final physical
realization of the required state transformations.

The interpreter then is that program written for the host
machine which takes a particular DEL and causes, corresponding
to the DEL transformation rules, appropriate state transformations in the DEL name space. In order to accomplish this, the
interpreter must have its own name space and cause its own
host machine state transitions. The name space of the interpreter and the DEL should be separate, the interpreter for
example residing in "control store" which is otherwise
unaddressable by any other entity.

V. SYNTHESIS OF SIMPLE HOST MACHINES

A. Simple Host Machine Structures

Since the host machine will undergo a number of state
transitions before it completes the interpretation of a
single DEL instruction unit, and since presumably the host
machine will not be designed uniquely for the interpretation
of a single DEL, the need for speed in interpretation is
obvious. The program for the interpretation of the DEL must
be stored in high speed read write storage. Since this
storage will by and large determine host machine state transition times, it will therefore also determine the interpretation speed of the host machine. Since the traditional machine
instructions premise of slow memory access is no longer true,
at least for small memory sizes, a new arrangement of host
machine instructions seem to be in order. This would stress
(1) multiple simultaneous access to resources of the system,
(2) overlapped access to fast interpretive store which contains

interpreter parameters.

Additionally, a number of specific host machine attributes have been identified [5] which are significant in producing interpretive performance. We mention several of these below:
- (1) Flexible field extraction and manipulation for generalized decoding
- (2) Residual control for dynamically reconfiguring both internal and external environment
- (3) Capability for constructing complex address mapping functions
- (4) Large amount of writeable interpretive storage with simple mechanisms for reading or writing any portion
- (5) Flexible host instruction sequencing with comprehensive facility for bit setting and testing which can be used for sequencing
- (6) Parallelism within a host instruction and host environment arranged to aid in eliminating host overhead instructions.

B. A Sample Host Architecture

Consider the organization outlined in Fig. 2. The general purpose registers contain the instruction register and instruction counter. Assume that the instruction width is the same as the data word width (perhaps 32 bits). A typical host instruction is partitioned into three fragments, each of which is essentially a primitive instruction with simultaneous action of typical host instruction fragments shown below:

I. (F) $C(R_1)$ OP $C(R_2) \rightarrow C(R_1)$

II. (M) $C(R_3)$ $\xleftarrow{\text{LOAD}}\xrightarrow{\text{STORE}}$ C(MICROSTORAGE ADDRESS)

III. (P) IF   (TEST = 1)
         THEN $* \leftarrow * + \Delta$
         ELSE $* \leftarrow * + 1$

(a) A register-to-register operation of the F-type. OP uses the contents of R_1 and the contents of R_2 as arguments, placing the result in R_1.

(b) A load or store from microstroage into the general purpose registers. Immediate values can be contained in the address field in this structure fragment.

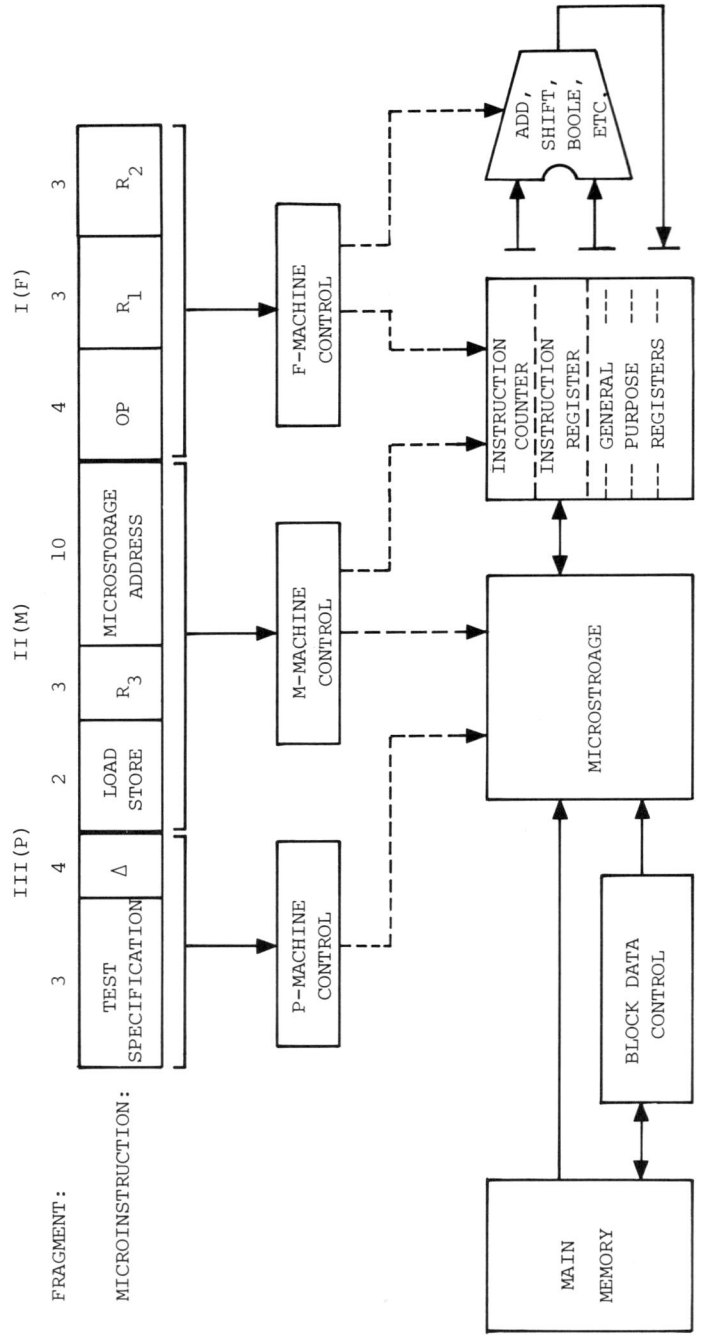

Fig. 2: Sample Host Machine

(c) The branch instruction or P-type. This includes specification of a test mask and an offset value (Δ) relative to the location counter (*).

The net effect is to simultaneously control the operation of three finite state machines; an F machine, an M machine, and a P machine. Actually it will not always be possible to exploit concurrent operations. Inconsistent use of the registers by two of the fragments could cause a conflict. Also it may not be possible in many instances to write code which uses all three fields.

The concurrency gives use to an interesting type of overlapped operation: while the F fragment transforms current data values, the P fragment tests the results of the preceding instruction and the M fragment fetches ahead new data for the following F instruction fragment. Notice that while a split name space is still used, no additional time is required to manage the partition; since every F fragment carries an M fragment with it. (We make no pretense here that a split name space is always required in an efficient host or that the above is the only way to handle it.) In any event, the foregoing instruction resembles a familiar microinstruction. This instruction executes in essentially one machine cycle--perhaps 200 nanoseconds--using ordinary circuitry. Depending upon the arrangement of microstorage, conflicts between the load/store fragment and next-instruction-fetch mechanism could double the instruction execution time.

For transfer of input data to and from main memory, an alternate instruction format is used. This instruction format is block--oriented and asynchronously moves blocks of data between microstorage and main storage. Thus, main memory is in many ways treated as an I/O device. Notice that this treatment, except for its explicit nature, is very similar to cache-based memory systems already in use.

The example is actually an abstraction of a machine in use at Stanford called EMMY [6,7]. EMMY word size, timing and parallel host instruction philosophy are similar to this example. Other host machine structures designed for similar interpretive purposes should also be mentioned [5], especially Burroughs B1700 [8].

VI. DEL SYNTHESIS[1]

A. Terms and Assumptions

In order to synthesize simple "quasi-ideal" DELs, let us make some fairly obvious straight forward assignments and

---

[1]The material presented in this section is a much simplified and shortened version of [9].

assumptions:
> (1) The DEL program representation lies in the main storage of the host machine.
> (2) The interpreter for the DEL lies in a somewhat faster, smaller interpretive storage. The interpreter includes the actual interpretive subroutines as well as certain parameters associated with interpretation.
> (3) A small number of registers exist in the host machine which contain local and environmental information associated with the interpretation of the current DEL instruction. Further assume that communications between interpretive storage and this register set can be overlapped with transformations on the register set (Fig. 3a).

Before preceding, an elaboration on some notions concerning DEL instruction structure will be useful. A <u>template</u> is a binary string partitioned into <u>containers</u> by action of the interpretive program. A <u>container</u> is an element of the vector bit string. It is an identifier for either a format, operand field, or operation field. In general, the containers specify the following information:
> (1) format and (implicitly) the number of operands
> (2) the operands
> (3) operations to be performed (of at most binary order) on the identified operands
> (4) sequencing information, if required.

A <u>format</u> is a transformation rule identifying:
> (1) template partition (i.e. number and meaning of containers)
> (2) the order of the operation: i.e. whether the operation in nullary, unary or binary
> (3) ordering precedence among operands

The container size is the maximum size that a field may take on. Container size is determined by the number of elements required in a locality, thus, the structure of the DEL instruction unit might consist of a template outlined in Fig. 3b.

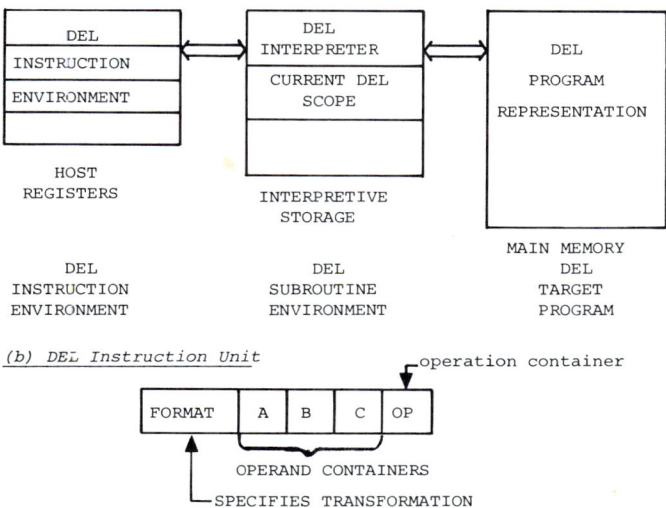

Fig. 3: DEL Model

B. DELs Which Approach Canonic Form

There are four notions useful in defining a DEL which approaches canonical form: environment, contour, operation and format.

1. Environment

The notion of environment is fundamental not only to DELs but also to traditional machine languages as evidenced by widespread adoption of cache and virtual memory concepts. What is proposed here is akin in some respects to the cache concept and yet quite distinct from it. We recognize locality as an important property of a program name space and handle it explicitly under interpreter control. Thus, locality is transparent to the DEL name space but recognized and managed by the interpreter. Properties of the environment are:

(1) The DEL name space is homogeneous and uniform with an a priori unbounded range and variable resolution.
(2) Operations, involving for example the composition of addresses which use registers, should not be present in the DEL code but should be part of the interpreter code only. Thus, the register name space and the interpreter name space are largely not part of the DEL name space and it is the function of the inter-

preter to optimize register allocation.
(3) The environmental locality will be defined by the higher level language for which this representation is created. In FORTRAN, for example, it would correspond to function or subroutine scope.
(4) Unique to every environment is a scope which includes:
   (i)   a label contour,
   (ii) an operand contour,
   (iii) an operation table.

2. Contours

Following the model of J. Johnson [10], <u>contour</u> is a vector (a table) of object descriptors. When an environment is invoked, a contour of label and variable addresses must be placed (or already present) in the interpretive storage. For a simple static language like FORTRAN this creation can be done at load time. For languages that allow recursion, etc., the creation of the contour would be done before entering a new environment. An entry in the contour consists of the (main memory) address of the variable to be used; this is the full and complete DEL name space address. Type information and other descriptive details may also be included as part of the entry.

The environment must provide a pointer into the current contour. Environment further must provide an index of width of the container for labels and variables. Typically, the environment pointer and width index would be maintained in the registers of the host machine. If W is the index of width of the environment and EP is the environmental pointer into the current contour contained in interpretive storage, then Fig. 4a illustrates the accessing process. Both labels and variables may be indexed off the same environmental pointer. The DEL source instruction unit, then, has containers which define indices in the current contour that identify a target name space address.

3. Operations

Each verb or operation in the higher level language identifies a corresponding interpretive operator in the DEL program representation (exclude for the moment control actions which will be discussed shortly). The routines for interpreting all familiar operations are expected to lie in the interpretive storage. Certain unusual operations, such as the trigonomentric functions may not always be contained in the interpretive storage. A pointer to an operator translation table must be part of the environment; the actual operations used are indicated by a small index container off this pointer (Fig. 4b). The table is also present in the interpretive storage. For simple languages, this latter step is probably unnecessary since the total number of operations may be easily contained in, for example, a six bit field and the saving in DEL program representation may not justify the added interpretive step.

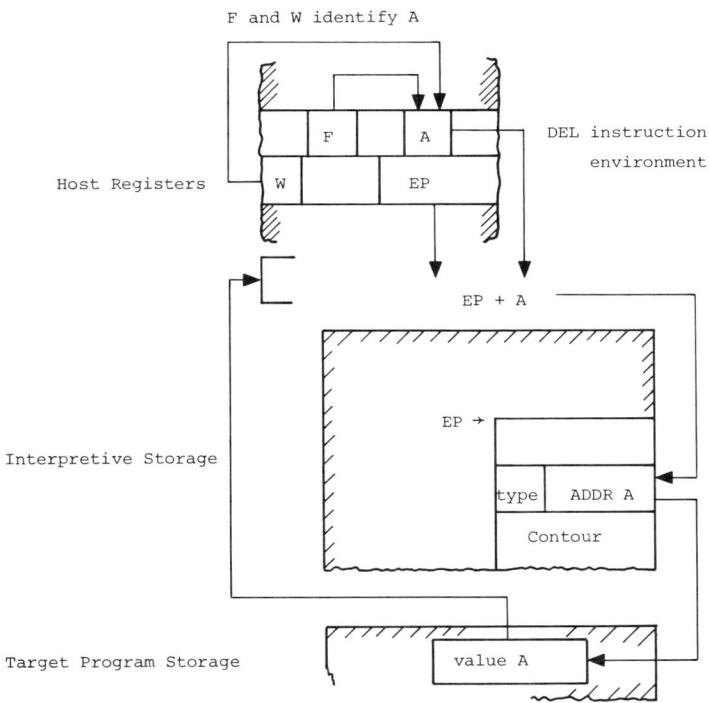

Fig. 4a: Variable Accessing in DEL

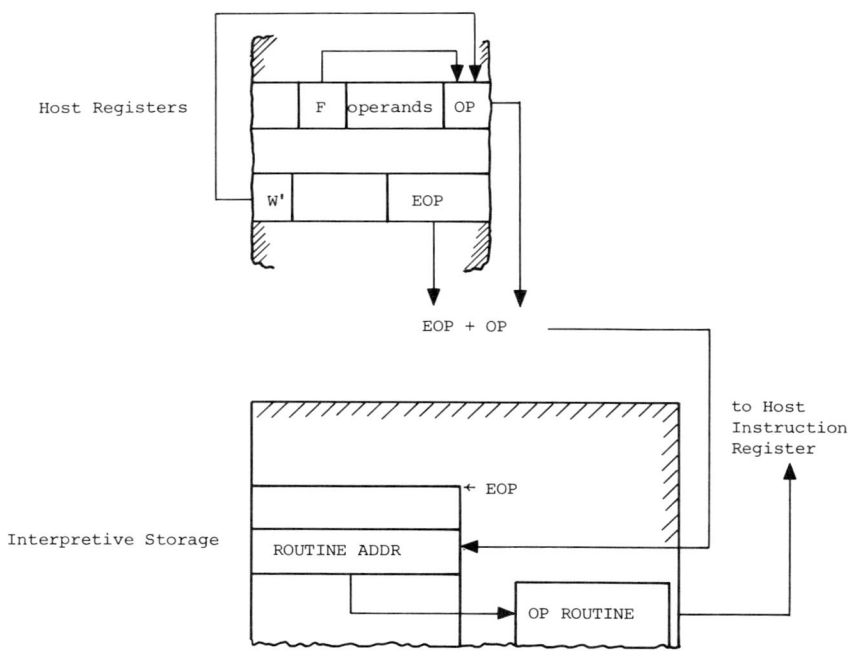

Fig. 4b: Operation Access in DEL

3. Formats for Tranformational Completeness

In order to achieve a form of transformational completeness property mentioned earlier, three distinct kinds of transformation must be considered based on the order of the operation--the nullary operation which assumes no operand, the unary operation which assumes one source and produces one result, and the binary operation which takes two source operands and produces a single result. In order to achieve completeness, a stack should also be available. However, the DEL formats should contain no "overhead instructions" for handling the stack. That is, the stack will always be "pushed" when used as a sink and always be "popped" when used as a source.

Then for transformational completeness we have the following formats:

nullary case, one format

$F_{0,1}$	OP

unary case, five formats (T is top of stack)

$F_{1,1}$	A	B	OP
$F_{1,2}$	A	OP	
$F_{1,3}$	A	OP	
$F_{1,4}$	A	OP	
$F_{1,5}$	OP		

OP A → B
OP A → T
OP T → A
OP A → A
OP T → T

binary case, formats (T,U are top and under the top elements of the stack, respectively)

$F_{2,1}$	A	B	C	OP
$F_{2,2}$	A	B	OP	
$F_{2,3}$	A	B	OP	
$F_{2,4}$	A	B	OP	
$F_{2,5}$	A	OP		
$F_{2,6}$	A	B	OP	
$F_{2,7}$	A	B	OP	
$F_{2,8}$	A	B	OP	
$F_{2,9}$	A	OP		
$F_{2,10}$	A	OP		
$F_{2,11}$	A	OP		
$F_{2,12}$	A	OP		
$F_{2,13}$	A	OP		
$F_{2,14}$	A	OP		
$F_{2,15}$	A	OP		
$F_{2,16}$	OP			

A OP B → C
A OP B → B
A OP B → A
A OP A → B
A OP A → A
A OP B → T
A OP T → B
T OP A → B
T OP A → A
A OP T → A
A OP A → T
A OP T → T
T OP A → T
T OP T → A
T OP U → A
T OP U → T

The binary formats vary from all explicit ABC type formats to all stack oriented formats, TUT format. Note that A, B and C are explicit variables, T infers the top of the stack, U the element underneath the top of the stack. While there are a total of over three hundred format transformations possible, it is easy to show more formally that the above 21 accomplish all possible valid transformations without overhead. Note that transformations such as U OP B → A, U OP T → T do not follow a uniform stack discipline while transformations such as C OP B → A are merely identifier permutations and unnecessary.

Furthermore, the size of a transformational complete (to a binary order) set can be minimized by observing that the trailing OP container can specify the order of the operation. This allows F_0 and F_1 formats to be subsumed into the binary. Also the four "identical" source formats (such as A OP A → B) require the compiler to identify argument equivalence. Given such a compiler, it would more likely optimize the source to eliminate the redundancy rather than require such formats for representation.

Thus, practical <u>binary transformational completeness</u> is achievable with twelve formats. So far we have ignored the control problem; statements such as IF, DO or GOTO actually represent a transformation on the sequencing structure and are more appropriately recognized as distinct formats rather than functional operations. A format for each of the aforementioned procedures would add three to the twelve previously discussed totaling fifteen formats as a useful complete set of formats.

C. AN EXAMPLE

Again consider the example previously considered:

```
1    I = I+1
2    J = (J-1)*I
3    K = (J-1)*(K-I)
```

This might be implemented as follows:

		4	2	2	2	
1		$F_{2,3}$	I	1	+	I+1 → I
		4	2	2	2	
2		$F_{2,6}$	J	1	−	J−1 → T
		4	2	2	2	
		$F_{2,8}$	I	J	*	T*I → J
		4	2	2	2	
3		$F_{2,6}$	J	1	−	J−1 → T
		4	2	2	2	
		$F_{2,6}$	K	I	−	K−I → T
		4	2	2		
		$F_{2,15}$	K	*		T*U → K

where T and U are again the top and under the top stack elements. Note that the stack is "pushed" automatically by the 5th instruction and the 6th instruction "pops" the stack for further use.

The canonic rules apply directly to container size--two bits are allowed to identify the four variables and two bits are used for the four operations.

Note that the canonic number of instructions are achieved as are the variable and operation container sizes. However, 4 bits additional instruction are required to identify one of fifteen formats discussed in the preceding section. Also, note the difference between transformation completeness at the statement level (required by the canonic rules) and achievable transformational completeness which is always accomplished only on single order statements. Thus, the additional $<J>$ container in instruction 3 and the additional $<K>$ container in instruction 6. These data containers do not, however, represent additional memory references--since separate domain and range references are also required in the CIF if a single variable is so used. The comparison with the CIF measures are shown in Table 6.

TABLE 6

Comparison With CIF

	achieved	CIF
# of i.u.	6	6
operand containers	11	9
container size	2 bits	2 bits
program size	30^b+6*4+2*2 (formats) = 60 bits	30 bits
memory reference (assume 32 bits/refr.)	2 for instr. + $\underline{12}$ for data 14	1 for instr $\underline{12}$ for data 13

In the table we have assumed 32 bits per instruction reference. Note that while the program size has grown with respect to CIF it is still substantially less than System 370 represnetation (Table 6); other measures are comparable to CIF.

VII. DELTRAN AND FURTHER RESULTS [11]

The example discussed in the preceding section may be criticized as being non-typical in its DEL comparisons:
1. The container sizes are quite small, thus, reducing size measures for the DEL code.
2. Program control is not included.
3. The program reduction in space may come at the expense of host machine interpretation time.

In response to the first criticism, it is interesting to note that the program representation grows as a log function of the number of variables and operations used in an environment. Suppose there were sixteen variables, this might increase overall program size to 90 bits, an increase of 50%. It is even more interesting, however, to observe what happens to the same three statements when they are interspersed in a larger context with perhaps 16 variables and 20 statements and compiled into System 370 code. The size of the object code produced by the compiler for either optimized or unoptimized versions increases by almost exactly the same 50%--primarily because the compiler is unable to optimize variable and register usage.

The absence of program control also plays no significant statistical affect. A typical FORTRAN DO or IF is compiled into between 3 and 9 System 370 instructions (assuming a simple IF predicate) depending upon the size of the context in which the statement occurs. Thus, the inclusion of program control will not significantly alter the statistics and may even make the DEL argument more favorable.

The third criticism is more difficult to respond to. We submit that host interpretation time should not be noticeably increased over a traditional machine instruction if the same premises are made, since (1) 16 DEL formats must be contrasted against perhaps 6 or 8 System 370 formats (using the same definition of format)--not a significant implementation difference. (2) Some features are required by a 370 instruction even if not required by the instruction, e.g. indexing. Name completion through base registers is a similar situation since the base values remain the same over several instructions. (3) Approximately the same number of state transitions are required for either a DEL instruction or a traditional machine instruction if each is referred to its own "well mapped" host interpreter. In fact, for an unbiased host designed for interpretation the interpretation time is approximately the same for either a DEL instruction or a System 370 instruction.

The language DELtran, upon which the aforementioned example was based, has been developed by my colleague Lee Hoevel as a FORTRAN DEL. The performance and vital statistics of DELtran on the host EMMY is quite interesting especially when compared to the 370 performance on the same system (Table 7).

The table is constructed using a version of the Whetstone benchmark which was developed by the National Physical Laboratory (U.K.). It is widely accepted and used for FORTRAN machine evaluation. The EMMY host system referred to in the table is a very small system--the processor consists of one board with 305 circuit modules and 4096 32 bit words of interpretive storage. It is clear that the DELtran performance is significantly superior to the 370 in every measure.

TABLE 7

DELtran - System 370 Comparison on Whetstone Benchmark

Whetstone source - # of statements - 80 (static)
- # of statements interpreted - 15,233
- program size - 8,624 bits
        (excluding comments, etc.)

	System 370 FORTRAN H Opt 2	DELtran	Ratio 370/DELtran
Program Size (static)	12,944 bits	2,428 b	5.3:1
Instructions Executed	101,016	21,843	4.6:1
Instructions/Statement (as Executed)	6.6	1.4	4.6:1
Memory References Required	220,561	46,939	4.7:1
EMMY Execution Time (EMMY 370 emulation = 360 Model 50)	0.70 sec	0.14 sec	5:1
EMMY Interpreter Program Size	2100 words (for emulator excludes I/O)	800 words (excludes I/O and Trig. fcts.)	

Before concluding, a further comparison is in order, Wilner [12] compares the S-language for FORTRAN on the B-1700 as offering a 2:1 space improvement over System 360 code. The FORTRAN S-language instruction consists of a 3 or 9 bit OP code container followed by operand containers of (usually) 24 bits--split as descriptor, segment and displacement (not unlike our interpretive storage entry). Apparently the formats are limited in number without completeness. However, even this early effort offers noticable improvement of static program representations.

VIII. CONCLUSION

   Traditional machines built on the premise of slow access to storage and fixed interpretive sequences require program representations (instruction sets) which are inefficient in spacial representation and interpretation time. New host machine processors, specifically designed for the task of interpretation coupled with environmentally organized program representation, promise significant improvements in representation space and execution time for typical scientific programs. Much additional work needs to be done on speeding up--overlapping--host and target machine instructions in this new environment.

ACKNOWLEDGEMENTS

   The work described is an outgrowth of ongoing research in the Stanford Emulation Laboratory. The host processor in the Lab, EMMY, was designed and implemented at Palyn Associates, San Jose, CA. The Lab has come to be largely thru the efforts of Charles J. Neuhauser. The insight into the DEL problem is largely a result of studies by Lee W. Hoevel, in developing the DELtran interpreter for FORTRAN at the Lab.

IX. REFERENCES

 1. Flynn, M. J., "Some Computer Organization and Their Effectiveness," IEEE Transactions on Computers, Vol. C-21, No. 9, pp. 948-960, Sept. 1972.
 2. Hammerstrom, D. W. and Davidson, E. S., "Information Content of CPU Memory Referencing Behavior," Proceedings of Fourth Symposium on Computer Architecture, March 1977.
 3. Flynn, M. J., "Trends and Problems in Computer Organizations," IFIP Proceedings 74, North-Holland Pub., pp.3-10.
 4. Lunde, A., "More Data on the O/W Ratios," Computer Architecture News, Vol.4, No. 1, pp.9-13, March 1975, Pub. ACM.
 5. Rossman, G., Flynn, M., McClure, R., and Wheeler, N.D., "The Technical Significance of User Microprogrammable Systems," Technical Report, Palyn Associates, San Jose, CA., for U.S. National Bureau of Standards Contract

No. 4-36045, Nov. 74.
6. Flynn, M. J., Neuhauser, C. J., and McClure, R. M., "EMMY--An Emulation System for User Microprogramming," AFIPS, Vol. 44, NCC, 1975, pp. 85-89.
7. Flynn, M. J., Hoevel, L. W., and Neuhauser, C. J., "The Stanford Emulation Laboratory," Digital Systems Lab., Technical Report No. 118, Stanford University, June 76.
8. Burroughs Corp., "B-1700 Systems Reference Manual," Burroughs Corpl, Detroit, Mich., 1972.
9. Hoevel, L. W. and Flynn, M. J., "The Structure of Directly Executed Languages: A New Theory of Interpretive System Support," Digital Systems Lab., Technical Report No.130, Stanford University, March 1977.
10. Johnson, J. B., "The Contour Model of Block Structured Processes," SIGPLAN Notices, Vol. 6, pp. 52-82, Feb.71.
11. Hoevel, L. W., "DELtran Principles of Operation," Digital Systems Lab., Technical Note No. 108, Stanford Univ. March 1977.
12. Wilner, W., "Burroughs B-1700 Memory Utilization," AFIPS Proceedings, Vol. 41-I, FJCC, 1972, pp. 579-586.

AN EVALUATION OF THE CRAY-1 COMPUTER[*]

Forest Baskett
Tom W. Keller

Los Alamos Scientific Laboratory

A summary of the organization of the CRAY-1 computer is given together with an evaluation of its strengths and weaknesses based on current user experience with the machine. Some of the unique features of the organization of this computer are its vector registers, its intermediate scalar and address registers, and its use of only four different integrated circuits and only two different resistors. Its small number of distinct components leads to economy through volume purchases of parts, even for a single machine, and to reliability through simplified circuit design and mass production testing of components. Its vector registers lead to vector processing that has the same speed advantage over memory-to-memory vector processing that scalar processing in high speed registers has over memory-to-memory scalar processing. Its intermediate scalar and address registers lead to very high speed scalar processing, a valuable characteristic uncommon in other vector and parallel computers. These registers are like a programmable data cache; a simple scheme is described which makes them easily usable by compiler generated code. Reliability estimates for the machine in a production environment are made based on results from a test workload. The increased reliability predicted for memory error correction is found to far outweigh its additional cost. Without any vector processing at all, the speed and price-performance advantage over older architectures is between a factor of two and a factor of three. For problems that make good use of the vector processing capabilities of the machine, the advantage is between a factor of two and a factor of ten.

---

[*]Work performed under the auspices of the U.S. ERDA.

I. SUMMARY OF MACHINE CHARACTERISTICS

The CRAY-1 is a general purpose computer with special features to enhance its performance when solving scientific problems, particularly problems dealing with arrays of numbers. It is a parallel computer only in the sense that it can automatically provide significant overlap of different operations from its single instruction stream and its single data stream. The overlap capabilities are of several sorts. It has multiple functional units so that different operations such as multiplications and additions can take place in parallel. Each functional unit is completely segmented or pipelined so that any functional unit can accept a new set of operands each clock period (every 12.5 nanoseconds) even though some operations take several clock periods to complete. It has vector instructions that cause element by element operations on vector registers. The vector instructions make it easy to supply new operands to the pipelined functional units at each clock tick. The vector registers allow many vector operations to take place for each main memory reference. An instruction buffer allows a new instruction to be issued each clock tick with minimal main memory delays. Scalar registers and address registers can access data from "backup" scalar registers and "backup" address registers which form a programmable cache for scalars and addresses. The backup registers can be block loaded from and block stored to main memory very rapidly. A diagram of these features of the machine organization is given in Figure 1.

The use of vector registers for results and operands in vector operations has implications about the class of problems that can use the vector operations to greatest advantage. Those problems that can "slice" arrays into 64 element pieces and perform a substantial amount of vector computing on each slice are those that are most likely to make excellent use of the vector operations. It is possible for up to six vector operations to take place in parallel. Even if multiple operations do not appear to be independent because the results of one operation are operands to another, the vector functional units can pass the results to other vector functional units as operands as soon as they are available. Hence, under ideal circumstances the machine can deliver up to 240 million 64 bit floating point results per second. Under good circumstances, such as a matrix multiply, the machine can deliver 100 million floating point results per second. Under circumstances that appear to be vector oriented but do not quite fit into the multioperation per vector memory reference

COMPUTER SYSTEM DESIGN AND THEORY

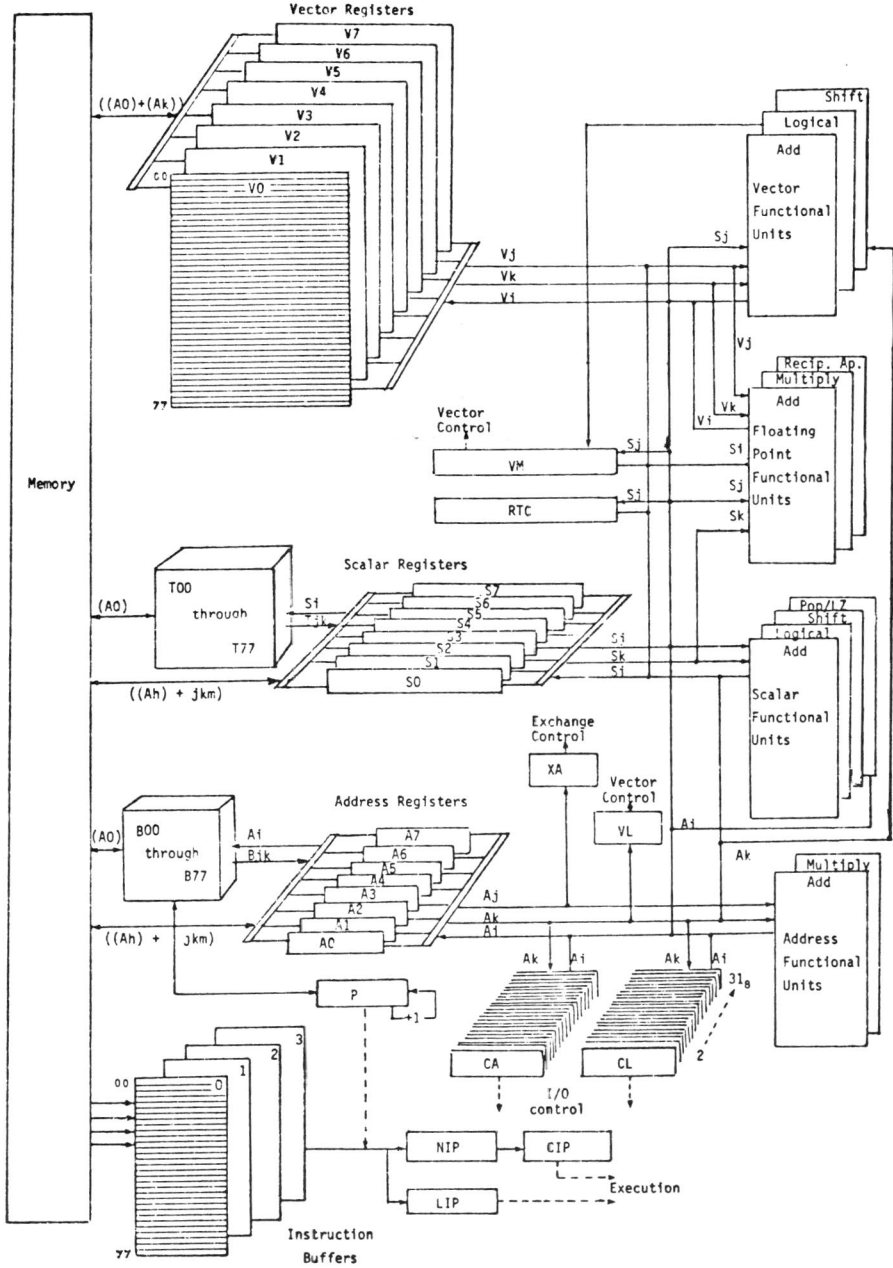

Fig. 1. CRAY-1 Organization

category, the machine can deliver up to 70 million floating point results per second. These last two cases compare with CDC 7600 times as follows: the good case is roughly ten times faster than the equivalent 7600 program, the other case is roughly five times faster than the equivalent 7600 program. For programs that are not able to use the vector instructions at all, CRAY-1 programs may average two and one-half times the speed of equivalent CDC 7600 programs (or equivalent IBM 370/195 programs).

The input/output structure of the machine has several important and unusual features. The machine has 12 full duplex high speed channels. The channels can transfer data at a rate of up to 250 megabits per second. Up to four channels can be operating at this speed simultaneously. Thus the channels have the potential of supplying the CPU with sufficient data if there were input/output devices that could match their speed. In the absence of such devices, the disk controllers built for the machine use internal high speed buffers. This allows the disk to be automatically read ahead or written behind the CPU, while allowing full speed channel-buffer transfers. This potentially enables I/O bound programs to run at full disk speed with little programming effort and little buffering effort.

II. USE OF INTERMEDIATE SCALAR AND ADDRESS REGISTERS

The CRAY-1 has 64 24-bit intermediate address registers, called B registers and 64 64-bit intermediate scalar registers, called T registers. The only operations that can be performed on these registers are move operations. Individual values may be transferred between any of the 8 primary address (index) registers, the A registers, and any of the 64 B registers. Likewise, individual values may be transferred between any of the 8 primary scalar registers, the S registers, and any of the 64 T registers. These move operations are one cycle (12.5 ns) instructions. The contents of contiguous blocks of B or T registers may be moved to or from main memory with block load and block store instructions. The block load and the block store instructions specify a beginning B or T register, an A register containing the initial memory address and an A register containing the number of words to be transferred. The block load instructions issue in 13 cycles plus one cycle per word transferred. The data is available in the affected intermediate registers one cycle later. The block store instructions issue in 7 cycles plus one cycle per word transferred. The direct data path from A and S registers to memory makes use of instructions that

transfer one word. The direct load instructions issue in
2 cycles and the data is available in 10 cycles. The direct
store instructions issue in 2 cycles.

Because the block load and block store instructions can
drive the memory at a 5 gigabits per second rate, it is desirable to use the B and T registers as a programmable cache of
main memory values needed for computation in the A and S
registers. The timings of the competing operations are such
that there is no obvious best way of programming such a cache.
When we consider the problem of having a compiler generate
code to take advantage of these intermediate registers,
we see the need for a systematic method of use.
We think that eventually the techniques of global data flow
analysis across procedure (subroutine) boundaries will be
sufficiently well developed (1) to allow these intermediate
registers to be used for storage of appropriate values
throughout a program. In the meantime, compiler usage of
these registers inside a given procedure or subroutine means
that conventions must be developed for the status of the
values contained in these registers across calls to other
procedures or subroutines. For some popular programming
languages (the only ones currently available on the CRAY-1)
we have devised conventions and a procedure call and return
code sequence that allow a straightforward exploitation of
these intermediate registers.

In the programming languages FORTRAN, MODEL, and PASCAL
it is possible for the compiler to completely allocate and
arrange the local data storage of each routine. In most implementations of FORTRAN, this local storage is in a fixed
place in memory, while in MODEL and PASCAL it is in the activation record of an invocation of a routine (procedure). In
either case, it is possible to use the B and T registers as a
cache for much of the local storage of each routine. The
goal is to have most memory references turned into one-cycle
references to B or T registers and avoid the possibility
of having to wait 10 cycles for data to arrive at a working
register from memory. The price paid for such an organization
is the time required for block stores at routine entry and
block loads at routine exit.

We now describe a method we are using in two compilers
to keep local values in the B and T registers and the resulting procedure calling sequence this method entails. The
compiler sorts the local storage for a routine so that the
return address and associated information and local addresses,
indexes, and pointers are in the first part of the local
storage block for the routine. All this information is held

in the B registers as a cache. In the next block of the local storage are held all the "long" integers, simple floating point numbers, masks, and other items of information, each of which will fit in one 64-bit word. This part of the local storage block is held in the T registers as a cache. The rest of the local storage block consists of the overflow from the first two blocks and all local arrays. Arrays cannot be held in B or T registers because there is no mechanism for indexing into them. When a routine calls another routine, these caches must be returned to the locations in main memory allocated for them with block store instructions. When the called routine returns, the B and T register cache image of the calling routine can be reloaded from memory with the block load instructions.

The block stores and loads are done in the called procedure prologue and epilogue, respectively, for the following reasons. While the same number of instructions are executed as would be executed if the B and T register save and restore were done by the calling routine, a smaller number of instructions are generated; there is only one save and restore pair for each routine, rather than one per call. Assembly language subroutines that do not use B and T registers and whose parameters are certain to be in memory do not need to save and restore those registers. Thus the overall calling sequence overhead is significantly smaller.

The calling sequence that results from this approach is as follows: set an address register to the address of the beginning of the block of local storage where the B and T registers are to be saved; set another address register to the number of B registers to save; set another address register to the number of T registers to save. Set an address register to the address of the parameter list for the routine being called. Then call the routine to be called. On return from the routine called, there is no additional work to be done. At the beginning of the called routine it is necessary to execute eight instructions to save the B and T registers in the designated locations. At the end of the called routine eight instructions are needed to restore the B and T register cache of the calling routine. With a block structured language such as MODEL or PASCAL a total of five additional instructions are sometimes needed to manipulate the display in the appropriate way.

Combining some standard conventions about where the appropriate counts and pointers are kept with this calling sequence results in all interesting values being easily locatable in memory. Thus symbolic debugging and symbolic dumps

are straightforward. In fact, the successive blocks of
local storage are all chained together according to the sequence of calls.

The prologue and epilogue required for each routine may
seem long but occupy only two words each of CRAY-1 memory.
In addition, since reference to B and T registers are 16 bit
instructions while references to memory are 32 bit instructions, using the B and T register cache makes most routines
substantially shorter. Of course, these cache references
are also significantly faster than references to memory. We
feel that this scheme makes for quite a reasonable programmable data cache. Note that a similar scheme would be appropriate for microprocessors where it is easy to add high
speed memory to the chip containing the CPU but hard to
determine how to integrate such high speed memory into the
architecture of the machine.

III. RELIABILITY EVALUATION

The reliability of the CRAY-1 computer was investigated
during a formal six month evaluation period at the Los Alamos
Scientific Laboratory (LASL). A complete report on that
evaluation is available (2); some of the results are summarized here. The main instrument in the reliability study
was a program written to solve for the vector x in the matrix
equation $Ax = y$ by LU decomposition. This program was
called the Exerciser. The program made heavy use of most
of the vector operations, most of the main memory (501,000
words out of 524,288), and all of the functional units. The
Exerciser program was run from five to eight hours per day,
five days a week, throughout the entire six month period. The
distribution of time between failures is given in Figure 2.
The overall mean time to failure for the machine during the
evaluation was approximately 4 hours. The standard deviation
was 5 hours.

An analysis of failures occurring during the Exerciser
runs revealed that unreproducible memory parity errors dominate. The first CRAY-1 computer, the one evaluated, has only
memory parity error detection. Almost all of the memory
parity errors were shown to be due to a single bit failure
in a word. The memory is implemented with 1024-bit high
speed bipolar semiconductor chips. The observed memory
failure rate translates into a mean time to failure for a
single chip of 150,000 hours. This corresponds to a chip
failure rate that is between "improved commercial" grade and

"JAN Class C screened" grade, according to reliability estimates by Rome Air Development Center (3). This roughly corresponds to the type of screening being done by the manufacturer, Cray Research, Incorporated (CRI). Thus the machine failure rate appears to be dominated by the raw memory chip failure rate. Hence machine reliability could be substantially improved by either improving the reliability of the memory chips (more rigorous screening) or by adding a single bit error correcting code to the memory.

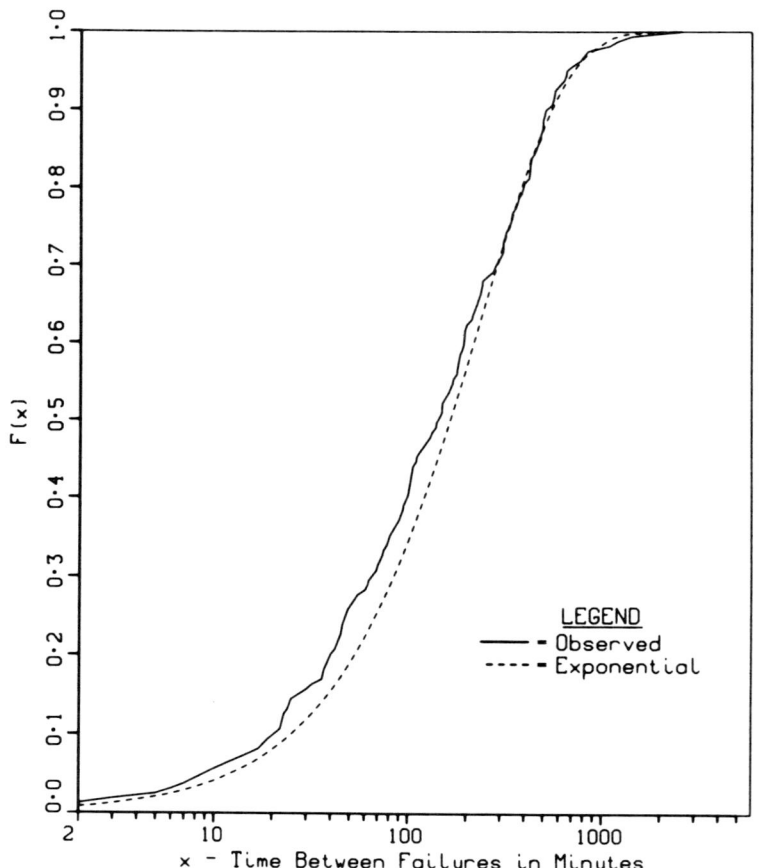

Fig. 2. *Cumulative Distribution of Intervals Between Failures*

If one assumes that all unreproducible memory failures could have been avoided by a single bit error correction code, the mean time to failure would have increased by a factor of 5.5. If one assumes, in addition, that all the reproducible single bit failures could have been avoided and fixed during scheduled maintenance, the mean time to failure would have been increased by a factor of 9.4. A single bit correction, double bit detection error code on the memory increases the memory cost by less than 15 percent. This is substantially more economical than the cost of the more rigorous screening that would be required to reach the same increase in reliability.

The results of the LASL reliability study were instrumental in prompting the announcement by CRI of the availability of such a code as an optional memory feature on the CRAY-1. With the error correcting code on the memory, the reliability study would suggest a mean time to failure on the order of one and one-half days. This is reasonable for a machine as complex as the CRAY-1. The mechanical construction and the circuit design seem to be outstanding in their reliability.

IV. SCALAR PERFORMANCE EVALUATION

As part of the formal performance evaluation of the CRAY-1 (2), a number of FORTRAN kernels were implemented on both the CDC 7600 and the CRAY-1. Vector instructions were not used in the CRAY-1 implementation so as to obtain a "scalar" speed ratio, thought to represent a lower bound for the overall performance of the machine relative to a machine without a vector processing capability. Steps were taken to ensure that each kernel was implemented as efficiently as was feasible in the assembly language of each machine, in order to eliminate the impact of the efficiency of compiler-generated code upon the comparison. The kernels were selected from five production programs by a sampling scheme which weighted the probability of drawing a specific kernel by its contribution to the total execution time of the program. The five programs were selected by criteria which ensured that they would comprise the most likely workload for a CRAY-1, should a CRAY-1 be installed at LASL. Both the kernel selection scheme and the program selection criteria were defined such that an unbiased, representative sample of kernels would be drawn for the comparison. Interested readers should consult (2) for a complete description of the elaborate procedures used to select the FORTRAN kernels, to define the assembly language representations, to ensure the efficient coding of the kernels, and to minimize the bias due to individual programmers.

The 23 kernels coded were not sufficient to determine a "scalar" speed ratio between the two machines with statistical significance. Their number was sufficient to

establish that the scalar speed of the CRAY-1 relative to the
CDC 7600 was greater than a factor of two with 90% confidence
over the workload defined. A sorted histogram of the kernel
speed ratios is given in Figure 3. Each kernel was named according to the program it was drawn from. Some kernels are
named twice because the sampling scheme resulted in their
being selected twice, due to their (relatively) heavy contribution to the total execution time of the program.

The speed ratios ranged from 4.12 to 2.03. The high
ratios were unexpected by the following simple analysis. The
ratio of CPU cycle times for the two machines is 2.2, while
the ratio of memory access times is 1.8 (both ratios favor
the CRAY-1). If one factors out the vector architecture of
the CRAY-1 from the analysis, which is exactly what the kernel implementation did, then the instruction sets are similar.
Since the cycle counts for instructions are roughly equivalent, one would expect the speed ratios to fall in the range
of 1.8 to 2.2. A careful analysis of the coded kernels
revealed that certain architectural features of the CRAY-1
resulted in some kernels executing in fewer CRAY-1 instructions than CDC 7600 instructions. Perhaps the most important
feature was the more uniform instruction set of the CRAY-1.
In contrast to the CDC 7600, results and operands may be
transferred between memory and all scalar registers. Some
kernels required Large Core Memory to Central Memory
transfers on the CDC 7600, an overhead unnecessary on the
CRAY-1. The CRAY-1's larger instruction buffer (64 words
versus 12 words) and different buffer management technique
further contributed to its relative advantage over the CDC
7600. Finally, it was assumed that many recently used
results would still remain in the CRAY-1's B and T cache
registers, since storage to memory can be accomplished
through the cache. This resulted in some operands being
fetched from the cache instead of memory, if the operands had
been stored to the cache a reasonable number of instructions
previously.

V. PRINCIPAL MACHINE STRENGTHS

The two most obvious strengths of the CRAY-1 are its
vector register organization and its speed (one machine
cycle every 12.5 nanoseconds, with many instructions executing
in only one cycle). The fully pipelined nature of the multiple functional units, together with the vector registers
and the vector operations, make it possible to achieve re-
markable result rates for a machine which is conceptually

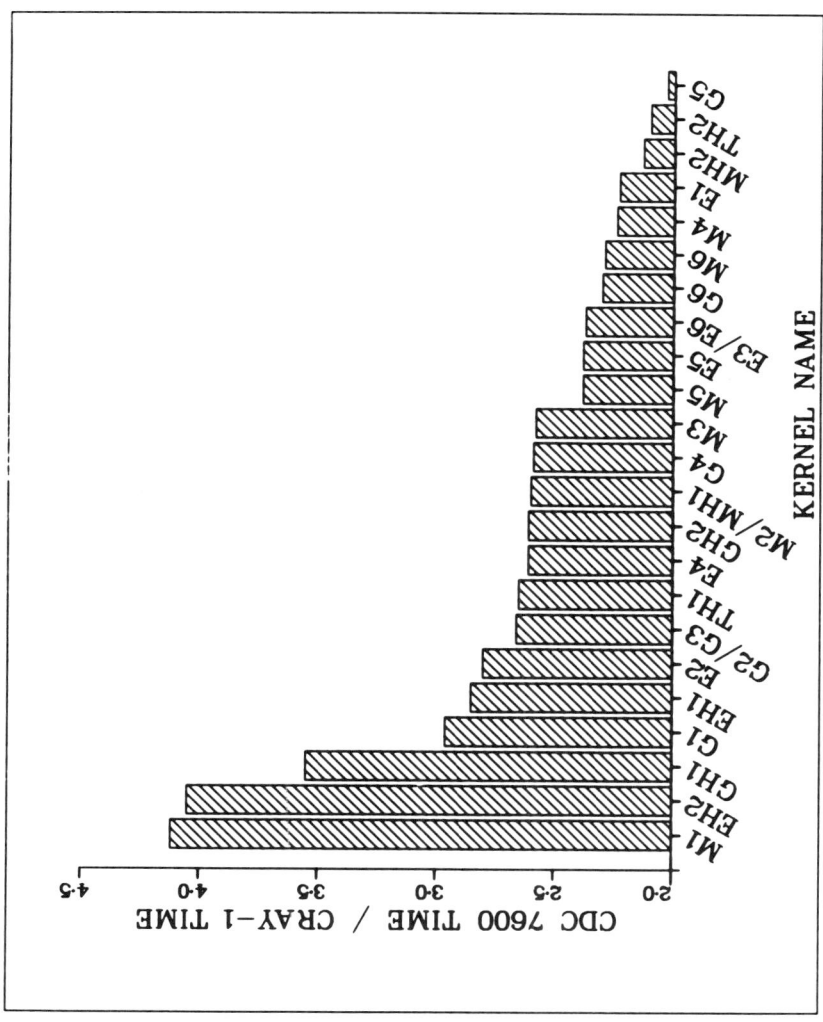

Fig. 3. Sorted Histogram of Kernel Speed Ratios

serial. It is theoretically possible to write a program
that would produce 500 million 64-bit results per second.
While it is hard to imagine what such a program would be doing
in the way of useful work, it is not difficult to write meaningful programs which produce 100 million 64-bit floating point
results per second (4).

While the machine is conceptually serial in that the
programmer may think of only one thing happening at a time,
in a sequential order, the machine is in fact similar in a
number of respects to at least one machine which is inherently
parallel, the ILLIAC IV. Because of the similarities, much
of the work that has been done to automatically detect and
exploit parallelism that has been inspired by the ILLIAC IV
(5) is applicable to the CRAY-1. Thus techniques for making
recurrence relations parallel, for dealing with IF statements in DO loops, and wave front methods can be applied
to the CRAY-1. In addition, once vector operations have been
introduced into a program, tree height reduction techniques
on vector register expressions are even more important for
exploiting the (multiple) fully pipelined functional units,
the multiple vector registers, and the chaining of one vector
operation to another. Of course, many of the details of such
techniques will be different. For example, the chaining
of one vector operation to another sometimes conflicts with
full tree height reduction.

The use of vector registers is a major step forward
for vector machines, quite comparable to the first use of
scalar registers in early computers. Previous vector machines,
in which vectors were all memory resident, have been severely
constrained by main memory bandwidth limitations. Vector
registers provide buffering to alleviate this problem.

Other less obvious strengths of the machine are its
excellent code density, its reliability, and its scalar
speed. The high code density is an indication of the clean
and relatively uniform nature of the instruction set. It is
a "cleaner" design in many respects than earlier efforts by
the same designer. Its reliability can surely be partly
attributed to the very small parts count and the resulting
economy of design rules, coupled with the affordability of
mass production screening and testing. Its scalar speed
means that even programs that find it difficult to use the
vector operations can still be run with no cost penalty.

VI. PRINCIPAL MACHINE WEAKNESSES

An obvious weakness of the machine is the lack of a vector compress operation. While it is clear that an operation that selectively compresses one vector down into a shorter vector does not easily fit into the pipelining-chaining scheme of the machine, it is also clear that some algorithms cannot profitably use the other vector operations as a consequence. The most obvious example is sorting. No one has yet been able to devise an internal sorting algorithm on the CRAY-1 that makes more than trivial use of the vector operations and still runs faster than a good scalar internal sort. The vector comparison operation exists but there is no convenient way to make use of the result of that comparison for sorting.

The vector registers are both a blessing and a curse. While they clearly provide a great deal more speed potential than main-memory based vector architectures, they are fixed length registers and carry with them the usual register problems. They must be allocated and deallocated; there are still no good register allocation algorithms. The dimension of the problem is also different for vector registers since the logical vectors being manipulated may be longer than the vector registers.

A number of other weaknesses in no special order follow. It is possible with a vector operation to add the elements of a vector together and it is possible to multiply the elements of a vector together, but these possibilities are accidents of the implementation and hence are tricky and awkward to use. Their use is important since the first gives a fast inner product and the second gives a fast polynomial evaluation. The machine has no special provision for multiple precision. Thus multiple precision must be done by keeping multiple words of half precision quantities. The error in floating point operations is difficult to categorize and hence quite difficult to analyze. There are no complete provisions for full word integers. Integers are used most efficiently if represented as 24 bits or less and next most efficiently used if represented as 46 bits or less. There is no concept of a vector of indexes as on some other vector machines. One of the most serious bottlenecks in the implementation of the machine that we have found for carefully coded programs is in the scalar register file. Only one scalar result can be stored in the scalar register file per machine cycle. Many programs have been implemented that generate excessive conflicts at this gate.

VII. CONCLUDING REMARKS

The CRAY-1 is an important step forward in the development of vector type high speed computers with its use of vector registers. However, we have found that the machine is an impressive general purpose computer even if its vector capabilities are ignored. The traditional folklore that high speed computers with unusual processing capabilities do not make good general purpose computers does not seem to be true in this case. With our currently naive PASCAL compiler, we achieve a code density within ten percent of the code density achieved by a similar PASCAL compiler on an IBM 370/168 computer. In addition, we achieve approximately the same speed ratio with that computer doing character processing as we do doing "number crunching." These indicators, together with the I/O capacity of the machine and its price, suggest that it would be a very attractive general purpose computer if it were available with a sufficient amount of general purpose software.

VIII. REFERENCES

1. Barth, J. M., "An Interprocedural Data Flow Analysis Algorithm," Fourth ACM Symposium on Principles of Programming Languages, Los Angeles, Jan. 1977, pp. 119-131.

2. Keller, T. W., "CRAY-1 Evaluation Final Report," Los Alamos Scientific Laboratory, Los Alamos, NM, LA-6456-MS, Dec. 1976, Chapter 5.

3. Rome Air Development Center, "Reliability Analysis for the CRAY-1," Reliability Branch, Sept. 1975, Chapter 1.

4. Buzbee, B., Golub, G., and Howell, J., "Vectorization for the CRAY-1 of Several Methods for Solving Elliptic Difference Equations," Symposium on High Speed Computer and Algorithm Organization, Academic Press, April 1977.

5. Kuck, D. J., "A Survey of Parallel Machine Organization and Programming," ACM Computing Surveys, Vol. 9, No. 1, March 1977, pp. 29-59.

6. Rudsinski, L., and Worlton, J., "The Impact of Scalar Performance on Vector and Parallel Processors," Symposium on High Speed Computer and Algorithm Organization, Academic Press, April 1977.

BURROUGHS SCIENTIFIC PROCESSOR

Richard A. Stokes
Burroughs Corporation

I. INTRODUCTION

The Burroughs Scientific Processor is designed to provide very high speed execution of algorithms used to help solve complex scientific and engineering problems in such fields as meteorology, nuclear energy, seismic data analysis, structure analysis, and econometric modelling.

The BSP is capable of performing 50 million floating point operations per second. This speed is achieved primarily through the utilization of 16 arithmetic units that operate in parallel. Other significant features that contribute to the high computation rate are:

- conflict-free memory that allows access to vectors of arbitrary length and skip distance at full bandwidth

- a pipeline that allows overlapping of array operations

- overlapped array and scalar operations

- a charge coupled device auxiliary memory

- in-line processing of input and output

II. SYSTEM MANAGER

The Burroughs Scientific Processor (BSP) is intended to be used in conjunction with a sophisticated system manager, such as the Burroughs B 7800 or B 7700 computer system. This allows the BSP to execute scientific and engineering programs at high speed with a minimum of interruption to perform ancillary tasks.

On the other hand, the user is provided with a complete sophisticated computing facility that is easy to use because the management processor provides:

- time sharing

- data and program file editing

- data communications to remote job entry stations, terminals, and networks

- compiling and linking of BSP programs

- long-term data storage and data base management

- general purpose data processing utilizing languages such as COBOL, BASIC, APL, ALGOL, PL/I, and FORTRAN

III. SYSTEM COMPONENTS

The Burroughs Scientific Processor consists of a control processor (CP), 16 arithmetic elements (AE), an array memory (AM) consisting of 17 memory units, an alignment network to interface the AE's and AM, a file memory (FM), and a file memory control unit. The components are shown in Figure 1.

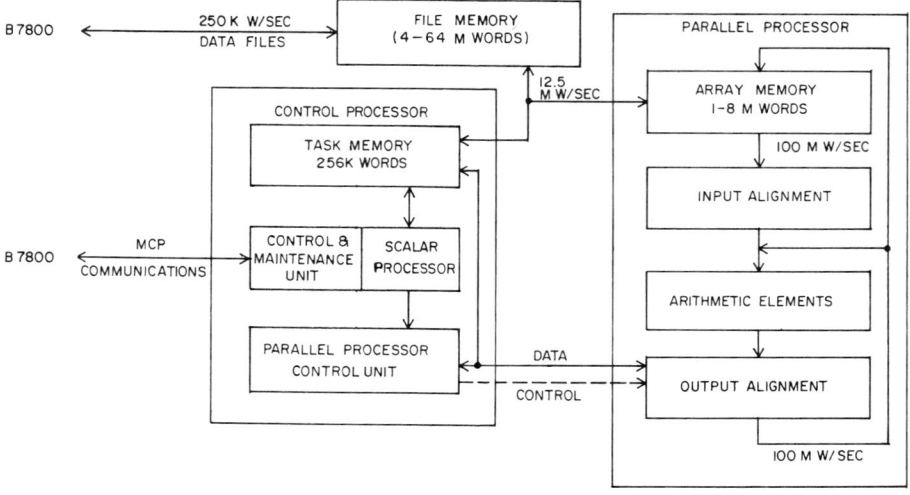

Fig. 1. Burroughs Scientific Processor Block Diagram

A. Control Processor

The control processor (CP) is a high-speed asynchronous element of the BSP that provides the supervisory interface to the system manager in addition to controlling the parallel processor and the file memory. The CP consists of a scalar processor unit (SPU), a parallel processor control unit (PPCU), a task memory (TM), and a control and maintenance unit (CMU).

The control processor executes some serial or scalar portions of user programs utilizing an arithmetic element similar to one of the 16 arithmetic elements in the array processor, but containing additional capabilities to perform integer arithmetic and indexing operations. The CP also performs task scheduling, file memory allocation, and I/O management under control of the BSP operating system.

1. Scalar Processor Unit

The scalar processor unit processes all operating system and user program instructions, which are stored in task memory. It has a clock frequency of 12M Hz and is able to perform up to 3 million floating point operations per second. All array instructions and certain scalar operations are passed to the parallel processor control unit, which queues them for execution on the parallel processor.

2. Parallel Processor Control Unit

The parallel processor control unit receives array operations from the scalar processor unit. The instructions are validated and transformed into microsequences that control the operation of the 16 arithmetic elements in the parallel processor.

3. Task Memory

The task memory is used to store portions of the operating system and user programs as they are being executed. It is also used to store program data values that are operands for those instructions executed by the scalar processor unit.

The task memory is a 4K-bit bipolar memory with a 160 ns cycle time. Four words are accessed simultaneously. Capacity of the memory is 256K words; each word consists of 48 data bits and 8 bits for error detection and correction.

4. *Control and Maintenance Unit*

The control and maintenance unit (CMU) serves as the direct interface between the system manager and the rest of the control processor for initialization, communication of supervisory commands, and maintenance. It communicates with the input/output processor of the system manager.

The CMU has access to critical data paths and registers of the BSP, so that it can perform state analysis and circuit diagnostics under control of maintenance software running on the system manager.

B. Parallel Processor

The parallel processor performs array oriented computations at high speeds by executing 16 floating point operations simultaneously in its 16 arithmetic elements. Data for the array operations are stored in an array memory (AM) consisting of 17 memory modules. Array memory is accessed by the arithmetic elements through an array memory alignment network (AN).

1. *Arithmetic Element*

At any time, all of the arithmetic elements are executing the same instruction on different data values. The arithmetic elements operate at a clock frequency of 6.25M Hz and are able to complete the most common arithmetic operations in two clock periods. Each arithmetic element can perform a floating point add, subtract, or multiply in 320 nanoseconds, so the BSP is capable of executing up to 50 million floating point operations per second. Each arithmetic element can perform a floating point divide in 1280 ns and extract a square root in 2080 ns.

2. *Array Memory*

The array memory consists of 17 memory units, each of which may contain from 32K to 512K words, making a total of from .5 to 8 million words. Like the control processor memory, it is a 4K bit bipolar memory. Each word contains 48 data bits and 8 bits for error detection and correction. The rate of data transfer between the array memory and the arithmetic elements is 100M words/second.

The organization of the array memory is unique in that it permits simultaneous access to almost any consecutive 16 elements of the commonly referenced components of an array, such as rows, columns, and diagonals.

3. The Alignment Networks

The Alignment Network is functionally divided into two parts: The Input Alignment network for data fetching and the Output Alignment network for data stores. Both units are full crossbar switching networks, which permit general purpose interconnectivity between the arithmetic array and the memory storage modules. It is the combined function of the memory storage scheme and the alignment networks which support the "conflict-free" capabilities of the Array Memory.

Other inter-arithmetic element switching is provided to support special functions such as the data COMPRESS and EXPAND operations and Fast Fourier Transform algorithm.

C. File Memory

The file memory (FM) is a high-speed secondary storage device. The FM is loaded by the system manager with BSP tasks and task files. These tasks are then queued for execution by the control processor. The FM is also used to store scratch files and output files produced during execution of a BSP program. It is the only peripheral device under the direct control of the BSP; all other peripheral devices are controlled by the system manager.

The FM utilizes high-speed charge coupled devices (CCD) as its storage media. The CCD memory combines a one millisecond access time with a 12.5M word/second transfer rate. Since it is entirely electronic, the reliability of the file memory is much greater than that of conventional rotating storage devices.

NETWORKS AND INTERCONNECTION SCHEMES

James E. Thornton
Network Systems Corporation

It appears that large computer centers have adopted multi-computer configurations to provide more compute power and especially greater availability. The potential exists for many additional benefits, such as specialized computers and memories, if this trend continues. The first multi-computer networks have utilized conventional computers and memories to build primitive, but useful, systems. Limitations of conventional channels, the number of ports to memory, and the reliability of key units represent the principal hurdles to continued progress in this direction. It is expected that this area of development will be one of the most active in the next few years.

Since the end of the 1960's, the explosion of terminal networks connected to large-scale computer centers has set the stage for major changes within those centers. Optimization of large computers has moved from the single central processing unit to aggregates of CPUs. As a result, the procedures and mechanisms for configuring these aggregate computer systems are expected to come under more serious review.

I.   EVERYBODY'S DOING IT

The number of telephone-oriented terminal networks providing access to computers is staggering. A major industry has been built in a few short years, even to the point of impacting the largest company in the world, AT&T, which has asked the United States Congress for legislative relief to reduce competition.

These terminal networks take several forms depending upon traffic level, distance and complexity. Most often, the network is a star configuration, with a single central computing facility supporting direct-connected terminals. In this case, control over the network is vested in the computing center.

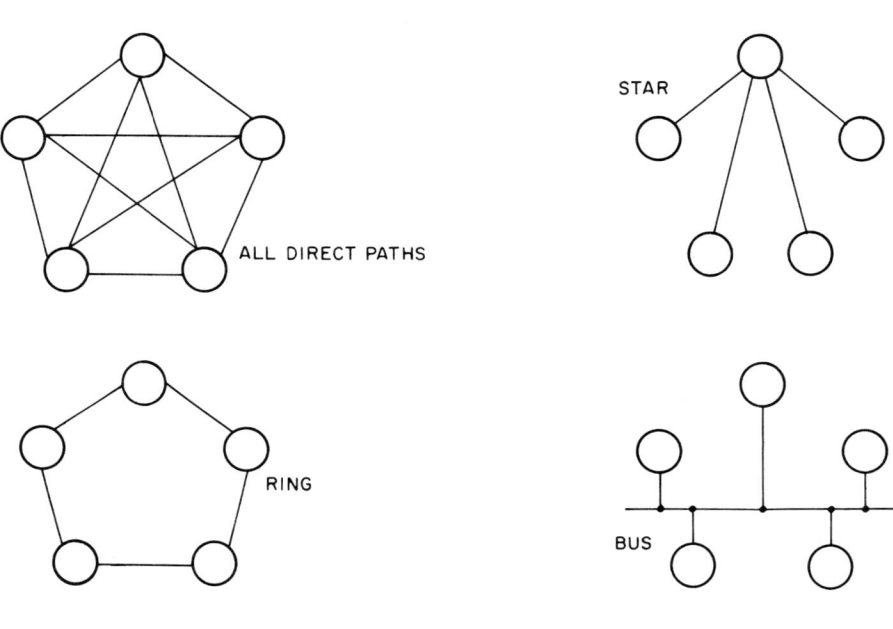

Fig. 1

More complicated structures, such as the ring and bus open the opportunity to provide very interesting properties, at the risk of problems of control and conflict. Mixtures of the star, ring and bus configurations are readily found in many networks.

Along with the time-sharing terminal networks have been efforts to allow computers to directly communicate with other computers in real time. These have utilized communications processors as front-ends to the host computer. One of the most sophisticated networks of this type is TYMNET owned and operated by Tymshare, Inc. The configuration consists of a backbone of multiple rings, with some nodes connected in stars or straight runs.

With a ring configuration, data for a computer is addressed to that computer and sequentially sent, link by link, one direction on the ring. At each step around the circuit, the data is examined by the interface processor. When the data reaches the interface processor connected to the destination computer, it is removed from the ring. All elements in the ring must operate for the network to operate. Redundant paths can be added, but we now perceive the need for more flexible routing.

A very ambitious system, ARPANET, employs store-and-forward switching of blocks of data, "packets," through a number of separate paths through the network. This significantly differs from the centralized system in the control of the flow of data.

In the centralized system, nearly all controls reside in the central computer, which will simply slow down the call rate or prevent additional calls in order to handle the flow. The distributed control of ARPANET provides routing adaptation for high traffic or node failure where the path through the network is not chosen in advance, but is a dynamic function of the conditions in the network at any time.

In order to construct these time-sharing and packet switched networks, several classes of new products have been developed. These include multiplexers, concentrators, front-end processors, port sharing units and interface processors. One can easily understand that functions performed in each of these products may complement, support, off-load or eliminate functions in the host computer. The combination of these new hardware products and the hardware/software functions executed in them and the CPU are now the basis for new "network architectures."

II. IMPACT ON LARGE COMPUTERS

After the five to ten years of this front-end networking activity, it is possible to assess some of the impact on the large host computers. To some extent, they have become schizophrenic in an attempt to function well in the batch environment, as well as in the transaction and interactive environment. Added to this has been the critical requirements of reliability. It is striking that the average large computer site over the entire reported population of U.S. sites contains 1.6 + mainframe computers. Probably the single most significant reason is the need for redundant CPUs in order to account for the failure rate of the large machines.

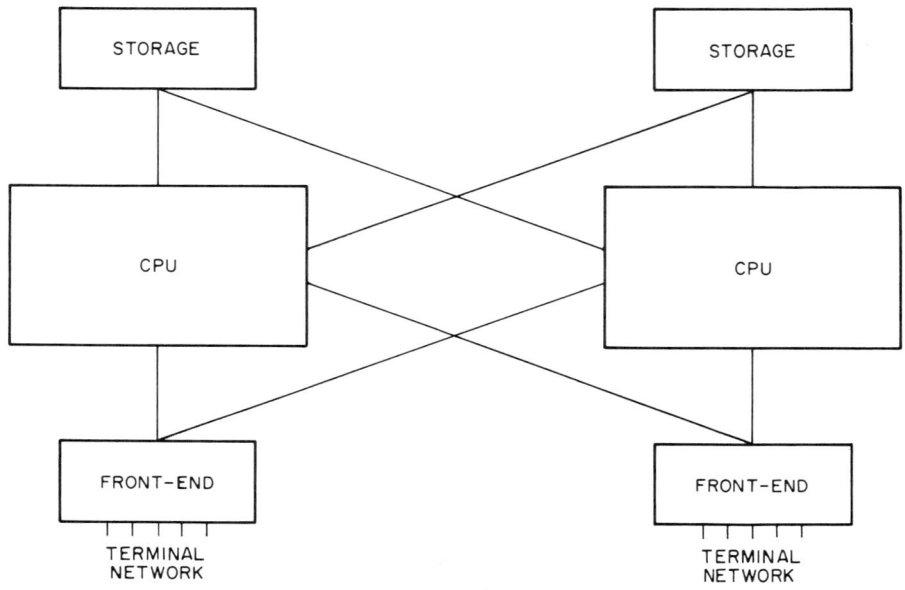

Fig. 2

In adding second machines to each site, there has grown a serious duplication of support equipment. In some instances, as shown in Fig. 2, the CPUs have been interconnected to share support equipment. On the record, however, very little real sharing has been achieved due to the added complexity.

In some cases, the batch/interactive schizophrenia mentioned above has been addressed by assigning different operating systems to each of the two machines in Fig. 2.

III. THE OTHER NETWORK

It is apparent that the large site has established the need for a "local" network, more or less a mirror of the phone network, which addresses the problems associated with aggregates of computers and their support systems. Some new words are appearing, such as "back-end," symbolizing the local network counterpart to "front-end," which is the designation for the terminal network. We can expect to see the "back-end network," and the "back-end processor."

A number of differences exist between the front-end and the back-end. The front-end has been normally associated with byte and character traffic, although the introduction of packet switching is modifying that. The back-end is block oriented, especially with regard to magnetic disk storage. Fixed block sizes make optimum use of the disk surface. Virtual memory addressing concepts also utilize fixed blocks.

A second difference of considerable consequence is the data rate. Data rates in the front-end range to the thousands or tens of thousands of bits per second. This is, of course, limited most by the nature of phone line electronics. An interesting future impact of satellite communications could change this radically. The data rates in the back-end range in the millions to tens of millions of bits per second. This is driven mostly by the data rates of magnetic disks, but also by central computer data-channel electronics.

A third difference is the serial transmission of the phone lines in the front-end versus parallel transmission in the back-end. It is unthinkable, in the economic sense, to go parallel in the front-end. In the back-end, the high data rate has precluded use of serial transmission.

Efforts to construct back-end networks have been difficult, although not impossible. Primitive back-end networks have provided a degree of back up protection but little sharing, load leveling or throughput improvement.

Most of the active efforts in the architecture have concentrated on the front-end and the terminal networks. This has necessarily addressed byte-oriented, serial, low-speed traffic. It has been geared to terminals sharing a computer, not to computers sharing a disk, or a tape transport. This writer believes that a significant effort should, and will, be directed to this important area.

IV. COMMON MEMORY

One of the methods used in the primitive networks of computers is a multiport common memory. This has definite merit and has been effective in allowing several computers to share common system programs and tables. This writer is most familiar with the approach taken by Control Data Corporation with its Extended Core Storage. This unit has four ports with a very high data transfer rate. Mainframe computers share this core memory by point-to-point connection, one each to a memory port. This memory was large when introduced, but new super-computers now have central memories this large.

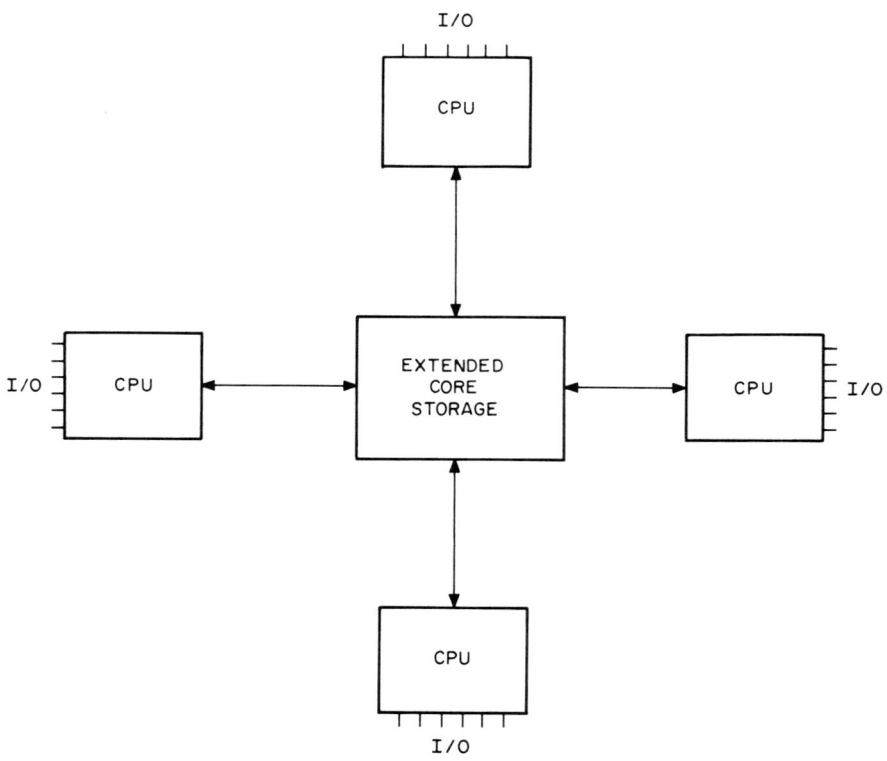

Fig. 3

To the benefits and advantages this common memory approach has, we must add some basic disadvantages.

The most serious disadvantage is similar to that of the early super-computers: the single point of failure. This was solved in the case of the large computer by adding another. However, adding another common memory with high data rate parallel connections is very difficult.

A second difficulty of the common memory as a switching center is the vulnerability of the memory to a "berserk" mainframe and other memory protection problems. These are solvable but with very little flexibility.

V. SWITCHING COMPUTER

Another method used to create a local computer network is the use of a switching computer. In many multi-computer sites, one or more of the mainframe computers is used to service other computers, either for the delivery of data files or the routing of jobs. This writer has attempted to determine what level of activity this represents with marginal results thus far. Estimates range up to 25 percent of the "compute cycles" at the site involved in what might be called a file delivery service.

As more attention is focused on this area, a form of the store-and-forward switching network may become a permanent part of the large computer center.

VI. CHANNELS

Conventional mainframe data channels can be connected to subsystems, such as controllers, by channel switch units allowing more than one channel to access the subsystem. As a practical matter, usually only two channels are given access by this method in high data rate units. The parallel channels connected by channel switches and by "daisy-chaining" do provide a primitive networking capability.

Conventional channels are generally restricted to very short distances, especially as the transfer rate is increased to the limit. The difficulty arises from the method of asynchronously signalling the presence of each channel word. A control signal must make one round trip pass for each channel word. Most channels are limited to as small a channel word as possible, in order to reduce the number of wires in the cable. Even so, standard channels require 50 to 100 wires. At one hundred feet, assuming 2.5 nanoseconds per foot, the round trip time (not counting any time for the electronics) would be 500 nanoseconds. An eight-bit channel word would be limited to 16 million bits per second, and, with electronics delay times counted, would be in the order of 12 million bits per second.

The practical reality of conventional channels is that those now represent one of the more serious limitations on the effectiveness of the computer system. Examples can be cited in which the congestion of data traffic on conventional channels represents a larger factor in throughput than the computational speed of the mainframe.

VII. MAXIS AND MINIS

A widespread movement to interconnect super-computers with mini-computers for more effective operation of large computer centers introduces an even greater strain on the common memory and conventional channel approaches. Going further, the movement to provide "intelligent" controllers and controllers so inexpensive that each disk may have its own will add the final death blow to our current systems architecture built around conventional channels.

This writer believes that the computer industry is about to see major partitioning of large centers in which separate units will provide such functions as data base management, front-end preprocessing, message switching and, of course, bigger and better computation.

VIII. THE VALUE OF A SHORT-HAUL NETWORK

Consideration of the "short-haul" network of about one mile and under has only recently been possible. Semi-conductor technology has now reached the point that very high-speed, single-wire serial transmissions are cost effective. Today's high-speed channels operate in the region of 10 to 40 million bits per second. Distance limitations have become so restrictive, that computer centers are approaching spherical volumes of very high density. Relieving the distance restrictions from current 50 to 100 feet to the 1000 feet region would unquestionably allow more convenient use of facilities.

Sharing the physical units, such as magnetic tapes, disks and so on over a more relaxed physical environment should also encourage <u>real</u> sharing - something that has not been done much. Certainly one can point to increases in efficiency arising from simply the physical sharing (as opposed to the actual data sharing) of these storage devices. Idle tape transports and idle disk drives on one machine complex can be put to work.

A short-haul network can also use the store-and-forward buffer memory to great advantage in performing a speed change function. For example, super computers utilizing high bandwidth disks can allow direct access to these disks by mini-computers through the use of such buffer memories.

A short-haul network utilizing the BUS configuration appears the most attractive. Groupings of super-computers, mini-computers, disk storage units, magnetic tape units and "electronic parking lots" can be serviced through such a network with great flexibility.

My company, Network Systems Corporation, (I simply cannot resist a short commercial) has developed a short-haul site network of this kind.

We call it HYPERnet^{TM}.

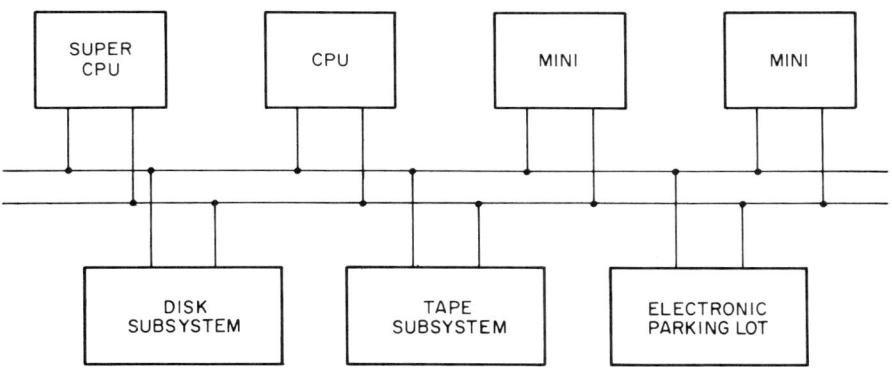

Fig. 4

A DISCOURSE ON A NEW SUPER COMPUTER, PEPE

Hiram G. Martin
System Development Corporation

ABSTRACT:

PEPE, a parallel array processor with distributed and associative logic, is capable of floating point computation rates in excess of 500 MIPS. PEPE tied to a CDC 7600 is operational at the Huntsville Advanced Research Center. Support software includes a Parallel FORTRAN compiler and machine emulator (both executing on the 7600) and operating executives. The distributed and associative logic was modeled after the Bell Lab Integrated Circuit PEPE. The parallel logic has been augmented with three sequential processors each with separate data and program memories. Although the machine was developed to solve the BMD problem, it has potential in other problem areas.

I. PREAMBLE

System Development and Burroughs Corporations under contract to the Ballistic Missile Defense Technology Center (BMDATC) has just completed the development of a new super computer, the Parallel Element Processing Ensemble or PEPE. PEPE is a parallel array processor with distributed and associative logic. In parallel mode with maximum configuration and all elements active, the PEPE system is capable of computation rates in excess of 500 millions of instructions per second. This discourse covers the development of this powerful system from inception through demonstration. It includes a definition of the system from a programmer's point of view, a description of the research center, discussions on the support software, a sampling of the programming language along with the problems attendant with execution. Concluding remarks cover total system capabilities and potential uses.

II. HISTORY OF PEPE

PEPE's history began in the late 1960s when a group of Bell Telephone scientists headed by Jack Githens were looking for a solution to the Ballistic Missile Defense (BMD) Problem. The associative and distributed array logic (still prevalent in the latest PEPE) was implemented in an integrated circuit

(IC) model that required instruction streaming from a host computer. The machine was developed for the Army Ballistic Missile Defense Agency (ABMDA) as a candidate machine for solution of the Preliminary Hardsite BMD problem. The concept was proven as part of those studies. It was at this point that System Development Corporation (SDC) became involved. Bell asked SDC to complete the application study and Honeywell Industries (HI) to take over development of the prototype hardware. SDC and HI successfully demonstrated the Hardsite software on the IC Model PEPE in 1971.

SDC and HI continued to study and to design the next generation PEPE until the fall of 1973 when SDC put together a functional specification for a new computer system. The Burroughs Corporation won the development contract and under a subcontract to SDC built the machine that is now installed in BMDATC's Huntsville, Alabama, Advanced Research Center. Using a functional simulation model, a SDC/TRW team has predicted that a PEPE augmentation of the old Site Defense system could easily increase the data throughput of the Site Defense System by 40%. This improvement is accomplished with almost no software breakage by simply moving computations from the CDC 7700 to PEPE, relaying the data to PEPE, and sending results back to the host machine. Subsequent tests on the live and emulated PEPE have verified timings used in the simulations. In fact the simulations were carefully conservative. The PEPE concept can in the next decade be used to produce systems with over 1,000 MIPS performance.

At the end of the 1971 experiments, the IC Model was given to Auburn University in Alabama. It is now part of a system of mini- and microcomputers in Auburn's graduate school research laboratory. It has become one of their teaching tools, and the PEPE concept is now appearing in textbooks on computers. The new model is a working part of BMDATC's Research Center. The new model was demonstrated and turned over to the government in December of 1976. A complete operational and documented support software system will be delivered in the fall of 1977. Much of this software has been in use since September of 1976.

III. BMDATC ADVANCED RESEARCH CENTER (ARC)

PEPE is an addition to an ARC that already included several powerful computers. PEPE is attached to the CDC 7600 by three multiplexor channels; the Texas Instrument (TI) pipeline computer (Advanced Scientific Computer) is connected to the 7600 via a TI Data Coupler; a CDC 6400 is attached to the 7600 by Satellite Couplers. The 6400 is the system support machine. It is the system's primary input/output; card reading/punching, tape reading/writing, interactive terminal servicing, and color graphics interfacing.

Notice that PEPE is the only machine connected directly to a 7600 multiplexor channel. All other machines are interfaced by a peripheral processor. This direct connection reduces the data turn around time to and from PEPE and provides better real-time response and shorter, port-to-port performance.

IV. DESCRIPTION OF PEPE

From a programmer's point of view, PEPE is a system of three sequential processors with access to the same parallel memory units, via parallel control units: Arithmetic Control Unit (ACU), Associative Output Control Unit (AOCU), and Correlation Control Unit (CCU). Each sequential processor has an associated parallel processing unit: Arithmetic Unit (AU), Associative Output Unit (AOU), and Correlation Unit (CU). Each parallel unit has its own access ports into all parallel element data memories, and each parallel element has a set of operating registers, Figure 1.

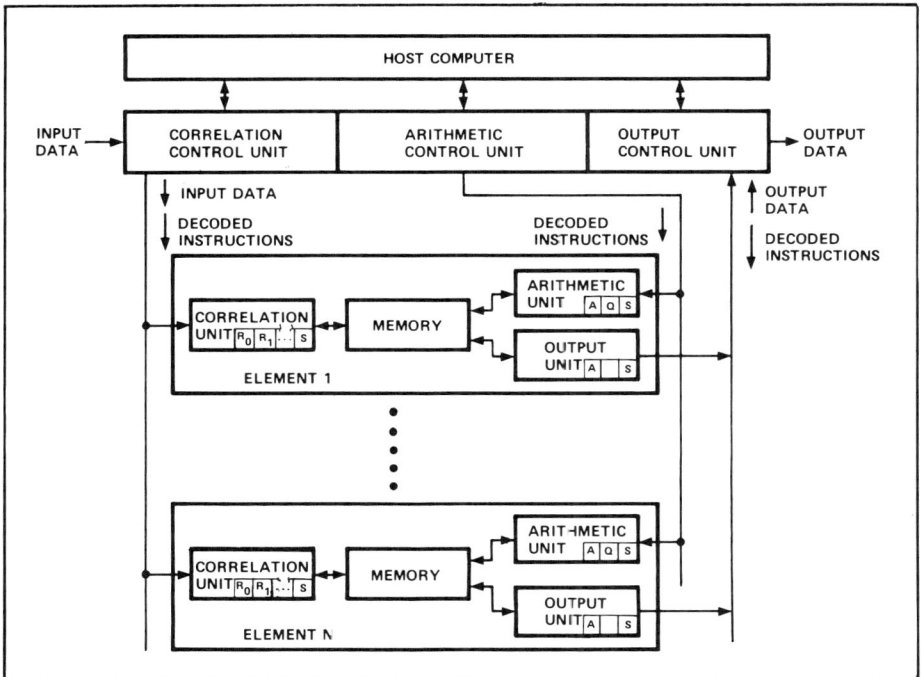

Figure 1. PEPE Architecture

The three sequential control units effect program execution. Each unit has a program and data memory. Both parallel and sequential instructions are intermixed in program memory. Referenced data may be fetched from or stored in sequential data memory or program memory or parallel data memory. As the sequential control logic (SCL) for each unit steps its way through the program in its own program memory, sequential instructions are handed to the parallel control unit (PICU) together with any required sequential data. In the auxiliary units (CCU, AOCU) the parallel instructions are executed as encountered. In the ACU, parallel instructions are placed in a queue from where they are executed in order of entry. The queue allows the ACU to proceed with sequential execution while longer running parallel instructions are being executed from the queue. The queue holds up to 16 instructions and, with proper mixture of sequential and parallel instructions, allows execution of parallel instructions in as little as one machine cycle. The ACU, the main computation unit, can, therefore, almost completely overlap the execution of parallel code with the execution of sequential code. The Interface Units (IU) replicate the CDC channel signals and perform simultaneous independent I/O for PEPE. When accepting data from the 7600, each IU uses the first 60 bit word as a channel command. Each PEPE unit can have four IU's. The installed system has two: one to the 7600, one to the Burroughs Test and Maintenance Computer (a Burroughs B-1700).

PEPE is a system of many computers that function as three independent sequential control units (ACU, CCU, AOCU) each with its own PICU that hands parallel instructions to its parallel execution unit (AU, CU, AOU). Thus, PEPE has six similar but distinct instruction sets. The sequential set is typical; the parallel set includes powerful new forms.

V. PEPE SUPPORT SOFTWARE

The bulk of the support software will be delivered in fall 1977. The PEPE high level language, Parallel Fortran or PFOR, is a single language that includes language forms for all three units. The forms, extensions of Basic Fortran, are translated into a mixture of sequential and parallel code. The code expansions are dependent upon data residency: Sequential Data Memory, Parallel Data Memory, or Correlation Register Data. The PEPE code Catenator provides object module file editing as well as load consolidation and memory allocation. An Emulator Preprocessor is used when an emulated PEPE run is to be made. This program examines each instruction in the load file and attaches codes used to simplify simulated execution. PEPE loading is not a typical load and go procedure. Compilation is done on the host, so the load file must be transmitted to each PEPE program memory prior to execution. If operational data are included in the load file, loading may be independent with no host resident code to control PEPE execution or to respond to PEPE outputs. This is a rare case. Most PEPE execution is under control of the host machine with the loading process as part of the total execution preparations.

Two modes of execution are possible. Both modes require host code to support the process. The system mode uses the real-time executive (RTE) components to control process task execution and to handle I/O. The special mode requires process specific loading, execution controls, and I/O procedures. Both modes must operate within the constraints imposed by the 7600 operating system (a modified SCOPE 2). The SCOPE modifications are superficial, affecting only the I/O and system dedication. The system is intended to run short bursts (less than 5 minutes) of real-time experiments, so the 7600 operating system was modified to give quick response to I/O messages with minimal operating system overhead. Output to PEPE is moved directly from Large Core Memory to Small Core Memory channel buffers. Inputs from PEPE are moved directly from Small Core Memory channel buffers to a single Large Core Memory circular buffer.

The system mode of execution assumes that each process to be developed will be gradually produced as a BMD tool. As such it is subject to algorithm changes, schedule changes, and total process redefinition (exclusion/addition of tasks). Task execution orders may change dynamically. Thus, the process writer does not write a master control routine (a FORTRAN Program). He writes a separate solution task (a control subroutine that may or may not call other subroutines) to perform each defined step (filtering, tracking, guidance, battle planning, data routing, etc.) of the total process. The sequences of execution is established at the time of execution. This is accomplished by building and maintaining a set of process control tables. A real-time executive determines which task to run next by examining the contents of the process control tables. The system mode of execution provides a research base in which a BMD analyst can operate on a given threat base without wholesale reprogramming. The existing file or library of tactical routines may contain many practical alternative solutions, and the analyst can pick the desired solution for each run.

The special mode of execution requires that the user build total communications and executive controls in both the 7600 and PEPE units. PEPE Interface Unit Commands must begin each message sent to any of the three PEPE units and code must be resident in each of those units that will respond to the message. The PEPE loader must be specifically called with the proper load file attached, after the system has been initialized. A Large Core Memory input area must be identified to receive data from PEPE, and the received data must match system protocol. There is no interrupt mechanism provided for input servicing, so the user must service the input area periodically. On the PEPE side, the ACU is the major problem. It has 16 possible I/O, timer, and error interrupts that must be handled. The special mode is frequently used when a specific PEPE feature is to be tested or used exclusively.

Postrun support is provided by 7600 utility programs. Execution time history, PEPEDUMP data, message recordings, and emulated PEPE trace data can be printed and plotted. Trace output selection controls are provided at both the recording and printing levels.

VI. PFOR LANGUAGE

Parallel Fortran or PFOR is a combination of parallel and sequential language forms. The parallel forms take advantage of available parallel instructions. The sequential forms are USA Standard Fortran. The total language is consistent if one is cognizant of data residency at all times. For example, parallel operations on sequential data is seemingly inconsistent, yet it may be desirable, and it is sometimes permissible. It is incorrect, however, to set a sequential variable equal to a parallel variable when more than one element is active. This is tantamount to parking two or more autos in the same space. Problem solution with PFOR is easy when the data definitions and residencies are kept in mind.

Data are assigned with typical Fortran statements. Sequential data assignments are made with standard Fortran specifications within each program unit. Each program unit is assigned to a specific PEPE unit by attaching unit identifiers to the end of the subroutine statements.

Parallel data specifications are also Fortran like:

```
PAR REAL PRV, PRA(4,6)
PAR INTEGER PI, PIA(3,2)
```

```
PAR LOGICAL PL
PAR COMMON /PARDAT/ PRV, PRA, PI, PL
PAR DIMENSION PLA(3)
PAR EQUIVALENCE ( ... , ...)
PAR DOUBLE PDI
```

CCU program units may also delcare Correlation Register data. Each parallel element associated with the CCU has 16 correlation registers. Data are assigned to these registers with similar statements:

```
PAR COR INTEGER PCI1, PCI2
PAR COR REAL    PCR, PCR2
PAR COR LOGICAL PCL
PAR COR DOUBLE  PCD
DESCRIPTOR (PCI1,01),(PCR,02),(PCD,03),(PCL,05)
DESC (PCI2,06),(PCR2,07)
```

VII. PARALLEL STATEMENTS

An important concept of parallel language that is not uniformly handled is the technique used to skip redundant data or unused elements. The PEPE concept that is reflected in the PFOR language forms is twofold: (1) elements taking part in parallel activity are associatively selected or activated--inactive elements do not participate; or (2) all elements are allowed to perform the parallel action--there is no additional time cost for their participation, and unwanted results are simply ignored. The following statements will clear the parallel variables in all elements that are active when the subroutine TCIN is executed in the CCU:

```
      SUBROUTINE TCIN, CCU
C     DATA DEFINITIONS
C                              In all active parallel elements,
                               parallel integer PIN is set to 0,
      PIN=0                    parallel logical PLHERE is set
                               false.
      PLHERE= .FALSE.
      RETURN                   A sequential return of control is
      END                       made.
```

More example code shows the use of CCU statements to set parallel data from sequential input data:

```
      WHERE (PIN.EQ.0) 10
        WHERE FIRST 10     )
          PIN= CXBINT(1)  * )
          PRA= CXBUFS(2)  * )
```

```
          PRB= CXBUFS(3)      * )
          PRC= CXBUFS(4)      * )
          PLIMAG= .FALSE.     * )
          PLEQUL= .FALSE.     * )
10        CONTINUE            * )
          RETURN
          END
```

* These statements are executed in the first active element only.

) These statements are executed only in a subset of the elements where the parallel integer PIN is equal to 0.

These statements show the versatile capabilities of ACU resident code:

```
          WHERE (PIN .NE. 0) 160      In els where PIN is not 0:
          PRD= (PRB*PRB -(4.*PRA*PRC))
          WHERE (PRD .LT. 0.) 20
20            PLIMAG= .TRUE.          & PRD less than 0.
          WHERE (PRD .EQ. 0.) 30
30            PLEQUL= .TRUE.          & PRD equal 0.
          WHERE (.NOT.PLIMAG) 40
              PRX= PSQRT(PRD)         & PLIMAG is not true.
              PRR1= (-PRB +PRX)/(2.*PRA)       "
              PRR2= (-PRB -PRX)/(2.*PRA)       "
40        CONTINUE
          ...
160       CONTINUE
          PLYES= .FALSE.              In all elements.
          DO SEQ 200 (.TRUE.)9,I      From the first 9 elements se-
              PLYES= .TRUE.           lect one at a time and set the

              PRSN= I -1              parallel variables in that
                                      element. I varies from 1 to 9.
200       CONTINUE
          MOVE 210 (PLHERE) TO (PLYES)     Where PLHERE is true,
              PRXMIN .TO. PRXMIN           move the parallel real
                                           variable PRXMIN to the
                                           elements where parallel
                                           logical PLYES is true.
210           PRC  .TO. PRCO               PRC to PRCO.
          ...
```

VIII SUMMARY OF PFOR LANGUAGE FORMS

The following summary shows the complete forms of the more important PFOR forms. The lower case letters represent user supplied names or expressions. The square brackets surround optional parts. The s# represents a numeric statement number. The s represents a PFOR statement.

The WHERE Forms.
All these forms utilize save activity (PUSH).
WHERE (ple) s# [,NONE]   Uses conditional select instr.
WHERE FIRST s# [,NONE]   Uses Select on First instr.
WHERE MAX (pae) s# [,NONE] Uses Select Highest.
WHERE MIN (pae) s# [,NONE] Uses Select Lowest.
WHERE NOT s# [,NONE]   Uses activity complementing.
WHERE SET (ple) s# [,NONE] Uses Activate All.
                       All use restore activity (POP)

As the name implies, the WHERE is a form for subsetting a parallel data base. The various forms provide further capabilities utilizing PEPE hardware features. The optional NONE clause provides a time saving skip around the range of the WHERE when no elements are active as the result of evaluating the parallel logical expression (ple) or parallel arithmetic expression (pae). The WHERE FIRST selects just one of the active set. The statements in the range of the WHERE MAX statement are executed only in those elements where the pae has a maximum algebraic value. If two or more of the active elements have the same maximum value, the statements are executed in all those active elements having the identical maximum value of the pae. The WHERE MIN is the same except the minimum value is used. The WHERE MAX/MIN are not legal in the CCU since it has no floating point capability needed to evaluate the pae. A WHERE NOT statement must appear within the range of a WHERE, WHERE FIRST, WHERE MAX, or WHERE MIN. The statements within the range of the WHERE NOT statement will be executed only by those elements made inactive by the containing WHERE-class statement. The WHERE SET statement saves the current activity status and activates all available elements; then the ple is used to select a new set. After the range terminating statement is executed, the saved activity is restored. The WHERE SET makes it possible to create an entirely new set in the midst of processing.

The CONVERGE Form.
  CONVERGE (ple) s#   ,NONE

The CONVERGE form is simply a WHERE form that requires less machine level code to save and restore element activity. Because of this saving, one restriction exists. The range statement number, s#, must be the same for all nested CONVERGE forms.

The Parallel DO Forms

DO ASC s# (pae) n, m	All these use PUSH, POP to save/restore activity. Uses Select Lowest, First, Branch on None.
DO DESC s# (pae) n, m	Uses Select Highest, First, Branch on None.
DO SEQ s# (ple) n, m	Uses Select Equal, First, Branch on None.
DO UP s# (pae) n, m	Uses Select Lowest, Branch on None.
DO DOWN s# (pae) n, m	Uses Select Highest, Branch on None.

The DO SEQ is legal in all three PEPE units (ACU, CCU, AOCU). The other forms are legal only in the ACU and AOCU. The CCU is not able to evaluate a parallel arithmetic expression.

If one or more elements are active after evaluating the ple of a DO SEQ statement, the statements within its range are executed (looped) in at most the first n elements of the new active subset. One and only one element is active each iteration through the loop. The parameter m is a programmable index through the loop.

The statements in the range of the DO ASC and DO DESC statements are executed in at most the first n active elements as selected in algebraic order (ascending or descending) according to the results of evaluating the pae. If more than one element has the same resulting value, the tie is resolved by selecting the first available element, then the next, etc.

The DO UP and DO DOWN are similar to the DO ASC/DESC. The difference is the single selection of the DO ASC/DESC. The DO UP/DOWN do not require single element activity for each loop. If all of the selected set had the same result after evaluating the pae, all statements within the range would be executed by all of the elements at once. There is one evaluation or execution of the in range statements for each unique result from the pae. The executions are performed in order of either the increasing values (UP) or decreasing values (DOWN).

The Parallel IF Forms

IF ALL (ple) s	Uses Branch On None Active.
IF ANY (ple) s	Uses Branch on Any Active.
IF MANY (ple) s	Uses Branch on Many (>1)
IF NONE (ple) s	Uses Branch on None.
IF ONE (ple) s	Uses Branch on One.

If the indicated condition exists after selecting the set of elements where the parallel logical expression is true, the appended statement is executed. For example:

```
IF ALL  (PLYES) GO TO 100
IF ANY  (PLA .EQ. PLB) PLC= .TRUE.
IF MANY (PRX .GT. 1.) PIE= PEPECOUNT(PRX .GT.0)
IF NONE (PRY) GO TO 25
IF ONE  (PRDELX .NE. 0.) PIF= 1
```

The evaluation of the parallel logical expression does not result in a permanent subset. The activity is restored to the pre-evaluation state before the s statement is executed and before any subsequent statements are executed.

The MOVE Form.
```
     MOVE s#1 (ple1) to (ple2)   s#2
          pva   .TO.   pvb
          pvc   .TO.   pvd
                ...
s#1       pvx   .TO.   pvy
```

The MOVE form effects a data move from the single element selected by the left parallel logical expression (ple1) to all elements selected by ple2. All data listed through the range terminating statement number (s#1) are moved from the single element variables listed on the left to the one or more element variables listed on the right. A transfer of control to statement label #2 occurs when the from set is a null set (no active elements) or has more than one active element or when the to set is a null set. Without the optional s#2 parameter, a from set with multiple activity will result in an ACU Error Interrupt and possible run abort.

The PEPEDUMP Form.
PEPEDUMP (flag, format, entities)

The PEPEDUMP form is the only system supplied dynamic diagnostic that is available to a real hardware system run. An instruction trace is also available during a simulated PEPE run. The PEPEDUMP form includes parameters that define the source of the data to be printed (flag), the format to be used, and a list or description to a subroutine call that effects data transmission to the host. The data messages are of unique type that are passed to the host for recording. A postrun program extracts and prints the requested dump.

The PEPESTAT Form.   The PEPESTAT form provides the
PEPESTAT (f, pv)   capability to save and restore
                     parallel activity status.

The MODE Forms.
  MODE ACU   ... MODE OFF
  MODE DIRECT ... MODE PFOR

The MODE ACU/OFF brackets provide access to the ACU floating point and other capabilities from the AOCU and CCU. In effect, the statements between the MODE ACU and the MODE OFF are executed in the ACU via an interrupt mechanism. The MODE DIRECT/PFOR brackets allow the use of direct or machine level code.

The PEPE Functions. Some parallel functions may be used in parallel arithmetic expressions: Absolute Value (PABS), Unfloat (PFIX), Float (PFLOAT), Square Root (PSQRT).

The PEPECOUNT Function.
    siv=PEPECOUNT or
    siv=PEPECOUNT (ple)

Both forms produce a sequential integer (single value) activity count. The first form produces the number of active elements. The second form produces the number of active elements after subsetting by the parallel logical expression (ple).

IX. PEPE AND THE FUTURE

With all three PEPE units operating on a typical instruction mix, PEPE can easily perform one million instructions per second (MIPS) per element per unit. This puts the current system in the 800 MIPS range with a full 288 element ensemble. System experts are predicting future performance in the 1,500 MIPS area with ensemble capacities in the thousands of elements. Proposed improvements in element to element data exchange rates and reductions in fabrication costs will make PEPE a strong contender for such applications as weather processing, fluid dynamics, nuclear computations, and air traffic control.

EFFICIENT HIGH SPEED COMPUTING WITH THE
DISTRIBUTED ARRAY PROCESSOR

P.M. Flanders, D.J. Hunt, S.F. Reddaway, D. Parkinson
International Computers Limited

The Distributed Array Processor (DAP) is a SIMD
(Single Instruction - Multiple Data) machine which
distributes a few thousand very simple bit-organised
processing elements throughout a store module of a
conventional computing system. The design is presented,
together with details of its arithmetic and logical
capability and of the software system being implemented.
Some algorithms have been run on a pilot 32 x 32 DAP
and their performance is discussed. The size and
performance of probable future models are also
considered. The results of some application studies
are presented illustrating the high performance
achievable with this flexible and cost effective
processor.

I. PRINCIPLES

The Distributed Array Processor (DAP) is a computer
architecture capable of achieving high performance on a
variety of large computing jobs. It comprises a few thousand
Processing Elements (PEs) arranged in a two-dimensional array.
The PEs are very simple but high processing power is achieved
by having many of them. They execute a common instruction
stream broadcast by a Master Control Unit (MCU); the DAP is
thus classified as a SIMD (Single Instruction - Multiple Data)
machine.
Various sizes of PE array can be made, offering a range
of processing powers. It is most natural for the array to be
a square whose side is simply related to standard store
highway widths. The design aims for cost-effectiveness
rather than speed at any price.
The PEs are bit organised giving great flexibility.
Hence parallelism can be exploited in operations such as
table lookup, scanning data, symbol processing and sorting
as well as arithmetic. Each PE has associated with it a few

thousand bits of fast random access storage. The fast parallel transfer between stores and PEs balances the high processing speed.

The totality of PE stores form a standard store module of a conventional computer. Hence there is no need for separate transfer of data between host and DAP. DAP processing is under the control of the host via a simple interface. Being part of a general purpose system has two related advantages. It gives access to the facilities of that system, in particular the operating system, languages and input-output, and it allows users progressively to take advantage of DAP processing.

A pilot model having 1024 PEs arranged 32 x 32 each with 1K (expandable to 2K) bits of bipolar store has been working since Spring 1976. It has a total of 89 boards, most of which are "array" boards each having 79 16-pin off-the-shelf TTL integrated circuits forming the logic and storage for 16 PEs. The total power dissipation excluding fans and power supply losses is under 1.5K Watts

The next model will achieve about five times more processing power with a 64 x 64 array. Each PE will have 4K bits giving a 2 MByte store module. The DAP architecture is ideal for custom LSI, so a 128 x 128 model could be built using today's semiconductor technology.

A. Processing Element

Figure 1 shows the essential features of one PE with some of the control and data paths omitted for clarity (the PE has been simplified since (1)). All data paths are one bit wide.

The top multiplexor selects the input to the Arithmetic and Logic Unit (ALU), which may be either the PEs own output or that from its North, East, South, or West neighbour. The bottom multiplexor selects the PE output, which may be an ALU output, or store output, and may go to the store, another PE or to the MCU. The two multiplexors also allow input of data broadcast from the MCU along row or column highways.

The ALU has three one-bit registers (A, Q and C) and a one-bit full adder. The low level software allows total flexibility in the use of ALU facilities but most common usage is as follows.

Register A provides 'activity' control; certain store write operations are only effective if this register is true. This allows application of a function to selected elements of an array and is also used for bit level implementation within functions. The A register incorporates a logical AND facility which allows conditions to be combined rapidly and

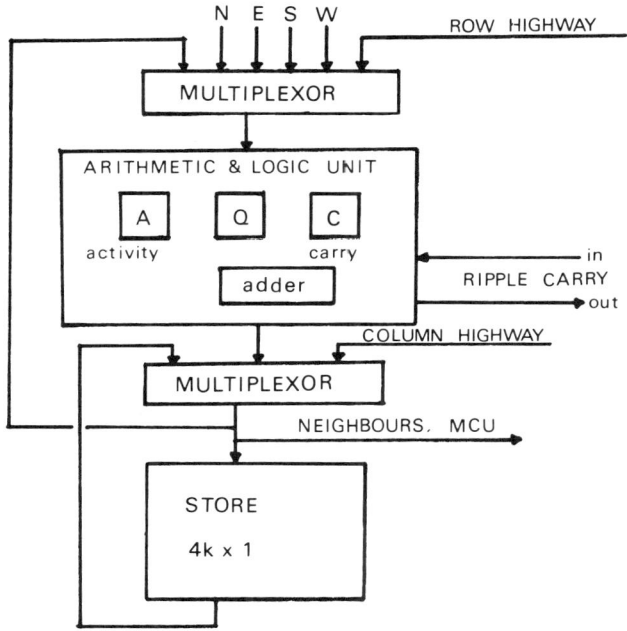

Fig.1. Processing Element.

may also be used in its own right for implementing general logic functions.

The Q register acts as a one bit accumulator and the C register as a carry store. The adder adds Q, C and the ALU input and its sum output may be written back to Q and its carry output to C.

B. Master Control Unit

Figure 2 is a schematic of the MCU, which may be likened to the instruction sequencing and control sections of a small computer. Implementation of an array instruction involves a Fetch phase, during which the instruction is fetched from the array store, and an Execute phase, during which appropriate control signals are broadcast to the array. Each phase uses one basic machine cycle.

Each instruction occupies 32 bits along one row of PEs and successive instructions are held in successive rows (or part rows) so that code is spread evenly among the PE stores. It must be emphasised that instructions can only be

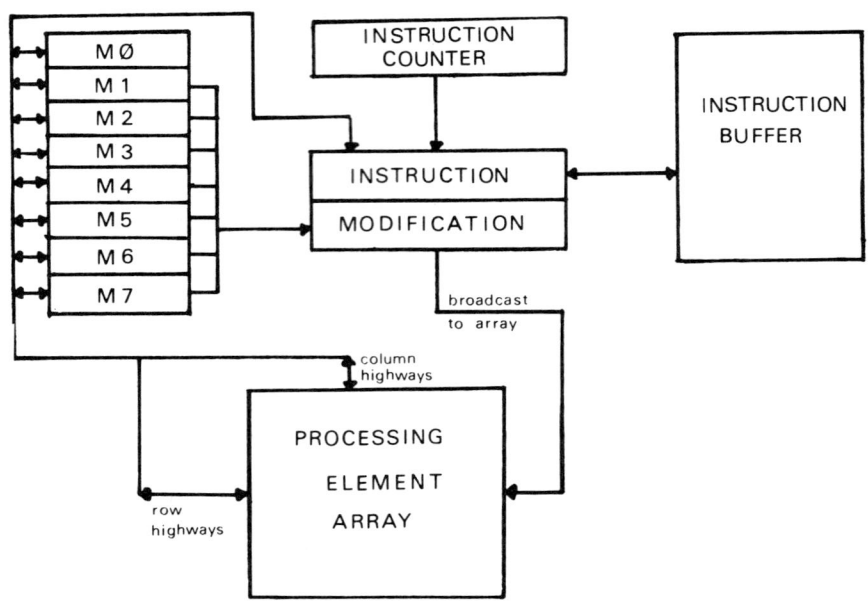

Fig.2. Master Control Unit

interpreted by the MCU; the PEs cannot recognise instructions themselves.

An important feature is the instruction buffer which stores loops (of up to 15 instructions on the pilot) explicitly specified by low level coding. Hence the instructions need to be fetched only once prior to the first time found the loop. Automatic stepping of addresses is possible for operating on successive bits of a word.

There are eight general purpose registers, MØ to M7 with length equal to the side of the PE array. These may hold data or addresses used in instruction fetching or execution. The register contents may be transferred to or from the array along the row or column highways.

The normal control transfer instructions GOTO, LINK and EXIT and facilities for address arithmetic are provided.

The MCU also contains the store and control interfaces (not shown in Figure 2) to the host. When the DAP is processing, the host can still access the store by cycle stealing.

C. Modes of Storage and Processing

There are two formats in which data are held in the DAP store. In the 'vertical' format each number is held entirely within one PE with successive bits in successive store locations. In the 'horizontal' format each number is spread along a row of PEs, in a manner similar to the storage of DAP instructions. Words as seen by the host are also in this format.

The most powerful processing mode, known as matrix mode, operates on data in vertical format.

Vector mode processing is used where problem parallelism is lower but makes less effective use of the PEs. This operates on data in horizontal format and makes use of instructions which allow carrys to ripple along each row.

Small amounts of scalar processing may be done in the array to avoid the overhead of returning to the host. This uses the horizontal format and is faster than vector processing since more use is made of data dependent jumps and advantage is taken of any parallelism within the arithmetic operations.

Transformations between horizontal and vertical format are done by DAP processing and take less time than a multiply operation. Thus the overhead is normally negligible.

II. ARITHMETIC AND BASIC OPERATIONS

Since the PEs are bit organised, arithmetic is built up by low level software. This software is continually being improved and is now substantially faster than a year ago. Table 1 gives the times for some operations in standard ICL 2900/IBM 360 floating point format, based on a 200 nSec cycle time as in the pilot 32 x 32 DAP. Unbiased rounding is used for greater accuracy than truncation towards zero. The operations are on matrices or vectors which match the DAP size.

For the operations in Table 1 both operands and the result have the same rank. In cases where the ranks are different the operation may be significantly faster, as indicated by the examples in Table 2.

The time for multiplication of every element of a matrix by a scalar is strongly dependent on the value of the scalar and on whether it is known at compile time. It is always significantly less than the time to multiply corresponding elements of two matrices.

Surprisingly, the sum of all elements of a matrix can be computed in a time only slightly longer than to add two matrices. The method involves converting the array to block

TABLE 1

Some Operation Times for the Pilot DAP in μSec.
Estimates for a 64 x 64 DAP are in Brackets.

Operation	Matrix	Vector	Scalar
Floating Point (32 bit):			
Z←X+Y	148(135)	54(32)	27(21)
Z←X*Y	305(250)	50(45)	34(27)
Z←X/Y	390(330)	100(90)	
Z←X**2	155(125)	40(35)	
Z←SQRT(X)	215(180)		
Z←X	14(13)	1	
Z←MAX(X,Y)	34(33)		
Fixed Point (32 bit):			
Z←X+Y	23(22)	4	

TABLE 2

Some Times in μSec for 32-bit Floating Point Mixed
Rank Operations. X and Y are Matrices; S is a Scalar

Operation	Time
Y←X*S	40-150 (35-125)
S←ΣX	170 (160)
S←MAX(X)	46 (45)

floating point, enabling the ten stages of addition to be done essentially as fixed point operations. At each stage the number of partial results is halved. During each of the first five stages, each partial result field is split into two fields such that twice as many PEs are devoted to each partial sum. The last five stages, with the partial results in horizontal format, are somewhat similar to vector mode fixed point additions except that a carry save technique is used. Finally the scalar result is normalised. Sufficient guard bits are used that both the worst case and average rounding errors are less than if floating point were used throughout.

A bit level algorithm is used to find the maximum element of an array.

The DAP offers complete flexibility of function so the time taken by a function depends only on its complexity. Some important consequences of the flexibility are:
(a) More complex functions such as square root and logarithm are faster in comparison with basic arithmetic operations

than on a conventional computer.
(b) The DAP can take advantage of symmetries within a function so that, for example, the time for the squaring operation is about half that for general multiplication.
(c) Operations that are inherently simple may be several orders of magnitude faster than on conventional computers. For example, to replace every element of a matrix by its modulus takes less than 1 μSec for the whole matrix. Also, data dependent jumps in conventional programs are usually implemented on the DAP as conditional assignments of the result of an arithmetic operation. Thus the jumps are essentially replaced by setting the activity; this takes negligible time and the routines in the tables all incorporate activity control. Global tests, resulting in a branch if all elements of a boolean matrix are true, take less than 1 μSec.

The complete flexibility of precision of data stored in vertical mode gives continuous space and speed trade-offs. Arithmetic function times vary approximately linearly with precision: multiplication more sharply, addition less sharply.

The flexibility of representation allows radix 2 or radix 4 floating point representations to be used with consequent improvements in the arithmetic times. Still larger gains may often be made by using block floating point representation in which all elements of an array are normalised to a common exponent. In this case addition and subtraction are approximately four times faster.

III. SOFTWARE

The different modes of processing available in a computer system incorporating an NxN DAP are given below along with the associated storage mode and degree of parallelism:

Processing Mode	Storage Mode	Data Parallelism
Host - Scalar	Horizontal	1
DAP - Scalar	Horizontal	1
DAP - Vector	Horizontal	N
DAP - Matrix	Vertical	N^2

The key to using such a system effectively is to allow the mode appropriate to the degree of parallelism to be selected at any instant provided that the cost of switching modes is not dominant. The high level language system which is being implemented satisfies this requirement in a natural and efficient way.

A. Program Structure

A program to be run on the DAP comprises a standard FORTRAN program and a number of subprograms written in a language developed for the DAP called DAP-FORTRAN. The standard FORTRAN part is processed by the host and gives access to all the facilities of the host including input-output and fast scalar processing. When a subroutine written in DAP-FORTRAN is called, the host processor activates the DAP to process the subroutine and any further levels of DAP-FORTRAN routines. Processing of the FORTRAN part by the host computer may proceed asynchronously, including access to data held in the DAP store.

Data communication between FORTRAN and DAP-FORTRAN is by common blocks held in the DAP store. Since these are immediately accessible to both the host and DAP, no time is required for data transfer. Any changes in the format of stored data necessitated by different processing modes are performed either explicitly or implicitly by the DAP-FORTRAN code.

B. The Language DAP-FORTRAN

DAP-FORTRAN provides a good match between problem and hardware and encourages users to rethink algorithms to good effect. It is an array processing dialect of FORTRAN permitting vectors and matrices, as well as scalars, as the basic elements of an expression. Much of the explicit coding of inner loops of a program is thus eliminated with consequent advantages in code conciseness and readability.

The vectors and matrices of the language have their dimensions constrained to match directly the size of the DAP and are mapped in horizontal mode and vertical mode respectively. Implicit mode changes occur during the processing of statements when a row or column is selected from a matrix or when a vector is expanded to a matrix. Larger arrays are represented as indexed sets of vectors or matrices. When handling such arrays the code tends to expand to about the size of the equivalent FORTRAN code.

Operators are provided for arithmetic, logical and relational operations as in standard FORTRAN and they are also applied in an element-by-element manner to arrays. Standard functions provide regular mappings of arrays as well as element-by-element application of arithmetic functions such as logarithm.

Indexing operations are a powerful generalization of the conventional single element selection; in particular they permit the selection of elements by logical masks, a task particularly suited to the DAP.

Indexed assignment, where subscripts are used to select arguments for updating, is generalized in a way compatible with the generalized indexing. In particular the use of a logical mask as a subscript is directly implemented via the activity control of the DAP hardware.

C. DAP Code Translation

As well as DAP-FORTRAN, there is a macro-assembly language for the DAP in which all code run to date has been written. The DAP-FORTRAN compiler will produce target code in a form suitable for input to the assembler. This intermediate form is the assembly language itself, supplemented by a number of system macros.
After assembly the DAP subprograms, including any common blocks to be held in the DAP store, are consolidated into a contiguous block of code and data to be loaded into the DAP store. Entries from the host processor to specific DAP-FORTRAN subroutines within this block are engineered by "interface procedures" which enable the subroutines to be called by the standard FORTRAN subroutine calling mechanism. These interface procedures are generated by the DAP-FORTRAN compilation system but are executed by the host.

D. Operating System Software

The DAP makes minimal demands on the host operating system. The only special actions required are:
(a) The DAP program block is loaded into a contiguous area of the DAP store where it resides for the duration of the program (i.e. it is non-paged and locked into store).
(b) The host treats sub-blocks of the program block as data areas corresponding to FORTRAN common blocks.
(c) The host controls the DAP in a peripheral-like manner. This entails initiating processing by the DAP, after setting up store protection registers in the DAP, and servicing interrupts generated by the DAP when it stops processing.

IV. ALGORITHMS IMPLEMENTED ON THE PILOT DAP

A. Matrix Multiply

The usual method of calculating matrix products is to compute each element in turn as the inner product of a row of one operand with a column of the other. However the method implemented calculates all elements in parallel by using outer products.

The DAP-FORTRAN code for multiplying 32x32 matrices A and B to produce result C on a 32x32 DAP is:

```
         C = 0.0
         DO 100 I = 1,32
100      C = C + A( ,*I) * B(*I, )
```

The expression A(,*I) selects column I of matrix A and forms a new matrix each of whose columns is equal to this column. At the hardware level this is done by extracting and re-broadcasting each bit of the numbers in turn using the row highways. Similarly row I of matrix B is extracted and broadcast using the column highways. These and all other non-arithmetic operations account for only about 10% of the total time. The two temporary matrices are multiplied element by element and added to the partially accumulated result. It is interesting to note that this method makes no use of the nearest neighbour connections.

Performance details are given in section 4.5.

B. Matrix Inversion

The matrix inversion program run on the DAP uses the algorithm of Gauss Jordan (i.e. complete elimination above and below the pivot elements in a single forward sweep). In each of the N steps required to transform an NxN matrix into its inverse the elements of the new value A' are given in terms of the current value A by the equations:

$$A'_{pq} = \frac{1}{A_{pq}} \; ; \quad A'_{ij} = A_{ij} - \frac{A_{iq} A_{pj}}{A_{pq}} \quad \text{for } i \neq p \text{ and } j \neq q$$

$$A'_{pj} = \frac{A_{pj}}{A_{pq}} \quad \text{for } j \neq q; \quad A'_{iq} = -\frac{A_{iq}}{A_{pq}} \quad \text{for } i \neq p$$

where p and q are the numbers of the pivot row and column respectively.

The DAP-FORTRAN code to invert a 32x32 matrix on a 32x32 DAP, along with some explanation, is given below. It minimizes the number of arithmetic operations since these account for most of the execution time. At each step the pivot element is selected from all the remaining elements. All row and column interchanges are left until the end.

DAP-FORTRAN Code for Matrix Inversion with Pivoting

```
01      SUBROUTINE INVP(A)
02      REAL A(,),B(,)
03      LOGICAL PROW(,),PCOL(,),PMASK(,),PIV(,),MASK(,),PIVS(,)
04      INTEGER RN( )
05      MASK=.TRUE.
06      PIVS=.FALSE.
07      DO 1 K=1,32
08      PIV=FRST(MAXP(ABS(A),MASK))
09      S=A(PIV)
10      PIVS=PIVS.OR.PIV
11      PROW=MATC(ORC(PIV))
12      PCOL=MATR(ORR(PIV))
13      PMASK=.NOT.(PROW.OR.PCOL)
14      A(PIV)=1.0
15      A=MERGE(A,0.0,PMASK)-A(,*PCOL)*MATR(A(PROW,)/S)
16      A(PROW)=-A
17    1 MASK=MASK.AND.PMASK
18    C RESHUFFLE ROWS AND COLUMNS
19      RN=ROWN(PIVS)
20      DO 2 K=1,32
21    2 B(K,)=A(RN(K),)
22      DO 3 K=1,32
23    3 A(,RN(K))=B(,K)
24      RETURN
25      END
```

Line 2 declares A, the matrix to be inverted, and B to be 32x32 matrices of 32-bit floating point numbers. Line 3 declares a number of 32x32 matrices with logical elements. Line 4 declares RN to be a 32-element vector of 32-bit integers.

In lines 5 and 6 the elements of MASK and PIVS are all set to TRUE and FALSE respectively.

Line 7 specifies the loop control in a way similar to FORTRAN.

Lines 8 and 9 select a pivot element equal to the element of the array with largest modulus, setting the scalar S equal to the value of the element and the logical matrix PIV equal to FALSE for every element except the one in the pivot row. and column. When selecting the pivot element, only elements for which the corresponding element of MASK have the value TRUE are considered.

PIVS records the positions of all the pivot elements and is used later in the reshuffling of rows and columns. Line 10 sets the element of PIVS to TRUE at the position of the current pivot element.

The elements of PROW and PCOL are set in lines 11 and 12 to have the value TRUE if and only if they are in the pivot row and pivot column respectively. The elements of PMASK are set in line 13 to have the value TRUE if and only if they are in neither the pivot row nor the pivot column.

Line 14 sets the pivot element equal to one. Line 15 contains the arithmetic operations of the loop and accounts for most of the execution time. The standard function MERGE with arguments A, 0.0 and PMASK produces a matrix whose elements are the same as the elements of A where PMASK has the value TRUE, and 0.0 elsewhere. The indexing operation A(,*PCOL) produces a matrix with every column equal to the value of the pivot column of A. The expression MATR(A(PROW,)/S) produces a matrix with every row equal to the value of the pivot row of A divided by S.

Line 16 negates the values of A in the pivot row only. This is a trivial operation for the DAP and has negligible execution time.

The last statement of the loop in line 17 sets the elements of MASK in the pivot row and pivot column to FALSE so that subsequent pivot elements are not selected from this row or column.

Lines 18 to 25 perform the reshuffling of rows and columns.

C. Fourier Transformation

The Fast Fourier Transform (FFT) of an initial set of N points involves $\log_2(N)$ steps each of which is as follows:
(a) Divide each set into two equal sets;
(b) Interchange adjacent sets in pairs;
(c) Multiply by a factor dependent on set number;
(d) Add to data at beginning of step.

For a DAP implementation with one data point per PE interchanging the data sets involves shifting using the neighbour connections. The algorithm considers the data as a linear chain, but advantage is taken of the two-dimensional connectivity of the DAP to reduce the amount of routing.

Consider a 1024 point complex transform on a 32x32 DAP. In step 1, the interchange is done in a single shift by a distance of 16 PEs making use of a cyclic connection at the array edges. The multipliers are (1,-1) so it is only necessary to negate half the array which can be done very rapidly. In step 2 there are two shifts by 8 PEs in opposite directions with the results being merged. The multipliers are (1,-1,i,-i) which are implemented as conditional negation and conditional interchange of real and imaginary parts. Subsequent multiplications require arithmetic work. For steps 6 to 10, the routing is similar to that for steps 1 to 5 respectively but is in the orthogonal direction.

Further routing is needed to arrange the results in a natural order. However, in many applications, such as convolution, the forward transform is followed ultimately by a backward transform, making the intermediate order irrelevant.

The alogrithm implemented uses a standard radix four technique to reduce the arithmetic compared with the basic description given above. Data routing accounts for about 10% of the overall time (or 20% with re-ordering).

D. Convolution using Fermat Number Transforms

It is well known that a fast convolution may be achieved by multiplying the Fourier Transforms of the operand vectors term by term and taking the inverse transform of the result. There are however other transforms which can be used in this way and one which is particularly attractive for the DAP is based on the use of Fermat Numbers (2). In this, addition and multiplication in the field of complex numbers, as in the FFT, are replaced by addition and multiplication modulo F_t in the ring of integers, where F_t is the Fermat Number $2^{2^t} + 1$. The advantage is that for suitable choices of t and the number of points N, all the multiplier factors have very simple binary representation; in almost all cases the multiplies are implemented simply as cyclic shifts. The DAP takes advantage of this at the bit level and hence achieves very fast transforms. Since integers are used throughout, the convolution obtained is exact, in contrast to the FFT method which is subject to rounding error.

The code implemented carries out cyclic 2-D convolution on 32x32 points using t=4, i.e. F_t = 65537, so all numbers occupy 17 bits.

E. Performance Summary

The measured times for routines written in the assembly language on the pilot 32 x32 DAP are as follows:

Routine	Time on Pilot
Matrix Multiply: 32-bit floating point (32x32)	16 mSec.
Matrix Inversion: 32-bit floating point with full pivoting (32x32)	29 mSec.
Fast Fourier Transform: 32-bit floating point including re-ordering (1024 point complex)	14 mSec.
Convolution: 16-bit integer (32x32)	4.3 mSec.

These times can be reduced by:
(a) improving standard functions;
(b) making functions more specific to the application;
(c) using an internal number representation better suited to the DAP;
(d) improving the algorithms.

A DAP-FORTRAN implementation should only be slightly slower than the corresponding assembly language implementation since most of the time is spent in arithmetic routines rather than in organisational work.

V. APPLICATIONS

Most problems, especially large ones, have a lot of parallelism - usually much more than is apparent at first. Mapping of applications on to the DAP is best done at the problem level and with re-appraisal of the algorithms used; it is less effective to look at sections of an existing program in isolation. In nearly every case studied, almost all the computation can be written efficiently in DAP-FORTRAN and executed in the DAP. Performance estimates, derived from detailed studies, for a number of complete calculations are listed below. The comparisons are with existing implementations on particular machines.

Application	Estimated Performance (64x64 DAP)
Finite Element Analysis	2-6 x 360/195
Simple relaxation	20 x 360/195
	5 x ILLIAC IV
Meteorology - complete suite of operational programs	13 x 360/195
3-D Magnetohydrodynamics	14-30 x 360/91
Many Body Simulation (Galactic Simulation)	10 x 7600
A data re-organisation problem	10 x 7600
A table look-up problem	3 x CRAY 1
A pattern matching problem	300 x 360/195
Operations Research (The Assignment Problem)	1200 x 370/145

Much of Finite Element Analysis involves matrix manipulations which are well suited to the DAP but the performance on other parts is less clear. Overall the performance is expected to be good, particularly on large problems.

The simple relaxation calculation (3) is an elementary method for solving Laplace's equation on a 64x64 grid. Reference 3 gives the code in CFD for ILLIAC IV and in FORTRAN for the 360/195 and gives times for 10 iterations as 17.2 and

67.2 mSec respectively. The problem can be programmed easily in DAP-FORTRAN, with each iteration needing only two additions and a multiplication by 0.25. Thus 10 iterations would take 3.3 mSec using standard floating point. On the DAP, fixed boundary conditions on an arbitrarily shaped area are dealt with by using the activity control, with no increase in computation time. Further dramatic performance improvements are possible by adopting block floating point, and by using an "average" routine to combine the addition and multiplication. The next three problems are essentially more complex grid calculations. All these are very natural for the DAP.

The Table Look Up problem studied was used recently by the Los Alamos Scientific Laboratory to measure the scalar performance of CRAY 1 (4). Conditional operations and table look-up caused the code to be regarded as "scalar" despite the fact that it is used to process arrays. Logarithm and exponential functions are also involved. Table look-up in this context means performing a number of indexing operations in parallel on a single array. In the DAP a matrix of indices is used to produce a matrix of corresponding selected elements. Successive elements of the table are written selectively to the result matrix, using as a mask a different boolean matrix for each table element. Each boolean matrix is formed by testing for equality between the index of the table element and the matrix of indices. Global tests on the indices are used to reduce the amount of work. Also, regularities of this problem allow four result matrices to be generated in one pass through the table.

The last two applications in the table are non-scientific and achieve outstanding performance because they involve mainly boolean operations.

A general observation is that the DAP performs well on many tasks which might appear to be unsuitable for parallel processing. This is a consequence of the flexibility of a bit organized array processor. Our studies, many of which are complete problems, indicate that virtually all the computation can be done effectively in the DAP and hence there is no necessity for a powerful host.

Applications studied so far cover only a subset of all computing, but it is expected that high performance will be obtained on a wide range of CPU bound activities.

VI. REFERENCES

(1) Reddaway, S.F., "DAP - A Distributed Array Processor", First Annual Symposium on Computer Architecture, Florida, December 1973.

(2) Agarwal, R.C., Burrus, C.S., "Fast Convolution Using Fermat Number Transforms with Application to Digital Filtering", Vol. ASSP-2, No.2, pp 87-97, IEEE Transactions on Acoustics, Speech and Signal Processing, April 1974.
(3) Walkden, F., McIntyre, H.A.J., Laws, G.T., "A User's View of Parallel Processors", CERN School of Computing, 1976.
(4) Keller, T.W., "Report of the CRAY-1 Evaluation", LA-6456 MS, Los Alamos Scientific Laboratory, 1976.
(5) Flanders, P.M., Hunt, D.J., Parkinson, D., Reddaway, S.F.. "Experience Gained in Programming the Pilot DAP, A Parallel Processor with 1024 Processing Elements", IMACS (AICA)-GI-Symposium on Parallel Computers - Parallel Mathematics, Munich, March 1977.

VII. ACKNOWLEDGEMENTS

ICL wish to thank the Department of Industry for permission to publish this information, which results from work which was supported by a normal cost-sharing contract by the Department's Advanced Computer Technology Project.

The many contributions by other members of the DAP project are gratefully acknowledged.

A COMPLEXITY RESULT ON A PIPELINE PROCESSOR DESIGN PROBLEM

Michael Schlansker
D. E. Atkins
The University of Michigan

I. TASK STRUCTURE

This paper presents significant features of a model of synchronous pipeline computation and shows its application to the study of the complexity of an algorithm which is useful in the design of pipelined processors.

We assume that the task to be implemented is specified by a computation graph. Figure 1 is a computation graph which describes the computation of the length of a 3-component vector.

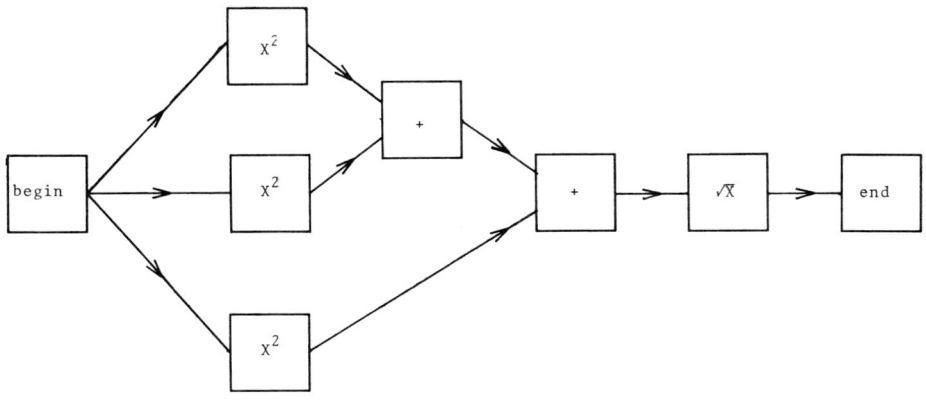

Figure 1

Formally, a <u>computation graph</u> G is an ordered pair

$$G = (N, E)$$

N   is the set of nodes, including two special nodes begin and end; and

$E \subseteq N \times N$ is the set of edges. If $(n_1, n_2) \in E$, we write $n_1 \to n_2$.

A <u>computation node</u> is a member of $N - \{begin, end\}$.

Computation graphs have the following properties:

1) They are acyclic.

2) There exists a path from the begin node to every computation node and from every computation node to the end node. This is a control restriction forcing all nodes to be served after initiation and before termination.

A time-processor assigned graph describes at what time and on which processor all nodes are served.

Definition: A <u>time-processor assigned graph</u> TPAG = $(G, \Delta N, NA)$ is an ordered triple where:

1) G is a computation graph.

2) $\Delta N: N \to \{0, 1, 2, \ldots\}$ maps each node of G into the time at which the node is served (relative to task initiation).

3) $NA: N \to P$ maps each node $n \in N$ into the processor serving the node $NA(n) = p \in P$.

A TPAG satisfies the following two properties:

1) Any two adjacent computation nodes n_1, n_2 with $n_1 \to n_2$ have $\Delta N(n_2) > \Delta N(n_1)$. Thus, at least a 1 clock delay is introduced to insure proper pipeline isolation.

2) A TPAG is <u>consistent</u> when no two nodes are served on the same processor simultaneously. Thus, $\forall n_1, n_2 \in N$ $NA(n_1) = NA(n_2) \to \Delta N(n_1) \neq \Delta N(n_2)$.

II. MAXIMAL RATE SCHEDULES

A TPAG describes the execution of a single task on a set of processors P. Typically, a stream of tasks is to be executed at the highest possible rate to optimize system throughput. However, the task execution sequence must not cause two tasks to use the same processor simultaneously.

The pattern of processor utilizations induced by the execution of a TPAG may be modelled by a reservation table [4].

It has been observed that the maximum rate execution sequence can be determined by finding minimum average latency cycles in a modified state diagram [2]. Thus, the maximum rate execution sequence is specified by a cyclic list of latencies describing the inter task initiation time. For example, $<\ell_0, \ell_1>$ represents initiations at time $\{0, \ell_0, \ell_0 + \ell_1, \ell_0 + \ell_1 + \ell_0, \ldots\}$. For ease of constraint formulation, we choose to represent the periodic initiation sequence by a schedule.

Definition: A schedule S_p is a mod p set of instruction initiation times.

Thus, the initiation cycle $<\ell_0, \ell_1>$ may be represented by: $S_p = \{0, \ell_0\}$ with $p = \ell_0 + \ell_1$. It is presumed that tasks are initiated at all times $\{t | t \in \mathbb{Z}, \text{ with } t \bmod p \in \{0, \ell_0\}\}$. $\mathbb{Z}$ denotes the set of integers.

III. A MINIMAL DELAY ASSIGNMENT PROBLEM

The following minimal delay assignment problem will be developed to illustrate one of the inherent difficulties in designing pipeline processors. While a solution algorithm is presented, the major result of this work illustrates that solution times are likely to be exponential in the number of nodes in the TPAG.

A. The Problem

Let a TPAG describe a single task to be repeatedly executed. Assume that the TPAG is completely specified except for the delay assignment ΔN. Find a delay assignment $\Delta N : N \rightarrow \{0, 1, \ldots\}$ such that:

1) If the TPAG is executed at all times indicated by a given schedule S_p, no two concurrently active tasks simultaneously use the same processor.

2) The TPAG is consistent.

3) $\Delta N(\text{end})$ is minimal among all solutions satisfying 1) and 2).

B. Constraint Formulation

In order to characterize the minimal delay assignment

problem a formulation of constraints must be developed. Let m denote the number of processors. Index these processors $P = p_1, p_2, \ldots p_m$. Node n is served on the jth processor iff $NA(n) = P_j$. Let Δ_j be the set of distances of all nodes served on the jth processor from the begin node. Thus

$$\Delta_j = \{\Delta N(n) \mid n \in N, NA(n) = P_j\}.$$

Since a steady state flow of identical tasks is considered, it is sufficient to keep only the mod p distances. That is, if a processor is used in any particular clock cycle, it is used in all mod p equivalent clock cycles. Conflict is the use of the same processor by distinct nodes in any two clocks equivalent mod p.

If any two nodes n, n' $\in N$, n $\neq$ n' have $NA(n) = NA(n') = P_j$ and $\Delta N(n) = \Delta N(n')$ then our computation graph has been constructed so as to utilize processor p_j to serve both n and n' at the $\Delta N(n)^{th}$ clock after task initiation. The TPAG is inconsistent. Thus, if for any processor p_j

1) $|\{\Delta N(n) \mid n \in N, NA(n) = p_j\}| < |\{n \mid n \in N, NA(n) = P_j\}|$,

there is a processor conflict. Further, if any two nodes n,n' $\in N$, n $\neq$ n' have:

2) $NA(n) = NA(n') = p_j$ and $(\Delta N(n) \bmod p) = (\Delta N(n') \bmod p)$, then

the computation will also exhibit a conflict since, given any time $t \in \mathbb{Z}$, the same computation graph is initiated at all clocks $z \in \mathbb{Z}$ with $z \bmod p = t \bmod p$. Let us define:

$$\tilde{\Delta}_j = \{i \bmod p \mid i \in \Delta_j\}.$$

Thus, $\tilde{\Delta}_j$ is the set of mod p distances from the begin node to all nodes served by the jth processor. 1) and 2) above can be rewritten as follows:

3) $|\tilde{\Delta}_j| < |\{n \mid n \in N, NA(n) = p_j\}| \rightarrow$ processor conflict.

So far, we have considered only conflicts caused by initiating a single computation graph or, two distinct computation graphs at equivalent times mod p. Recall the definition of our schedule S_p - the list of task initiation times mod p.

Consider any two $s, s' \in S_p$ with $s \neq s'$, then $s \oplus_p \tilde{\Delta}_j$ and $s' \oplus_p \tilde{\Delta}_j$ characterize utilization times mod p for processor p_j due to task initiations at clock times equivalent mod p to s and s' respectively. The operation $\oplus_p$ denotes mod p summation extended to sets. Hence, to eliminate conflict on processor p_j we require:

$$(s \oplus_p \tilde{\Delta}_j) \cap (s' \oplus_p \tilde{\Delta}_j) = \emptyset \text{ for all } s, s' \in S_p \text{ with } s \neq s'.$$

We can see that the $s \oplus_p \tilde{\Delta}_j$ must form distinct sets of size $|\tilde{\Delta}_j|$ for all $s \in S_p$. Therefore, for any processor P_j,

4) $|S_p \oplus_p \tilde{\Delta}j| < |S_p||\tilde{\Delta}_j| \rightarrow$ processor conflict

It can be shown that 3) and 4) are both necessary and sufficient conditions to describe processor conflicts for the steady state initiation identical tasks. We conclude that:

5) There is a processor conflict on p_j iff

$$|\tilde{\Delta}_j| < |\{n | NA(n) = p_j\}| \text{ or } |S_p \oplus_p \tilde{\Delta}_j| < |S_p||\tilde{\Delta}_j|.$$

Further, a simple complexity analysis reveals that these constraints can be tested in time no worse than polynomial in the number of nodes.

We now formally state the minimal delay assignment design problem: given S_p, a steady state schedule, and a TPAG totally specified except for delay assignment ΔN, the minimal delay assignment problem is that of assigning non-negative integers to the $|N|$ variables $\Delta N(n)$, $n \in N$ such that $\Delta N(\text{end})$ is minimal over the set of feasible solutions. Feasible solutions satisfy the following constraints:

1) $|\tilde{\Delta}_j| = |\{n | n \in N, \Delta N(n) = p_j\}| \quad 1 \leq j \leq m$ and

2) $|S_p \oplus_p \tilde{\Delta}_j| = |S_p||\tilde{\Delta}_j| \quad 1 \leq j \leq m$.

We also require that $\Delta N(n) < \Delta N(n')$ between any two adjacent computation nodes $n, n' \in N$ with $n \rightarrow n'$. Frequently the end node may violate this constraint allowing the end node to be served simultaneously with the last computation node.

IV. PREVIOUS WORK

In [4], Shar uses a fixed description of a task (reservation table) to characterize the state space structure of the scheduler. A reservation table is a matrix of reservations (X's) where an X in the i, j position represents the use of the ith functional unit in the jth clock. A reservation table describes the resource needs of a totally specified TPAG.

In [3], Patel and Davidson extend the definition of a reservation table to model a space of reservation tables. The minimum delay assignment problem is formulated on this space. As we shall see, this parameterization of the space of reservation tables is insufficient to model the partial ordering induced by nodal data dependence. In Patel's work, a variable d_{ij} is introduced for each X in the reservation table. The subscripts i and j represent the row and column of the X associated with d_{ij}. Where no X occurs in the reservation table, d_{ij} is implicitly zero.

The columns of reservation tables are served sequentially. The first column is completed before the second is initiated. Each X within a column is served d_{ij} time units after the column begins. A column can be said to be finished when the last processor usage within that column is completed. The next column begins during the next clock. Thus, the processor usages in the jth column will take $(\max_{i} d_{ij}) + 1$ clocks. The total delay from a task's initiation to its termination is $\sum_{j}((\max_{i} d_{ij}) + 1)$. This is the function which Patel minimizes under the constraint that the task be conflict free for the given schedule of task initiations.

Briefly consider the space of representable partial orderings spanned by a reservation table. In Figure 2, every X in an arbitrary reservation table has been replaced by the node it represents. We have then ordered the nodes using edges which represent ordering restrictions imposed by the model (columns are served sequentially). Thus, reservation tables

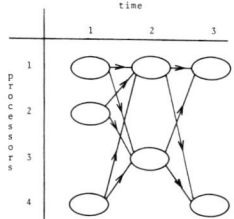

Figure 2

will only represent columns of unordered events with complete ordering between columns. No two nodes served by the same processor may appear in the same column. Hence, two utilizations of the same processor must be ordered.

The following results suggest the utility of a graph model for the solution of the delay assignment problem. A branch and bound algorithm for the solution of the minimal delay assignment problem will be presented. While solution times for this algorithm are exponential, solution times are also exponential for Patel's algorithm which operates over a restricted solution space. Further, the minimal delay assignment problem is NP complete, thus, it should not be surprising that solution times are exponential.

For the purpose of discussion, Patel's algorithm from [3] has been reproduced.

Patel's Algorithm

Let the number of X's in the reservation table be n and let the n variables, d_{ij}, be stored in any arbitrary order in a one dimensional array V. Let D(i) represent the value of the objective function for given values of V(1) through V(i), with V(i + 1) through V(n) taken to be 0.

Algorithm B:

B1. [Initialize] i ← 0; BOUND ← (p - 1) · J;

B2. [Advance] i ← i + 1; V(i) ← 0;

B3. [Check bounds and constraints] if (V(i) = p) or (D(i) > BOUND) then go to B6; if a completely assigned constraint is violated then go to B5;

B4. [Solution found?] if i < n then go to B2 else output the solution V(1) through V(n) and D(n); BOUND ← D(n);

B5. [Try another value] V(i) ← V(i) + 1; go to B3;

B6. [Backtrack] i ← i - 1; if i > 0 then go to B5 else terminate the algorithm.

The last value of BOUND is the minimum value of the objective function over all possible solutions and therefore the output solutions meeting this bound are all the minimum added delay solutions. If only one optimum solution is desired, the condition D(i) > BOUND in step B3 should be changed to D(i) $\geq$ BOUND.

The representation of delays within the system was chosen so that the objective function is non-decreasing in d_{ij}. This property is critical to the branch and bound algorithm. The variable p represents the period of a sequence of task initiations. It can readily be shown that there exists a constraint satisfying solution with $0 \leq d_{ij} < p$ for all i, j. Thus, Patel's solution space is finite. Checking bounds is the process of insuring that the current partial solution is shorter than the best known complete solution. Checking constraints insures that the current partial solution is conflict free under the given schedule of task initiations.

Problems can be constructed which illustrate that this solution algorithm has running times which may be exponential in the number of nodes. It is straightforward to construct problems with an exponential number of optimal solutions all of which must be inspected to verify that no better solution exists.

V. MORE GENERAL SOLUTION

In this section, a modification of Patel's algorithm is presented for use with the computation graph model. First, it is necessary to parameterize the design space.

As the parameterization of the design space, delays V(n) are defined on nodes n ε N where V(begin) = V(end) = 0 is assumed. For all V(n), n ε (N - {begin,end}), we will choose V(n) ≥ 1. ΔN can be uniquely defined from V(n) as follows:

1) ΔN(begin) = 0

2) ΔN(n) = V(n) + Max {ΔN(n') | n' ε N, n' → n}.

Thus, ΔN(n) = V(n) + the ΔN(n') such that n' is the last served predecessor to n. Here, the solution variable V has been introduced to explore exactly the space of ΔN's such that,

if n → n' then ΔN(n) < ΔN(n').

The objective function, ΔN(end'), is again nondecreasing in the V(n). The solution space vector V defined here assumes the same role as Patel's solution space vector, however, the range of the functions differ as follows: in our formulation we have, 1 ≤ V(n) ≤ p, in Patel's, 0 ≤ V(i) ≤ p-1. This difference is notational. While Patel counts excess delays, we count delays.

Although our formulation searches a somewhat different finite design space, it is compatible with a branch and bound solution scheme. Bounds and constraints may be evaluated after the computation of ΔN under the given assignment of integers to $V(n)$. By examining the method of computation of $\Delta N(n)$ from $V(n)$, one can see that the complexity of evaluating this function is at worst linear in the number of edges.

VI. NP COMPLETENESS OF STEADY STATE SCHEDULE, MINIMAL DELAY ASSIGNMENT PROBLEM

This section shows that the optimal assignment of delays is an NP complete problem. This proof should support the choice of a branch and bound algorithm for the solution of the pipeline delay assignment problem. The proof is a modification of a proof by Ullman in [6]. This proof does not work when restricted to Patel's design space.

We will show that, given a 3-satisfiability problem, one can construct a TPAG and a task schedule S_p such that, if one can optimally assign delays in $\Delta N(n)$, one can answer the 3-satisfiability question. Further, this construction can be done in polynomial time. Let's begin by describing the 3-satisfiability problem as presented by Ullman.

3-Satisfiability: Given a set of variables X_i, $1 \leq i \leq m$, and a collection of sets $D_1, \ldots, D_n$ where $m \leq 3n$, such that each D_j consists of exactly three of the elements X_i or $\bar{X}_i$ (called literals), does there exist a map f from $\{1, 2, \ldots, m\}$ to $\{true, false\}$ such that for each j, $1 \leq j \leq n$, either some $X_i \in D_j$ and $f(i) = true$ or $\bar{X}_i \in D_j$ and $f(i) = false$.

The assumption is made that the encoding of the 3-satisfiability problem is at least $O(n)$ in length and at most polynomial in n.

Proof: Given an instance of 3-satisfiability, we construct the following computation graph G. The notation $n_1 \rightarrow n_2$ will be used to define an edge from n_1 to n_2. The nodes of the graph are enumerated as follows (nodes will be named with a ' to distinguish them from literals):

1) begin', and end'

2) X_i' and $\overline{X}_i'$ for $1 \leq i \leq m$,

3) D_{ij}' for $1 \leq i \leq n$ and $1 \leq j \leq 7$.

We assume the following assignment of nodes to processors.

1) $NA(X_i') = NA(\overline{X}_i') = P_i \quad 1 \leq i \leq m$.

2) $NA(D_{ij}') = NA(D_{ik}') = P_{i+m} \quad 1 \leq i \leq n, 1 \leq j \leq 7,$
   $1 \leq k \leq 7$.

Thus, m processors each serving two nodes an X_i' and its corresponding $\overline{X}_i'$. We also have n processors each serving seven nodes from the array D_{ij}' (D_{ij}', $1 \leq j \leq 7$). Assume that we wish to schedule tasks at times 0, 7, 14, 21... Since the D_{ij}' are served in groups of seven, this is a maximum throughput schedule. In the following discussion, the first computation node will be assumed to begin at time 1. The NP complete question we will study is: Are there any solutions with $\Delta N(end') \leq 8$.

We define the following edge connections between nodes.

1) begin' $\rightarrow X_i' \quad 1 \leq i \leq m$

2) begin' $\rightarrow \overline{X}_i' \quad 1 \leq i \leq m$

3) $D_{ij}' \rightarrow$ end' $\quad 1 \leq i \leq n, 1 \leq j \leq 7$.

4) The edges into D_{ij}' are defined as follows:
   Let $a_1 a_2 a_3$ be the binary representation for j.
   (Note that the case $a_1 = a_2 = a_3 = 0$ does not occur.)
   Let D_i consist of literals Z_{k_1}, Z_{k_2}, Z_{k_3} where each Z independently stands for X or $\overline{X}$. Then for $1 \leq r \leq 3$, if $a_r = 1$, we have $Z'_{k_r} \rightarrow D_{ij}'$. If $a_r = 0$, we have $\overline{Z}'_{k_r} \rightarrow D'_{ij}$, where $\overline{Z}$, stands for $\overline{X}$, or X should Z be X or $\overline{X}$ respectively.

Let us explain this assignment of edges into D'_{ij}. First notice that nodes X'_i and $\overline{X}'_i$ may not be served simultaneously since they are served by the same processor. In fact, in any length 8 delay assignment, they will be served at times 1 and 2. Let us establish the correspondence that if $\Delta N(X_i') = 1$, then literal X_i is true. If $\Delta N(X_i') = 2$, literal X_i is false. We claim that $\exists j\ 1 \leq j \leq 7$ such that D'_{ij} can be served at time 2 iff D_i from the 3-satisfiability problem is true under the corresponding assignment of {true, false} to literals X_i.

Assume that D'_{ij} can be served at time 2. Let $a_1\ a_2\ a_3$ be the binary representation for j. At least one of these three bits must be a 1. Thus, $\exists r\ 1 \leq r \leq 3$ such that $a_r = 1$. By our construction of edges into D'_{ij}, we have $Z'_{k_r} \to D'_{ij}$. But since Z'_{k_r} precedes D'_{ij}, it must be served at time 1. Thus, according to our assignment of {true, false} to literals, Z_{k_r} will be true whether it represents X or $\overline{X}$. But Z_{k_r} is one of three literals in D_i. Hence, D_i is true.

Assume that D_i from the 3-satisfiability problem is true. Let Z_{k_1}, Z_{k_2}, Z_{k_3} be the three literals in D_i. Let $a_r = 0$ if Z_{k_r} is false, $a_r = 1$ if $Z_{k_r} = $ true $(1 \leq r \leq 3)$. Let j be the integer represented by the binary digit string $a_1 a_2 a_3$. Claim: node D'_{ij} can be served at time 2. First, note that at least one of Z_{k_1}, Z_{k_2}, Z_{k_3} must be true, thus $1 \leq j \leq 7$. By our definition of edges into D'_{ij}, we know that the three edges into D'_{ij} are defined by:

for $1 \leq r \leq 3$ if $a_r = 1$, $Z'_{k_r} \to D'_{ij}$

if $a_r = 0$, $\overline{Z}'_{k_r} \to D'_{ij}$.

If literal Z_{k_r} is true, then node Z'_{k_r} is served at time 1. Further, $a_r = 1$ and node $Z'_{k_r} \to D'_{ij}$. If literal Z_{k_r} is false, then node Z'_{k_r} was served at time 2 also, $\overline{Z}'_{k_r}$ is served at time 1. Further, $a_r = 0$ and $\overline{Z}'_{k_r} \to D'_{ij}$. Hence, all three nodes with edges into D'_{ij} are served at time 1.

Since the proof above holds for each of the D_i separately, one node can be scheduled (at time 2) from each row of D'_{ij} iff all D_i are true. At time 2, the second member of all X'_i

$\overline{X}'_i$ pairs is served. Thus, by time 3, any D'_{ij} may be served. The six remaining D'_{ij} are served one at a time beginning at time 3 and finishing at time eight. We conclude that the D_i are all satisfiable iff a solution of length 8 exists.

Above, we only considered restrictions on the delay assignment imposed by the partial ordering. We must also show that the above mentioned delay assignment of length 8 has no processor conflicts given that tasks are initiated at times 0, 7, 14... This should be clear since a processor conflict occurs iff two nodes are served by the same functional unit at times which are equivalent mod 7. But each row i of D'_{ij} is served during 7 consecutive clocks. Further, the X'_i, $\overline{X}_i$ pairs were served during consecutive clocks.

In Figure 3, the correspondence is shown between a 3-satisfiability problem and a minimum delay assignment problem of "equivalent difficulty." Note that each node is labelled with its name. A satisfying assignment of {01} to variables has been selected and illustrated. For this satisfying assignment, V(n) and ΔN(n) is given in the upper left and right corners of each node n. Arcs into the D_{2i} are not shown.

In representing a m-literal, n-clause 3-satisfiability problem, we require 2m + 7n + 2 nodes and 2m + 28n edges. Any 3-satisfiability problem can be encoded (in polynomial time) into a minimal delay assignment problem which can be represented by a string at most polynomial in the length of the encoding of the 3-satisfiability problem. Further, solving the minimal delay assignment problem trivially solves 3-satisfiability. The minimal delay assignment problem can be solved on a non-deterministic turing machine in polynomial time since the NDTM can inspect each potential solution simultaneously and any potential solution can be tested in polynomial time (testing bounds and constraints). We conclude that the minimal delay assignment problem is NP complete.

VII. APPLICATIONS

The authors are currently investigating the design of optimal schedulers which monitor an incoming sequence of tasks described by a fixed set of TPAG's. Thus, each TPAG represents a task type. Stochastic arrival assumptions are made about the composition of the incoming task sequence. The scheduler must determine when each of the tasks in the arrival sequence can be initiated without possibility of processor conflict.

COMPUTER SYSTEM DESIGN AND THEORY

A 3-SATISFIABILITY PROBLEM

M = 3   N = 2

VARIABLES X_1, X_2, X_3

$D_1 = \{X_1, X_1, \overline{X}_2\}$ $D_2 = \{X_3, X_2, X_3\}$

A SATISFYING ASSIGNMENT

X_1 = true, X_2 = true, X_3 = false

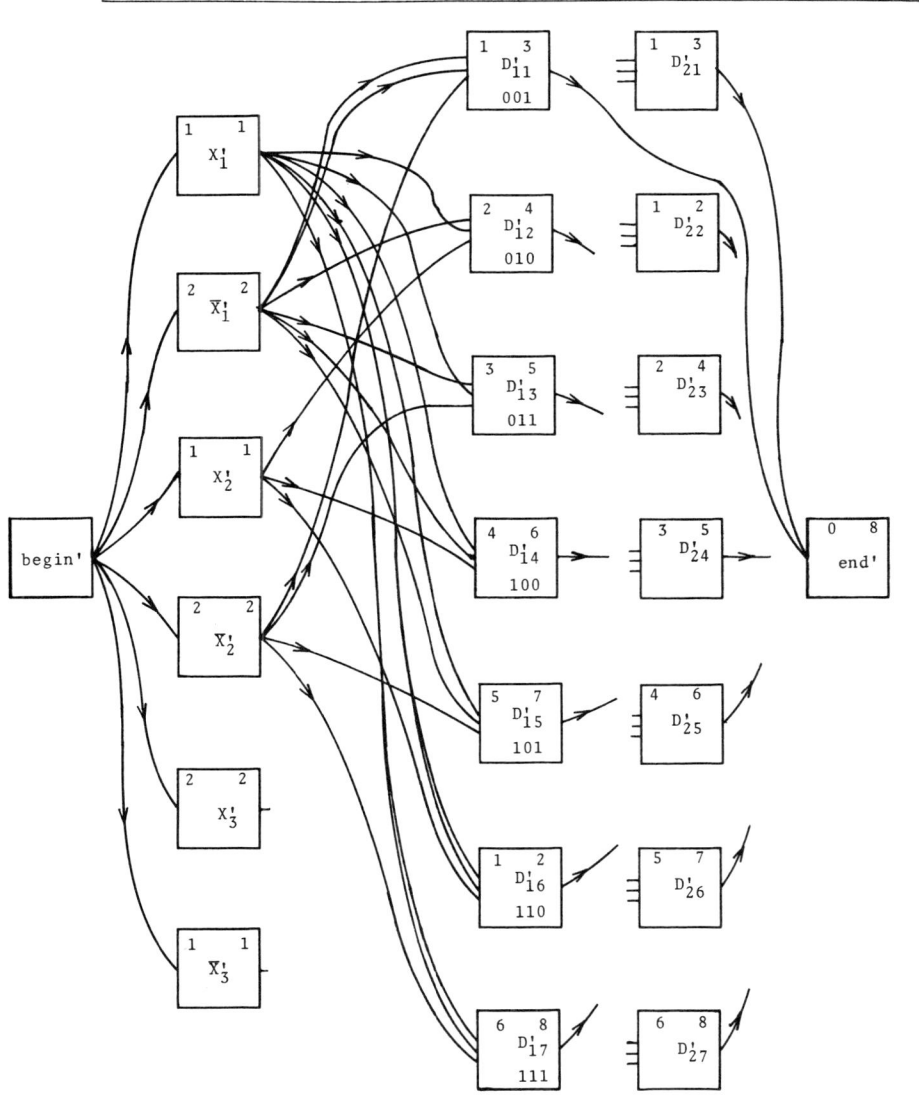

Figure 3

Algorithms have been formulated which optimize the design of such schedulers where the goal is to optimize throughput under stochastic arrival conditions. After establishing measures of the performance and cost of the implementation, one would hope to alter either the processor assignment or time assignment of a TPAG to find a better solution. The above proof shows that delay minimization problems will be quite difficult even when given a processor assignment and task schedule. This result applies to the more general stochastic arrival environment because the proof uses a simple subcase in which a single task type is re-executed with probability 1. It would also apply to any periodic arrival of distinct tasks types stemming from a program loop.

The optimality function $\Delta N(end)$ can be justified on the basis of performance. Performance optimization requires task duration minimization if data dependence (non-overlapped processing) exists among the stream of incoming tasks.

REFERENCES

[1] Aho, A.V., Hopcraft, J.E., and Ullman, J.D., <u>The Design and Analysis of Computer Algorithms</u>, Addison-Wesley Publishing Co., 1974.

[2] Davidson, E.S., "The Design and Control of Pipeline Function Generators," Proceedings of the 1971 Conference on Systems, Networks and Computers, Oaxtepec, Mexico, January 1971.

[3] Patel, J.H, and Davidson, E.S., "Improving the Throughput of a Pipeline by Insertion of Delays," 3rd Annual Symposium on Computer Architecture, Clearwater, Florida, January 1976.

[4] Shar, L.E., "Design and Scheduling of Statically Configured Pipelines," Technical Report No. 42, Stanford Electronics Laboratories, Stanford University, September 1972.

[5] Thomas, A.T., and Davidson, E.S., "Scheduling of Multi-Configurable Pipelines," Proceedings of the Twelfth Annual Allerton Conference on Circuit and System Theory, October 1974.

[6] Ullman, J.D., "Polynomial Complete Scheduling Problems," Proceedings of the Fourth Symposium on Operating Systems Principles, pp. 96-101, 1973.

APPLICATION OF DATA FLOW COMPUTATION TO THE WEATHER PROBLEM[1]

Jack B. Dennis
Ken K.-S. Weng
MIT Laboratory for Computer Science

ABSTRACT

Computer processors and memory systems organized to execute programs in data flow form show promise of overcoming the barrier to highly parallel computation without concomitant loss of programmability. The principles and advantages of data flow programming and computer architecture are illustrated in this paper by their application to a general atmosphere circulation model for numerical weather forecasting. The paper develops the structure of a data flow program for a basic global circulation model and discusses the performance achievable for this computation by a data flow computer.

I. INTRODUCTION

The past decade has witnessed the evolution of data flow languages from primitive concepts of data driven instruction execution [1, 2, 3] to fully developed schemes for representing algorithms in a form that exposes the natural concurrency of their parts [4, 5, 6, 7]. Recently, several interesting proposals have been advanced for organizing computer hardware to interpret data flow programs in a data driven mode [8, 9, 10, 11]. Although each of these authors makes a good case that his proposed system implements a well defined level of data flow language, their effectiveness as instruments for performing practical computations has not been demonstrated.

---

[1] This research was supported in part by the National Science Foundation under grant DCR75-04060, and in part by the Advanced Research Projects Agency of the Department of Defense under contract N00014-75-C-0661.

The aim of the present paper is to help fill the gap by studying the performance potential of a data flow computer. In an earlier study [12] submitted for publication, we evaluated the performance of a limited data flow machine for the fast Fourier transform computation. Here we use a more general data flow language that includes data structure operations on arrays, and we describe the structure of a corresponding extended data flow computer. Since data flow computers differ radically in structure from conventional machines, meaningful comparisons are only possible through the study of specific applications. For the present study, we have chosen a global general circulation model (GCM) for numerical weather forecasting.

In Section II of the paper we describe the general circulation model; the structure of a corresponding data flow program is developed in Section III. Section IV presents the overall structure of a data flow computer appropriate for the language used to express the GCM computation. In Section V the manner in which array operations are handled by the machine is studied in detail because efficient processing of arrays is crucial to realizing high performance in the GCM computation. Our performance study is presented in Section VI; this analysis shows how a one hundred-fold improvement in computation rate for the GCM computation may be achieved by a data flow computer.

II. THE GENERAL CIRCULATION MODEL

The General Circulation Model used in this study is the GISS fourth order model developed by Kalnay-Rivas, Bayliss and Storch [13] in which the atmospheric state is represented by the surface pressure, the wind field, temperature, and the water vapor mixing ratio. These state variables are governed by a set of partial differential equations in the spherical coordinate system formed by latitude (ϕ), longitude (λ) and normalized atmospheric pressure (σ). In this fourth order model, the computation is carried out on a three-dimensional grid that partitions the atmosphere vertically into K levels and horizontally into M intervals of longitude and N intervals of latitude of size $\Delta\lambda$ and $\Delta\phi$, respectively.

We denote a value of a state variable (the temperature for example) by $T(i, j, k)$ where i, j and k index over the ϕ, λ and σ coordinates, respectively. The model computes each state variable for the next time instant using "leap frog" integration: Thus the temperature $T^N(i, j, k)$ for the next time instant is computed from the temperature $T^P(i, j, k)$ for the preceding time instant and the time derivative $\partial/\partial t\, T^C(i, j, k)$ evaluated for the current time instant

$$T^N(i, j, k) = T^P(i, j, k) + 2\Delta t\, \frac{\partial}{\partial t} T^C(i, j, k)$$

The main computation is the evaluation of the time derivatives of the state variables from the current atmospheric state using the physical laws that govern the atmosphere.

In addition to the main computation, three additional computations must be performed to make the scheme workable: (1) Polar computation -- computation of state variables at the poles is treated as a special case; (2) Filtering -- to ensure stability in spite of the convergence of longitude lines toward the poles, spatial filtering is used to suppress high frequency waves at high latitudes; (3) Sum-of-Neighbors -- since the leap frog integration rule is inherently unstable, an averaging computation is performed once every so many time steps.

The GISS model has been implemented in Fortran and runs on an IBM 360/95 machine equipped with 4 megabytes of addressable core memory. Using a grid having nine vertical levels, 72 intervals of longitude, 45 intervals of latitude, and a time step of five minutes, this implementation can simulate one day of atmospheric activity in about one hour of computer time. Reliable long-range forecasts require that the simulation be carried out on a finer grid for more time steps, and thus demand a much faster processing rate.

III. THE DATA FLOW PROGRAM

To present the structure of the data flow program for the General Circulation Model, we shall use the language of data flow schemas [5] in terms of which the concurrency of execution of the computation on a data flow processor can be easily seen. In practice we envision that programs prepared for execution on a data flow computer will be written in a high-level textual language. The design of a high level language that permits straightforward translation into data flow schemas has been studied by Weng [14].

To construct a data flow program for the GCM computation, we represent the atmospheric state by a nested array data structure; for example, the temperature component T of the state is of type A1 where

<u>type</u> A1 = <u>array</u> 0..M+3 <u>of</u> A2
<u>type</u> A2 = <u>array</u> 0..N+3 <u>of</u> A3
<u>type</u> A3 = <u>array</u> 0..K+1 <u>of</u> real

The South and North poles correspond to latitude indices $i = 1$ and $i = M+2$, and the values for longitude indices $j \in [N-1..N+3]$ are copies of the values for $j \in [0..4]$.

The new values of each state variable are computed for $i \in [2..M+1]$, $j \in [2..N+1]$, and $k \in [1..K]$; the remaining components of the data structure provide neighboring values for the fourth order spacial difference formulas along the boundaries of the horizontal grid.

The overall structure of the GCM computation, represented as a data flow schema, is shown in Fig. 1. In this figure, the notation $T(i, j, *)$ denotes the K+2-element array containing the temperature values for horizontal grid point (i, j); $T(i, *, *)$ is the array containing all temperature values on the ith line of latitude; and $T(*, *, *)$ is the complete data structure of temperature values. The figure shows the blocks making up the data flow computation of the next temperature state $T^N(*, *, *)$ from the preceding state $T^P(*, *, *)$ and current values of all state variables including $T^C(*, *, *)$. The next state data structure and the current state data structure become the current state and preceding state for the next cycle of computation (the data paths and control for this are omitted in Fig. 1 for simplicity).

The data flow schema in Fig. 1 is organized so the parallelism of the GCM computation is exposed in two major ways: First, in the main computation, evaluation of the time derivative is carried out concurrently for all K atmospheric levels. This is accomplished by using K copies of the data flow program appropriate for a single grid point. Second, the main computation program block is coded so sets of data values for successive cells of the horizontal grid are processed concurrently by the several stages of the program block. Thus the streams of K+2-element arrays entering the main computation block are processed in pipeline fashion.

The function of each <u>get</u> operator (defined in Fig. 2a) is to convert each array arriving at its a-input into a stream of component values selected from the array by successive elements of the sequence of integers presented at the s-input. Each <u>get</u> operator in the first rank of Fig. 1 converts the temperature data structure $T(*, *, *)$ into a stream of M arrays where each

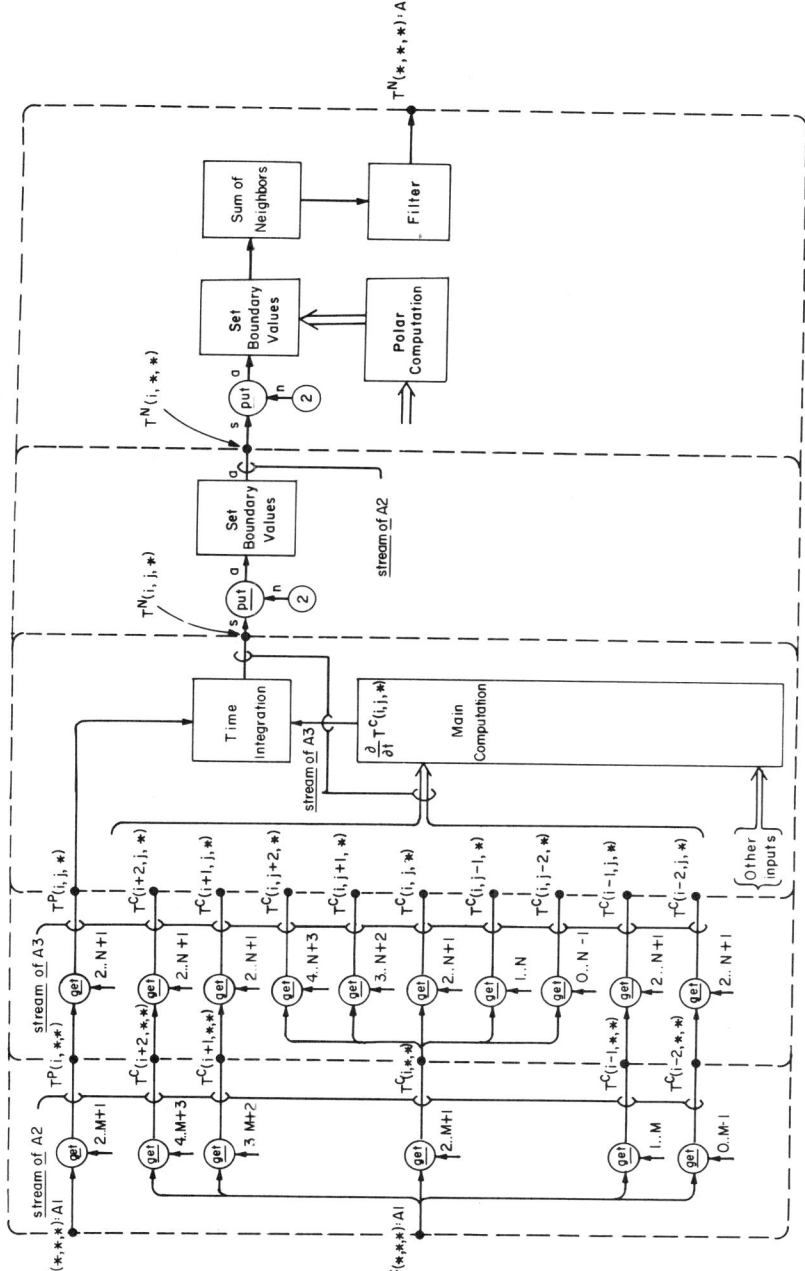

Fig. 1. Structure of a data flow program for the General Circulation Model.

array holds the temperature values for one latitude line. The second rank of <u>get</u> operators further converts the state data structure so each element of the resulting streams is a K+2-element array of values for all grid points having the same horizontal coordinates.

The output of the main computation and time integration is M streams of N arrays apiece, each containing the K+2 temperature values $T^N(i, j, *)$ for one horizontal grid point. The <u>put</u> operator converts each stream into an array of type <u>array</u> 2..N+1 <u>of</u> A3 with components representing $T^N(i, j, *)$, for $j \in [2..N+1]$, the set of new temperature values for the ith latitude line. The block labelled Set Boundary Values adds to the resulting array the temperature values for the boundary indices $j \in [0, 1, N+1, N+3]$, yielding an array of type A2 representing $T^N(i, *, *)$. A final <u>put</u> operator generates the array containing as components the temperature values $T^N(i, *, *)$ for $i \in [2, .., M+1]$. The full array of temperature values $T^N(*, *, *)$ is obtained by adding boundary values for $i \in [0, 1, M+2, M+3]$ using the results of the polar computation. This array is further averaged and filtered to ensure computational stability before becoming the next value of the current atmospheric state.

Data flow schemas for the <u>get</u> and <u>put</u> operators are shown in Fig. 2. These schemas are composed of data flow *actors* [5] interconnected by links that convey data and truth values from one actor to another. In addition to the basic actor types introduced in [5], these schemas use some special actors to implement operations on streams of values [14]: A stream is represented in a data flow schema by a sequence of value-bearing tokens followed by a special token called an *end-of-stream token*. The actor <u>est</u> generates an end-of-stream token; the predicate <u>eos</u> yields <u>true</u> if an end-of-stream token is received and <u>false</u> otherwise.

IV. THE DATA FLOW COMPUTER

Now we are ready to explain how our data flow program for the GCM computation will run on a data flow computer. The organization of a computer that implements the appropriate level of data flow language is shown in Fig. 3. This machine is similar in structure to the data flow processor described in [12], but the machine provides, in addition to the basic scalar operations and control mechanisms, support for data structure operations in its Structure Processor.

Before discussing operation of the Structure Processor, let us review the basic scheme of operation of the data flow

(a) the get module : get (a,s) ⟶ r

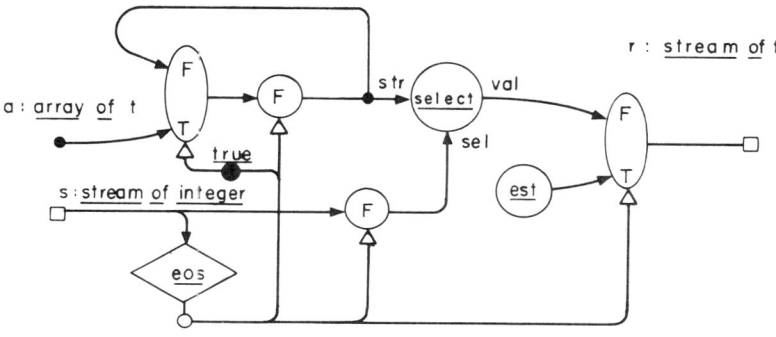

(b) the put module : put (s,n) ⟶ a

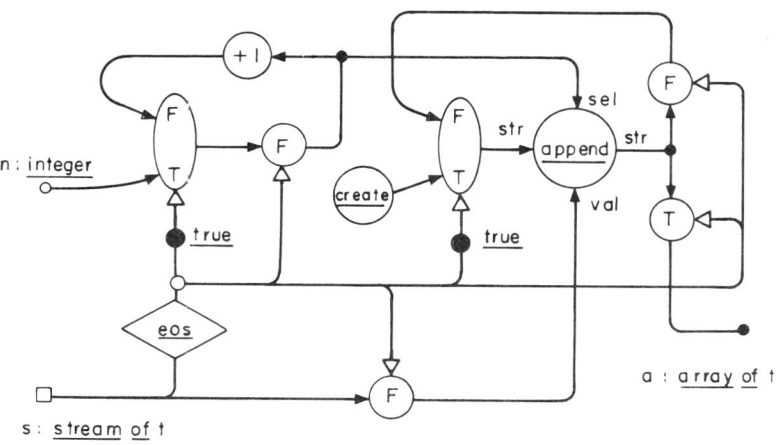

Fig. 2. The get and put operators as data flow schemas.

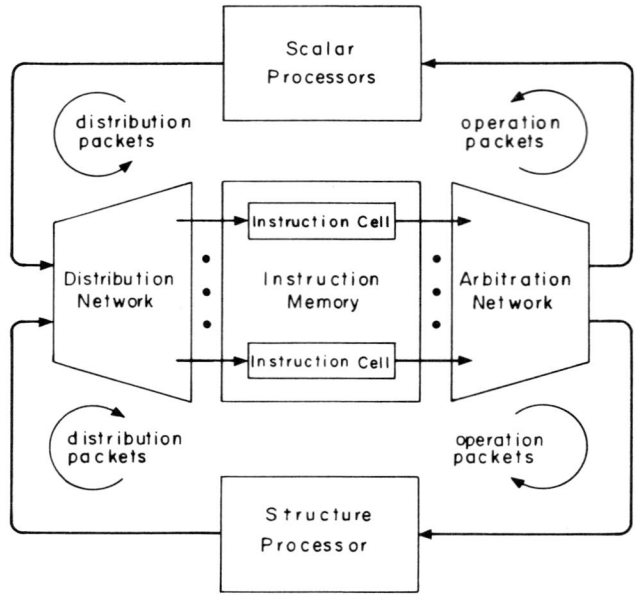

Fig. 3. Structure of the data flow computer.

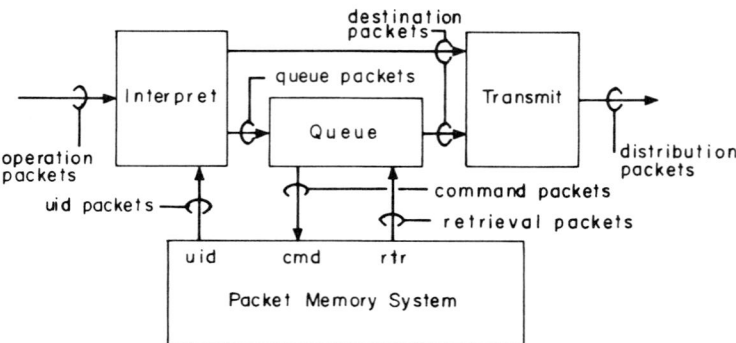

Fig. 4. The Structure Processor.

machine. Each Instruction Cell in the Instruction Memory holds one instruction which corresponds to an actor of a data flow program. Once an Instruction Cell has received (via the Distribution Network) all required operand values and the necessary number of acknowledge signals, the Cell is *enabled* and delivers its contents to the Arbitration Network for transmission to the appropriate Processor. The result value produced by the Processor is transmitted through the Distribution Network to the Instruction Cells which require it as an operand, and *acknowledge* signals are sent to control the enabling of Cells. Even though roughly 20 microseconds may be required for an instruction to be enabled, sent to the Processing Section, executed, and the results transmitted back to other Instruction Cells, the computer is capable of high performance because a large number of instructions may be in various stages of execution simultaneously.

In this form of data flow processor, congestion of the Distribution Network is possible if Instruction Cells are reenabled repeatedly without waiting for previously generated results to be consumed by other Instruction Cells; this congestion can even lead to deadlock -- the complete cessation of computation (see [12]). We avoid these problems of congestion and deadlock by requiring that an Instruction Cell not be reenabled until the data and control packets generated by the previous execution of the instruction have been absorbed by their destination cells. Machine language programs which satisfy this condition are said to be *safe*. Safety is achieved through the use of acknowledge signals generated by an instruction to control the enabling of instructions that produce the data required by the instruction.

V. THE STRUCTURE PROCESSOR

The Structure Processor receives operation packets calling for the data structure operations <u>create</u>, <u>select</u> and <u>append</u>. Earlier concepts for the design of structure processors have been given by Rumbaugh [10] and by Misunas [15]. As shown in Fig. 4, the Structure Processor consists of a Packet Memory System [16] and three units -- the Interpret, Queue and Transmit units -- which make up the Structure Controller.

<u>The Packet Memory</u>: The function of the Packet Memory System is to hold representations of data structures and to provide the means for storing and accessing their components. Each data structure value held in the Packet Memory has a *unique identifier* which serves to represent the structure value in all units outside the Structure Processor. Within the Packet Memory, a data structure value (we consider here only arrays) is represented by

an *item* of the form

$$(i, (c_m, \ldots, c_n), r)$$

in which

- i is the unique identifier of the data structure value.
- $c_m, \ldots, c_n$ are either all real number representations, or all unique identifiers of component structure values. Some components may be undefined, and c_k is then <u>nil</u>.
- r is a reference count used to detect when all references to the item have disappeared indicating that the item may be deleted from the Packet Memory.

The state of the Packet Memory is fixed by giving the collection of items held and the set of unique identifiers available for creation of new items. The behavior of the Packet Memory is conveniently specified by giving the state changes for each of the five basic transactions:

Store Transaction: In response to a *store* command packet
$\langle$STO, i, k, c$\rangle$ at port <u>cmd</u> the item having unique identifier i is modified to have a component $c_k = c$ (the previous value of c_k is lost). If no item exists with unique identifier i, then a new item is created having $c_k = c$ as its sole component, and with its reference count set to one.

Retrieval Transaction: If a *retrieval* command packet
$\langle$RTR, i, k$\rangle$ arrives at port <u>cmd</u> and an item $(i, (c_m, \ldots, c_n), r)$ exists where $m \leq k \leq n$, then a retrieval packet $\langle i, k, c_k \rangle$ is sent at port <u>rtr</u>.

Up and Down Transactions: The command $\langle$UP, i$\rangle$ adds one to the reference count of item i; the command $\langle$DWN, i$\rangle$ decrements its reference count by one. If the reference count is reduced to zero by a down command, the item is deleted from the collection of items held by PM and its unique identifier i is added to the set of available unique identifiers, and the reference count for each data structure component is decremented.

Unique Identifier Generation: A unique identifier packet $\langle i \rangle$ is sent at port <u>uid</u>, and the unique identifier i is removed from the set of available unique identifiers.

In [16] we have shown how the Packet Memory can be structured to handle many transactions concurrently at a high throughput rate.

The Structure Controller: The function of the Structure Controller is to implement the data structure operations create, append and select in terms of the memory transactions supported by the Packet Memory System. In the GCM data flow program these data structure operations occur only in the blocks labelled Set Boundary Values and the get and put routines which transform arrays into streams and vice versa; these routines have been specified as data flow schemas in Fig. 2.

To achieve the desired level of performance, it is important to exploit the capability of the Packet Memory to handle many transactions concurrently, while permitting the memory system to be slow in responding to individual retrieval requests. Thus the get routine as written in Fig. 2a is unsatisfactory because the select actor is not reenabled until after the result of its previous execution has been sent. Consequently, repeated execution of the select actor can occur only at a rate determined by the retrieval delay of the Packet Memory, and no overlap of retrieval requests is realized.

The desired overlapped execution of select operations can be achieved through the choice of an appropriate machine level instruction set and careful design of the Structure Controller. The Interpret unit of the Structure Controller interprets the data structure operations producing sequences of commands that it sends to the Packet Memory System. The Transmit unit generates result and acknowledge packets for distribution to Instruction Cells as called for by the instructions in operation packets. The Queue unit is the heart of the Structure Controller; it holds an entry for each select operation that has been initiated but not completed. Each entry includes the unique identifier and selector that specify the value to be obtained, and the destinations to which copies of the result are to be sent. Operation of the Structure Processor must be such that the results of selection are sent to the destination cell exactly in the order of select actor initiation even though variations in retrieval delay cause retrieval packets to be returned out of sequence from the Packet Memory. Otherwise, the components of the arrays constructed by the put operators of the GCM program would be incorrectly indexed. The function of the Queue module is to ensure that results of select operations are sent by the Structure Controller in the same order as the corresponding operation packets are received. When a retrieval packet is received from the Packet Memory, a matching entry in the Queue is found and the retrieval value appended to the entry. Result packets are generated from entries containing retrieved values as they reach the end of the queue.

Correct pipelined operation of select actors in the data flow program requires that after a result packet is sent to an Instruction Cell by the Structure Processor, no further result packet is sent until an acknowledge signal has been received indicating that the Instruction Cell is ready to receive it. This provision requires a machine level get routine that is more elaborate than a direct encoding of the scheme in Fig. 2a, but the details will not be covered here. Further discussion of the machine encoding of safe data flow programs may be found in [12].

The put routine in Fig. 2b generates an array by appending successive elements to the empty data structure. If each result of an append operation is viewed as a distinct value, as in the usual data flow semantics, a new copy of the partial array must be created in the Packet Memory each time an append operation is executed. In most cases, as in the put routine, each new partial array value is used only as input to the next instance of append, and it is unnecessary to retain the input array after execution of append. Therefore the append operation is implemented by the Structure Controller by adding a component to an existing item in the Packet Memory System. It is the responsibility of the programming system to ensure that no attempt is made to reference the old data structure value once the append operation is initiated.

VI. PERFORMANCE

We now turn to the analysis of the processing capacity of the data flow processor necessary to achieve the desired one hundred-fold performance over IBM 360/95 on which the GISS model is implemented. The 360 implementation simulates one day of atmospheric activity in about one hour using a 9 x 45 x 72 grid and a five-minute time step. To increase this performance by two orders of magnitude implies that our data flow computer must be able to complete all operations for computing new values of the state variables for one group of K grid points at the same latitude and longitude each 40 microseconds.

For the data flow computer shown in Fig. 3, the computation rate will be determined by which part of the machine is the bottleneck for the flow of operation and result packets. We proceed by determining the throughput required of each part of the machine if the desired performance level is to be achieved.

Analysis of the complete data flow program partially sketched in Fig. 1 reveals that the machine level program will occupy about 13,000 Instruction Cells and that computation of the new state for all grid points with the same horizontal coordinates requires processing approximately 7000 operation packets, of which 2700 are multiplications or divisions, 2700 are additions or subtractions, 900 are data structure operations, and 700 are other miscellaneous operations. If the data flow computer is to complete this processing in 40 microseconds, the Scalar Processors must be able to handle operation packets at 150 MHz and the Structure Processor must be capable of handling data structure operations at 25 MHz. The routing networks must be able to perform packet switching at 175 MHz. These rates may be achieved by using many processors and structuring the Arbitration and Distribution Networks for concurrent transmission of many packets.

In addition to these throughput requirements, we must ensure that the instruction processing time (the time interval from the instant an Instruction Cell becomes enabled to the instant all result and acknowledge packets have been received by other Instruction Cells) is small enough that instructions are enabled at the necessary rate. If a block of a data flow program is constructed to make the most effective use of the pipeline capability of the data flow computer, the period of repeated use of any actor is twice the instruction execution delay. This is because one execution cycle is needed to compute a result value and forward it to the next actor, and a second cycle is needed to return an acknowledge signal. We conclude that the two routing networks (the Arbitration and Distribution Networks) must be constructed so the instruction execution delay is no more than 20 microseconds.

Finally, the memory access time for retrieval requests handled by the Packet Memory must not be so large that values of the new atmospheric state are not available when they are needed. Since a time step is completed only once every 125 milliseconds, this requirement is easily met. However, the Queue unit of the Structure Controller must be large enough to hold all retrieval requests which have not been completed by the Packet Memory. For the arrival rate of 25 MHz even a one millisecond retrieval delay would require a capacity of 25,000 entries in the Queue, thus the Packet Memory should be implemented with storage devices having an access time well under a millisecond.

VII. CONCLUSION

Our study of the General Circulation Model as a data flow computation shows that a very high computation rate can be realized if the units of our proposed data flow computer operate at the assumed rates. This level of performance results from exposing and exploiting the inherent concurrency of the computation on a global basis. In contrast, the "lookahead" machines such as the IBM 360/195 attempt to discover parallelism through execution-time analysis of data dependencies in a small fragment of a sequential program. The vector and array machines can effectively use their highly parallel operation only to the extent that the programmer (or the compiler) can invent ways of encoding problem data into vectors or arrays that take advantage of the machine's power. Since the high performance of a data flow computer results from exposing large numbers of operations for concurrent execution, the speed with which each operation is executed is not crucial; thus a very powerful machine could be built using a large number of relatively slow logic devices. Since our data flow machines are composed of many units of similar type, these machines are ideal for effective application of LSI technology.

The open questions concerning the feasibility of practical data flow computers are: What physical structure should the Structure Controller and the Packet Memory System have? Can these units, which make up the Structure Processor, achieve the throughput assumed in our analysis? How difficult will it be to construct and debug such a large asynchronous system? How much will it cost to build data flow computers? The last question can be answered only by developing complete logic designs for the critical components of the machine. Each of these questions is under study in the Data Flow Project at the MIT Laboratory for Computer Science.

REFERENCES

1. Seeber, R. R., and Lindquist, A. B., "Associative Logic for Highly Parallel Systems," *Proc. of the AFIPS Conference* 24, 489-493 (1963).

2. Shapiro, R. M., Saint, H., and Presberg, D. L., "Representation of Algorithms as Cyclic Partial Orderings," Report CA-7112-2711, Applied Data Research, Wakefield, Mass., 1971.

3. Miller, R. E., and Cocke, J., "Configurable Computers: A New Class of General Purpose Machines," Report RC 3897, IBM Research Center, Yorktown Heights, N. Y., June 1972.

4. Rodriguez, J. E., "A Graph Model for Parallel Computation," Technical Report MAC TR-64, Laboratory for Computer Science, Mass. Inst. of Technology, Cambridge, Mass., 1969.

5. Dennis, J. B., "First Version of a Data Flow Procedure Language," Lecture Notes in Computer Science 19, 362-376, Springer-Verlag, New York, 1974.

6. Kosinski, P. R., "A Data Flow Language for Operating Systems Programming," SIGPLAN Notices 8, 89-94 (1973).

7. Bährs, A., "Operation Patterns," Lecture Notes in Computer Science 5, 217-246, Springer-Verlag, New York, 1974.

8. Dennis, J. B., and Misunas, D. P., "A Computer Architecture for Highly Parallel Signal Processing," Proc. of the ACM 1974 National Conference, 402-409 (1974).

9. Dennis, J. B., and Misunas, D. P., "A Preliminary Architecture for a Basic Data-Flow Processor," Proc. of the Second Annual Symposium on Computer Architecture, IEEE, 126-132 (1975).

10. Rumbaugh, J. E., "A Data Flow Multiprocessor," IEEE Trans. on Computers C-26, 138-146 (February 1977).

11. Arvind, and Gostelow, K., "A New Interpreter for Data Flow Schemas and Its Implications for Computer Architecture," Technical Report 72, Department of Information and Computer Science, University of California, Irvine, 1975.

12. Dennis, J. B., Misunas D. P., and Leung, C. K., "A Highly Parallel Processor Using a Data Flow Machine Language," submitted for publication.

13. Kalnay-Rivas, E., Bayliss, A., and Storch, J., "Experiments with the 4th Order GISS Model of the Global Atmosphere," Proc. of the Conference on Simulation of Large-Scale Atmospheric Processes, Hamburg, Germany (1976), to be published.

14. Weng, K.-S., "Stream-Oriented Computation in Recursive Data Flow Schemas," Technical Memo 68, Laboratory for Computer Science, Mass. Inst. of Technology, Cambridge, Mass., 1975.

15. Misunas, D. P., "Structure Processing in a Data-Flow Computer," Proc. of the 1975 Sagamore Computer Conference on Parallel Computation, IEEE, 230-234 (August 1975).

16. Dennis, J. B., "Packet Communication Architecture," Proc. of the 1975 Sagamore Computer Conference on Parallel Processing, IEEE, 224-229 (August 1975).

AN INVESTIGATION OF FAULT-TOLERANT ARCHITECTURES
FOR LARGE-SCALE NUMERICAL COMPUTING[1]

Algirdas Avižienis, Miloš Ercegovac, Tomás Lang
Pierre Sylvain, Alexander Thomasian

UCLA Computer Science Department

This paper presents a discussion of the current results of a study of high-speed computer architectures intended for large-scale numerical computing. The emphasis of the study is on the incorporation of fault-tolerance techniques and on the attainment of longevity for autonomous parts of the system. The choice of methodology for the study is discussed, followed by the description of two distinct approaches: the use of a reconfigurable set of processing elements and the use of tagging with an unstructured set of processing elements. A major goal of the study is to arrive at both qualitative and quantitative assessments of the relative merits of the two approaches with respect to fault-tolerance, longevity, and computing efficiency.

I. GOALS AND A GENERAL MODEL

The principal goals of the investigation whose current results are being reported here are: (a) the systematic incorporation of fault-tolerance, and (b) the attainment of longevity characteristics in very large, high-speed computer systems of the future. The attributes of fault-tolerance and longevity are discussed in the companion paper (1).

It is evident that neither fault-tolerance, nor longevity can be effectively studied without postulating an overall system architecture of the computing system. Our model assumes an environment in which an entire user community will share the services of a HIgh-SPeed ARithmetic System (HISPARS) to perform various large-scale numeric computations. Examples are: a university, a government research institute, the computing center of an industrial organization, etc. The HISPARS

---

[1]This research is supported by NSF Grant MCS 72-03633 A04.

itself consists of several types of elements: a set of arithmetic units, a large modular memory, sets of auxiliary units to interpret computing requests and to manage memory access, and interconnection networks for intra-system communication. More detailed descriptions of typical HISPARS organizations are presented in later sections.

Speaking figuratively, the HISPARS serves as a "supercalculator" to be used by a computing system of growing sophistication in the aspects of programming languages, operating systems, storage, and man-machine interaction. The entire system is postulated to be a heterogeneous and changing set of "Program Processors" (PP's), which are complete computers of differing size, speed, and design. Each computer serves one user and executes its own set of programs. Whenever a large computing task is to be executed, a request in a standard (internal language) format is issued to the HISPARS. Prior to the request, the operand arrays are placed into the large, high-bandwidth memory associated with the HISPARS. The requests are enqueued, interpreted, executed, and the result arrays are returned to the memory. The execution of the request is bound to specific elements of the HISPARS only during the interpretation. This allows a run-time adjustment to fault-caused losses of system elements (or an increase in their number due to repair or expansion) within the HISPARS that does not require a participation of the PP's.

Several advantages may be gained by such a separation of large-scale calculations from program execution in user computers, which also perform all other calculations. They are: (a) the HISPARS can be conveniently shared by an entire user community; (b) the HISPARS attains longevity with respect to various changes in user computers (PP's), and the entire computing complex can be refined by evolution; (c) fault-tolerance is more readily incorporated in the system; (d) user requests are interpreted with respect to the calculating resources available at run time. The problems to be solved in order to attain fault-tolerance, longevity, and evolution capabilities with respect to the HISPARS are: (a) efficient communication of work requests from user computers (PP's) to the autonomous HISPARS; (b) interpretation of requests for efficient execution on presently available HISPARS resources; (c) the coupling of the arithmetic units to the main memory for maximum memory bandwidth utilization; (d) the internal HISPARS design for modularity, efficient hardware utilization, and fault-tolerance.

The origins of various features of the HISPARS model may be traced to the Fixed-Plus-Variable Structure computer (2), the Supermachine system (3), the universal Arithmetic Building Element (4) and the Self-Testing-And-Repairing (JPL-STAR) computer (5). Useful insights have come from descriptions of the properties and users' experience with current-generation systems, especially ILLIAC IV, CDC STAR-100, TI ASC, and CRAY-1.

II. METHODOLOGY OF THE STUDY

There is a large number of built or proposed systems for high-speed computing but relatively little explicit knowledge is available concerning design methodology. Our efforts are devoted to (a) an investigation identifying the desirable characteristics of high-speed systems; and (b) the development of analytic and experimental models and their effective use in performance measurement and evaluation. We are interested in studying the relationships existing between the representation of the problems being solved, a compatible system organization, the implementation constraints, and the desired overall functional properties such as speed of computation, fault-tolerance, implementation-independent modules, and longevity (1).

The choice of system organization depends on the implementation constraints and the desired system features. How to make good choices in practical design situations is a key point of the design methodology. The implementation constraints are determined by the cost-performance characteristics of the available hardware and software resources. Among the system features we are studying are system modularity, reconfigurability, structural uniformity, LSI realizability, implementation flexibility, and intermodule communication bandwidth. In particular, an implementation-independent specification of the system modules is important in order to keep up with the rapidly evolving hardware technology.

We employ both analytic models and simulation in this investigation. Efforts are being made to develop analytic models considering different system features and levels of abstraction. Thus far, a comprehensive model for the reliability evaluation of fault-tolerant computer systems, including "graceful degradation", transient fault-recovery and offline repair of failed modules has been developed and implemented by means of a set of interactive APL programs, called ARIES (6).

Simulation has remained the principal tool for verification of design decisions and for system improvement. Functional simulation is used to validate completeness and consistency of designs. For performance evaluation our present approach is to simulate the system operating on representative problems. For example, the weather circulation model (7) and the Fast Fourier Transform are used in evaluating the design described in Section V. Simulation was successfully applied in evaluating the Array Machine System (8). Discrete event stochastic simulation of a model of the system described in Section IV has been used to investigate design decisions (9).

III. EFFECTIVENESS OF MULTIPROCESSORS IN LARGE-SCALE NUMERICAL CALCULATIONS

The following factors influence the effectiveness of multiprocessor systems in large-scale numerical calculations:

(a) The first consideration is the amount of parallelism and sequentiality in the algorithm. It has been noted that even a very small amount of sequentiality might considerably reduce the effectiveness of the system. Research has been done to find parallel algorithms for some important applications and to extract parallelism from sequential programs (10).

(b) The system should have a memory with a high bandwidth capable of providing to the processors the required operands and of receiving from them the partial and final results. With today's technology, to have the desired bandwidth, the memory is partitioned into several modules that can be accessed simultaneously. The ability to use this bandwidth effectively depends on the way the data is stored in memory, so that operands that have to be accessed simultaneously reside in different modules. Efficient schemes for storing matrices and other vectors have been devised. To perform the access using these schemes requires sometimes complex index calculations and elaborate routing structures (11), (12), (13). Multiaccess memory modules could be a way to alleviate these difficulties (14).

(c) The system requires an interconnection network to provide the processors with the required operands. If the number of processors is large, cost and implementation considerations impose a limited interconnection network. This network has to be chosen in a way that reduces routing time in a large class of important applications (15). Also, methods have to be developed to partition the computation among the processors in a way that reduces this routing time (13).

(d) The rigid structure that is imposed by the interconnection network and the storage schemes usually makes the computation efficient only for some specific sizes of the operand arrays. For other sizes a severe underutilization of processors can occur.

(e) Due to the large number of processors included in some proposed or built systems, the mean time between processor failures may be quite low. Fault-tolerance features should be introduced to permit the operation of the rest of the system when some processors fail. Dynamic redundancy

techniques are very appropriate due to the modular structure
of these systems but the high-bandwidth interconnection network with a rigid structure makes the introduction of spares
more difficult. It has been proposed to use a decoupling
network between the processors and the interconnection network
to facilitate the introduction of spares (16). Another possibility is the operation of the system with a reduced number of
processors (graceful degradation). Again, the interconnection
network might impose restrictions to this mode of fault-tolerance and some costly restructuring of data and programs
might be necessary to compute efficiently with the reduced
number of processors.

It should be clear that all these factors are interrelated. For example, the storage scheme used would depend on
the indexing facilities available; this storage scheme would
influence the partitioning of the computation among processors
(which also depends on the interconnection network). All
these factors would determine the amount of restructuring to
be done in case of a processor failure. The merits of a proposed architecture should be measured by its capability to
reduce the inefficiencies mentioned for a large set of important computations. In the next sections we discuss two architectures that represent a step toward this goal.

IV. THE SCR SYSTEM: A RECONFIGURABLE PROCESSING ARRAY

One HISPARS design under study is the Shared Computing
Resource (SCR), which is a high-bandwidth array processing
system composed of two sets of special purpose modules: arithmetic processors and address generators. These modules
are connected by dedicated links to accomodate commonly occurring array computations. The modules required for the execution of an array computation are allocated dynamically by a
scheduler within the SCR and interconnected according to the
data-flow graph of the computation (17, 9).

a. Basic organization and operation. Fig. 1 gives a
block diagram of the SCR as part of the multiprocessing system. It consists of: multiple multifunctional, high performance pipelined Arithmetic Processors (AP's); a high-bandwidth
shared memory; an Interconnecting Network (IN) among processors; and a set of Address Generators (AG's) connected to the
processors by a Switching Network (SN).

The PP's executing user programs send requests for array
computations to the Scheduling/Interface Unit (SIU) of the
SCR. Several AP's are allocated to the evaluation of an
array expression and the IN is used to transmit the temporary
results among processors. The operands are obtained from the
shared main memory with the assistance of the AG's which are

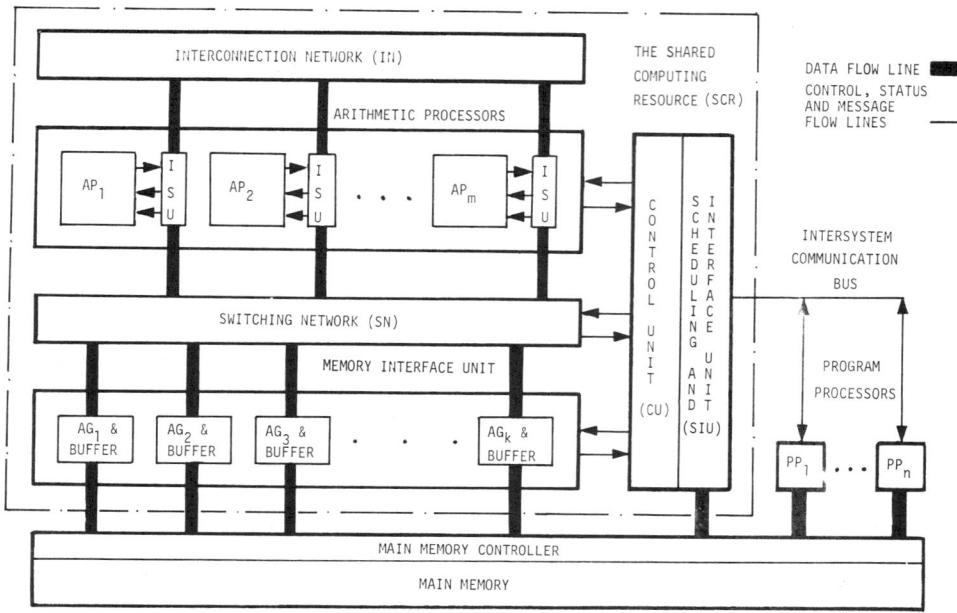

Fig. 1. The SCR System's General Organization

also used for memory remapping operations.

A task requests a subset of the SCR modules, hence several tasks execute concurrently in the SCR system. While the execution time of some tasks can be reduced by breaking them down into independent subtasks for concurrent execution, this approach is not viable when there are other tasks enqueued for execution because of the additional time overhead in setting up additional tasks. Once the task scheduler (implemented in the SIU) schedules a task for execution, actual task setup is performed by a Control Unit (CU) under the direction of the SIU. The components of the SCR are then reconfigured for the duration of an array computation into a virtual computing system according to the corresponding data-flow graph. Once the AP's and the AG's are set up to perform a computation, they can proceed autonomously (without assistance from the CU and SIU) in the streaming mode until the completion of the task. Thus the overhead associated with task scheduling and setup is prorated over the set of array operands which are operated upon in one step. The operation of the AP's and the AG's allocated to the execution of a task are coordinated by a set of registers whose status indicates the presence of operands in the buffers of the AG's. The alignment in time of corresponding data elements being inputted to the AP's is achieved by presetting the AG's so that the transmission of certain operands is delayed with respect to others or by introducing delays by means of buffers in the Input Switching Unit (ISU).

   b. *Dynamic task allocation in the SCR.* In a dynamic task allocation system it is important to consider the task allocation overhead. In this case, each task can be considered as a directed acyclic graph (dag) in which the nodes correspond to vector computations and the edges correspond to data transmissions among the nodes. The allocation of a task is tantamount to imbedding the dag into the interconnection structure of the SCR. This problem is related to the problem of finding isomorphic graphs with its related complexity. To reduce the dynamic task allocation overhead under intercommunication constraints the maximum number of operations in each task is limited to p (a design parameter) and the IN is designed so that the temporary results of all dags with p nodes or less can be transmitted directly. Obviously, the larger the value of p, the smaller is the number of memory accesses used up for temporary results. An acceptable value for p can be determined by studying a set of representative programs and the interconnection requirement of a task by using table lookup. The issue of allocating tasks is then analogous to dynamic storage allocation and a certain degree of resource underutilization is to be expected due to an effect similar to storage fragmentation.

   c. *Viability of the SCR System.* The SCR system has taken the following approaches with respect to factors influencing the effectiveness of a multiprocessing system as discussed in Section III:

   (a) The variability of parallel processing potential in user programs is resolved by sharing the array processing capability of the SCR system by the user programs executing simultaneously in the system.

   (b) The SCR system has extensive provisions to make effective use of memory bandwidth. The SCR operates in a streaming mode, thus reducing memory accesses for instructions. With respect to addressing, more complex address generation can be realized in the SCR by having functional units dedicated to this purpose (the AG's). This added flexibility in addressing results in efficient storage schemes which reduce memory contention and improve memory bandwidth utilization. Also, the number of memory accesses is reduced because temporary results are communicated directly to the AP's and common operands are distributed by an AG to all processors that require them.

   (c) The SCR system has two intercommunication networks, the IN for data transmission among the AP's and the SN for data transmission between the AP's and AG's. The expandability of the system is directly affected by the cost of these networks. In the case of the IN, the limited intercommunication among the AP's does not result in a significant degree of resource underutilization. With respect to overhead in task allocation under interconnection constraints, the approach taken in the SCR is to limit the sizes of tasks which can be executed directly in the system. A side-effect of this approach is the need for partitioning data-flow graphs of vector computations in user programs.

(d) As discussed in (c), the limited interconnections among the AP's limit the size of data-flow graphs of vector computations which can be executed in one step in the SCR. An interconnection network of moderate complexity is required to accomodate vector expressions with at most four operators. Since the percentage of vector expressions with a large number of operations in user programs is expected to be small, this limit does not significantly affect performance.

(e) The pooling concept contributes to the graceful degradation capability. The SCR is fault-tolerant with respect to failures of AP's and AG's. The degradation of the performance of the SCR is due (1) to the loss of the processing capacity of the failed unit, and (2) to indirect inefficiencies resulting from limited interconnections. These inefficiencies are reduced by the use of a certain amount of redundancy in the IN and by "short-circuiting" the failed unit when it is possible, depending on the type of failure.

A discrete-event, stochastic simulation program was used to assess system performance. The mean response time of the SCR (under a postulated workload) was taken as the performance measure. In the case of AP failures, the simulation program was used to determine the effect of limited intercommunication among the AP's on the system performance. A full discussion of all aspects of the SCR which have been summarized above can be found in (9).

V. THE UNSTRUCTURED PROCESSING ARRAY WITH TAGGED OPERANDS

As an alternative to structured arrays of processing elements like the SCR, we are investigating a HISPARS organization based on an unstructured set of arithmetic processors with self-identifying operands. The set of processors is characterized by the absence of fixed data links between arithmetic elements and by the anonymity of all processors. Operands are identified and control flow is specified by tags. The use of tags introduces flexibility in operation, an execution independent of hardware implementation, and an effective reconfiguration in the event of a failure. This approach transfers the complexity of computational task execution from the supervisory control level and overall programming to the generation and the processing of tags. In turn, the lowest level of execution, i.e., the set of arithmetic processors, is left conceptually very simple so that fault-tolerance and optimized resource utilization at that level can be carried out easily and independently of task structure and complexity. The fundamental concepts of organization and operation of this system are summarized below.

a. The main idea. A computational request or task is a computation which can be expressed as a tree and whose input operands are arrays (vector, matrix, etc.). The execution of a computational task in this processor is divided into two distinct and independent levels, the *task* level and the *arithmetic* level. As shown in Fig. 2, an interconnection network with storage capability called the Operand Buffer forms the interface between these two levels.

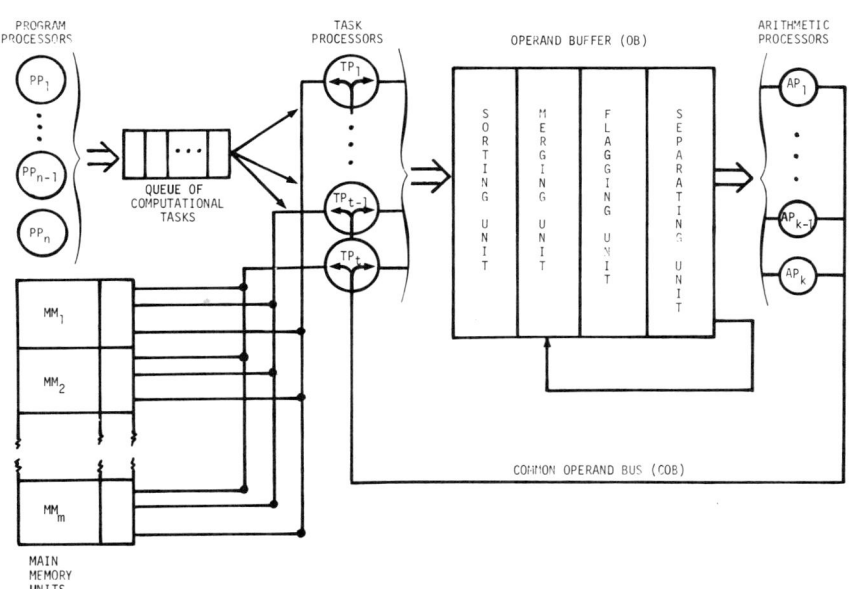

Fig. 2. Block Diagram of the Unstructured Processing Array

b. The task level. At the task level there is a set of Task Processors (TP), each one in charge of tag generation and operand acquisition for one computational task. Each TP is a dedicated microprogrammed control unit with limited arithmetic capabilities and two memories, a conventional RAM and an associative memory with associative processing capabilities. The TP receives as input a task descriptor which carries all the necessary information for task execution (task structure, operand description, number and address of results), and produces an output which consists of blocks of operands each of which carries a tag completely specifying the execution flow for that operand.

   c. *The Operand Buffer (OB) and the arithmetic level.* The OB forms the interface between the task level and the arithmetic level. Its functions are operand pairing, operand selection, and routing to the AP's. The arithmetic level consists of an ensemble of k Arithmetic Processors (AP's) which reduces a set of 2k operands to k results. These results are sent back to the TP through the Common Operand Bus (COB) where, according to tag specification, they are either fed back into the OB or, in the case of final results, they are sent to the main memory for storing. This design is characterized by a generalized use of tags, the logical separation of execution into two independent processing levels, and by a flexible interface between these two levels, the Operand Buffer.

   d. *The use of tags.* Tags are used for operand description, operation identification, task structure specification, and correct ordering of result generation. Shown below is the tag format with two fields, a control field and a dynamic field. The control field contains the information for task

TASK NUMBER	SUBTASK NUMBER	TREE LABEL	OPCODE	RESULT INDEX

                    CONTROL FIELD   DYNAMIC FIELD

and input operand identification. The computational task is transformed into a binary tree. A tree processing algorithm generates a binary label for each leaf, i.e., input operand. The label is stored in the operand tag and is used for correct operand pairing. Computational tasks are partitioned into directly executable subtasks, and the subtask number is stored in the control field. For each subtask, r result elements are generated. All input operands are tagged by the index of the result element they generate; this index is stored in the dynamic field.

   e. *Processing at two independent levels.* Task processing consists of scheduling the task, fetching operands, generating tags for each operand, and interfacing the arithmetic level. Task scheduling and tag generation is explained above. Operand fetching is preceded by memory address generation. It requires two functions which are part of the operand description:

      - the index function describes the relationship between each index of the input operand and the indices of the result.
      - the storage function defines the way the operand array is stored in memory.

Final formation of tagged operands is done by attaching the

tags to the operands coming from memory and sending them to the OB.

The arithmetic level operates independently of the task level. During every cycle, executable operand pairs appear at the output of the OB. They are executed by the pool of AP's according to a local scheduling rule. When results are ready, their tags are generated and they are broadcast on the Common Operand Bus. Tagged results are picked up on the bus by their originating TP which inspects the tag to determine where to send the result: back to the OB if it is an intermediate result or to the Main Memory if it is a final result to be stored.

f. Functions of the Operand Buffer. The OB consists of four units, a Sorting unit, a Merging unit, a Flagging unit and a Separating unit. The Sorting unit sorts (by their tag fields) operands coming out of the TP's, i.e., new tagged operands and intermediate results. The Merging unit sorts two ordered input sequences of operands by their tag fields. The Flagging unit first pairs off operands ready for execution, then selects and flags a variable number of them depending on AP's availability. The Separating unit forms two sequences, the flagged operands sent to the AP's for execution, and the unflagged operands sent back to the OB to be merged with new tagged operands and intermediate results. This organization allows dynamic matching of operand delivery rate with the execution rate of the AP's through adjustment of the number of tagged operands to be flagged and sent to the AP's. The fundamental trade-off here is size of the buffer vs. transfer time. In case of AP failure immediate reconfiguration and rollback are implemented by reducing the number of available AP's and re-circulating the operands from the failed AP.

g. Concluding remarks. There are two basic concepts which apply specifically to this approach: (a) the use of multiple levels of execution, and (b) the use of tagged operands. The processing array is designed with two logically independent levels, the task level and the arithmetic level. System modeling is patterned after the structural design approach with a distinct model at each level. The use of tagged operands has the following consequences: (a) it enhances the logical isolation of the different levels thereby facilitating system modularity, reconfigurability and resource utilization, and (b) it affects the representation and the efficiency of algorithms. Modeling and simulation are being used to determine for which classes of computations the greatest gains in efficiency can be expected. A complete discussion of this design will be found in (18). The use of tagged operands is a generalization of the tagging scheme devised by Tomasulo (19). The design of the Operand Buffer is based on (20) and the general approach offers similarities with the Data Flow Processor (21).

VI. CONTINUING EFFORTS

The near-term goal of this investigation is to compare the competing HISPARS organizations with respect to: (a) fault-tolerance; (b) modularity for longevity and evolution; (c) efficiency of implementing fast algorithms; and (d) implications to the user community with respect to cost-effectiveness and convenience of use. The representative problems chosen for this purpose are the Mintz-Arakawa weather circulation model (7) and digital signal processing using FFT algorithms.

The principal long-term goals are: (a) evolution of a more formal methodology for the design and evaluation of computer systems; (b) development of analytic and empirical tools for the modeling, evaluation and refinement of "paper designs", and (c) search for support to construct an experimental system which would employ and demonstrate the desirable approaches identified in our "paper designs".

VII. REFERENCES

1. Avižienis, A., "Fault-Tolerance and Longevity: Goals for High-Speed Computers of the Future," in these Proceedings.
2. Estrin, G., "Organization of Computer Systems: the Fixed Plus Variable Structure Computer," Proc. WJCC, 33-40, 1960.
3. Chen, T.C., "Unconventional Superspeed Computer Systems," AFIPS Conf. Proc., 38, 365-371, 1971.
4. Avižienis, A., and Tung, C., "A Universal Arithmetic Building Element (ABE) and Design Methods for Arithmetic Processors," IEEE Trans. Comp., C-19, 8, 733-745, Aug. 1970.
5. Avižienis, A., et al., "The STAR (Self-Testing-And-Repairing) Computer: An Investigation of the Theory and Practice of Fault-Tolerant Computer Design," IEEE Trans. Comp. C-20, 11, 1312-1321, Nov. 1971.
6. Ng. Y.W., and Avižienis, A., "ARIES - An Automated Reliability Estimation System," Proc. of the 1977 Annual Reliability and Maintainability Symposium, 108-113, Jan. 1977.
7. Gates, W.L., et al., "A Documentation of the Mintz-Arakawa Two-Level Atmospheric General Circulation Model," ARPA Report R-877, Rand Corp., Dec. 1971.
8. Sylvain, P. and Vineberg, M., "The Design and Evaluation of the Array Machine: a High-Level Language Processor," Proc. of the Second Annual Symposium on Computer Architecture, 119-125, Jan. 1975.
9. Thomasian, A., "A Design Study of a Shared-Resource Array Processing," Technical Report UCLA-ENG-7702, Computer Science Department, UCLA, Apr. 1977.
10. Kuck, D., "Parallel Processing of Ordinary Programs,"

Report UIUCDCS-R-75-767, Department of Computer Science, Univ. of Illinois at Urbana-Champaign, 1975.
11. Budnick, P. and Kuck, D., "The Organization and Use of Parallel Memories," IEEE Trans. Comp., C-20, 12, 1566-1569, Dec. 1971.
12. Swanson, R., "Interconnections for Parallel Memories to Unscramble P-ordered Vectors," IEEE Trans. Comp., C-23, 11, 1105-1116, Nov. 1974.
13. Lang. T., "Vector Computations in an Array Computer," Ph.D. Dissertation, Stanford University, Aug. 1974.
14. Korff, P., "A Multiaccess Memory," Technical Report UCLA-ENG-7607, Computer Science Department, UCLA, July 1976.
15. Lawrie, D., "Access and Alignment of Data in an Array Processor," IEEE Trans. Comp., C-24, 12, 1145-1155, Dec. 1975.
16. Baqai, I.A., and Lang, T., "Reliability Aspects of the ILLIAC IV Computer," Proc. of the 1976 Int. Conf. on Parallel Processing, 123-131, Aug. 1976.
17. Thomasian, A. and Avižienis, A., "A Design Study of a Shared-Resource Computing System," Proc. of the Third Annual Symposium on Computer Architecture, 105-112, Jan. 1976.
18. Sylvain, P., "A Fault-Tolerant Large-Scale Processing System Based on Tagged Architecture with an Unstructured Set of Processors," Ph.D. Dissertation in progress, Computer Science Department, UCLA, 1978.
19. Tomasulo, R.M., "An Efficient Algorithm for Exploiting Multiple Arithmetic Units," IBM J. of Res. and Dev., 11, 25-33, Jan. 1967.
20. Rohrbacher, D.L., "Advanced Computer Organization Study," Air Force Contract Report AD631870 and AD631871, Apr. 1966.
21. Dennis, J.B., and Misunas, D.P., "A Preliminary Architecture for a Basic Data-Flow Processor," Proc. of the Second Annual Symposium on Computer Architecture, 126-132, Jan 1975.

FAULT-TOLERANCE AND LONGEVITY: GOALS FOR
HIGH-SPEED COMPUTERS OF THE FUTURE[1]

Algirdas Avižienis

UCLA Computer Science Department

A rationale and methods of investigation applicable to systems design research in a university environment are discussed. Fault-tolerance and longevity are identified as desirable attributes of future high-speed systems. Some techniques for the attainment of these attributes are described.

I. A RATIONALE FOR RESEARCH

The question: "Can university research make significant contributions to advances in computer system design?" has been the subject of debate at research-sponsoring government agencies as well as among practicing researchers and designers in industry and academia. While it is conceded that universities have pioneered with innovative designs in the 1940's and 1950's, the argument is often made that this role now has been preempted by industrial research and development laboratories of computer manufacturers.

The major arguments against university research are: (a) universities lack the budget for the extensive repertoire of design tools and the technical support needed for this type of research; and (b) the pressure to produce publications frequently leads to the study of trivial problems or to superficial and incomplete "paper designs" that are never subjected to a trial by construction and use.

The viewpoint of this paper is that once they are recognized, the above objections can be largely overcome and that universities can provide a uniquely suitable environment for in-depth studies of desirable innovations. This is due to some specific advantages of the university environment which are: (a) there is no motivation to conceal good new results,

---

[1]This research is supported by NSF Grant No. MCS 72-03633 A04.

since rewards are given for publication rather than for delivering a better product than the competition; (b) there are no pressures to rush completion of studies in order to meet manufacturing deadlines; (c) there is no limitation on innovations imposed by the need to remain compatible with the current product line, company tradition, or maintenance and support policy.

The principal challenge to the academic researcher in system design is to recognize and to relate several important aspects of the "real world" of the manufacturer and the user. The key questions are: Which urgent problems need systems superior in some sense to those that are available today? What are the new algorithms, data structures, and performance measures that can be applied? What are the coming innovations in design tools, implementation technologies, and manufacturing techniques? What are the observed strengths and weaknesses of the generation of machines currently in use?

The remaining sections of this paper discuss a method used to investigate these questions and identify two attributes--fault-tolerance and longevity--that may provide better performance of high-speed computers in the future. A companion paper (1) describes a currently ongoing investigation of fault-tolerant high-speed computer architectures.

II. METHOD OF INVESTIGATION

Our university environment currently does not provide the means for the construction of experimental systems and therefore limits computer architecture studies to "paper designs". Furthermore, details of the problems encountered in design and use of present-generation high-speed machines usually remain unpublished, and they have to be acquired by private communication or from miscellaneous working papers of manufacturers and users.

In order to keep in touch with the experience of computer builders and users, we have followed a pragmatic method of investigation, containing the following steps: (a) successful features of existing machines are noted and studied; (b) information is collected on all known and suspected deficiencies, difficulties and oversights; (c) desirable features are identified that are not found in working systems, but promise better performance; (d) a new design is described at two or more levels with increasing amounts of detail; (e) two or more dissimilar classes of typical problems are selected to be used in its evaluation; (f) a qualitative evaluation is carried out: is the design reasonable? is it complete?, etc.; (g) analytic models and simulation are applied to evaluate the design qualitatively; (h) the design is compared to other designs; (i) the design is modified to eliminate observed inadequacies or to take advantage of new insights. Following these guidelines we expect to accomplish not only an exercise in "paper design", but also to raise interest in the implementation of experimental machines which, in turn, would serve as sources of new concepts for the design of the next generation of high-speed computers.

In addition to devising new designs by means of the heuristic approach described above, we are also concerned with the long-range development of a more formal design methodology. The goal is to devise analytic models that would quantitatively relate the major aspects of the system: problem representation, system organization, implementation constraints, and the desired attributes, e.g.: speed, ease of programming, high throughput, fault-tolerance, etc.

III. FAULT-TOLERANCE: A KEY TO FULL AVAILABILITY

One evident problem of current high-speed machines is global vulnerability to component failures. A simple single-circuit failure in a processor usually requires testing, fault location, and manual repair of frequently unpredictable duration. In cases in which operation resumes after fault location in a "degraded" mode (with fewer processing elements), a loss of efficiency takes place because the computation had been compiled for execution on a full set of processors. Some reasons for such global effects of a local failure are evident. First, current designs do not provide immediate and localized detection of a fault (i.e., a failure, or an error due to a transient malfunction) in a processor. The symptoms of the fault have to be recognized externally, by means of special software. Second, the design of the very fast pipelined processing units is highly centralized. There are no provisions to recover by bypassing a failed part of the pipeline, and the entire pipeline is lost due to a failure.

Past experience with smaller, specialized machines (2), (3) suggests that the use of fault-tolerance techniques can lead to a major reduction of global vulnerability to failures and thus increase the availability of large-scale, high-speed computing systems of the future to very near 100%. The remaining challenge is to select those fault-tolerance techniques that are best suited to high-speed computing systems and to devise the means to incorporate them into future designs. *Fault-tolerance* is an attribute of the system that allows it to carry out the desired operations regardless of the occurrence of a specified set of faults (3). A *fault* is an abnormal condition of the system which may disrupt its operation. The set of faults may be limited to *physical* faults caused by adverse physical phenomena (component failures, physical interference from the environment, etc.), or it may also include *man-made* faults caused by human mistakes (errors in design, manufacturing, programming, man-machine interaction, etc.) The form of fault-tolerance that is most suitable for large-scale computing systems is known as "graceful degradation". Recovery from a fault consists of an immediate exclusion of the failed part (hardware module, or program, or both) of the system from further use, followed by a resumption of efficient operation with a diminished set of system parts.

In order to attain such fault-tolerance, the entire system must be partitioned into sets of autonomous functional units. Well-defined communication interfaces between the autonomous units serve as boundaries to stop the propagation of fault-caused errors. Furthermore, they allow the use of self-contained fault detection and recovery mechanisms for each set of units, avoiding the need for a complex central clearinghouse for fault detection and recovery. A second requirement is run-time mapping of the computing algorithms onto the currently available sets of units. Such mapping allows immediate continuation of efficient operation after the exclusion of a failed unit.

The most important areas of investigation for each functional part of the system are: internal partitioning into a set of units, choice of local fault-detection techniques, and fast hardware-controlled implementation of recovery. A highly promising technique for designing building-block arithmetic units suitable for LSI implementation is signed-digit arithmetic (4). Key fault-detection techniques for immediate (concurrent) fault detection are arithmetic error-detecting codes (5) and self-checking logic design (6), (7). Implementation of recovery has been studied using the concepts of a specialized Test-And-Repair Processor (8), (9).

IV. LONGEVITY: A KEY TO EVOLUTIONARY GROWTH.

The history of computer development shows that the implementation of arithmetic algorithms has changed much less than the other functional parts (storage management, instruction processing, input and output devices, etc.) over three generations of computers. Several novel ideas, such as significance arithmetic, use of redundancy to get faster algorithms, residue arithmetic, signed-digit arithmetic, and use of arithmetic error codes have emerged in this period (10), but their acceptance has been quite slow. Pipelining has been the major exception in this trend to stay with "tried and true" approaches in the implementation of arithmetic in high-speed machines; otherwise, faster logic elements in larger quantities were used to speed up computing.

The arithmetic units of computers have been discarded because they were embedded in a system in which other functional parts and the component technology became obsolete. Given the possibility that components will evolve more gradually in the future, it may be conjectured that the arithmetic units and some other system parts can remain useful over considerably longer periods than a specific system configuration. This property of *longevity* will be attained only if these units are made autonomous, that is, if they are to a certain extent decoupled from the other parts of a total system. Such systems could be modified, expanded, and kept up-to-date by the process of *evolution*, i.e., the deletion of obsolete and the introduction of new functional parts, rather than the replacement of an entire system. The autonomous arithmetic units of a large and costly high-speed computer are an example of units that would be able to serve for relatively long periods of time within an evolving system.

The fault-tolerance and longevity properties of arithmetic units are significantly enhanced when an entire arithmetic unit for any specified word length is assembled from identical standard building blocks. Such a building block, called the ABE (Arithmetic Building Element), is available when a signed-digit (S-D) number system is used to represent the operands during computation (4). The fully self-contained nature of an ABE has some major advantages for the design of autonomous and fault-tolerant arithmetic units. First, each digit of the S-D representation can be encoded in an arithmetic error-detecting code (5). The carry-free nature of the algorithms assures that checking of the output result requires only an independent digit-by-digit check of each output digit by the receiving ABE. Second, operands of arbitrary length may be processed beginning with their most significant digits. This allows a "graceful degradation" feature within the arithmetic array itself. The failure of one ABE does not require the shutdown of the entire arithmetic unit; instead it only reduces the number of digits that can be processed in parallel at once. Conversely, expansion or reorganization for an evolutionary improvement of the system is also possible and enhances its longevity. The modular nature of ABE blocks provides a basis for local error detection, local recovery (degradation), evolutionary expansion, and restructuring of algorithms that are not possible with conventional arithmetic now used in high-speed computers.

In conclusion, it is important to note that the functional partitioning of the system into autonomous units is a key prerequisite for both fault-tolerance and longevity. Both attributes are closely interrelated and reinforce each other in attainment of their respective goals. A general model of a High-Speed Arithmetic System (HISPARS) with fault-tolerance and longevity attributes is described in a companion paper appearing in these Proceedings (1).

V. REFERENCES

1. Avižienis, A., Ercegovac, M., Lang, T., Sylvain, P., and Thomasian, A., "An Investigation of Fault-Tolerant Architectures for Large-Scale Numerical Computing", in these Proceedings.
2. Avižienis, A., et al., "The STAR (Self-Testing-And Repairing) Computer: An Investigation of the Theory and Practice of Fault-Tolerant Computer Design", IEEE Trans. Comp., C-20, 11, 1312-1321, Nov. 1971.
3. Avižienis, A., "Fault-Tolerant Systems", IEEE Trans. Comp., C-25, 1304-1312, Dec. 1976.
4. Avižienis, A., and Tung, C., "A Universal Arithmetic Building Element (ABE) and Design Methods for Arithmetic Processors", IEEE Trans. Comp., C-19, 733-745, Aug. 1970.
5. Avižienis, A., "Arithmetic Error Codes: Cost and Effectiveness Studies for Application in Digital System Design", IEEE Trans. Comp., C-20, 1322-1331, Nov. 1971.
6. Carter, W. C., "Theory and Use of Checking Circuits", in Computer Systems Reliability, Infotech Information Ltd. (Maidenhead, England), 413-454, 1974.
7. Sum, E. K. S., and Avižienis, A., "A Probabilistic Model for the Evaluation of Signal Reliability of Self-Checking Logic Circuits", Proc. Sixth Int. Symp. on Fault-Tolerant Computing, 83-87, June 1976.
8. Rennels, D. A., "Fault Detection and Recovery in a Redundant Computer Using Standby Spares", Technical Report UCLA-ENG-7355, UCLA Computer Science Dept., July 1973.
9. Avižienis, A., and Parhami, B., "A Fault-Tolerant Parallel Computer System for Signal Processing", Digest Fourth Int. Symp. on Fault-Tolerant Computing, 2-8 - 2-13, June 1974.
10. Avižienis, A., "Digital Computer Arithmetic: A Unified Algorithmic Specification", Proc. Symposium on Computers and Automata, Polytech. Institute of Brooklyn, 509-526, Wiley-Interscience, 1971.

SEMIGROUPS OF RECURRENCES[*]

Daniel D. Gajski
University of Illinois at Urbana-Champaign

Abstract

A method for solving logic design problems for high-speed computers is given. It is shown that the class of problems characterized by the recurrence relations can be decomposed into modularly structured networks. The structure of the module and the network interconnections are obtained using semigroups of recurrence systems. Such network computes a given function in logarithmic time. The method is universal and can be very easily adapted for automization of logic design problems. The modularity of the generated network is very suitable to present-day LSI technology. The same method can be used outside the logic design area. In all cases considered, the best known time and processor bounds are obtained.

I. MOTIVATION

Winograd [1] and Spira [2] considered the construction of combinatorial networks using modules with a fixed number of input lines to each module. They obtained a general lower bound on time delay required by any network to compute a given function. Their lower bound is based on cardinality of input lines that influence the state of the output lines. Since only cardinality of the input and not the structure of the computing network is involved, the lower bound obtained by Winograd and Spira are difficult to realize in practice, in general. However, they succeeded in obtaining very tight bounds on the complexity of multiplication in finite groups.

This paper is concerned with the expansion of the above

---

[*] This work was supported in part by the National Science Foundation under Grant No. MCS73-07980 A03.

problem in the following ways:

(a) We would like to obtain some realizable lower bounds together with the structure of the computing network for a general class of problems.

(b) The function to be computed should be given in a simple form and easy to comprehend by humans.

(c) There should be a class of algorithms to generate the computational network out of description (b). It is assumed that this process is carried out by a computer, therefore, automating the logic design by use of another computer.

(d) The algorithms in (c) should minimize the time delay through the network by taking advantage of the parallelism of the given function, and obtaining the speed at the expense of gate quantity.

(e) The design of the computational network should be modular in such a way that increased demands for speed and size can be met through increased parallelism and increased number of modules, and not through the redesign of the circuit. This way logic design becomes technology independent.

(f) Gate minimization should be last on the list of priorities, since today's logic design is not usually limited by solid state technology. The multitude of gates provided by present LSI technology is not exploited completely because of the limited number of external connections to a package.

II. BASIC IDEA

We have chosen to express the function to be computed with recurrence equations. A recurrence system of first order is a triple $R(1) = <K, X, F>$ where $K = K_1 \times K_2 \times \ldots \times K_s$ is the product of finite sets of coefficients, $X = X_1 \times X_2 \times \ldots \times X_t$ is a product of finite sets of variables and $F: K \times X \to X$ for every instance of recurrence system. Usually the set F is given in a compound form. For example, a carry-lookahead function in a binary adder can be expressed as a first-order linear recurrence system

$$R_1(1) = <A \times B, C, F_1> \tag{1}$$

where F_1 is given by

$$F_1: \quad c_i = a_i b_i + (a_i + b_i) c_{i-1} = y_i + x_i c_{i-1} \tag{2}$$

Similarly, the comparison of two binary numbers is first-order recurrence system $R_2(1) = <A \times B, C \times D, F_2>$ with

$$F_2: \quad \begin{aligned} c_i &= c_{i-1} + \overline{d}_{i-1} \, a_i \cdot \overline{b}_i \\ d_i &= d_{i-1} + \overline{c}_{i-1} \, \overline{a}_i \cdot b_i \end{aligned}$$

The function F of the first-order recurrence system can be interpreted as a set of functions f_k from X into X for all $k \in K$

$$F = \{f_{k_i} : X \to X \mid k_i \in K\} \tag{3}$$

Therefore, every instance of recurrence can be written as

$$\begin{aligned} x_i &= f_{k_i}(x_{i-1}) = f_{k_i}(f_{k_{i-1}}(x_{i-2})) \\ &= f_{k_i}(f_{k_{i-1}}(\ldots f_{k_2}(f_{k_1}(x_0)) \ldots)) \\ &= f_{k_i} f_{k_{i-1}} \ldots f_{k_2} f_{k_1}(x_0) \end{aligned} \tag{4}$$

since functional composition is an associative operation.

The above observation has a profound influence on computation time. Let τ_R be the time to compute f_k, $k \in K$, and let τ_s be the computation time in $<F>$, the semigroup generated by F. Then for every integer n, x_n can be computed in $\lceil \log_2 n \rceil \tau_s + \tau_R$ instead of $n \, \tau_R$ when substitution into recurrence equation is used. However, it must be noted that computation in $<F>$ is more complicated than the computation of recurrence equation, particularly when cardinality of $<F>$ is greater than cardinality of F. As an example, for $R_1(1)$ the semigroup multiplication in $<F_1>$ is defined as follows

$$f_{(y_2,x_2)} \cdot f_{(y_1,x_1)} = f_{(y_2 + x_2 y_1,\ x_2 x_1)} \tag{5}$$

and from equation (2)

$$f_{(y_i,x_i)}(c_{i-1}) = y_i + x_i\, c_{i-1} \tag{6}$$

If only 2-input AND and OR gates are used, the above algorithm will compute any linear recurrence of the first order in $2\lceil \log_2 n \rceil$ gate delays. This is the best possible time, precisely the lower bound reported by Winograd [1]. This bound is an improvement over the one reported by Chen and Kuck [4], and gives better time than any commercially available carry-lookahead function. The same decomposition has been reported by Kogge and Stone [3].

It should be observed that the above procedure is not limited to only linear recurrences. It works with any kind of recurrences as well. It was conjectured by Chen and Kuck [4] that nonlinear recurrences can be computed by an array of modules where all nonlinearities are computed inside the module and the overall structure is that of linear recurrences. The above procedure proves the idea of Chen and Kuck to be correct. The modules are at least of the complexity expressed by the recurrence relation, and the overall structure, that is, the connection among modules, is that of an associative operation (semigroup multiplication).

Semigroups of recurrences can be generated for linear as well as nonlinear recurrence systems of order m, m being any integer. However, the complexity and the quantity of computation inside a module realizing semigroup multiplication increases not only with the cardinality of <F> but with the order m as well.

The sets K and X in the definition of a recurrence system do not have to be defined over Boolean constants and Boolean variables. The set of integers or the set of real numbers may be chosen. The algorithm using recurrence semigroups will still be valid. In particular, for linear recurrences of any order we obtain the best known time and processor bounds, the same as those reported by Sameh and Brent [5]. At the same time, the modularity of the obtained result can be exploited successfully in the design of vector or parallel processors.

III. CONCLUSION

In conclusion, we should mention that the present algorithm has several advantages over work previously reported.

Firstly, it is an universal algorithm that can be used in automation of logic design problems. The concept of recurrence semigroups can be applied to other areas outside logic design. The algorithm works for any kind of recurrence system.

Secondly, the algorithm leads to a modular design that is very amendable to present-day LSI technology. Generally, modular designs are conceptually simpler, easier to understand and more flexible.

Thirdly, the presented approach achieves the best known time and processor bounds in cases considered.

IV. REFERENCES

[1] Winograd, S., "On the Time Required to Perform Multiplication," J. Assoc. Comp. Mach., Vol. 14, pp. 793-802, 1967.

[2] Spira, P. M., "The Time Required for Group Multiplication," J. Assoc. Comp. Mach., Vol. 16, pp. 235-243, 1969.

[3] Kogge, P. M., and Stone, H. S., "A Parallel Algorithm for the Efficient Solution of a General Class of Recurrence Equations," IEEE Trans. Comput., Vol. C-22, pp. 786-793, 1973.

[4] Chen, S. C., and Kuck, D. J., "Combinatorial Circuit Synthesis with Time and Component Bounds," to appear in IEEE Trans. Comput., 1977.

[5] Sameh, A. H., and Brent, R. P., "Solving Triangular Systems on a Parallel Computer," to appear in SIAM J. Numer. Anal.

ARRAY PROCESSORS AND THEIR APPLICATION

T. E. Rudy
Lawrence Livermore Laboratory

For over a decade the signal processing community has effectively utilized array processors for their computational needs. The algorithms implemented on the array processors such as the Fast Fourier Transform, convolution, etc., require several arithmetic operations for each data point. Hence, the rather slow transfer rate of a host channel was not a limiting factor. Other considerations which made the array processor an attractive alternative to maxi computers for the seismic community were the relatively low cost of array processors for pure number crunching capabilities, the fact that the algorithms to be implemented on an array processor were stable, relatively small in instructions and could be stored in a separate memory or ROM. In fact, the array processor was essentially a "black box" which, when initialized, accessed host memory for a block of data, converted the data from host to AP format "on the fly", performed the required computation and returned the results from AP memory to host memory.

Today there are several computer firms which market array processors. The common features incorporated in array processors such as the CSPI, Data West, Floating Point Systems, SPS and CDC AP's are:

- a) Cycle time: 50-200 nanoseconds.
- b) Floating point multiply: 100-500 nanoseconds.
- c) Pipelined arithmetic units and/or parallel instruction execution.
- d) Multi processor and/or memories.
- e) Interface to mini computer channel, bus, etc., with format conversion capability.
- f) Programmable with a cross-assembler and usually a simulator provided.
- g) Overlap of data transfer from host computer to AP instruction execution.
- h) Library of frequently used algorithms provided by vendor.

When the above features are compared to the performance of mini computers such as the PDP-11/45, SEL 32, Interdata 8/32 the array processor is 10 to 20 times faster than the host computer. Indeed, for some applications the AP is two orders of magnitude faster than typical mini computers.

For the effective utilization of the computational capability of an array processor a user must balance the data transfer limitation with AP arithmetic throughout. Since channels on mini computers operate at approximately one microsecond per word and an AP such as the FPS AP-120B can perform six floating point multiplies in one microsecond the potential degradation in AP performance is apparent. From the host's point of view the host cpu could be effectively blocked from accessing its own memory if the AP is continually issuing requests for host memory cycles.

An additional constraint for effective utilization of an AP is the necessity of vector or array operations and/or highly specialized application programming.

From LLL's point of view the performance of array processors on vectorized finite difference algorithms is of interest. A comparison of the performance of a one dimensional hydrodynamics program and a two dimensional electron conduction scheme on the FPS AP-120B versus other computers is presented below:

1-D Hydrodynamics	5000 cycles execute time	100 zones (seconds)
KI-10 Fortran		205.0
7600 Fortran		11.3
STAR-100 Vector		3.4
Array Processor		37.1

2-D Electron conduction		42 × 82 Grid Milliseconds/cycle
KI-10		1900.0
7600 Vector		78.0
STAR-100		30.6
CRAY-1		5.2
Array Processor		259.4

To attain the performance for the AP described above the data must reside in the AP's memory and the issue of vector instructions must be controlled by the AP. This requires the host to define descriptor blocks for all vector instructions and the AP to process a sequence of descriptors without host communication.

The operational sequence envisioned would facilitate the interaction of the host computer with the user without degradation of the computations performed by the AP. The host computer would perform I/O operations and respond to user inquiries while the AP is busy computing.

The primary limitations encountered with the system described are the necessity of the user to vectorize the application program to attain optional performance and to restructure his application code to allow parallelism in the computational and user response phases of the program.

Although the throughput potential of array processors approaches, and for a few applications exceeds, that of a CDC 7600 the cost effectiveness and actual performance level attained is dependent on the user's ability to restructure his application for the hardware and software environment.

THE USE OF LADDERS FOR THE EXECUTION OF APL

Charles R. Minter
Yale University

APL is a very expressive programming language that is well suited for some classes of problems. There are some problems for which a solution in APL is both natural and simple but requires too much storage or computation time. The work described here uses special structures called ladders to improve the execution of APL.

A ladder is a structure, introduced by Perlis [1], that combines a data-access mechanism for array-structured data with computational and linkage capability. One ladder is associated with each occurrence of an array in an APL statement. The ladders for the arrays referenced by a statement are connected to form a ladder network for the statement. A ladder can be divided into two parts, a fixed part and a variable part. The fixed part handles the accessing of the array elements and the check for completion. The variable part performs the computation specified by the operators in the statement. The variable parts of each ladder are generated in much the same way code is generated by a standard compiler. If the ladder network for a statement is saved after the statement has been executed, it is likely that the same network can be used the next time the statement is encountered.

An APL implementation based on ladders offers several advantages. First, the ladder addressing mechanism allows the selection operators discussed by Abrams [2] to be implemented very efficiently. Second, ladders can drastically reduce the intermediate storage used during the execution of an APL statement. The third advantage of a ladder-based APL system is that a ladder network generated when a statement is executed can often be saved and reused.

The implementation of a ladder-based APL system can be based on software, firmware, or hardware.

In a software implementation, an APL interpreter/compiler translates an APL statement into a program in the machine language of a general-purpose computer that executes the statement by simulating a ladder network. A rough comparison based on data given by Breed and Lathwell [3] indicates that a software implementation of APL using ladders is as efficient in its use of the machine as the Breed implementation.

A firmware implementation is possible on a microprogrammable machine and with this technique special microprograms are written for the most common and time-consuming operations. The execution time and the storage required for the ladders can be reduced by about a factor of two.

Finally a ladder-based APL system can be based on specially designed hardware to take advantage of the characteristics of the ladder mechanism. In one such approach, a commercially available computer (the host processor) is used with a specailly designed computer (the ladder processor) to execute ladder networks. The host computer generates ladder networks and loads them into the small memory used by the ladder processor. The ladder processor references array data residing in the main memory of the host. The parts for a moderate performance ladder processor to be connected to a PDP-11 as the host cost a few thousand dollars. Simulations indicate that such a system would run about five times faster for some problems than an IBM 370/158 running APL.SV [4]. For APL statements using selection operators the speed-up can be much more significant.

REFERENCES

1. Perlis, A.J., "Steps toward an APL Compiler", Yale University Computer Science Department Report No. 24, 1975.
2. Abrams, P.S., "An APL Machine", SLAC-114, 1970.
3. Breed, L.M., and Lathwell, R.H., "The Implementation of APL/360", Proceedings of ACM Symposium on Interactive Systems for Experimental Applied Mathematics, (M. Klerer and J. Reinfelds, Eds.), p. 390. Academic Press, New York, 1968.
4. Minter, C.R., "A Machine Design for Efficient Implementation of APL", Yale University Computer Science Department Report No. 81, 1976.

DISTRIBUTED SIGNAL PROCESSING AS IMPLEMENTED IN THE
L-2000 REMOTE RADAR TRACKING STATION

Frank P. Hiner, III
Litton Data Systems Division

I.   BACKGROUND

The development of special-purpose (hardwired) processors required for modern radar and IFF equipments has historically necessitated the design and development of many small units of specialized digital equipment. These units are integrated together to perform the total digital task. In each subsequent design effort, a virtually new design is required and the result is often a complex machine which requires arduous checkout, is understood chiefly by its original designer, and is difficult to maintain and modify.

Recognizing that the complete signal processor is made up of a set of functions coordinating to perform some total job (e.g., the detection of radar targets), then a distributed or federated processor approach towards signal processing implementation was sought. Required for such implementation is a processing element which would be physically small and be instructionally powerful enough to perform a reasonably large function. The Building Block Signal Processor is such an element.

II. THE BUILDING BLOCK SIGNAL PROCESSOR

The Building Block Signal Processor (BBSP) was first designed and developed in 1972 as a set of seven 4" x 5" logic boards.[1] By 1975, the machine had evolved to a single 8" x 8" logic board.

Having the complete processor on a single board (including instruction and data memory) meant that automatic maintenance to the single card level was readily attainable in a distributed processor incorporating a goodly number of processors. For the designer, the single-card machine meant that if another function had to be added to the machine, he could simply add another BBSP to the system with small impact on system size.

The single card BBSP is a 12-bit processor constructed of off-the-shelf low-power Schottky devices netting a power consumption from 12 to 15 watts. The machine runs relatively slowly (but noise free) at a 2 MHz clock speed but gains instruction power with a wide (40 bit) instruction word which allows, in effect, parallel microprogramming. The BBSP contains a 2048-word instruction memory (stored in PROM after program debug), a 1024-word data memory, 8 general registers, a wide set of arithmetic instructions, 16 conditions for JUMP and CALL and a 16-level return address stack.

III. THE L-2000 REMOTE RADAR TRACKING STATION

The L-2000 Remote Radar Tracking Station was developed at Litton Systems as a distributed processor using the BBSPs as the processing elements. The L-2000 interfaces with a wide variety of pulse search radar sets, accepting the analog videos, timing triggers and azimuth synchro voltages and outputting the cartesian position and velocity of moving aircraft within the surveillance volume. The system must perform digital detection on radar signals, the automatic control of threshold voltages for quantization of the analog video, synchro-to-digital conversion, automatic mapping of the radar clutter (i.e., those echoes from mountains, clouds, etc.) and tracking (estimation and prediction) of the aircraft positions. Each of these functions is performed by one or two BBSPs plus peripheral cards such as multiplies, memories, and A-D converters. The L-2000 employs a total of 10 BBSPs.

A. Inter-Processor Communication in the L-2000

Several of the processors within the L-2000 communicate directly with each other in "star" fashion in real time, all processors are interconnected in a single continuous loop and most of the intersystem communication takes place on this loop. Timing of loop communication in the L-2000 is based on the radar timing trigger to which the L-2000 is synchronized. Upon receiving the timing trigger, all BBSPs are interrupted, breaking them out of their real time functions and selecting the communication routines. Common system data is then passed throughout the system in bucket brigade fashion. Not only does this provide an easy means of system intercommunication, but all processors have access to a large and common data base.

B. Fault Detection and Maintenance in the L-2000

   System fault detection is facilitated by injecting test targets at the input of the system and monitoring system outputs. Moreover, during intersystem transfers, advantage is taken of the loop nature of the transfer path to pass test data throughout the system. Upon detection of a fault, audible and visual alarms are enabled. The local maintenance personnel may then, by switch action, perform the Automatic Troubleshooting Sequence (ATS). ATS is initiated by pressing the system reset button sending all BBSPs into ATS simultaneously. Each machine contains its own ATS program which performs an exhaustive diagnostic test on that machine. Upon a BBSP's passing its test, it checks out its dedicated peripheral cards such as multiply arrays or mass memories. The developed system is able to isolate failures to the single card to a confidence level of 95 percent with an MTTR of one minute.

IV. SUMMARY

   The L-2000 is an operational remote radar tracking station implemented as a distributed processor with a set of 10 BBSPs.

   High-speed functions formerly requiring hardwired implementation have been programmed producing a machine which is intrinsically modular and easily modifiable. The communication scheme allows processing to be truly distributed.

   The single-card processing element has allowed the immediate development of maintainability to the single replaceable unit level.

References

[1] F. Hiner, "Distributed Processing for Signal Processing using the Building Block Signal Processor", Proceedings of the 1976 International Conference on Parallel Processing (140-144).

A FAMILY OF SPECIAL-PURPOSE PROCESSORS
FOR
DISTRIBUTED DEDICATED COMPUTER SYSTEMS[*]

Maniel Vineberg
Naval Ocean Systems Center

I. SUMMARY

A distributed dedicated computer system, used to integrate and control a variety of complex subsystems, groups functions according to the subsystems which require them [1]. Functional requirements for any subsystem may be partitioned into (1) process control functions and (2) computation and correlation functions. The first category of functions can then be allocated to sequential controlling processors and the second category to dedicated special-purpose processors. The rapid development and programming of dedicated special-purpose processors is therefore of considerable interest.

The Programmable Algorithm Machine (PAM) has been proposed [2] as a dedicated special-purpose processor. The PAM will feature a processor composed of multiple processing elements, separate instruction and operand memories, and instruction pipelining. It is designed to execute efficiently over a class of algorithms that exhibit (1) a high frequency of independent operations and (2) a low frequency of branching. The first property offers operations whose order of execution is arbitrary and which therefore can be allocated efficiently to the PAM processor and may be executed concurrently. The second property offers program statements which are intended to follow one another in sequence and which may therefore be allocated to the PAM processor in large blocks, to take best advantage of processing elements. Arithmetic algorithms, signal processing, array processing, and character string manipulation are examples of applications which exhibit these properties.

---

[*]This research was supported by the Naval Electronics Systems Command under Project No. 720.

The PAM represents a family of machines. Each PAM <u>version</u> (family member) is characterized by the following: a <u>version processor</u>, including a number of processing elements defined in terms of the operators (e.g., "+", "-", etc.) that each accepts and the times required for the execution of the respective operations; a <u>version operator set</u>, comprising the union of operators implemented by the version processor; <u>version parameters</u>, specifying such machine characteristics as memory sizes, cycle times, transmission times, etc. To be valid, a version operator set must be a superset of the <u>PAM primitive operator set</u>, a set of basic operators from which more complex operators are defined.

The PAM will normally be programmed in an algorithmic language (e.g., a subset of ALGOL). The PAM will also be programmable in the PAM Assembly Language (PAL). Each PAL instruction includes a postfix assignment part and a sequencing part (optional). This representation is convenient for exploiting the PAM architecture and as an intermediate representation for the algorithmic language.

The PAM will be supported by a unified software system. A compiler will translate algorithmic language programs into PAL. A parameterized assembler, capable of accepting a PAM version specification and a PAL program, will produce code executable by the specified PAM version. A parameterized simulation will allow translated programs to be executed and verified on a specified version of the PAM. Compilation, assembly, and simulation time are less important in the dedicated environment of the PAM than is execution efficiency. Therefore, the PAM software will be used to optimize PAM application programs and to verify and measure the performance of those programs on various versions of the PAM, in order to produce a PAM version tailored to the application.

Once optimization is complete, the actual PAM hardware version will be assembled. As a dedicated special-purpose processor, the PAM will perform preprogrammed, preoptimized algorithms at the request of a controlling device. Versions of the PAM, tailored to specific applications, will be expected to perform time-critical functions now performed by costly fixed-program hardware.

II. REFERENCES

1. Eddington, D., "SEAMOD: Distributed Combat Direction Systems Partitioning for a Modular Ship - Feasibility Study", NELC/TN 3281, Naval Ocean Systems Center, San Diego, CA, February 1977.

2. Vineberg, M., "The Programmable Algorithm Machine (PAM): Part 1 - Theory, Part 2 - Applications", NELC/TD 478, Naval Ocean Systems Center, San Diego, CA, 4 June 1976.

THE PARALLEL PROCESSING OF LARGE APPLICATIONS

Harvey S. Koch
The Ohio State University

This paper summarizes the results of a research project that has been active for about a year. We have directed our efforts toward the processing requirements of large applications operating in dedicated multiprocessing systems. Formal definitions and proofs of results discussed in this paper can be found in [1].

In our multiprocessing model, each processor is devoted to executing one particular process or a set of processes of an application. At any given time only one process is operating on each query or input request to the system. When processes are being concurrently processed, each of these processes is operating on a different query. As a result, one query is not being parallel processed; several queries are being parallel processed.

We have identified two system processing requirements and have proven that if either or both are violated, interference can occur. This can cause either a temporary or permanent loss of data integrity. Assume that Q and R are two queries, where Q is submitted before R. The <u>influence requirement</u> says: if Q affects R in sequential processing, then Q should affect R the same way during multiprocessing. The <u>antecedence requirement</u> says: R should not affect the processing of Q.

There is a simple method whereby the system designer or compiler can determine which processes should not be parallel processed together; otherwise interference could occur. Stated in simple terms, all processes from the first reference of a shared variable to the last reference of that variable cannot be parallel processed with each other. They can, however, be parallel processed with other processes. Two interesting results we have shown are that mutual exclusion is not a sufficient synchronization method to prevent interference from occurring in our model and that even some disjoint processes cannot be executed in parallel.

A <u>reference set</u> of a shared variable x is the set of all processes included in the sequence Pm,...,Pn where Pm is the first process that references x and Pn is the last process that references x. The <u>concurrency set</u> is the set of all processes not included in the union of all reference sets over all shared variables. The concurrency set of a system represents the set of all processes that can be parallel processed with any other processes of the system. In general, two processes from the same reference set cannot be concurrently processed whereas two processes that are not in the same reference set can be concurrently processed.

Some design guidelines that we have identified are: 1) the concurrency set can be made larger if the reference sets are small and have many processes in common, 2) the reference sets can be made smaller by having references to the same shared variable in processes that are close to each other, and 3) the maximum number of processors needed is the cardinality of the concurrency set plus the number of disjoint reference sets.

Research is currently being conducted to formalize more software engineering principles for applications executed in dedicated multiprocessing systems. We expect that our results will not only yield better response time, more throughput and higher processor utilization, but will also help the system designer measure the amount of multiprocessing his system can attain before implementation. At present, we are also proceeding to identify the conditions under which some of the processes in the same reference set can be multiprocessed without having interference occur. This means that some processes which reference the same shared variable can be processed concurrently.

We believe that conditional critical regions are both a necessary and sufficient method of synchronization in our model. We are in the process of showing that a compiler of the sequence of processes that represents the application can determine without special language constructs: 1) which processes need to be synchronized, and 2) the conditions for synchronization.

REFERENCES

1. Koch, H. S., "Information System Design for Real-Time Multiprocessing Systems", International Journal of Computer and Information Sciences, Vol. 6, No. 3, September 1977.

PROCESSOR INTERCONNECTION NETWORKS, SOME NEW RESULTS

David Stevenson
Gary Feierbach
Institute for Advanced Computation

The mechanism for interprocessor communication in a single instruction stream array processor is a critical component in determining the computer's suitability for various applications. It is desirable to preserve the flexibility and ease of control of a crossbar but without the high cost and component count (proportional to N^2 where N is the number of processors). In particular, the permutation network (PN)[1] still has this flexibility with a total gate count proportional to 2N(logN).

The paper reviews the advantages of a PN and compares them with other possible interconnection networks -- a full crossbar switch, the omega network,[2] the barrel switch, and the boolean cube.[3] It then considers an implementation of a large PN using today's (1977) high speed technology and also presents a new control mechanism.

A systematic study of cost, MTBF with one bit error correction, and network delay time was conducted for the PN. Network costs for a 1024 PE network of word width 21 lie in the range of one million dollars. Such a PN would transmit words by segments in a pipelined fashion. The best times for the full transmission of one word -- 80 bits of information and error coding -- are around 250 ns. The major delay involved transmission to a centralized portion of the PN, assumed to be 40 feet from the most distant PE. A network of width 21 has an acceptable MTBF (>600 hours); the driving factor is that of connectors. Connectors of very high reliability could improve this picture a great deal.

Previous fast or parallel methods of network control[2,4] involve sending the address through the network before the data and having the network actively sort the addresses, setting switches on its way through. One disadvantage of this approach lies in the implementation. The devices in the setting network are not the same as the devices in the data carrying network, so one cannot take full advantage of the cost/integration benefit achievable with today's technology.

If the switch settings are stored in the processors or are computed by the processors, the control of the PN is associated with the processors. Since equivalent networks arise from various rearrangements within the levels of the network, the control of the PN should be invariant with respect to such rearrangements. This goal can be accomplished by setting all switches to straight-through. The resulting path from a processor can be associated with that processor. For a given switch setting, associate the following control bit vector with a path: if at the ith level the path coincides with the switch setting, the ith position of the bit vector is 0; else it is 1.

Algorithms are known for setting central switches of the PN to form smaller arrays of possibly non-contiguous processing elements (which is of interest for electronically reconfiguring the array in the presence of faulty processors). Also presented is a technique for emulating on a smaller array a permutation specified for a larger array. Finally, fast algorithms to calculate the switch settings for each processor's control slice of the PN are presented for the most frequently occurring interprocessor communication patterns: shifting a distance of k, perfect shuffle, and broadcasting.

REFERENCES

1. Waksman, A., "A Permutation Network," JACM 15(1968) 159-163.
2. Lawrie, D.H., "Access and Alignment of Data in an Array Processor," IEEE Trans. Comput. C24(1975) 1145-1155.
3. Sullivan, H., and Bashkow, T.R., "A Large Scale, Homogenous, Fully Distributed Parallel Machine, I," Proc. Symp. Computer Architecture (1977) 105-117.
4. Batcher, K.E., "Sorting Networks and their Application," S.J.C.C. AFIPS 32(1968) 307-314.

A MASSIVELY PARALLEL PROCESSING COMPUTER*

Lai-wo Fung
NASA Goddard Space Flight Center

This paper reports recent activities at NASA Goddard Space Flight Center on an ultra high-speed data processing system especially suitable for processing images or other two-dimensional data. The system, called the MPP *(Massively Parallel Processor)* is a computer with an aggregation of 16,384 processing elements (PE's) arranged as a 128x128 array. Procurements leading to the fabrication of this computer have been initiated. It will be built as an experimental peripheral processor for processing images from earth sensing spacecrafts.

The concept of highly parallel processing arrays dated back to the late fifties and early sixties (1). Recently, an electro-optical implementation of massively parallel array computers was proposed (2). With the advent of high-speed low-power LSI technologies, electrical implementations of such array systems have become viable. The following contains a summary of the MPP architecture and its expected performance.

The MPP Computer is an SIMD (single-instruction-multiple-data stream) system. It is under the control of a central control unit which provides identical control signals and memory addresses to all PE's. Every PE in the processing array has three basic constituents: (A) *Arithmetic, Logic and Routing Unit,* with a four-neighborhood PE-interconnections for routing data (such interconnection scheme is the familiar SOLOMON computer configuration), (B) *Memory Unit* composed of 256 bits of random-access memory, and (C) *Input/Output Unit,* containing one bit of storage with the connections for "left-to-right" 128-bit parallel input-output data transfer. These three components within each PE communicate with each other through a bidirectional data-bus.

Arithmetic is on variable-wordlength integer or floating-point operands. Arithmetic operations are based on a novel design consisting of a binary counter (which

---

*This research is sponsored by the National Research Council.

downshifts the lowest bit to the data-bus), a logic processing component, and a mask component which inhibits the counter and logic processing component under control of a mask register when the system is operating in the Masked Mode. In general, the counter downshift function is for changing the weights of the digits in the sum, product and cross-correlation function during computations. The sum of two operands is formed by using the lowest two stages of the counter as a full adder. With both the counter and mask component, an individual PE computes the product of two unsigned integer operands starting from the lowest bit, using the counter as an accumulator for the carry bits, and the mask register as a means of checking coincidence of a pair of digits. This approach is different from the conventional procedure in which one operand is shifted and a new partial product is formed by adding the shifted operand to the old partial product.

Such a bit-serial arithmetic unit is extremely efficient for arithmetic operations and image processing tasks. Based on a 10 Mc clock rate, performance of the size 128x128 MPP system on integer arithmetic is summarized below (in million operations/second):

Wordlength	8	12	16	20	24	32	64
2's-Complement Adds/Subtracts	5851	4096	3151	2560	2156	1638	836
Unsigned Multiplies	1130	522	301	195	136	78	20

The effective rates of 32-bit (IBM Format) floating-point operations are approximately 160 MFLOPS for adds and 100 MFLOPS for multiplies. Cross-correlation of a 128x128 image and a 20x20 image, both quantized in 6 bits, is computed in 3 milliseconds. The correlation algorithm requires a feedback condition from the P-register in the PE corresponding to one of the four corners of the two-dimensional PE array.

Details of the MPP system and other optional features will be given in a NASA Technical Note under preparation.

REFERENCES
(1) Murtha, J.C., in "Advances in Computers" (F. L. Alt and M. Rubinoff, Eds.), Vol. 7, p.1, Academic Press, New York, 1966.
(2) Schaefer, D. H., and Strong, J. P., Proc. IEEE, 65, 129, (1977).

II
Numerical Algorithms

NUMERICAL PARALLEL ALGORITHMS -- A SURVEY[*]

Ahmed H. Sameh
University of Illinois at Urbana-Champaign

I. INTRODUCTION

Many of the available sequential numerical algorithms make poor use of parallel and vector computers that have appeared recently. Efforts have been going on for some time for developing parallel algorithms for various applications. Some success has been realized judging by the papers published on the subject. Several excellent surveys have also appeared. Miranker [71] summarized the situation as it existed in the late 1960s, recently Heller [77] has given an up-to-date account of parallel algorithms in numerical linear algebra, and Ortega and Voigt [77] gave a detailed account of available algorithms for solving partial differential equations on vector computers. Much work remains to be done. For example, we are still far from obtaining a collection of such high quality algorithms as those available for sequential computers as in Wilkinson and Reinsch [71], the EISPACK package (Smith, et al [74]), or LINPACK package which is still under development. Great efforts have been expended in developing and analyzing such reliable sequential algorithms, and we do not expect the job of developing corresponding parallel algorithms to be any easier.

In this brief survey we present an account of numerical algorithms suitable for parallel computers. We do not include the various algorithms developed for vector computers such as the CDC-STAR and the CRAY-1. To facilitate the analysis and presentation of these algorithms, we adopt the following model of a parallel computer:

---

[*]This work was supported in part by the National Science Foundation under Grant No. MCS75-21758.

(i) an unlimited number of processors are available,
(ii) each processor can evaluate any of the four arithmetic operations and the maximum (or minimum) of two numbers in one time step, and
(iii) no memory or data alignment time penalties are incurred.

While assumptions (i) and (iii) may be unrealistic, the algorithms presented here can be easily modified if only a limited number of processors are available. As for assumption (iii), it is not difficult to add to the arithmetic time required by any algorithm the additional time due to memory conflicts and data alignment on a certain realizable computer. Admittedly, such extra time ("overhead") may overshadow the time required by arithmetic, and comparing the speedup of two algorithms cannot be complete without taking overhead into account. In some recent computers such as the BSP, see Stokes [77], pipelining does mask much of this time.

In section II, we briefly review algorithms for evaluating arithmetic expressions. With the exception of this section, all the algorithms presented here have been originally developed for single-instruction, multiple-data (SIMD) computers (adopting Flynn's notation, Flynn [72]), rather than multiple-instruction, multiple-data (MIMD) computers. In section III, we present a comprehensive summary of direct linear system solvers, and in section IV we discuss the few algorithms available for solving the algebraic standard eigenvalue problem. We do not consider iterative linear system solvers, or algorithms for the numerical handling of differential equations. Such subjects are adequately covered by Heller [77] and Ortega and Voigt [77].

Throughout this paper, we define the speedup of a parallel algorithm as the ratio of the corresponding sequential and parallel times. For example, if τ is the time required by an algorithm using π processors, and σ is the minimum time required by the same algorithm using one processor, then the speedup is given by $\sigma/\tau \geq 1$. We also define the efficiency of the calculation by $\sigma/(\pi \bar{\tau}) \leq 1$. Another important parameter is the redundancy of a parallel algorithm. If the parallel algorithm requires ω arithmetic operations, then its redundancy is defined by $\rho = \omega/\sigma \geq 1$; ($\omega$ is the number of distinct nodes in the computational graph of the parallel algorithm). The larger the redundancy of a parallel algorithm, the larger the probability that the parallel algorithm is not as numerically stable as its sequential counterpart. Several people are investigating the numerical stability of parallel algorithms and we report such available results here.

We use Householder's notation (Householder [64]), so unless otherwise indicated, lower case Greek letters represent scalars; lower case Latin letters, column vectors; capital letters, Greek or Latin, matrices. In what follows, A is a real matrix of order n. We also denote the bandwidth of a matrix by (m + 1). Without loss of generality, we assume that both m and n are powers of 2, and log x denotes $\lceil \log_2 x \rceil$.

II. EVALUATION OF ARITHMETIC EXPRESSIONS

By an arithmetic expression E(n) we mean any well-formed string composed of the four arithmetic operations (+, -, x, /), left and right parentheses, and n distinct atoms which are constants or variables. By distinct, we mean that each atom appears just once in the expression. On a sequential machine such an expression can be evaluated in O(n) time steps. If we have a parallel computer with an unlimited number of processors, then by a simple fan-in argument the lower bound on the evaluation time of E(n) is log n steps. One important arithmetic expression that can be evaluated in a time close to this lower bound is the inner product of two n-vectors. Let x, y be such vectors, then the inner product $x^t y = \sum_{i=1}^{n} \xi_i \eta_i$ can be computed sequentially in (2n - 1) steps, (n multiplications and n - 1 additions). On a parallel computer with n processors, this inner product can be computed in (1 + log n) steps, (one multiplication and log n additions). This results in an approximate speedup and efficiency of (2n/log2n) and (2/log2n), respectively. Note that the number of operations is the same as the sequential algorithm, i.e., no redundancy.

A comparison of the rounding errors in the sequential and parallel algorithms is of interest. Let * denote any of the four arithmetic operations, then a floating-point operation satisfies $f\ell(\xi_1 * \xi_2) = (\xi_1 * \xi_2)(1 + \delta)$ where $|\delta| \leq \varepsilon$ in which ε is the unit roundoff. If β is the radix of the machine and d is the length of the fraction, then $\varepsilon = (1/2) \beta^{1-d}$ for rounded operations, and β^{1-d} for chopping. An error analysis of the sequential algorithm, e.g., see Wilkinson [63] or Stewart [73], shows that if σ_s is the computed inner product, then

$$\sigma_s = \sum_{i=1}^{n} \xi_i \eta_i (1 + \gamma_i) \qquad (2.1)$$

where $|\gamma_1| < 1.06\, n\, \varepsilon$ and $|\gamma_j| < 1.06\,(n - j + 2)\,\varepsilon$ for $j \geq 2$. Here we assume that $n\,\varepsilon < 0.1$ which is not restrictive for computers with reasonable word length. An error analysis of the parallel algorithm has been given by Linz [70], if σ_p is the computed value, then

$$\sigma_p = \sum_{i=1}^{n} \xi_i\, \eta_i\, (1 + \rho_i) \qquad (2.2)$$

where $|\rho_i| < 1.06\,\varepsilon\,\log 2n$ for $i \geq 1$. For values $|\xi_i\, \eta_i|$ that do not vary greatly, the parallel algorithm certainly has a lower absolute error bound than that of the sequential algorithm, and generally yields more accurate results.

A direct application of inner products is in computing matrix-vector and matrix-matrix products. Let A, B be two matrices of order n and x be an n-vector. Then the products $f = Ax$ and $C = AB$ can be obtained in $(1 + \log n)$ steps provided we have n^2 and n^3 processors, respectively. The respective speedups are $O(n^2/\log n)$ and $O(n^3/\log n)$ with the same efficiency as an inner product. Note also that the number of operations is identical to the sequential process in each case, i.e., no redundancy.

Various parallel algorithms have been developed for evaluating more general arithmetic expressions $E(n)$. All these algorithms show that, given enough processors, $E(n)$ can be evaluated in $O(\log n)$ steps resulting in $O(n/\log n)$ speedup over the sequential algorithm. In what follows, we present a brief survey of the fundamental results. Brent [74] has shown that, given $3(n - 1)$ processors, $E(n)$ may be evaluated in time no more than $4\log n$ steps with $O(n)$ operations, i.e., redundancy $\rho = O(1)$. It was also indicated, via Miller's software package for automatic roundoff error analysis, e.g., see Miller [75], that the algorithm is not stable in the presence of division. Muller and Preparata [76] reduced the time to $2.88\log n + 1$ steps at the cost of increasing the processors and operations to $O(n^{1.44})$ yielding a redundancy $\rho = O(n^{0.44})$. For expressions $E(n)$ that do not contain division, some savings can be realized. Brent [73] showed that given only $(n - 1)$ processors, an algorithm requiring no more than $4\log n$ steps and $O(n)$ operations is numerically stable. Muller and Preparata [76] reduced the time to $2.08\log n$ for such expression but again at the cost of increasing the processors and operations to $O(n^{1.817})$

resulting in an even higher redundancy of $O(n^{0.817})$. This leads us to believe that their algorithm is likely to be less stable than Brent's. An error analysis of the algorithms in Muller and Preparata [76] is not yet available.

Brent [74] also showed that if any computation can be completed in τ time steps with ω operations and sufficiently many processors π, then for $\hat{\pi} < \pi$ processors it can be completed in time $\hat{\tau} \leq \tau + (\omega - \tau)/\hat{\pi}$. Thus, using $\hat{\pi}$ processors $E(n)$ can be evaluated in time $4\log n + 10(n-1)/\hat{\pi}$. If $E(n)$ does not contain division the time reduces to only $4\log n + 2(n-1)/\hat{\pi}$. For small number of processors $\hat{\pi}$, Winograd [75] has improved on Brent's results: $(3n/2\hat{\pi}) + O(\log^2 n)$ for expressions without division, and $(5n/2\hat{\pi}) + O(\log^2 n)$ for general expressions.

Finally, we consider matrix expressions. Muraoka and Kuck [73] solved the problem of minimizing the time to evaluate the product of a sequence of conformable arrays on a parallel computer. Kuck and Maruyama [75] showed that, given enough processors, any matrix expression including addition, multiplication, and matrix inversion requires $\alpha \log n + O(1)$ steps where $\alpha = 3\tau_m + 2\tau_a + \tau_i$ in which τ_m, τ_a and τ_i denote time for matrix multiplication, addition, and inversion, respectively.

III. DIRECT LINEAR SYSTEM SOLVERS

In this section we discuss direct parallel algorithms for solving linear systems $Ax = f$ where A is a nonsingular matrix of order n. Usually, the first step in solving such systems is to factor the matrix A. The two familiar factorizations are: (i) $PA = LU$, and (ii) $QA = R$. Here P is a permutation matrix, L is lower triangular, U and R are upper triangular, and Q is an orthogonal matrix. Once such factorizations are realized, solving the system $Ax = f$ reduces to solving triangular systems of equations. Therefore, we start this section by reviewing the various parallel algorithms for solving triangular systems, followed by algorithms for dense and tridiagonal matrices.

A. Triangular Systems

The problem of solving triangular systems of equations arises in many situations. One important case is the evaluation of linear recurrences of order $m \leq n - 1$

$$\xi_1 = \phi_1$$

$$\xi_i = \phi_i - \sum_{j=k}^{i-1} \lambda_{ij} \xi_j \quad \begin{array}{l} i = 2, 3, \ldots, n \\ k = \max\{1, i - m\} \end{array} \quad (3.1)$$

In matrix notation, (3.1) may be written as $x = f - \tilde{L}x$, where $x^t = (\xi_1, \xi_2, \ldots, \xi_n)$, $f^t = (\phi_1, \phi_2, \ldots, \phi_n)$, and $\tilde{L} = [\lambda_{ij}]$ is strictly lower triangular. Denoting $(I + \tilde{L})$ by L we obtain the unit lower triangular system of equations

$$Lx = f \quad (3.2)$$

where L is of bandwidth $m + 1$, i.e., $\lambda_{ij} = 0$ for $i - j > m$.

The sequential algorithm (3.1) requires $O(mn)$ steps. If we have m processors, a parallel scheme (column sweep algorithm, Kuck [76]) can be easily developed requiring $2(n - 1)$ steps. It also has the same stability properties as the sequential algorithm. If $\tilde{x}$ is the computed solution then $(L + \delta L) \tilde{x} = f$ where $||\delta L|| \leq m ||L|| \varepsilon$, Wilkinson [63], where $||\cdot||$ denotes the ∞-norm and ε is the unit roundoff error. The column sweep algorithm has a speedup of approximately m with efficiency $O(1)$ and no redundancy ($\rho = 1$). Heller [74], Orcutt [74], Borodin and Munro [75], and Chen and Kuck [75] presented three different algorithms for solving (3.2) for $m = n - 1$ in $O(\log^2 n)$ time steps using $O(n^3)$ processors. The resulting speedup over the sequential algorithm is $O(n^2/\log^2 n)$ with efficiency proportional to $1/(n \log^2 n)$. Among the above algorithms, the one given by Chen and Kuck [75] requires the lowest number of processors, $(n^3/68) + O(n^2)$ and $(1/2) \log^2 n + (3/2) \log n$ time steps. We sketch briefly this algorithm as described in Sameh and Brent [77]. The inverse of L can be written as $L^{-1} = M_{n-1} M_{n-2} \ldots M_2 M_1$, where each M_i is an elementary lower triangular matrix given by $M_i = [e_1, e_2, \ldots, e_{i-1}, \ell, e_{i+1}, \ldots, e_n]$ with $\ell = (0, \ldots, 0, 1, -\lambda_{i+1,i},$

$-\lambda_{i+2,i}, \ldots, -\lambda_{n,i})^t$. Thus the solution can be expressed as

$$x = M_{n-1} M_{n-2} \ldots M_2 M_1 f \qquad (3.3)$$

This product can be evaluated in parallel in log n stages, obtaining the above time and processor bounds. An error analysis of this algorithm, Sameh and Brent [77], shows that if $\tilde{x}$ is the computed solution then $(L + \delta L) \tilde{x} = f$ where $||\delta L|| \leq \varepsilon \alpha(n) \kappa^2(L) ||L||$, in which $\kappa(L)$ is the condition number of L and $\alpha(n) = O(n^2 \log n)$. This bound on δL can be large compared to the sequential algorithm. Many experiments show that both the sequential and this parallel algorithm yield identical results. Certain ill-conditioned problems, however, show that the sequential algorithm indeed yields more accurate results. Consider problem (3.2) with,

$$L = \begin{bmatrix} 1 & & & \\ 1.07 & 1 & & \\ 1.02 & 1.10 & 1 & \\ \alpha & \beta & \gamma & 1 \end{bmatrix}, \text{ and } f = \begin{bmatrix} 1 \\ 2.07 \\ 3.12 \\ -4.00017 \end{bmatrix}$$

where $\alpha = 0.993 \times 10^{14}$, $\beta = -(\alpha + 4.0)$, $\gamma = -0.34 \times 10^{-3}$. The sequential algorithm (forward substitution) yielded the exact solution, $\xi_1 = \xi_2 = \xi_3 = 1.0$ and $\xi_4 = 0.00017$, on an IBM 360 with long precision (machine epsilon $\simeq 2.22 \times 10^{-16}$). The parallel algorithm also obtained the correct result for the first three components of the solution, but gave the value -0.0039 for ξ_4 (not even the correct sign). Using a software package developed by Miller [75] for automatic roundoff analysis, M. Heller [76] and Larson [76] independently observed such instability of the parallel algorithm. Finally, we note that the parallel algorithm has a redundancy $\rho = O(n)$.

Orcutt [74], and Chen and Kuck [75] also showed that if $m \leq (n/2) - 1$, then system (3.2) may be solved in $O(\log m \log n)$ steps using $O(m^2 n)$ processors. The algorithm in Chen and Kuck [75] is described in matrix notation in Sameh and Brent [77] as follows. Let L be partitioned as a block bidiagonal matrix with diagonal submatrices L_i, $i = 1, 2, \ldots, n/m$, and subdiagonal matrices

R_j, $j = 1, 2, \ldots, (n/m) - 1$, where L_j and R_j are lower and upper triangular, respectively. Premultiplying both sides of (3.2) by $D = \text{diag } (L_i^{-1})$ we obtain the system $L^{(0)} x = f^{(0)}$ where $L^{(0)}$ is block bidiagonal with identities of order m on the diagonal and matrices $G_j^{(0)} = L_{j+1}^{-1} R_j$ on the subdiagonal, and $f^{(0)} = Df$. Note that we do not invert the L_j's, but obtain $f^{(0)}$ and $G_i^{(0)}$ by solving triangular systems using the previous parallel algorithm. We repeat the process by multiplying both sides of $L^{(0)} x = f^{(0)}$ by $D^{(0)} = \text{diag}$ $(L_i^{(0)})^{-1}$ where,

$$L_i^{(0)^{-1}} = \begin{bmatrix} I_m & 0 \\ -G_{2i-1}^{(0)} & I_m \end{bmatrix}.$$

Now $L^{(1)} = D^{(0)} L^{(0)}$ and $f^{(1)} = D^{(0)} f^{(0)}$ are obtained by simple multiplication. Eventually, $L^{(\log(n/m))} = I_n$ and $f^{(\log(n/m))} = x$. For $m \ll n$, such an algorithm yields approximate speedup and efficiency of $(2mn/\log 4m \log n)$ and $(4/m \log 4m \log n)$, respectively. The required number of operations is $O(m^2 n \log(n/2m))$ resulting in a redundancy $\rho = O(m \log(n/2m))$. Furthermore, for a given m the upper bound on the absolute error $||\tilde{x} - x||$ grows exponentially with n, Chen, Kuck, and Sameh [76]. Numerical experiments again indicate that except for few ill-conditioned cases the results obtained by this algorithm are identical to those of the sequential algorithm.

Chen [75], Chen and Sameh [75], and Hyafil and Kung [75] have discussed parallel algorithms for solving (3.2), with $m = n - 1$, when only a limited number of processors are used. Chen [75], and Chen, Kuck, and Sameh [76] have also described parallel algorithms for the banded case with a limited number of processors $2m \leq \hat{\pi} \leq n$, showing that the time reduces to $O(m^2 n/\hat{\pi})$. For m, $\hat{\pi} \ll n$, the speedup is approximately $(\hat{\pi}/m)$ with efficiency $(1/m)$. The required number of operations is $O(m^2 n)$ yielding a redundancy $\rho = O(m)$. Moreover, it was shown that if $\hat{\pi} \leq m \log n$ the bound on the absolute error is proportional to a low degree polynomial in n.

If these triangular systems are Toeplitz, i.e., $\lambda_{ij} = \alpha_{i-j}$, then savings in the number of processors are realized. Chen [75] has shown that the time remains the same for the dense and banded cases, but the numbers of processors reduce to $O(n^2)$ and $O(mn)$, respectively, instead of $O(n^3)$ and $O(m^2 n)$. For the banded case with limited number of processors $2m \leq \hat{\pi} \leq n$, the time reduces to $O(mn/\hat{\pi})$ instead of $O(m^2 n/\hat{\pi})$.

We present our own interpretation of the algorithm for the dense Toeplitz case. First, we observe that if L is Toeplitz, then L^{-1} is Toeplitz, Lafon [75]. Hence, if we determine the first column of L^{-1}, the whole inverse is also determined. Now the algorithm presented in Borodin and Munro [75] can be applied efficiently. Consider a leading principal submatrix

$$\begin{bmatrix} L_1 & 0 \\ G_1 & L_1 \end{bmatrix}$$

of L, where L_1, G_1 are of order q and $L_1^{-1} e_1$ is known. The inverse of this principal submatrix is given by

$$\begin{bmatrix} L_1^{-1} & 0 \\ -L_1^{-1} G_1 L_1^{-1} & L_1^{-1} \end{bmatrix},$$

and can be computed in $2(1 + \log q)$ steps using q^2 processors. Starting with a leading principal submatrix of order 4, where

$$L_1^{-1} = \begin{bmatrix} 1 & 0 \\ -\alpha_1 & 1 \end{bmatrix},$$

and doubling the size every stage, we obtain the inverse of the leading principal submatrix M of order n/2 in
$\sum_{q=2}^{n/4} 2(1 + \log q) = (\log^2 n - \log n - 2)$ steps with $n^2/16$ processors. Thus the solution of (3.2), or

$$\begin{bmatrix} M & 0 \\ N & M \end{bmatrix} \begin{bmatrix} x_1 \\ x_2 \end{bmatrix} = \begin{bmatrix} f_1 \\ f_2 \end{bmatrix},$$

is given by $x_1 = M^{-1} f_1$, $x_2 = M^{-1} f_2 - M^{-1} N M^{-1} f_1$. Both x_1 and x_2 can be computed in $(1 + 3\log n)$ using no more than $n^2/4$ processors. This yields a total of $(\log^2 n + 2\log n - 1)$ steps with only $n^2/4$ processors. A scheme for the banded case can be similarly developed. It is of interest to note that evaluating a polynomial $p_{n-1}(x)$, of degree $(n - 1)$, at a given point $x = \xi$ reduces to obtaining the last element of the solution vector of a Toeplitz banded unit lower triangular with m = 1. In this case the time is only $1 + 2\log n$ steps with $(n/2)$ processors.

B. Dense Systems

We consider first the most popular factorization, i.e., LU-factorization via Gaussian elimination, e.g., see Stewart [73]. Without pivoting, such an algorithm requires $3(n - 1)$ steps with $(n - 1)^2$ processors. The method fails, however, if any leading principal minor is zero. A pivoting strategy is necessary for the completion of the factorization. Observing that, for many models of parallel computers the maximum of n elements can be determined in log n steps using n/2 processors, then the factors L and U in Gaussian-elimination with partial pivoting, can be obtained in $O(n \log n)$ steps with $(n - 1)^2$ processors. This results in a speedup of $O(n^2/\log n)$ and efficiency proportional to $1/\log n$. Note also that the sequential and parallel algorithms have the same operation count, and stability properties.

Several methods are available for orthogonal factorization of A, e.g., see Stewart [73] or Wilkinson [65]. It is not difficult to show that using $O(n^2)$ processors, direct implementation of Householder's reduction and the Gram-Schmidt algorithm require $O(n \log n)$ steps. Givens' reduction, however, can be modified to produce a parallel algorithm of $O(n)$ steps with $O(n^2)$ processors, see Sameh and Kuck [76]. This yields a speedup of $O(n^2)$ with efficiency $O(1)$. Again we have no redundancy, $\rho = 1$, and the algorithm is as numerically stable as its sequential counterpart. Hence, Givens' reduction is the cheaper algorithm to use unless Gaussian elimination without pivoting does not fail. We describe the algorithm briefly. In the sequential algorithm the orthogonal matrix Q, in QA = R, is formed as the product of plane rotations each annihilating an element below the diagonal of A. In the parallel scheme, Q is the product of orthogonal matrices Q_j each being the direct sum of independent rotations. Thus, each Q_j can annihilate more than one element below the diagonal. There are several annihilation schemes. One such scheme achieves the reduction in (2n - 3) transformations, i.e., $Q = Q_{2n-3} \cdots Q_2 Q_1$. Each Q_j is a block diagonal matrix with 2×2 matrices (rotations) on the diagonal. These rotations are chosen such that Q_j does not destroy any zeros in $(Q_{j-1} \cdots Q_2 Q_1 A)$. In the figure below, we illustrate the pattern of element annihilation for n = 10. By an integer k we denote all the elements annihilated by Q_k.

*	*	*	*	*	*	*	*	*	*
9	*	*	*	*	*	*	*	*	*
8	10	*	*	*	*	*	*	*	*
7	9	11	*	*	*	*	*	*	*
6	8	10	12	*	*	*	*	*	*
5	7	9	11	13	*	*	*	*	*
4	6	8	10	12	14	*	*	*	*
3	5	7	9	11	13	15	*	*	*
2	4	6	8	10	12	14	16	*	*
1	3	5	7	9	11	13	15	17	*

Csanky [76] observed that the method of Leverrier (see Faddeev and Faddeeva [63] or Wilkinson [65]), for computing the characteristic polynomial of a matrix may be used to solve the system Ax = f. By the Cayley-Hamilton theorem we have

$$(-1)^n [A^n - \gamma_1 A^{n-1} - \gamma_2 A^{n-2} \cdots - \gamma_{n-1} A - \gamma_n I] = 0,$$

hence, $A^{-1} = (1/\gamma_n)[A^{n-1} - \gamma_1 A^{n-2} - \gamma_2 A^{n-2} - \cdots - \gamma_{n-2} A - \gamma_{n-1} I]$. The coefficients γ_i are given by the lower triangular system $\sigma_1 = \gamma_1$, and $\sigma_k = k \gamma_k + \sum_{i=1}^{k-1} \gamma_i \sigma_{k-i}$ (k = 2, 3, ..., n) where $\sigma_k = tr(A^k)$. Simultaneously, computing the various powers of A, and hence the σ_k's, and solving the lower triangular system (Newton's identities), we obtain the coefficients γ_i in $O(\log^2 n)$ steps. Csanky [76] required $n^4/2$

processors. Preparata and Sarwate [77] reduced the processors required to less than $2n^{3.31}/\log^2 n$ by observing all the powers of A need not be computed, since only the diagonal elements of A^k are required, $k \leq n$, and by using Strassen's method for matrix multiplication. Needless to say, the method is numerically unstable (see Wilkinson [65]).

C. Tridiagonal Systems

Stone [73] was the first to develop a parallel tridiagonal linear system solver that requires $O(\log n)$ steps using $O(n)$ processors. The algorithm is a parallel version of the sequential LDU-factorization of a tridiagonal matrix without pivoting, e.g., see Forsythe and Moler [67]. The parallel algorithm is usually referred to as "recursive doubling". An interpretation of Stone's algorithm follows. Let $A = [\gamma_i, \alpha_i, \beta_i]$ be a nonsingular tridiagonal matrix where α_i, $i = 1, 2, \ldots, n$, are the diagonal elements, and β_j, γ_{j+1}, $j = 1, 2, \ldots, n-1$, are the off-diagonal elements. Let D be a diagonal matrix with elements δ_i, L and U be unit lower and upper bidiagonal matrices with off-diagonal elements λ_{j+1} and μ_j, $j = 1, 2, \ldots, n-1$, respectively. From the relation $A = LDU$ we obtain the nonlinear recurrence relation $\delta_i + (\beta_{i-1} \gamma_i / \delta_{i-1}) = \alpha_i$, $i = 2, 3, \ldots, n$, with $\delta_1 = \alpha_1$. Multiplying both sides by $\tau_{i-1} = \delta_1 \delta_2 \cdots \delta_{i-1}$, we obtain the linear recurrence $\tau_i - \alpha_i \tau_{i-1} + \beta_{i-1} \gamma_i \tau_{i-2} = 0$, $i = 2, 3, \ldots, n$, with $\tau_0 = 1$ and $\tau_1 = \alpha_1$. Using the algorithm described in section A for solving banded triangular systems with $m = 2$, τ_i ($i = 2, 3, \ldots, n$) can be evaluated in $2\log n + O(1)$ steps using $(2n - 4)$ processors. Note here that we have taken advantage of the fact that the right-hand side is the first column of the identity of order $(n + 1)$, see Sameh and Kuck [77]. Thus, $\delta_i = \tau_i / \tau_{i-1}$ ($i = 2, 3, \ldots, n$), $\mu_j = \beta_j / \delta_j$, $\lambda_{j+1} = \gamma_{j+1} / \delta_j$ ($j = 1, 2, \ldots, n - 1$), and the decomposition is completely determined. Now we solve the systems, $Ly = f$, $Dz = y$, and $Ux = z$ using the appropriate algorithm in section A, in $4\log n + O(1)$ steps using no more than n processors. Hence, the total time for solving $Ax = f$ is $6\log n + O(1)$ steps using $2n - 4$ processors. Since the sequential algorithm is $O(n)$, we have a speedup of $O(n/\log n)$ with efficiency proportional to $(1/\log n)$. The number of operations required by this parallel algorithm is $O(n \log n)$, yielding a redundancy of $O(\log n)$. Clearly, the algorithm fails if any leading principal submatrix of A is singular. Observe that if pivoting is necessary for completing the factorization, the parallel algorithm reduces to its sequential counterpart, requiring time $O(n)$. Even if pivoting is not necessary, this parallel algorithm suffers from the possibility of over- or underflow; for example, if $\delta_j = j$ then $\tau_n = n!$. Furthermore, the bound on the absolute error in evaluating the second-order linear recurrence in τ_j grows exponentially with n, see Sameh and Kuck [77]. The stability of Stone's algorithm is also discussed by Dubois and Rodrigue [77].

The method of cyclic odd-even reduction, originally developed by Gene Golub, e.g., see Buzbee, Golub, and Nielson [70], proved to be a viable parallel scheme for solving tridiagonal systems of equations. Jordan [74], Stone [75], Lambiotte and Voigt [75], and Heller [76] (the scalar version), have all discussed such an algorithm. This parallel algorithm requires $O(\log n)$ steps with operation count of only $O(n)$, i.e., with redundancy $\rho = O(1)$. Stone [75] gave a comprehensive evaluation of the arithmetic complexity of cyclic odd-even reduction compared to "recursive doubling" (Stone [73]) and Buneman's algorithm (Buneman [69]) for solving tridiagonal systems. Jordan [74], Stone [75], and Heller [76] have also showed that if A is diagonally dominant, the cyclic reduction algorithm can be used as an iterative algorithm. For in this case the magnitudes of the off-diagonal elements relative to those of the main diagonal decrease quadratically, allowing the process to terminate early with an approximation to the solution. However, since cyclic reduction is equivalent to an LU-factorization without pivoting of PAP^t where P is a permutation matrix, the algorithm fails if any leading principal minor of PAP^t is zero.

Sameh and Kuck [76] proposed a parallel algorithm to circumvent the shortcomings of LDU-factorization without pivoting and cyclic odd-even reduction for general tridiagonal systems. The algorithm is based on the orthogonal factorization, $QA = R$, of a tridiagonal matrix, e.g., see Reinsch [71]. Here Q is an orthogonal matrix and R is upper triangular with bandwidth 3. The nonlinear recurrence resulting from the orthogonal decomposition is reduced to two linear recurrences, of order 2 and 1, the solution of which determines the elements of Q and R. Once Q and R are determined, the solution x is obtained by solving Rx = Qf. The algorithm requires $9\log n + O(1)$ steps using less than $3n$ processors. While the time is larger than LDU-factorization without pivoting, it does not fail for any nonsingular matrix. It shares, however, the remaining two disadvantages of Stone's algorithm, namely, the possibility of over- and underflow and the exponential growth of the error bound. To overcome these difficulties the problem is decomposed, under the restriction that $\beta_i \gamma_{i+1} > 0$, so that the QR-factorization may be applied to submatrices of order no larger than $\log n$. This reduces the chance of over- or underflow and the error bound of the solution of second-order linear recurrences no longer grows exponentially, but only proportional to a low degree polynomial in n. This is achieved, however, at an additional cost in time and processors. The time becomes $O[(\log \log n)(\log n)]$ instead of only $O(\log n)$, and the number of processors is $5n$ instead of $3n$. The number of operations remains $O(n \log n)$, i.e., a redundancy of $O(\log n)$.

Bukhberger and Emelyaneko [73] presented a sequential algorithm based on Cramer's rule for obtaining the inverse of a general nonsingular tridiagonal matrix. The algorithm can be readily adapted for parallel computing. It solves unit lower triangular systems of bandwidth no more than 3 to obtain three vectors: $u = (\mu_1, \mu_2, \ldots, \mu_n)^t$, $v = (\nu_0, \nu_1, \ldots, \nu_n)^t$, and $w = (\omega_1, \omega_2, \ldots, \omega_n)^t$ such that the elements θ_{ij} of A^{-1} can be computed by $\theta_{ij} = \mu_i \nu_j \omega_j$. The vectors u, v, and w can be obtained in $3\log n + O(1)$ steps using no more than $4n$ processors. This algorithm is quite fast if only selected components of the solution vectors corresponding to several right-hand sides are desired. Swarztrauber [76] also presented an algorithm for solving tridiagonal systems based on Cramer's rule that requires only $O(n)$ operations. The numerical stability of the above two algorithms remains to be investigated.

All the algorithms in this section can be modified when the tridiagonal matrix is Toeplitz. An efficient and numerically stable algorithm, not discussed above, that does not fail for any nonsingular symmetric-Toeplitz tridiagonal system is the following. Let $A = [\beta, \alpha, \beta]$, then we can write it as $A = \alpha I + \beta(J + J^t)$, where $J = [e_2, e_3, \ldots, e_n, 0]$. The spectral decomposition $(J + J^t) = Q \Lambda Q^t$ is known, $\Lambda = \text{diag}(\lambda_k)$ with $\lambda_k = 2 \cos[k\pi/(n+1)]$, $(k = 1, 2, \ldots, n)$, and

$Q = [q_1 q_2, \ldots, q_n]$ is orthogonal with $q_k^t = [2/(n+1)]^{1/2}$ [sin $(k\pi/n + 1)$, sin $(2k\pi/n + 1), \ldots,$ sin $(nk \pi/n + 1)$]. Hence $A = Q \Omega Q^t$ where $\Omega = \alpha I + \beta \Lambda$. Since A is nonsingular Ω^{-1} exists, and the solution of $Ax = f$ is given by $x = Q \Omega^{-1} Q^t f$. Using a parallel algorithm for the fast Fourier transform, e.g., see Pease [68], $Q^t f$ may be obtained in $3\log n + O(1)$ steps with n processors (Sameh, Chen, and Kuck [76]). Also, with n processors $\Omega^{-1} (Q^t f)$ requires one step, and $Q^t (\Omega^{-1} Q^t f)$ requires another $3\log n + O(1)$ steps. Thus, the total time is $6\log n + O(1)$ using only n processors, the same time as LDU-factorization (without pivoting) using only half the number of processors.

IV. ALGORITHMS FOR THE EIGENVALUE PROBLEM $Ax = \lambda x$

Fewer parallel algorithms have been developed for handling this problem than for solving systems of linear equations. Those available are parallel versions of Jacobi and Jacobi-like algorithms (Sameh [71]), a multisectioning method (Kuck and Sameh [71]) and the QR-algorithm (Sameh and Kuck [77]) for obtaining selected or all eigenvalues of a symmetric tridiagonal matrix.

We discuss first Jacobi's algorithm for finding all the eigenvalues and eigenvectors of a real symmetric matrix. The sequential algorithm is described in detail in Wilkinson [65] and by Rutishauser, Contribution II/1 in Wilkinson and Reinsch [71]. A real symmetric matrix, A, can be reduced to the diagonal form by a sequence of plane rotations. Theoretically, we need an infinite number of plane rotations; in practice, however, the process is terminated when the off-diagonal elements become "negligible" compared to the main diagonal. In the classical Jacobi algorithm, each rotation $R_k = R(p, q, \alpha_{pq}^{(k)})$ eliminates the off-diagonal element in the position (p, q) and its symmetric counterpart. It is possible though to eliminate more than one element simultaneously. For example, for a matrix of order 4, an orthogonal transformation Q may contain two independent rotations

$$Q = \begin{bmatrix} c_1 & 0 & s_1 & 0 \\ 0 & c_2 & 0 & s_2 \\ -s_1 & 0 & c_1 & 0 \\ 0 & -s_2 & 0 & c_2 \end{bmatrix}$$

where $c_i \equiv \cos \alpha_i$ and $s_i \equiv \sin \alpha_i$, and α_1, α_2 are determined simultaneously such that the elements in positions (1, 3), (2, 4), and (3, 1), (4, 2) of $Q^t A Q$ are annihilated. For a matrix of order n, the maximum number of elements that can be annihilated simultaneously is (n/2). The task of choosing the sequence of transformations Q_k is simpler than that in Givens' reduction, discussed in section B, since we need not be concerned about destroying zeros that we previously introduced. However, for the sake of avoiding redundancy of the parallel computation, we annihilate each of the $(n^2 - n)/2$ pairs of off-diagonal elements only once during one sweep. Here, a sweep consists of (2w - 1) transformations, with $w = \lfloor (n + 1)/2 \rfloor$. Several annihilation regimes are possible. In the figure below we illustrate one such pattern of annihilation for a matrix of order 8, in one sweep.

```
  *  3  6  2  5  1  4  7
     *  2  5  1  4  7  6
        *  1  4  7  3  5
           *  7  3  6  4
              *  6  2  3
                 *  5  2
                    *  1
                       *
```

By an integer j we denote all the elements annihilated by the j-th transformation, $j = 1, 2, \ldots, 2w - 1$. If after ℓ sweeps (say) the matrix becomes practically diagonal, then the diagonal elements are taken as the eigenvalues and the product of the individual transformations Q_k is taken as the eigenvectors of A. Given $O(n^2)$ processors, one sweep requires $O(n)$ steps yielding a speedup over the sequential algorithm of $O(n^2)$ with efficiency $O(1)$, and no redundancy.

A related algorithm, norm reducing Jacobi-type method, has been developed by Eberlein [62] for handling any matrix,

complex in general. As before, let A be a real matrix of order n, then there exists a matrix $U = \Pi_\ell U_\ell(j, k)$ generated from a sequence of two-dimensional transformations $U_\ell(j, k)$, where (j, k) is the pivot pair, such that $A_L = U^{-1} AU$ is arbitrarily close to being normal, i.e., $(A_L A_L^t - A_L^t A_L)$ is arbitrarily small. At each stage of the iteration, based on the elements of the j-th and k-th rows and columns, the parameters of U_ℓ are chosen such that $||A_\ell||_F^2 - ||U_\ell^{-1} A_\ell U_\ell||_F^2$
$\geq [\frac{1}{3n(n-1)}] \, ||A_\ell A_\ell^t - A_\ell^t A_\ell||_F^2$ where $||A||_F$ denotes the Frobenius norm of A. The above norm-reducing procedure has been modified for parallel computation, Sameh [71]. The transformations U_ℓ are changed to n-dimensional with their parameters based on all the elements of the matrix A_ℓ. This results in a larger decrement in the Frobenius norm of A_ℓ,

$$||A_\ell||_F^2 - ||U_\ell^{-1} A_\ell U_\ell||_F^2 \geq (\frac{1}{4n}) \, ||A_\ell A_\ell^t - A_\ell^t A_\ell||_F^2$$

Since A is real, its eigenvalues are either real or complex conjugate. Consequently, we obtain a practically normal matrix A_L with pivotal elements $\alpha_{pq}^{(L)}$ such that either $\alpha_{pq}^{(L)} = \alpha_{qp}^{(L)}$; or $\alpha_{pq}^{(L)} = -\alpha_{qp}^{(L)}$ and $\alpha_{pp}^{(L)} = \alpha_{qq}^{(L)}$ to within a given tolerance. The matrix A_L can then be reduced to the diagonal form using the parallel Jacobi scheme described earlier, except for the case when $\alpha_{pq}^{(L)} = -\alpha_{qp}^{(L)}$ where the Jacobi rotation is replaced by $\frac{1}{\sqrt{2}} \begin{bmatrix} 1 & i \\ i & 1 \end{bmatrix}$, in which $i = \sqrt{-1}$.

Other "transformation" methods reduce the matrix under consideration to a condensed form via similarity transformations. The reduced matrix is either tridiagonal or upper Hessenberg (say) depending on whether the matrix is symmetric or not, see Wilkinson [65] for more details. Given $O(n^2)$ processors, it is not difficult to show that such methods require $O(n \log n)$ steps to achieve such reduction. Since the sequential algorithms require $O(n^3)$ steps, we obtain speedups of $O(n^2/\log n)$ with efficiencies proportional to $1/\log n$ and no redundancies. A result due to Kung [76], regarding nonlinear recurrence relations, indicates that we cannot achieve speedups higher than $O(n^2/\log n)$. Recent results by Parker [77], however, may show that the situation is not without hope.

If the reduced matrix is symmetric tridiagonal and we wish to obtain all the eigenvalues, then we may use the QR-algorithm, e.g., see Wilkinson and Reinsch [71], Contributions II/3, 4. A parallel version of the algorithm in Contribution II/3, TQL1, has essentially been given by Sameh and Kuck [77] and practically described in section C. In this algorithm we explicitly subtract the origin shift from the diagonal elements of the tridiagonal matrix. If the elements vary greatly in their orders of magnitudes, the algorithm yields poor approximations to the eigenvalues of smaller magnitudes. This is remedied in Contribution II/4, IMTQL1. In attempting to produce a parallel version of it, however, one is faced with nonlinear recurrences and the time for one iteration remains $O(n)$, rather than $O(\log n)$ as in the parallel version of TQL1. If only a few eigenvalues are desired, then a generalization of the bisection method, using the Sturm sequence properties, can be most effective on a parallel computer, e.g., see Kuck and Sameh [71], and Huang [74].

V. ACKNOWLEDGMENT

I wish to thank David J. Kuck for various discussions and comments regarding this paper. Special thanks go also to Mrs. Vivian Alsip for a good job in typing this manuscript.

VI. REFERENCES

Borodin, A., and Munro, I. (1975), Computational Complexity of Algebraic and Numeric Problems, American Elsevier.

Brent, R. (1973), "The Parallel Evaluation of Arithmetic Expressions in Logarithmic Time," pp. 83-102 in Complexity of Sequential and Parallel Numerical Algorithms, J. F. Traub, ed., Academic Press.

Brent, R. (1974), "The Parallel Evaluation of General Arithmetic Expressions," J. of the ACM, Vol. 21, pp. 201-206.

Bukhberger, B., and Emelyneko, G. (1973), "Methods of Inverting Tridiagonal Matrices," USSR Computational Math. & Math. Physics, Vol. 13, pp. 10-20.

Buzbee, B., Golub, G., and Nielson, C. (1970), "On Direct Methods for Solving Poisson's Equations," SIAM J. on Numer. Anal., Vol. 7, pp. 627-656.

Chen, S. (1975), "Speedups of Iterative Programs in Multiprocessing Systems," Ph.D. thesis, Dept. of Computer Science, University of Illinois at Urbana-Champaign.

Chen, S., and Kuck, D. (1975), "Time and Parallel Processor Bounds for Linear Recurrence Systems," IEEE Trans. Comput., Vol. C-24, pp. 701-717.

Chen, S., and Sameh, A. (1975), "On Parallel Triangular System Solvers," Proc. of the Sagamore Comput. Conf., T. Feng, ed., pp. 237-238.

Chen, S., Kuck, D., and Sameh, A. (1976), "Practical Parallel Triangular System Solvers," submitted for publication.

Csanky, L. (1976), "Fast Parallel Matrix Inversion Algorithms," SIAM J. on Computing, Vol. 5, pp. 618-623.

Dubois, P., and Rodrigue, G. (1977), "An Analysis of the Recursive Doubling Algorithm," this proceedings.

Eberlein, P. (1962), "A Jacobi-like Method for the Automatic Computation of Eigenvalues and Eigenvectors of an Arbitrary Matrix," J. of SIAM, Vol. 10, pp. 74-88.

Faddeev, D., and Faddeeva, V. (1963), Computational Methods of Linear Algebra, Freeman.

Flynn, M. (1972), "Some Computer Organizations and Their Effectiveness," IEEE Trans. Comput., Vol. C-21, pp. 948-960.

Forsythe, G., and Moler, C. (1967), Computer Solution of Linear Algebraic Systems, Prentice-Hall.

Heller, D. (1974), "On the Efficient Computation of Recurrence Relations," ICASE technical report.

Heller, D. (1976), "Some Aspects of the Cyclic Reduction Algorithm for Block Tridiagonal Linear Systems," SIAM J. on Numer. Anal., Vol. 13, pp. 484-496.

Heller, D. (1977), "A Survey of Parallel Algorithms in Numerical Linear Algebra," to appear in SIAM Review.

Heller, M. (1976), "Experiments on the Stability of Parallel Matrix Methods," Computer Science Dept., Technical Rpt. No. 212, The Pennsylvania State University.

Householder, A. (1964), The Theory of Matrices in Numerical Analysis, Blaisdell Publ. Co.

Huang, H. (1974), "A Parallel Algorithm for Symmetric Tridiagonal Eigenvalue Problems," Center for Advanced

Computation, Doc. No. 109, University of Illinois at Urbana-Champaign.

Hyafil, L., and Kung, H. (1975), "Parallel Algorithms for Solving Triangular Linear Systems with Small Parallelism," Dept. of Computer Science, Carnegie-Mellon University.

Jordan, T. (1974), "A New Parallel Algorithm for Diagonally Dominant Tridiagonal Matrices," Los Alamos Scientific Lab., Los Alamos, NM.

Kuck, D., and Sameh, A. (1971), "Parallel Computation of Eigenvalues of Real Matrices," IFIP Congress 1971, North-Holland, Vol. 2, 1972, pp. 1266-1272.

Kuck, D., and Maruyama, K. (1975), "Time Bounds on the Parallel Evaluation of Arithmetic Expressions," SIAM J. on Computing, Vol. 4, pp. 147-162.

Kuck, D. J. (1976), "Parallel Processing of Ordinary Programs," Advances in Computers, Vol. 15, pp. 119-179.

Kung, H. (1976), "New Algorithms and Lower Bounds for the Parallel Evaluation of Certain Rational Expressions and Recurrences," J. of the ACM, Vol. 23, pp. 252-261.

Lambiotte, J., and Voigt, R. (1977), "The Solution of Tridiagonal Linear Systems on the CDC STAR-100 Computer," ACM Trans. on Math. Software, Vol. 1, pp. 308-329.

Lafon, J. (1975), "Base tensorielle des matrices de Hankel (on de Toeplitz) applications," Numer. Math., Vol. 23, pp. 349-361.

Larson, J. (1976), Private communication.

Linz, P. (1970), "Accurate Floating-Point Summation," Comm. of the ACM, Vol. 13, pp. 361-362.

Miller, W. (1975), "Software for the Roundoff Analysis," ACM Trans. on Math. Software, Vol. 1, pp. 108-128.

Miranker, W. (1971), "A Survey of Parallelism in Numerical Analysis," SIAM Review, Vol. 13, pp. 524-547.

Muller, D., and Preparata, F. (1976), "Restructuring of Arithmetic Expressions for Parallel Evaluation," J. of the ACM, Vol. 23, pp. 534-543.

Muraoka, Y., and Kuck, D. (1973), "On the Time Required for a Sequence of Matrix Products," Comm. of the ACM, Vol. 16, pp. 22-26.

Orcutt, S. (1974), "Parallel Solution Methods for Triangular Linear Systems of Equations," Technical report No. 77, Stanford Electronics Labs., Stanford, CA.

Ortega, J., and Voigt, R. (1977), "Solution of Partial Differential Equations on Vector Computers," to appear in the Proc. of the 1977 Army Numerical Analysis and Computer Conf.

Parker, D. (1977), "Nonlinear Recurrences and Parallel Computation," this proceedings.

Pease, M. (1968), "An Adaptation of the Fast Fourier Transform for Parallel Processing," J. of the ACM, Vol. 15, pp. 252-264.

Preparata, F., and Sarwate, D. (1977), "An Improved Parallel Processor Bound in Fast Matrix Inversion," submitted for publication.

Reinsch, C. (1971), "A Stable Rational QR-Algorithm for the Computation of the Eigenvalues of an Hermitian Tridiagonal Matrix," Math. Comp., Vol. 25, pp. 591-597.

Sameh, A. (1971), "On Jacobi and Jacobi-like Algorithms for a Parallel Computer," Math. Comp., Vol. 25, pp. 579-590.

Sameh, A., Chen, S., and Kuck, D. (1976), "Parallel Poisson and Biharmonic Solvers," Computing, Vol. 17, pp. 219-230.

Sameh, A., and Kuck, D. (1976), "On Stable Parallel Linear System Solvers," submitted for publication.

Sameh, A., and Brent, R. (1977), "Solving Triangular Systems on a Parallel Computer," to appear in SIAM J. on Numer. Anal.

Sameh, A., and Kuck, D. (1977), "A Parallel QR-Algorithm for Symmetric Tridiagonal Matrices," IEEE Trans. Comput., Vol. C-26, pp. 147-153.

Smith, B., et al (1974), Matrix Eigensystem Routines--Eispack Guide, Spring-Verlag.

Stewart, G. W. (1973), Introduction to Matrix Computations, Academic Press.

Stokes, R. (1977), "BSP: The Burroughs Scientific Processors," this proceedings.

Stone, H. (1973), "An Efficient Parallel Algorithm for the Solution of a Tridiagonal Linear System of Equations," J. of the ACM, Vol. 20, pp. 27-38.

Stone, H. (1975), "Parallel Tridiagonal Equation Solvers," ACM Trans. on Math. Software, Vol. 1, pp. 289-307.

Swarztrauber, P. (1976), "A Parallel Algorithm for Solving General Tridiagonal Equations," National Center for Atmospheric Research, Boulder, CO.

Wilkinson, J. H. (1963), Rounding Errors in Algebraic Processes, Prentice-Hall.

Wilkinson, J. H. (1965), The Algebraic Eigenvalue Problem, Oxford.

Wilkinson, J. H., and Reinsch, C. (1971), Handbook for Automatic Computation, Vol. 2, Linear Algebra, Springer-Verlag.

Winograd, S. (1975), "On the Parallel Evaluation of Certain Arithmetic Expressions," J. of the ACM, Vol. 22, pp. 477-492.

THE INFLUENCE OF VECTOR COMPUTER ARCHITECTURE
ON NUMERICAL ALGORITHMS

Robert G. Voigt
ICASE

I. INTRODUCTION

Over the past 15 years the interest of numerical analysts in algorithms to exploit vector computers has been slowly increasing. In the 1960's most of the work took one of two approaches: either the algorithm was designed with the incomplete ILLIAC-IV in mind or the algorithm was discussed in the context of a model parallel computer with a large, sometimes unbounded, number of ideal processors. Some of this work is summarized in the review article of Miranker [1971]. In the 1970's as computers such as the Control Data Corp. STAR-100, the Texas Instruments Inc. Advanced Scientific Computer (ASC) and the Cray Research Inc. Cray-1 became operational, algorithmic development, somewhat surprisingly, did not shift noticeably toward these machines but remained centered around theoretical computers. This emphasis is reflected in the bibliography of Poole and Voigt [1974] and the linear algebra survey by Heller [1977]. The last year has seen an increase in the interest in existing vector computers as evidenced by the bibliography in the survey on solving partial differential equations by Ortega and Voigt [1977].

The purpose of this paper is to show that algorithms for the computers mentioned above must be developed with the specific architecture well in mind if anything approaching the full potential of these machines is to be realized. As will be seen, one of the most important aspects of the architecture is what each computer defines as a vector and what restrictions and costs are involved in operating within that definition. To demonstrate this we will discuss algorithms for the solution of the linear system

$$Ax = b . \tag{1}$$

The case when A is tridiagonal has already been discussed in detail for the ILLIAC-IV and vector computers like the STAR-100 in Stone [1975] and Lambiotte and Voigt [1975]; both studies point out how the architecture of the two computers influences the performance of various algorithms. For this paper we will assume that the system (1) results from the

discretization of a partial differential equation over a
square grid. In Section II we use the natural ordering of the
grid to produce a banded matrix A ; in Section III the
orderings known as one-way and nested dissection are
considered. In all cases the intent is not to show one
computer superior to another, but to demonstrate how different
manifestations of vector architecture can influence the
performance of algorithms. Finally, we conclude the paper
with some observations in Section IV.

The reader is assumed to be familiar with the basic
architecture of the ASC, STAR-100 and Cray-1; a brief
description of these and the ILLIAC-IV is contained in Ortega
& Voigt [1977]. A more complete description of the Cray-1,
ASC and STAR-100 may be found in Ramamoorthy and Li [1977].
The latter two computers have vector operation timing formulas
of the form $T = S + pm$ where S is the overhead referred to
as the start-up time, $1/p$ is the number of results per minor
cycle emerging from the pipelines, and m is the length of the
vector. The appropriate timing formulas will be used
throughout the remainder of this paper.

II. THE SOLUTION OF BANDED LINEAR SYSTEMS

In this section we assume that the matrix A of equation
(1) is banded with bandwidth $\beta(A)$ defined by

$$\beta(A) \equiv \max_{a_{i,j} \neq 0} |i-j| .$$

Such systems arise, for example, from the discretization of
partial differential equations. For definiteness we assume
that the domain of interest for the equation is a square
covered by an n by n grid consisting of $(n-1)$ small
squares called elements. After the partial differential
equation is discretized over this grid a row by row numbering
of the grid points gives rise to a banded linear system. In
fact, assuming linear quadrilateral elements, the n^2 by
n^2 matrix A has bandwidth $\beta \equiv \beta(A) = n+1$. We further
assume that the partial differential equation and the
discretization are such that A is symmetric and positive
definite. Orderings other than the row by row or natural
ordering will be discussed in the following section.

We consider the Cholesky decomposition $A = LL^T$, where
L is lower triangular; the solution of system (1) is then
obtained by solving the systems $Ly = b$ and $L^T x = y$. In
the algorithms that follow we exploit the zeros outside of the

band, but not those within the band since the band itself almost completely fills during the factorization.

The STAR-100, the ASC, and the Cray-1 each present different architectural features which dictate the use of different algorithms to obtain maximum efficiency. On the ILLIAC-IV the primary consideration is a storage scheme for A which permits efficient row and column access, rather than the algorithm; consequently we will not discuss this computer here. The interested reader is referred to Kuck [1968], for example.

The following algorithm for performing the factorization of A is a variant of one which was shown to be among the fastest by Lambiotte [1975] for a virtual computer patterned after the STAR-100. The lower half of the matrix A is assumed to be stored by columns and the factor L, with the modifications to A, is developed a column at a time using the appropriate linear combinations of the columns of A. For example, the following vector operations are involved in the modification of column k+j of A required when computing column k of L:

$$(a_{k+j,k+j}, \ldots, a_{k+\beta,k+j}) \leftarrow (a_{k+j,k+j}, \ldots, a_{k+\beta,k+j})$$
$$-a_{k+j,k} * (a_{k+j,k}, \ldots, a_{k+\beta,k}) \quad (2)$$

Expression (2) is executed for j ranging from 1 to β; hence the vector lengths vary from 1 to β with an average of $(\beta+1)/2$. Note that the STAR-100 concept of a vector as contiguous memory locations is not violated by the algorithm. The algorithm is not implemented in precisely the form given by (2); for details the reader is referred to Knight et al. [1975] and George et al. [1976b]. In the latter report a precise timing formula is given which, in terms of STAR-100 minor cycles of 40 nanoseconds, is approximately

$$T(n) \approx .75n^4 + 232n^3 + 274n^2 + O(n) . \quad (3)$$

Note that since $\beta = n + 1$ and the system is $n^2 \times n^2$, the leading term is as expected, namely $N\beta^2$ where $N = n^2$. What may not have been expected is the large coefficient of the n^3 term which causes that term to dominate the timing for all but very large problems. Thus, we see the danger of relying on highest order term approximations for timing comparisons. In the formula (3), almost all of the coefficient of the n^3 term is attributable to vector start-up times for the subtract-multiply operations which have a timing of 230 + 1.5m cycles.

Since the STAR-100 has an inner product instruction, one might wonder how an inner product based algorithm would compare. Because of the design of this instruction, its timing is 137 + 5.5m cycles; thus for vectors of length greater than 23, the instruction requires longer to execute than the subtract-multiply combination it would replace, and asymptotically, an inner product based factorization would be almost 4 times slower than the algorithm suggested by expression (2).

For the ASC an implementation of the algorithm discussed above would have a timing formula similar to that given in expression (3). In fact if we consider hypothetical computers with operation times of 100 + m, but with the STAR-100 and the ASC definitions of a vector, the timing formula for both becomes approximately

$$T(n) \approx n^4 + 200n^3 + 200n^2 + \mathcal{O}(n) \ . \tag{4}$$

On the ASC a vector consists of any string of memory locations that might be referenced by a triply nested FORTRAN DO loop where the inner most loop has an increment of one. This more general definition does not influence formula (4) for reasons discussed below.

Now the ASC has a fast inner product relative to the subtract-multiply time. If we reflect this on the hypothetical ASC-like computer with a timing formula of 100 + m cycles (as opposed to 120 + m cycles for 64-bit arithmetic on an ASC with four pipelines) an inner product algorithm would have a timing formula of approximately

$$T(n) \approx .5n^4 + 100n^3 + 200n^2 + \mathcal{O}(n) \ . \tag{5}$$

Expression (5) is an obvious improvement over expression (4), but as was noted in Calahan et al. [1976], the correct implementation on the ASC of an LU factorization of a full nxn matrix yields a timing formula where the start-up times contribute to the $\mathcal{O}(n)$ term rather than the $\mathcal{O}(n^2)$ term as on the STAR-100. Our goal here is to achieve that same improvement in the banded case by using an algorithm based on the faster inner product, whose timing has the start-up times contributing to the $\mathcal{O}(n^2)$ term rather than the $\mathcal{O}(n^3)$ term as with the STAR-100. Unfortunately the architecture of the ASC forces an unexpected premium to be paid for achieving this goal.

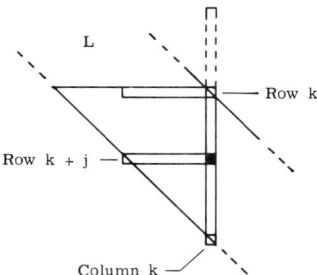

Fig. 1. *Inner product algorithm*

We first consider an inner product algorithm where at the k-th step of the factorization the k-th column of L is computed by $\beta + 1$ inner products. Figure 1 depicts the computation of element $\ell_{k+j,k}$. Conceptually the dotted portion of column k is used; however, by symmetry this is just $\ell_{k,k-j},\ldots,\ell_{k,k-1}$. The key point is that the inner product for element $\ell_{k+j,k}$ is of length j ; consequently, the computation of column k requires $\beta + 1$ inner products varying in length from $\beta + 1$ to 1 , and the ASC hardware cannot execute such a varying length sequence with a single instruction. The algorithm could of course be executed, but it would have a timing formula as given in expression (5) where the startup time appears in the $O(n^3)$ term. Note that the varying vector length problem also arose in expression (2) and was the reason that the implementation on the ASC-like computer produced the timing formula (4) with the startup time contributing to the $O(n^3)$ term.

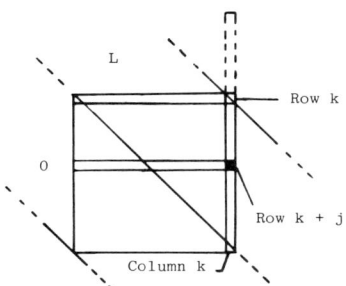

Fig. 2. *ASC algorithm*

Now if we are willing to perform more computation and use more storage, we can develop an algorithm for which the start-up time contributes to the $O(n^2)$ term. The idea is to use the algorithm suggested by Figure 1, but append a band of zeros so that the inner products are of constant length. This is depicted in Figure 2 where at the k-th step of the factorization the computation of each element of column k involves an inner product of length β. Assuming row by row storage the key operations are given by:

```
      DO 10 J = K+1,K+β
         DO 20 I = K-β,K-1
            TEMP = TEMP + A(K,I) * A(J,I)
20       CONTINUE
10    CONTINUE
```

Now because the lengths of the inner products remain constant, this nested DO loop can be executed on the ASC in one instruction on vectors of length β^2 rather than 2β instructions of average length $(\beta+1)/2$ as on the STAR-100. Again using operation times of $100 + m$ cycles, the timing formula for the factorization is approximately,

$$T(n) \approx n^4 + 300n^2 + O(n) . \qquad (6)$$

Note that about half of the computations reflected by the coefficient of the leading term are with zeros; thus the value of this algorithm clearly depends on n. The choice between the two algorithms will naturally depend also on the actual machine and how its instructions compare. If we use ASC timing information for four pipelines and 64-bit arithmetic, the algorithm based on Figure 1 has a timing formula, in cycles of 80 nanoseconds, of approximately,

$$T(n) \approx .5n^4 + 121n^3 + 365n^2 + O(n) ,$$

while the one based on Figure 2 becomes approximately,

$$T(n) \approx n^4 + 1.2n^3 + 485n^2 + O(n) .$$

Both algorithms include time for the scalar divides and square roots. Even though nearly twice as much computation is being done in the second algorithm, it is superior until $n > 238$.

We next consider the Cray-1 where a different architectural characteristic is dominant. On this computer the definition of a vector has some of the aspects of both the STAR-100 and the ASC definitions. With regard to memory, a vector may have its elements separated by a constant multiple which is slightly more restrictive than on the ASC; however, operations are performed not on the contents of memory but rather on the contents of eight vector registers each containing up to 64 words. A vector is defined as the contents of consecutive elements of one of the vector registers, always beginning with the first element of that register. Thus, for example, as on the STAR-100, arithmetic cannot be done on every other element of a vector; one must return the contents of the vector register to memory and then load every other element into a vector register. Since essentially all vector instructions obtain their operands from the vector registers, these registers must be loaded from memory and this can be a major influence on the effective computation rate as has been noted by Calahan et al. [1976] and Fong and Jordan [1976]. To be specific, there is one path between memory and the vector registers capable of transferring one operand or result per cycle. With the functional units capable of performing an add, a multiply and a reciprocal in a single cycle, the potential problem is clear. For example, consider an implementation of the STAR-100 algorithm given in expression (2) assuming $\beta \leq 64$. Denoting vector register p by VRp, and assuming VR1 contains $(a_{kk}, \ldots, a_{k+\beta,k})$, the sequence of instructions on the Cray-1 would be

$$j=1,\ldots,\beta \begin{cases} \text{LOAD} & (a_{k+j,k+j}, \ldots, a_{k+\beta,k+j}) \text{ into VR2} \\ \text{MULTIPLY} & a_{k+j,k} * \text{VR1}(k+j,\ldots,k+\beta) \text{ to VR3} \\ \text{SUBTRACT} & \text{VR2} - \text{VR3 to VR4} \\ \text{STORE} & \text{VR4 to memory} \end{cases}$$

Now the Cray-1 architecture permits the chaining of the first three operations so that the results of the subtract are available at a rate of one per cycle after a few cycles delay to fill the multiply unit and the add unit. However, the STORE must wait until the LOAD is complete, and because the sequence must be executed for j ranging from 1 to β, the operation after the STORE is another LOAD. Consequently, the arithmetic units will be busy only about half of the total time required by the algorithm. The algorithm points up another difficulty of the Cray-1. The multiply operation as indicated does not begin with the first element of the vector register. Thus the contents of this register must either be shifted, or as pointed out by Fong and Jordan [1976], all vectors can be stored in reverse order so that computation always begins with the first element. Conceptually, there is no difficulty with the latter approach, but the design of a compiler capable of recognizing the situation in general would not be a simple matter.

By redesigning the algorithm it is possible to keep both arithmetic units busy. This is accomplished by completely modifying the k-th column of the matrix at the k-th step of the factorization and leaving all other columns unchanged.

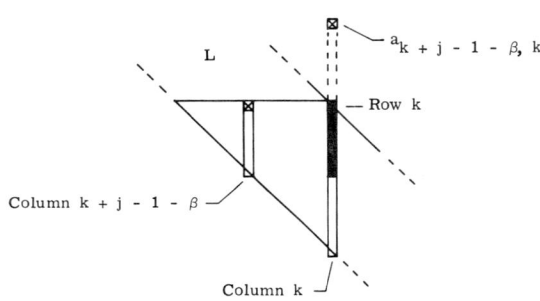

Fig. 3. *Cray-1 algorithm*

Following Figure 3, the key portion of the algorithm is given below where $j = 1,\ldots,\beta$:

$$(a_{k,k},\ldots,a_{k+j-1,k}) \leftarrow (a_{k,k},\ldots,a_{k+j-1},k) \tag{7}$$
$$-a_{k,k+j-1-\beta} * (a_{k,k+j-1-\beta},\ldots,a_{k+j-1,k+j-1-\beta})$$

Now assuming VR1 contains $(a_{k,k},\ldots,a_{k+\beta,k})$, the sequence of instructions on the Cray-1 would be

$j=1,\ldots,\beta$
$\begin{cases} \text{LOAD} & (a_{k,k+j-1-\beta},\ldots,a_{k+j-1,k+j-1-\beta}) \text{ into VR2} \\ \text{MULTIPLY} & a_{k,k+j-1-\beta} * \text{VR2 to VR3} \\ \text{SUBTRACT} & \text{VR1}(k,\ldots,k+j-1) - \text{VR3 to VR1} \end{cases}$

　　　　　STORE　　　　VR1 to memory

As before the three instructions in the j loop are chained so that a result is produced each cycle; however, the STORE does not occur until the j loop is complete so that there is no delay in performing the arithmetic of the j loop. It should be pointed out that the Cray-1 architecture does not permit the return of the result of an operation to a register containing an operand. Again, conceptually, this is no problem because the result can oscillate between two registers with the appropriate change in the instruction stream; however, it is at best a nuisance to the compiler writer.

In Calahan et al. [1976], algorithms similar to those given in expressions (6) and (7) for factoring a full matrix were compared by executing them on a Cray-1, and the times reported there bear out the contention that algorithm (7) is approximately twice as fast as algorithm (6).

III. DISSECTION METHODS

In this section we continue with the linear system of Section II which arose from the discretization of a partial differential equation over an n by n grid of linear quadrilateral elements. However, we will now consider orderings of the grid points other than the natural ordering discussed previously. Specifically, we are interested in the effect of vector computer start-up time on the performance of the orderings known as one-way and nested dissection.

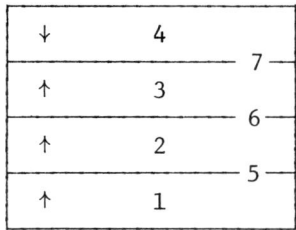

Fig. 4. *One-way dissection with the ordering indicated by the numbers and the arrows.*

Referring to Figure 4, the idea of one-way dissection is first to divide the grid with ℓ horizontal separators. The nodes in the $\ell+1$ remaining rectangles are numbered vertically toward a separator and then the nodes of the separators are numbered. For the proper choice of ℓ, George

[1972] and [1977] has shown that the number of arithmetic operations required for the factorization of the n^2 by n^2 system is reduced from $O(n^4)$ for the natural ordering to $O(n^{7/2})$, while the fill that occurs is reduced from $O(n^3)$ to $O(n^{5/2})$.

The nested dissection ordering further reduces the operation count and fill to $O(n^3)$ and $O(n^2 \log n)$ respectively as shown in George [1973] and [1977]. The idea here is to divide the grid with both horizontal and vertical separators as shown in Figure 5. Now regions 1 - 4 may be numbered in the usual way, or by again using horizontal and vertical separators. The idea may be applied recursively, and in the case $n = 2^k -1$, dissection will terminate in k-1 steps yielding the $O(n^3)$ operation count.

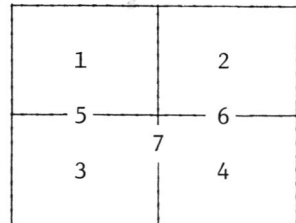

Fig. 5. One step of the nested dissection ordering

It should be clear that for both orderings as dissection proceeds at least some of the vectors involved in the factorization become shorter. This raises the question of whether a vector implementation of the two algorithms would not be more efficient if dissection were terminated earlier than in the scalar case. This question was studied in George et al. [1976b] by developing timing formulas parameterized in terms of the individual operation times and of the level of dissection. A result suggested by their work which we will expand here is that the quality of the vectorization of one-way and nested dissection differs significantly.

Using the timing formulas developed in George et al. [1976b], we obtain the estimates given in Figures 6 and 7 for one-way and nested dissection respectively with $n = 127$. We consider hypothetical computers with start-up times of 0, 10, 50 and 100 machine cycles and per-result times of 1 cycle. The curve for one-way dissection on the "0-1" computer is just

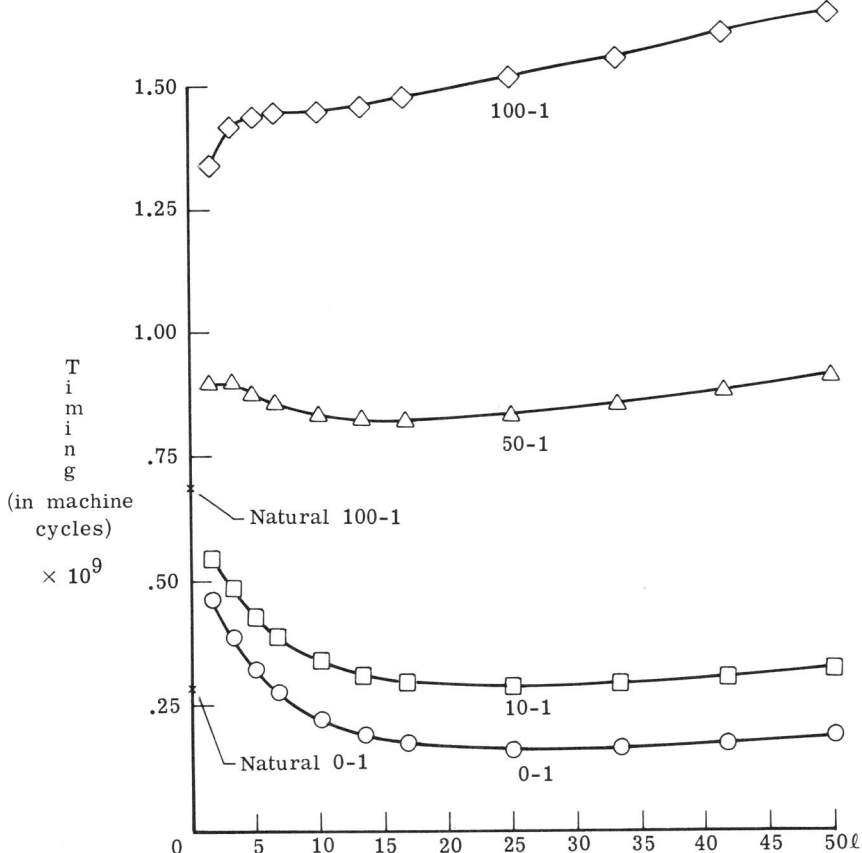

Fig. 6. Timing for factorization stage of one-way dissection ordering for n = 127

an operation count and exhibits the expected performance of the scalar algorithm attaining a minimum significantly less than the operation count for the factorization based on the natural ordering. This contrasts sharply with the timing on the "100-1" computer which always remains well above the point corresponding to the factorization based on the natural ordering.

Figure 7 shows the timing of nested dissection as a function of the amount of dissection; the point for $\ell = 0$ is the time for the factorization based on the natural ordering. The performance of this algorithm generally follows that of a scalar implementation although, as suggested earlier, it is more economical to stop the dissection short of completion. Stopping early also has advantages in both implementation and storage as pointed out in George et al. [1976a].

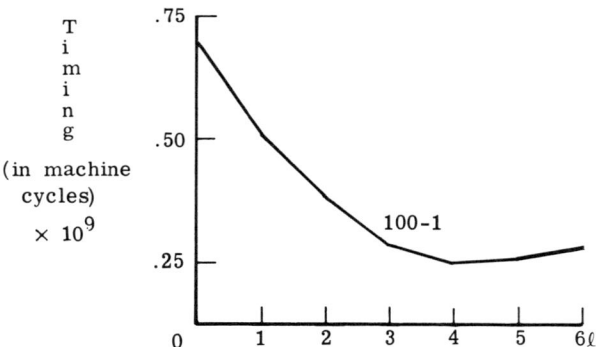

Fig. 7. Timing for factorization stage of nested dissection ordering for $n = 127$

It should be noted that there is nothing in scalar implementations of the two algorithms to suggest their contrasting performance on vector computers. In fact both of them appear to be well suited for these computers because they can be implemented almost entirely in vector instructions. Figure 6 suggests that the culprit in the poor performance of one-way dissection is the start-up time, for as we move from the "100-1" computer through the "50-1" to the "10-1", the performance becomes similar to that of the scalar algorithm. However, the question remains as to why the two algorithms behave so differently on the "100-1" computer.

The answer is provided by Figures 8 and 9 where the start-up time is separated from the total time by considering a "100-0" computer. In Figure 8 we see that for nested dissection both the start-up time and the number of arithmetic operations decrease as dissection continues until near completion when the startup time actually increases. Note that the "100-0" computer provides us with a count of the number of vector operations if the data is simply normalized by 100. Thus for nested dissection the number of vector operations decreases until a minimum is reached and then begins to increase. It should be pointed out that although one would expect that dissection should be terminated early because of some shortening vector lengths the much more significant influence of the increased number of vector operations was totally unexpected and became apparent only after some analysis of the timing formulas.

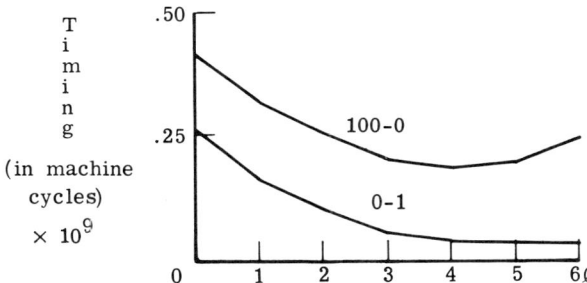

Fig. 8. *Start-up time and operation count for factorization stage of nested dissection ordering for* n = 127

In Figure 9 it now becomes clear why one-way dissection performs so poorly on a vector computer: the number of vector operations actually increases to a nearly constant level as dissection progresses while the number of arithmetic operations as depicted by the "0-1" curve decreases to the expected minimum. Again it is not the expected shortening vector length phenomenon that makes the algorithm inappropriate but the unexpected increase in the number of vector operations. It should be pointed out that even though the algorithm appears to perform as expected on the "10-1" computer in Figure 6 this is only because the start-up time is so small that the inefficiencies of increased vector operations are offset by the positive effect of decreased arithmetic operations.

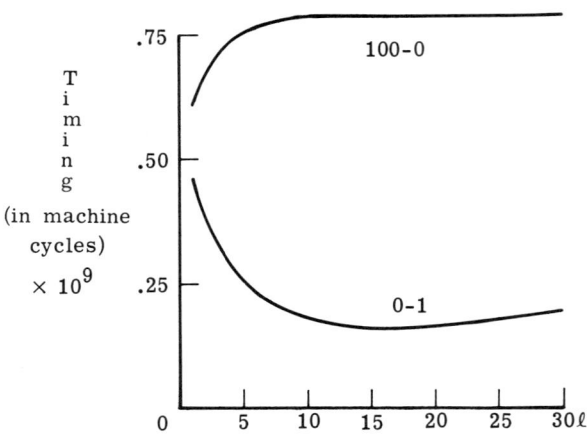

Fig. 9. *Start-up time and operation count for factorization stage of one-way dissection ordering for* $n = 127$

Finally, the poor performance of one-way dissection is not unique to $n = 127$. Of course, because of its lower arithmetic operation count, it will eventually be superior to the natural ordering. However, for the "100-1" computer this cross over does not occur until $n > 650$.

Clearly the above analysis was done with a computer like the STAR-100 in mind, and one might argue that start-up times of a 100 cycles are irrelevant for a computer like the Cray-1. However, it seems highly probable that for the foreseeable future vector computers will have nontrivial overhead associated with vector operations and this overhead may be viewed as a start-up time, albeit one that is less than 100 cycles.

IV. OBSERVATIONS

We have seen how the architecture of some current vector computers can significantly influence the performance of algorithms for a problem as routine as solving linear systems. We have also noted that algorithms which on the surface may appear quite attractive can turn out to perform poorly on vector computers because of inefficient vectorization and because of the overhead associated with vector operations.

Some say that the current hardware revolution makes all of this concern academic. They would argue that the current decline in the cost of hardware will guarantee computers with such arithmetic speed that one can afford to use them inefficiently. Ignoring the fact that most numerical analysts find such usage objectionable, the point is that that day has not yet arrived. We are currently seeing the first generation of vector computers and many of their idiosyncrasies will pass the way of the vacuum tube, but unless numerical analysts seriously consider the implication of the present architectures we cannot hope to influence the direction of the future designs.

V. ACKNOWLEDGEMENT

This paper was prepared as a result of work performed under NASA Contract No. NAS1-14101 while the author was in residence at ICASE.

VI. REFERENCES

Calahan, D., Joy, W. and Orbits, D. [1976]. Preliminary Report on Results of Matrix Benchmarks on Vector Processors. SEL Report No. 94, Systems Engineering Laboratory, University of Michigan.

Fong, K. and Jordan, T. [1976]. Some Linear Algebraic Algorithms and Their Performance on Cray-1. Report written under U.S. Energy Research and Development Administration Contract No. W-7405-ENG-36 at Los Alamos Scientific Laboratory, Los Alamos, New Mexico.

George, A. [1972]. An Efficient Band-oriented Scheme for Solving n by n Grid Problems. Proc. 1972 FJCC, AFIPS Press, Montvale, New Jersey, pp. 1317-1321.

George, A. [1973]. Nested Dissection on a Regular Finite Element Mesh. SIAM J. Numer. Anal. 10, pp. 345-363.

George, A. [1977]. Numerical Experiments Using Dissection Methods to Solve n by n Grid Problems. SIAM J. Numer. Anal., to appear in vol. 14, no. 2.

George, A., Poole, W. and Voigt, R. [1976a]. A Variant of Nested Dissection for Solving n by n Grid Problems. Report No. 76-16, ICASE, NASA Langley Research Center, Hampton, Virginia.

George, A., Poole, W. and Voigt, R. [1976b]. Analysis of Dissection Algorithms for Vector Computers. Report No. 76-17, ICASE, NASA Langley Research Center, Hampton, Virginia.

Heller, D. [1977]. A Survey of Parallel Algorithms in Numerical Linear Algebra. SIAM Review, to appear.

Knight, J., Poole, W. and Voigt, R. [1975]. System Balance Analysis for Vector Computers. Proc. 1975 ACM National Conference, pp. 163-168.

Kuck, D. [1968]. ILLIAC IV Software and Application Programming. IEEE Trans. Computer C-17, pp. 758-770.

Lambiotte, J. [1975]. The Solution of Linear Systems of Equations on a Vector Computer. Ph.D. Dissertation, University of Virginia.

Lambiotte, J. and Voigt, R. [1975]. The Solution of Tridiagonal Linear Systems on the CDC STAR-100 Computer. ACM Trans. Math. Software 1, pp. 308-329.

Miranker, W. [1971]. A Survey of Parallelism in Numerical Analysis. SIAM Rev. 13, pp. 524-547.

Ortega, J. and Voigt, R. [1977]. Solution of Partial Differential Equations on Vector Computers. Report No. 77-7. ICASE, NASA Langley Research Center, Hampton, Virginia. To appear in the Proceedings of the 1977 Army Numerical Analysis and Computers Conference.

Poole, W. and Voigt, R. [1974]. Numerical Algorithms for Parallel and Vector Computers: An Annotated Bibliography. Computing Reviews 15, pp. 379-388.

Ramamoorthy, C. and Li, H. [1977]. Pipeline Architecture. Computing Surveys 9, pp. 61-102.

Stone, H. [1975]. Parallel Tridiagonal Equation Solvers. ACM Trans. Math. Software 1, pp. 289-301.

ALGORITHMS FOR SOLVING TWO-POINT
BOUNDARY VALUE PROBLEMS

Victor Pereyra
California Institute of Technology

1. INTRODUCTION

We will consider the numerical solution of two types of boundary value problems

I.
$$y' = f(t, y), \quad t \in [a, b],$$
$$g(y(a), y(b)) = 0$$

with smooth vector functions $y, f, g \in \mathbb{R}^d$, and

II.
$$y_j^{(n_j)} = f_j(t, y_1, \ldots, y_1^{(n_1-1)}, \ldots, y_d^{(n_d-1)})$$
$$j = 1, \ldots, d; \; n_j \geq 1$$

$$g(y_1(a), \ldots, y_d^{(n_d-1)}(a), y_1(b), \ldots, y_d^{(n_d-1)}(b)) = 0,$$

$$g \in \mathbb{R}^{\sum_{j=1}^d n_j}.$$

We will concentrate on methods for which there are known, available, and reasonably tested computer implementations.

2. BASIC METHODS

For problem I we have two main kinds of methods:

i) Multiple shooting, with adaptive choice of shooting points [4, 9, 12, 30, 35].
ii) Finite differences or collocation with variable order and variable step [3, 13, 20, 22, 29].

For problem II there are many spline methods for

the case of a single equation (d = 1) but no general software is available that we know of. Some very recent developments using finite differences with variable order in the spirit of what exists for first order systems show some promise [15,16]. Also mixed finite difference - collocation methods are being developed which are promising [7,8].

Methods (i), (ii) are closely related. The main attraction of method (i) is that well understood available software for initial value problems form a considerable part of the algorithms core, thus diminishing the development costs.

Outside of that,(i) and (ii) share the same difficulties: solution of systems of nonlinear equations, mesh selection, and even the linear equations to be solved in iterative procedures have the same block structure. In general, though, the sizes of the discrete problems for (i) are smaller than for (ii) and therefore (ii) is more storage consuming. On the other hand, usually the implementations of (i) do not permit control on what the initial value problem solvers do between shooting points, and therefore method (ii) usually provides finer error control and more solution detail.

The nonlinear discrete equations are usually solved by Newton's method or some of its variations. Many routine, and otherwise simple problems, present great difficulties in the determination of suitable initial values and several techniques are used to increase the robustness and global convergence properties of the iterative method being used. Among others: continuation or embedding, step control, and forcing the iteration to be of descent for a norm of the residual [6,27,28].

Most iterations require the solution of a linearized set of equations at every step. For the methods mentioned above the resulting systems have sparse matrices of coefficients with a highly structured distribution of zeros. In fact, an intelligent ordering of the equations produces essentially block tridiagonal matrices, with some further sparseness within the nonzero blocks.

Special LU decomposition schemes with alternate pivoting have been developed which solve this type of systems efficiently and accurately [13,21,31].

The systems produced by the discretization of II are somewhat more complicated in structure. Band solvers with partial pivoting has been used so far [15], but there are probably more efficient algorithms [3], although they may be more space consuming.

It is in the solution of these special systems of linear equations where parallel or vector computation can be of use for this type of problems.

3. ERROR ESTIMATION AND VARIABLE ORDER

The implementations of algorithms in class (i) inherit the capabilities of their core initial value problem solvers in what error estimation and variable order is concerned. Usually error estimation and control will be limited to local truncation error as related to the shooting between station points, and therefore the relation with actual global error may be, at its best, tenuous. Of course, global error estimates similar to those employed by implementations of methods of class (ii) are possible, but no program that we know of bothers to pay the price to obtain this added, and we think, fundamental information.

Methods of class (ii), more specifically those using deferred corrections to increase the order of accuracy [20,22,24] have natural built in capabilities that provide asymptotic local and global error estimates with practically no extra cost. This is in the nature of global solvers, as opposite to marching techniques.

In our implementations the global estimates are used to steer the program through its logical tree, while the local ones are used to select dynamically a net that adapts itself to the problem at hand.

4. MESH SELECTION

The area of adaptive mesh selection for boundary value problems is one in which active research is being carried out [2,5,18,22,26,32].

Here again we have to separate the problems in two broad categories with fuzzy boundaries:

a) Regular problems with at worst moderately large gradients.
b) Boundary layer problems and quasi-singularities with extremely different time scales.

For this last class of problems, methods combining singular perturbation techniques [1,10], and others that make a very delicate study of the problem have been proposed [18], although no practical implementations are available at the time of this writing.

Problems of type (a) are amenable to methods that recursively adapt the mesh, building up information as the computation proceeds. A technique that has proven to be fairly successful and for which there is some theoretical backing [5,26,32] is that of asymptotically equidistributing some integral norm of the local truncation error [5,22]. Roughly speaking, equidistributing consists of making the net finer where the local truncation error (i.e. a multiple of some high order derivative of the solution) is large.

In [32], White has proposed a very appealing method for computing equidistributed meshes with respect to various monitor functions. Unfortunately the method as stated has found some unexpected difficulties in its implementation, but nevertheless we think it deserves further consideration. It is worth pointing out that the mesh selection algorithm in [22] is actually a successful implementation of White's idea for the case in which the local truncation error is used as a monitor function. We feel now that an implementation even more closely related to White's proposal could be achieved that might share the best of both approaches.

5. STRUCTURE OF PROGRAMS, MINIMUM CALLING SEQUENCES AND DESIRABLE OPTIONS

With the vague descriptions we have given in the former sections, complemented if necessary with the detailed versions to be found in the quoted literature, we would like now to indicate what we think the general skeleton of an implementation should be. To make things somewhat more precise we will have in mind problem I and finite difference methods for which we have direct experience, but it should be apparent that the basic techniques indicated in most of the black boxes can be fully exchanged by alternate ones, and also applied to problems of type II.

Also, we have tried to understress the amount of automatic decisions, providing some exit nodes ◊ which could be appropriate for inputing users decisions in a semi-interactive approach. This diminishes the algorithm's complexity and may provide the program with much greater flexibility. Present implementations are fully batch mode oriented, but allowing some user interaction could enhance the class of problems that can be solved effectively. Certainly the use of available interactive graphic facilities would be desirable in many specific applications.

A calling sequence for a subroutine of this type should contain at least the following parameters:

M = Number of differential equations in the system.
N = Number of mesh points in input net. On output this parameter could contain the number of points of the final net.
P = Number of initial conditions.
R = Number of coupled conditions.
A = Left end point of interval of integration.
B = Right end point of interval of integration.
TOL = Desired accuracy.
X = One dimensional array containing initial mesh. On output X may contain the final mesh.
Y = Array containing initial approximation (on the mesh X). On output Y may contain the answer.
F = Subroutine specifying the right hand sides of the equations.
JACOB = Subroutine specifying the Jacobian matrix of F with respect to y (in case explicit partial derivatives are used instead of some other type of quasi-Newton iteration).

Options. In our implementation [21] we have found useful to offer some options in order to facilitate the use of the program. We employ a one dimensional array OPT to input these options. If OPT(1) = 0 then default options will be activated and no other element of OPT need be specified. If OPT(1) = 1 then all the elements of OPT must be given values.

OPT(2) controls the use of an automatic continuation option for badly nonlinear problems.
OPT(3) controls intermediary printed output.
If OPT(4) = 0 the program will set the initial values for X and Y.
OPT(5) = 0 the problem is linear.
OPT(5) ≥ 1 the problem is nonlinear. By setting a larger value of OPT(5) the user can indicate that the problem nonlinearity should be treated more carefully. This will usually produce a less efficient performance, but in many cases it will solve the problem where a smaller value of OPT(5) would not.

'Dynamic' array dimensioning can be simulated in FORTRAN by adding two one-dimensional work arrays (one for integer and one for real variables) as in J. Bolstad's revised version of PASVA2 [34].

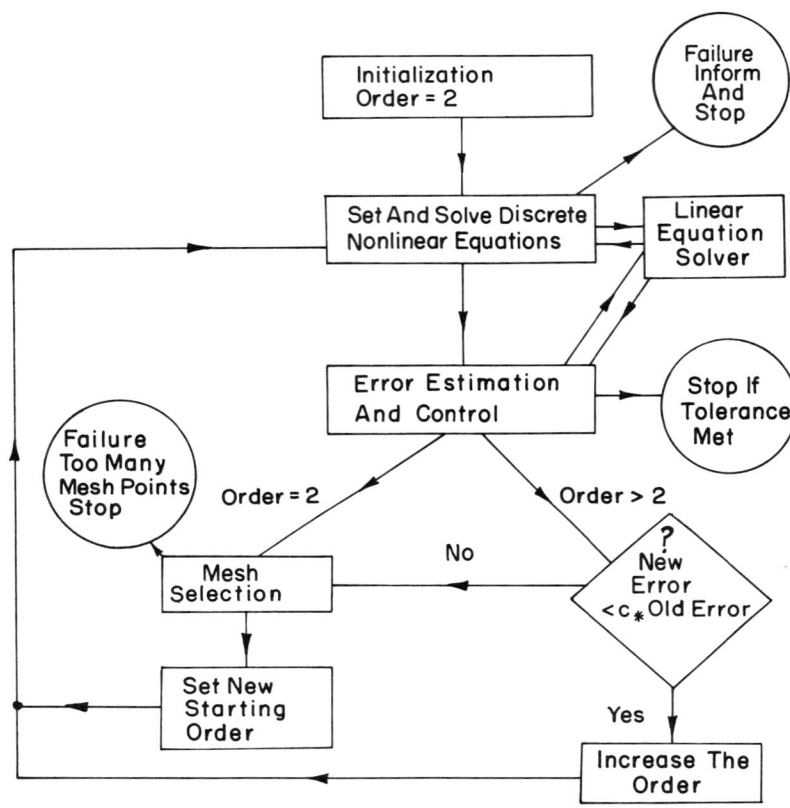

FLOW CHART FOR ADAPTIVE TWO-POINT BOUNDARY VALUE PROBLEM SOLVER

6. HIGH ORDER SYSTEMS

Problems of class II are fairly common in the applications, at least for $n_j \leq 4$. In the past we have adopted the position that since reduction to first order systems is always feasible, it is best to concentrate in providing high quality software for problems of class I.

This is the same attitude taken by the people working in software for initial value problems, with the exception of Krogh [19]. However, recent investigations [15] have shown that there might be significant gains in efficiency if high order systems are solved as they arise, instead of reducing them to lower order.

There is a large increase in complexity when passing from class I to II, and in our preliminary investigations we have concentrated in some simpler special cases in order to explore the feasibility and properties of the new approach.

Since any nonlinear solver is based on linear solvers, as a first step we have considered only linear systems.

The type of basic finite difference methods we use are symmetric, compact as possible, second order accurate ones, i.e. they use symmetric, $(n_j + 1)$ point formulas. Only uniform meshes are employed. In order to be able to obtain such methods we need to consider odd and even order equations separately, and to be able to use existing results on convergence [11,17] we have to concentrate in systems for which $n_j \equiv n$, $j = 1,\ldots,d$. So we have an even (fixed) order system solver, and an odd order one. Deferred corrections, providing variable order of accuracy have been implemented only for the even order solver so far.

All the finite difference formulas necessary in the basic approximation and in the correction procedure are constructed with precalculated weights. This preliminary work has been highly facilitated by the use of MACSYMA [23], a very powerful symbolic manipulation system available at MIT, and which we have accessed through the ARPA net.

This is in contrast with previous implementations where fast Vandermonde solvers [33] were used to generate weights whenever they were needed. A considerable saving is attained by this new approach.

Another new feature is the incorporation of Keller's modification of the deferred correction algorithm [14] that permits the use of symmetric correction formulas over the whole interval [a,b], by considering auxiliary mesh points external to this interval. This technique removes some theoretical difficulties and it also produces discrete solutions with orders of accuracy much closer to the theoretical ones than in earlier implementations.

REFERENCES

1. Abrahamsson, L.R., Keller, H.B. and Kreiss, H.O., "Difference approximations for singular perturbations of systems of ordinary differential equations," Numer. Math. 22, 367-391 (1974).
2. de Boor, C., "Good approximation by splines with variable knots II," Lecture Notes in Math. No. 363, 12-20. Springer-Verlag, Berlin (1973).
3. de Boor, C. and Weiss, R., "SOLVEBLOK: a package for solving almost block diagonal linear systems, with applications to spline approximation and the numerical solution of ordinary differential equations," MRC Rep. 1625, Math. Res. Center, U. of Wisconsin, Madison (1976).
4. Bulirsch, R., Stoer, J. and Deuflhard, P., "Numerical solution of nonlinear two-point boundary value problems I." To appear in Numer. Math., Handbook Series Approximation.
5. Christiansen, J. and Russell, R.D., "Adaptive mesh selection strategies for solving boundary value problems." To appear in SIAM J. Numer. Anal.
6. Deuflhard, P., "A modified Newton method for the solution of ill-conditioned systems of nonlinear equations with applications to multiple shooting," Numer. Math. 22, 289-315 (1974).
7. Doedel, E.J., "The construction of finite difference approximations to ordinary differential equations." To appear in SIAM Numer. Anal.
8. Doedel, E.J., "Finite difference method for nonlinear two point boundary value problems." Submitted for publication to SIAM Numer. Anal.
9. England, R., Nichols, N. and Reed, J., "Subroutine DD03AD." Harwell Lab., England (1973).
10. Ferguson, W.E. Jr., "A singularly perturbed linear two-point boundary-value problem." Ph.D. Thesis, App. Math. Caltech, Pasadena, Ca. (1975).
11. Grigorieff, R.D., "Die Konvergenz des Rand-und Eigenwert problems linear gewöhnlicher Differenzengleichungen," Numer. Math. 15-48 (1970).
12. Keller, H.B., "Numerical Methods for Two-Point Boundary-Value Problems," Blaisdell, Mass. (1968).

13. Keller, H.B., "Accurate difference methods for nonlinear two-point boundary value problems," SIAM J. Numer. Anal. 11, 305-320 (1974).
14. Keller, H.B., "Numerical Solution of Two-Point Boundary-Value Problems." Regional Conf. Series in App. Math. 24 (1976).
15. Keller, H.B. and Pereyra, V., "Difference methods and deferred corrections for ordinary boundary value problems." In preparation.
16. Keller, H.B. and Pereyra, V., "Symbolic generation of finite difference formulae." In preparation.
17. Kreiss, H.O., "Difference approximations for boundary and eigenvalue problems for ordinary differential equations," Math. Comp. 26, 605-624 (1972).
18. Kreiss, H.O., "Difference approximation for singular perturbation problems." Proc. NSF Symp. on Numerical Solution of Boundary Problems for Ordinary Differential Equations. Academic Press, New York (1975).
19. Krogh, F.T., "Variable order integrators for the numerical solution of ordinary differential equations." JPL Tech. Memo., Caltech, Pasadena, Ca. (1970).
20. Lentini, M. and Pereyra, V., "A variable order finite difference method for nonlinear multipoint boundary value problems," Math. Comp. 28, 981-1004 (1974).
21. Lentini, M. and Pereyra, V., "PASVA2 - Two Point boundary problem solver for nonlinear first order systems." Lawrence Berkeley Lab., Univ. of California (1975).
22. Lentini, M. and Pereyra, V., "An adaptive finite difference solver for nonlinear two point boundary problems with mild boundary layers," to appear in SIAM J. Numer. Anal., March (1977).
23. MACSYMA Reference Manual. Mathlab Group, Project MAC. MIT, Boston, Mass. (1975).
24. Pereyra, V., "Iterated deferred corrections for nonlinear operator equations," Numer. Math. 10, 313-323 (1967).
25. Pereyra, V., "High order finite difference solution of differential equations," STAN-CS-73-348, Comp. Sc. Dep., Stanford Univ., Cal. (1973).
26. Pereyra, V. and Sewell, G., "Mesh selection for discrete solution of boundary problems in ordinary differential equations," Numer. Math. 23, 261-268 (1975).
27. Pereyra, V. and Lee, W.H.K., "Numerical solution of nonlinear two-point boundary value problems and

its application to seismic ray tracing, Part I: The general numerical method and its implementation." Manuscript (1977).
28. Roberts, S.M. and Shipman, J.S., Two Point Boundary Value Problems: Shooting Methods, American Elsevier, New York (1972).
29. Russell, R.D., "Collocation for systems of boundary value problems," Numer. Math. 23, 119-133 (1974).
30. Scott, M.R. and Watts, H.A., "SUPORT - A computer code for two-point boundary-value problems via orthonormalization," SAND 75-0198, Sandia Labs., Albuquerque, N.M. (1975).
31. Varah, J.M., "On the solution of block-tridiagonal systems arising from certain finite-difference equations," Math. Comp. 26, 859-868 (1972).
32. White, A.B. Jr., "On selection of equidistributing meshes for two-point boundary-value problems." Rep. 112, Center Num. Anal., Univ. of Texas at Austin (1976).
33. Björck, Å. and Pereyra, V., "Solution of Vandermonde systems of equations." Math. Comp. 24, 893-903 (1970).
34. Bolstad, J., "Revised version of PASVA2," Comp. Sci. Dept., Stanford Univ. (1977).
35. Scott, M.R. and Watts, H.A., "Computational solution of nonlinear two-point boundary-value problems." SAND 77-0091, Sandia Labs., Albuquerque, N.M. (1977).

ACKNOWLEDGMENT

This work was supported under Contract No. AT-04-3-767, Project Agreement 12 with Energy Research and Development Administration.

VECTORIZATION FOR THE CRAY-1 OF SOME METHODS
FOR SOLVING ELLIPTIC DIFFERENCE EQUATIONS

B. L. Buzbee, G. H. Golub*, and J. A. Howell
University of California
Los Alamos Scientific Laboratory

ABSTRACT

In this paper, we discuss efficient implementation on the CRAY-1 of some familiar techniques for solving elliptic difference equations. We summarize CRAY-1 architectural features that are important when seeking to achieve optimum performance of the machine and show how to accommodate these in the implementation of point relaxation. Our discussion includes complications to vectorization caused by irregular regions. Finally, we provide quantitative measurements of algorithmic performance on the CRAY-1.

I. INTRODUCTION

Considerable experience has been acquired in the vectorization of numerical algorithms on such computers as the CDC 7600, the CDC STAR and Texas Instruments ASC. This experience consistently shows that successful vectorization requires careful attention to architectural features of the computer on which the vectorization is being done. Vectorization of algorithms for the Cray Research, Inc. CRAY-1 is no exception. In this paper we discuss efficient implementation on the CRAY-1 of several familiar techniques for solving elliptic difference equations. We summarize CRAY-1 architectural features that are important when seeking to achieve optimum performance of the machine and show how to accomodate

---
*
Computer Science Department, Stanford University, Stanford, CA 94302.
Work performed under the auspices of the U.S. Energy Research and Development Administration.

these in the implementation of algorithms such as successive overrelaxation (SOR). Our discussion includes complications to vectorization caused by irregular regions.

II. ARCHITECTURAL FEATURES

The eight vector registers or accumulators of the CRAY-1 central processing unit (CPU) are probably its most notable architectural feature. These registers represent an evolutionary advance in vector computers comparable to the introduction of accumulators into scalar CPUs. Vector registers enhance arithmetic efficiency on the CRAY-1 because they make possible very small overhead or vector start-up times, viz., the time required to obtain the first component of the result vector, and because they can be used to hold intermediate results thereby reducing data traffic between the CPU and the memory. These registers also introduce a complication because they can contain at most 64 numbers which means that vectors must be segmented modulo 64.

The presence of vector registers in the CPU facilitates manipulation of vectors whose elements are not stored contiguously in memory. This is another novel feature of the CRAY-1 and it is a feature which we will exploit. To transfer data between memory and a vector register, one specifies a vector segment length (VL) which cannot exceed 64, the starting address in memory of the segment, and the spacing in memory between elements of the vector. The transfer always starts with the first word of the associated vector register. Some caution is required in laying out vectors because a memory spacing of 8 or 16 will produce memory bank conflicts. The result will be degradation of memory access times.

The CRAY-1 CPU contains independent functional units for the vector operations of integer add, shift, logical, floating add, floating multiply, and reciprocal approximation. These units manipulate operands contained in vector registers and they always store their results in a vector register. One of the operands may be a scalar in the floating add and multiply units. These units involve the first VL elements of operand and result registers. This also causes complications in using the CRAY-1 computer. The notation $V_i = V_j$ "op" V_k indicates that the operation "op" is applied to corresponding elements of vector register V_j and V_k and the result stored in the corresponding element of V_i. The independence of these functional units makes possible their parallel operation in any situation where their operands are functionally independent. In situations where the results of a functional unit, say floating add, is the operand to another functional unit, say floating multiply, the hardware permits the results of the first to be transmitted directly to the second as they "come out of the pipe." This also provides significant parallelism in the machine and this process is called *chaining*. Four conditions must be satisfied before a vector instruction is executed:

1. The functional unit must be free.
2. The result register must be free.
3. The operand register must be free or at chain slot time.
4. Memory must be inactive if the instruction generates references to it.

Thus the sequence

$$V_0 = V_1 \cdot V_2$$
$$V_3 = V_4 + V_5$$

will proceed almost simultaneously since the required functional units, operand registers, and result register are independent. Similarly,

$$V_0 = V_1 \cdot V_2$$
$$V_4 = V_0 + V_3$$

may proceed almost simultaneously if the appropriate conditions are met. A *chime* is defined as the interval of time during which one or more functional units are in concurrent operation. The possibility of bank conflicts precludes chaining the store operation with the operation of any other functional unit in the CPU.

The maximum floating point arithmetic rate is achieved when the three floating point units are chained together. Since the cycle time of the CPU is 12.5 ns, the maximum rate is approximately 240 million floating point operations per second (megaflops).

In view of the above, our goals for vectorization and optimization on the CRAY-1 will be:

G.1. Formulate the algorithm in terms of vectors whose elements are functionally independent.

G.2. Formulate the algorithm to minimize complications from segmenting the vector modulo 64.

G.3. Structure the vectors in memory so as to avoid bank conflicts during their access.

G.4. Use the vector registers to hold intermediate results whenever possible.

G.5. Maximize parallel execution of the functional units.

III. ASSUMPTIONS

This paper will consider elliptic partial differential equations of the form

$$\frac{\partial}{\partial x}\left(\alpha(x,y)\frac{\partial u}{\partial x}\right) + \frac{\partial}{\partial y}\left(\beta(x,y)\frac{\partial u}{\partial y}\right) = f(x,y) \qquad (1)$$

with Dirichlet boundary conditions. We assume that the region is the unit square with boundaries parallel to the coordinate axes. We divide this region into N+1 vertical panels of equal width and label the boundaries of the panels 0 thru N+1 from left to right. Similarly we divide the region into M+1 horizontal panels with boundaries labeled 0 thru M+1. We assume the definition of a two-dimensional data array in the CRAY-1 memory and that the elements of this array correspond with the intersection of panel boundaries. The Dirichlet boundary data is stored __explicitly__ in this array and is assumed to be part of the input to the algorithm. The element $u_{i,j}$ indicates the numerical approximation to $u(x_i, y_i)$. Superscripts denote iteration number. When an algorithm involves predetermined iteration parameters, e.g., SOR, we assume that optimal values are available. Thus, we will compare the computation time required to update each $u_{i,j}$ per iteration of each algorithm.

IV. POISSON'S EQUATION

To simplify our discussion, we consider the vectorization of finite difference approximations to Poisson's equation. We assume the panel widths are the same in both directions and denote the panel width by h. One way to achieve G.1 is to use the familiar red-black point ordering. That is, if

i + j = 0 (mod 2), the point (i,j) is called *black*,

and if

i + j = 1 (mod 2), the point (i,j) is called *red*.

Figure 1 shows a subset of the array of grid points with "black" points denoted by ●'s and "red" by ◆'s. We do red-black relaxation "by lines." The notation u_i denotes the vector of black points along line i, and $u_{\underline{i}}$ denotes the vector of red points along line i. <u>We require that M be even.</u> Thus u_i and $u_{\underline{i}}$ always contain M/2 + 1 elements and they always contain a boundary value. If i is odd, the first element of $u_{\underline{i}}$ is a boundary value. If i is even, the last element of $u_{\underline{i}}$ is a boundary value. If w is a vector of k elements, we define

$$w^- = \text{vector of the first (k-1) elements of } w$$

and

$$w^+ = \text{vector of the last (k-1) elements of } w .$$

Since boundary values are given, we will always compute $u^+_{i\text{-odd}}$, $u^-_{i\text{-odd}}$, etc.

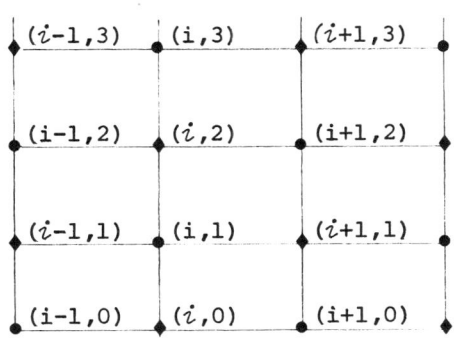

Fig. 1. Red-black ordering, i-odd.

We give explicitly the linear equations to be solved. Along line i-odd and with M even we have

$$\tilde{u}_{i,1} = .25\left[(u_{\underline{i-1},1} + u_{\underline{i},2}) + (u_{\underline{i},0} + u_{\underline{i+1},1})\right] - .25h^2 f_{i,1}$$

$$\tilde{u}_{i,3} = .25\left[(u_{i-1,3}^- + u_{i,4}^-) + (u_{i,2}^- + u_{i+1,3}^-)\right] - .25h^2 f_{i,3}$$

$$\vdots$$

$$\tilde{u}_{i,M-1} = .25\left[(u_{i-1,M-1}^- + u_{i,M}^-) + (u_{i,M-2}^- + u_{i+1,M-1}^-)\right] - .25h^2 f_{i,M-1}$$

or, in vector notation

$$\tilde{u}_i^- = .25\left[(u_{i-1}^- + u_i^+) + (u_i^- + u_{i+1}^-)\right] - .25h^2 f_i^-.$$

Thus for $i = 1, 3, 5, \ldots$,

$$\tilde{u}_i^- = .25\left[(u_{i-1}^- + u_i^+) + (u_i^- + u_{i+1}^-)\right] - .25h^2 f_i^- \tag{2a}$$

$$\tilde{u}_{i+1}^+ = .25\left[(u_i^+ + u_{i+1}^+) + (u_{i+1}^- + u_{i+2}^+)\right] - .25h^2 f_{i+1}^+ \tag{2b}$$

$$\tilde{u}_i^+ = .25\left[(u_{i-1}^+ + u_i^+) + (u_i^- + u_{i+1}^+)\right] - .25h^2 f_i^+ \tag{3a}$$

and

$$\tilde{u}_{i+1}^- = .25\left[(u_i^- + u_{i+1}^+) + (u_{i+1}^- + u_{i+2}^-)\right] - .25h^2 f_{i+1}^- . \tag{3b}$$

These "intermediate values" of u are then used in the relaxation process

$$u^{new} = u^{old} + \omega(\tilde{u} - u^{old}) . \tag{4}$$

Because of the difference in (2) and (3), <u>we also require N to be even</u>. This simplifies details of programming.

We achieve goal G.3 when loading (storing) u_i into (from) a vector register provided $u_{i,j}$ and $u_{i,j+2}$ have a memory spacing unequal to eight or sixteen. Consider the vector $w = (u_i + u_{i+1})$ of M/2 + 1 elements. w^- occurs in (2a) and w^+ occurs in (2b). Thus to achieve G.4, at line i-odd we can calculate w in a vector register and save it there for use at line i + 1. If N = 126, w has 64 elements. We obtain w^- by performing vector operations on w with VL = 63. To obtain

w^+ we shift the first element out of w and again perform computation with VL = 63. Similarly, $v = (u^-_{i+1} + u^+_{i+2})$ is saved from line i + 1 for usage in line i + 2. Note that w has one more element than v, (see Fig. 2). Since the vector registers have 64 elements, the length of w constrains M to a maximum value of 126. Otherwise, the vectors must be segmented. Because of the length of w, M should be equal to or slightly less than a multiple of 126 in order to obtain optimum hardware performance. The explicit inclusion of boundary values into the mesh, together with point relaxation "by lines" simplifies the segmentation process. To achieve G.4, we incorporate the relaxation process and a convergence test into the treatment of each line. Thus we make two sweeps through the mesh: 1) calculate relaxed u and check for convergence, 2) calculate relaxed u and check for convergence.

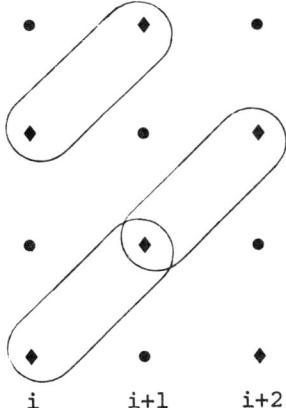

Fig. 2. Circled pairs are elements of
$(u_i + u_{i+1})$ and $(u^-_{i+1} + u^+_{i+2})$
for i-odd.

In order to achieve G.5 we will have to implement our algorithms with carefully written assembly language kernels. Thus we would prefer an algorithm which can be implemented with a single kernel. Implementation of (2) and (3) requires two kernels for red and black points, respectively. Also each kernel must process odd-even pairs of line segments. This leads us to investigate alternative difference approximations. Consider the skewed five-point star for Poisson's equation

$$4u_{i,j} = u_{i-1,j-1} + u_{i-1,j+1} \qquad (5)$$
$$+ u_{i+1,j-1} + u_{i+1,j+1} - 2h^2 f_{i,j} .$$

The truncation error of (5) is larger than the classical five-point star, so we must use a finer mesh. To obtain comparable accuracy, we need M'N' panels where M' = $\sqrt{2}$ M and N' = $\sqrt{2}$ N. This yields twice as many mesh points. However, if we again use the "checkerboard" ordering of Fig. 1, the resulting system of equations decouples into two systems - one for the red points and one for the black [5]. We focus on the system for the red points. The associated mesh is staggered as Fig. 3 illustrates. To solve this system we color even

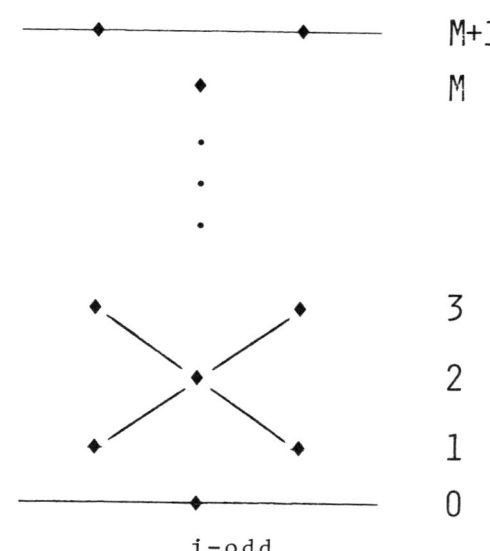

Fig. 3. Red points from checkerboard ordering with skewed approximation.

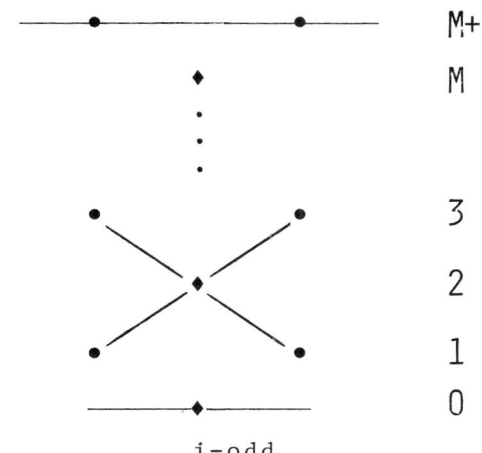

Fig. 4. Column coloring for a staggered mesh.

columns black as illustrated in Fig. 4. This yields

$$\tilde{u}_i^+ = .25\left[(u_{i-1}^- + u_{i-1}^+) + (u_{i+1}^- + u_{i+1}^+)\right] - .5h^2 f_i^+ \qquad (6)$$

for $i = 1, 3, 5, \ldots, N-1$ and

$$\tilde{u}_i^- = .25\left[(u_{i-1}^- + u_{i-1}^+) + (u_{i+1}^- + u_{i+1}^+)\right] - .5h^2 f_i^- \qquad (7)$$

for $i = 2, 4, \ldots, N$.

This system has $(\sqrt{2} N)(M/\sqrt{2}) = MN$ equations. The associated matrix of coefficients does not have point Property (A) [5], but it does have <u>block</u> Property (A). A short calculation shows that the optional choice of ω is

$$\omega = \frac{2}{1 + \sqrt{1 - \mu^2}}$$

where

$$\mu = \cos^2 \pi h.$$

Consequently, the rate of convergence of SOR on this system is $\sqrt{2}$ times that for the five-point star with MN points.

Only one assembly language kernel is required to process both (6) and (7). The segmentation problem can be solved in the same way as for the five-point star.

Since $(u_{i+1}^- + u_{i+1}^+)$ occurs in the equation for u_i and u_{i+2} it can be held temporarily in a vector register. Also, if we use (4), then δu can be held in a vector register for use in the convergence test

$$\text{if } |u_{i,j}^{\text{new}} - u_{i,j}^{\text{old}}| < \varepsilon \text{ for all } i \text{ and } j$$

then

$$\text{FLAG} = 0$$

else

$$\text{FLAG} \neq 0 \ .$$

To illustrate our attempt to achieve G.5, Table 1 displays an outline of a six chime CRAY-1 kernel for (6) and (7). The kernel begins with the assumption that V_0 contains $(u_{i-1}^- + u_{i-1}^+)$ and V_1 contains $(u_{i+1}^- + u_{i+1}^+)$. It ends with $(u_{i+1}^- + u_{i+1}^+)$ in V_0 and $(u_{i+3}^- + u_{i+3}^+)$ in V_1.

Since eight floating point operations are performed in six chimes, we can expect a maximum arithmetic rate of about 100 megaflops. Table 2 displays timing results as a function of vector length. Columns 2 and 3 of this table are conservative in that they were computed from the <u>total</u> time to solve a problem with

$$\varepsilon = \frac{1}{10 \ NM} \ .$$

Table 1

Kernel outline for skewed approximation

CHIME	ACTIVITY	UNIT USED	COMMENT
1	$V_2 \leftarrow 0.5h^2 \cdot F_i$	MEMORY	LOAD RHS
	$V_3 = V_1 + V_0$	FLOATING ADD	ADD PARTIAL SUMS
	$V_4 = 0.25 \cdot V_3$	FLOAT. MULT.	
2	$V_5 \leftarrow U_i^{old}$	MEMORY	LOAD
	$V_6 = V_4 - V_2$	FLOATING ADD	$V_6 = \tilde{U}_i$
	$V_0 = V_1$	SHIFT	
3	$V_7 \leftarrow U_{i+3}^-$	MEMORY	
	$V_3 = V_6 - V_5$	FLOATING ADD	$V_3 = \tilde{U}_i - U_i^{old}$
	$V_4 = \omega \cdot V_3$	MULTIPLY	$V_4 = \delta U$
4	$V_6 \leftarrow U_{i+3}^+$	MEMORY	
	$V_3 = V_5 + V_4$	FLOATING ADD	$V_3 = U_i^{new}$
5	STORE V_3	MEMORY	
	$V_1 = V_7 + V_6$	FLOATING ADD	$V_1 = U_{i+3}^- + U_{i+3}^+$
	$V_2 = ABS(V_4)$	LOGICAL	
6	$V_5 = \varepsilon - V_5$	FLOATING ADD	
	V_6 FORM MASK	LOGICAL	

Table 2
Timing Results for Skewed Approximation

VL	CPU CYCLES PER ELEMENT OF RESULT	TIME PER POINT PER ITERATION	MILLIONS OF FLOAT. PT. OPERATIONS PER SECOND
14	9.8	167 ns	47.8
30	7.6	112 ns	71.2
62	6.8	91 ns	87.9

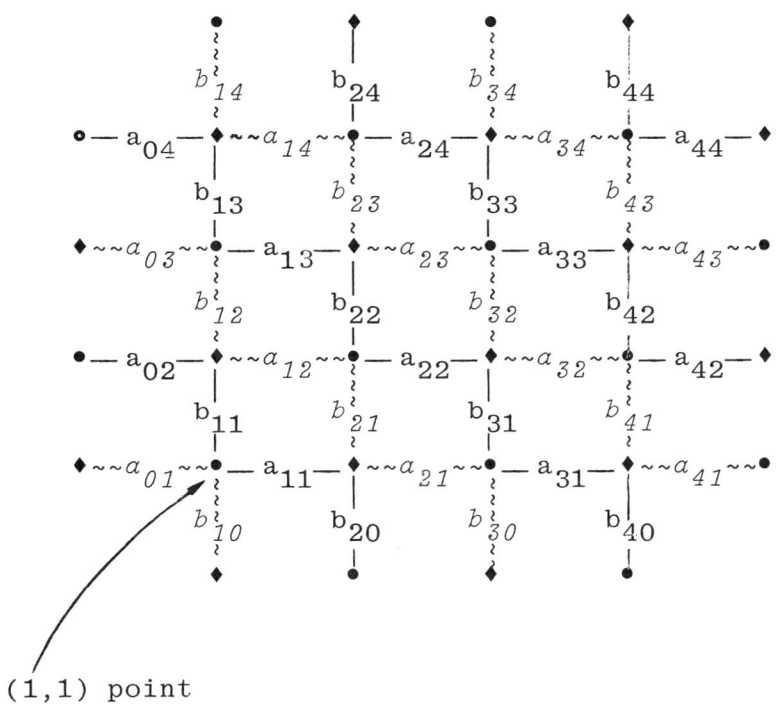

(1,1) point

Fig. 5. Coefficient coloring.

V. THE GENERAL CASE

We now consider the vectorization of the general equation (1). The difference approximation for (1) at $(i\Delta x, j\Delta y)$ is

$$a_{i,j}(u_{i+1,j} - u_{i,j}) - a_{i-1,j}(u_{i,j} - u_{i-1,j})$$

$$+ b_{i,j}(u_{i,j+1} - u_{i,j}) - b_{i,j-1}(u_{i,j} - u_{i,j-1})$$

$$= f_{i,j}$$

where

$$a_{i,j} \equiv a((i + 1/2)\Delta x, j\Delta y)/\Delta x^2$$

and
$$b_{i,j} \equiv b(i\Delta x, (j+1/2)\Delta y)/\Delta y^2 \ .$$

u_i and $u_{\tilde{i}}$ have the same meaning as in the Poisson case. a_i, $a_{\tilde{i}}$, b_i, and $b_{\tilde{i}}$ have similar meanings. The superscripts "+" and "-" also have the same meaning as in the Poisson case. Note that these superscripts only apply to $b_{\tilde{i}}$, i-odd, and b_i, i-even. We again require N and M to be even.

Using Figure 5, we have for i-odd

$$d_{\tilde{i},2}\tilde{u}_{\tilde{i},2} = a_{\tilde{i-1},2}u_{i-1,2} + a_{\tilde{i},2}u_{i+1,2} + b_{\tilde{i},2}u_{i,3} + b_{i,1}u_{i,1} - f_{i,2}$$

$$d_{\tilde{i},4}\tilde{u}_{\tilde{i},4} = a_{\tilde{i-1},4}u_{i-1,4} + a_{\tilde{i},4}u_{i+1,4} + b_{\tilde{i},4}u_{i,5} + b_{i,3}u_{i,3} - f_{i,4}$$

$$\vdots$$

$$d_{\tilde{i},M}\tilde{u}_{\tilde{i},M} = a_{\tilde{i-1},M}u_{i-1,M} + a_{\tilde{i},M}u_{i+1,M} + b_{\tilde{i},M}u_{i,M+1}$$
$$+ b_{i,M-1}u_{i,M-1} - f_{i,M}$$

or

$$d_{\tilde{i}}\tilde{u}_{\tilde{i}}^{+} = a_{\tilde{i-1}}u_{i-1}^{+} + a_{\tilde{i}}u_{i+1}^{+} + b_{\tilde{i}}^{+}u_{\tilde{i}}^{+} + b_i u_i^{-} - f_{\tilde{i}}^{+} \ .$$

Thus, for i = 1, 3, 5, ..., N-1

$$\tilde{u}_{\tilde{i}}^{+} = \left[a_{\tilde{i-1}}u_{i-1}^{+} + a_{\tilde{i}}u_{i+1}^{+} + b_{\tilde{i}}^{+}u_{\tilde{i}}^{+} + b_i u_i^{-} - f_{\tilde{i}}^{+} \right] d_{\tilde{i}}^{-1} \quad (6a)$$

$$\tilde{u}_{\tilde{i+1}}^{-} = \left[a_i u_i^{-} + a_{\tilde{i+1}}u_{i+2}^{-} + b_{\tilde{i+1}}^{+}u_{i+1}^{+} + b_{i+1}^{-}u_{i+1}^{-} - f_{i+1}^{-} \right] d_{\tilde{i+1}}^{-1} \quad (6b)$$

$$\tilde{u}_i^{-} = \left[a_{\tilde{i-1}}u_{i-1}^{-} + a_i u_{i+1}^{-} + b_i u_{\tilde{i}}^{+} + b_{\tilde{i}}^{-}u_{\tilde{i}}^{-} - f_i^{-} \right] d_i^{-1} \quad (6c)$$

and

$$\tilde{u}_{i+1}^{+} = \left[a_{\tilde{i}}u_{\tilde{i}}^{+} + a_{i+1}u_{\tilde{i+2}}^{+} + b_{i+1}^{+}u_{\tilde{i+1}}^{+} + b_{\tilde{i+1}}u_{\tilde{i+1}}^{-} - f_{i+1} \right] d_{i+1}^{-1} \ . \quad (6d)$$

As in the Poisson case these formulations for the red and black points achieve G.1, G.2, and G.3. Also, as in the Poisson case, we make two sweeps through the mesh: 1) calculate $\tilde{u}_i, u_i^{new}$, and check for convergence 2) calculate $\tilde{u}_i, u_i^{new}$, and check for convergence.

The $d_{i,j}$ are the "diagonal coefficients" from the difference approximation. Because the divide operation is rather slow, we will precompute and store the inverses of these diagonal terms. We assume the $d_{i,j}$ are not defined at boundary points. Thus the superscripts "+" and "-" will not apply to them.

Kernels for (6) have been designed, but not implemented. We estimate that they can be implemented in ten chimes and would achieve a maximum arithmetic rate of about 100 megaflops.

Conjugate Gradient Method

In the last several years, the conjugate gradient method has received extensive attention for solving sparse matrix equations [1],[2]. The method has the advantage that it does not require a priori estimation of parameters and that it takes advantage of the distribution of the eigenvalues of the matrix of coefficients. Reid [3] has shown how to utilize structure in the matrix of coefficients when it possesses Property (A) [5]. In particular by choosing the initial approximation appropriately, it is possible to eliminate the calculation of one of the two sequence of parameters and the calculation of the residual vector simplifies; for details see [3]. For solving the difference approximation to Poisson's equation on a rectangular region with the red-black ordering, a simple analysis shows that the amount of work required per iteration is at most twice that required using SOR. If the optimal ω is not known, it appears that the conjugate gradient method would be strong contender to SOR, especially since the asymptotic rate of convergence of SOR is extremely sensitive to the choice of ω.

VI. IRREGULAR REGIONS

A perhaps surprising aspect of the red-black ordering is that it enables relatively easy treatment of irregular regions. Given an irregular region, embed it in a rectangle. For simplicity, we assume that all boundary points are also mesh points. Since the red points are strictly functions of black, we sweep through the mesh on the rectangle in vector mode computing new values at all red points including red boundary points. At the end of the sweep, we restore all red boundary points to their specified value. This is an O(N+M) process. We repeat it for black points, etc. The O(N+M) restoration of boundary values does not interfere with our previously developed vectorization. In general the restoration must be done in scalar mode and this may substantially degrade the vector performance [4].

VII. CONCLUSION

Familiar relaxation procedures are easily implemented on the CRAY-1 including problems with irregular regions. With a rudimentary knowledge of the computer, efficient implementations can be obtained yielding arithmetic rates of up to 100 megaflops.

ACKNOWLEDGMENT

We are endebted to Professor David Young, The University of Texas at Austin, for showing us the decoupling that occurs when the skewed five-point approximation is combined with the checkerboard ordering. Dr. T. L. Jordan, Los Alamos Scientific Laboratory, kindly assisted us with developing the CRAY-1 kernel for (6) and (7).

REFERENCES

1. J. K. Reid, "On the method of conjugate gradients for the solution of large sparse systems of linear equations," Proc. Conference on "Large sparse sets of linear equations," Academic Press, New York, 1971.

2. P. Concus, G. H. Golub, and D. P. O'Leary, "A generalized conjugate gradient method for the numerical solution of elliptic partial differential equations," in Sparse Matrix Computation, J. R. Bunch and D. J. Rose (ed.), Academic Press, New York, 1976.

3. J. K. Reid, "The use of conjugate gradients for systems of linear equations possessing 'Property A'," SIAM J. Numer. Anal. 9 (1972), 325-332.

4. L. Rudsinski and J. Worlton, "The Impact of Scalar Performance in Vector and Parallel Processors", these proceedings.

5. D. Young, <u>Iterative Solution of Large Linear Systems</u>, Academic Press, 1972.

MINIMAL STORAGE BAND ELIMINATION

S. C. Eisenstat, M. H. Schultz[1]
Yale University
A. H. Sherman
University of Texas at Austin

A variation of Gaussian elimination is presented for solving band systems of linear equations on computers with limited core storage, without the use of auxiliary storage such as disk or tape. The method is based on the somewhat unusual idea of recomputing rather than saving most nonzero coefficients in the reduced triangular system, thus trading an increase in work for a decrease in storage. For a five-point problem on an nxn grid, the storage required is $\sim n^2$ versus $\sim n^3$ for band elimination, while surprisingly the work required at most doubles.

I. INTRODUCTION

Consider the system of linear equations
(S)   A x = b

where the coefficient matrix A is an NxN symmetric positive definite band matrix with bandwidth m, i.e., $a_{ij} = 0$ if $|i - j| > m$. Direct methods for solving (S) are generally variations of symmetric Gaussian elimination: Form the $U^t DU$ decomposition of A, where U is unit upper triangular and D positive diagonal, and then successively solve the triangular systems

---

[1] This research was supported in part by NSF Grant MCS 76-11460, ONR Grant N00014-76-C-0277, and AFOSR Grant F49620-77-C-0037.

$$U^t y = b, \quad D z = y, \quad U x = z.$$

The matrix U is again a band matrix with the same bandwidth as A. Variations of symmetric Gaussian elimination which take advantage of this structure to avoid storing and operating on entries outside the band are known as band elimination methods [6]. The total work (in terms of the number of multiplications and divisions) and storage required are given by

$$\theta_B(N,m) = 1/2\ Nm^2 + 7/2\ Nm - 1/3\ m^3 + 0(N + m^2)$$

and

$$S_B(N,m) = Nm + 0(N + m^2),$$

respectively [1].

As an example, consider the following model problem which arises from the familiar five-point finite difference discretization of the Poisson equation on the unit square with homogeneous boundary conditions. Given a uniform nxn grid in the plane we associate a variable u_{ij} with each mesh-point (i,j) and form the system of linear equations

$$4\ u_{ij} - u_{i-1,j} - u_{i+1,j} - u_{i,j-1} - u_{i,j+1} = f_{ij},$$

$$1 \leq i,\ j \leq n,$$

where

$$u_{ij} = 0 \quad \text{for} \quad i = 0,\ n+1 \text{ or } j = 0,\ n+1$$

There are $N = n^2$ unknown variables u_{ij}, and, with the natural row-by-row ordering, the bandwidth is m = n. Thus the work and storage required to solve the linear system are $\sim 1/2\ n^4$ and $\sim n^3$ respectively.

Our model problem illustrates the behavior one often encounters in using Gaussian elimination to solve large band systems: The storage required can easily exceed the core storage available for even moderately large N and m, even though the problem and solution (i.e., A, b, and x) CAN be represented in core. Thus, although we could store the nonzero coefficients, right hand side, and solution for our model problem in $\sim 5n^2$ locations, the factorization would require an additional $\sim n^3$ locations. More generally, although we could store x in N words of storage, we would still require an additional $\sim Nm$ words of storage for D and the band of U, even if we could recompute the nonzero entries of A and b as easily as store them.

In this paper we discuss several variations of band elimination which can solve (S) with minimal core storage. The methods are based on the following assumptions:

(1) The nonzero entries of A and b are inexpensive to generate on demand (e.g., A is sparse and can be represented more compactly than in band form, or A must be preserved for subsequent computations).

(2) There is enough core storage for the solution vector x, plus an additional $\gamma(N+m^2)$ words of working storage (for some small constant γ), but not enough to store the band of U.

We count only the working storage required to solve (S) in stating the storage requirements of such methods. All other storage (i.e., storage for A, b, and x) is associated with the linear system rather than the method of solution and is ignored.

In section II, we review the standard approach to this problem, the use of auxiliary storage, and indicate some of the disadvantages of auxiliary storage band elimination. In section III, we introduce minimal storage methods as a corollary of the somewhat unusual idea of recomputing rather than saving most nonzero entries in the factorization,[2] the effect being to trade a logarithmic increase in work for a factor of N/2m decrease in storage. Finally, in Section IV, we consider the special case of the model problem, and show that the work at most doubles while storage is reduced from $\sim n^3$ to $\sim n^2$.

---

[2] The same approach can be applied to sparse elimination, see [2].

II. AUXILIARY STORAGE BAND ELIMINATION

A standard approach to problems in which the storage required exceeds the amount of core storage available is to use auxiliary storage such as disk or tape. This approach works extremely well for band elimination [5], as can be seen by examining the process more closely.

In the classic view of Gaussian elimination, we use the kth equation to eliminate the kth variable from the remaining $N - k$ equations for $k = 1,\ldots,N$, and then solve the resulting triangular system. In terms of the factorization model, this corresponds to solving

$$U^t y = b, \quad D z = y$$

as A is factored, and then solving

$$U x = z$$

when the factorization is complete. A program fragment for symmetric band elimination using a scratch array M appears as Figure 1a.

Note that only those locations $M[i,j]$ for which $k \leq i \leq j \leq k+m$ are referenced in eliminating the kth variable. These locations form an $(m + 1) \times (m + 1)$ triangular window on the upper band of M. All the previous rows contain entries of U and will not be needed until back-solution; all subsequent columns contain entries of A and have not yet been used in the elimination process; and the window advances as each variable is eliminated (see Figure 1b).

This suggests an auxiliary storage band elimination algorithm. We use core storage as an $(m + 1) \times (m + 1)$ triangular window on the elimination process. After each variable is eliminated, the window is shifted; the row of U left behind is written to auxiliary storage; and the last column of the window is initialized to the next column of A. During back-solution, we retrieve the rows of U in reverse order and solve for the corresponding component of the solution. Since we do exactly the same operations as in band elimination, $\theta_{AS}(N,m) \cong 1/2\ N\ m^2$, yet the core storage required (other than that for A, b, and x which we have agreed

```
FOR k = 1 UNTIL N DO
   {imax = MIN (k+m, N);
    FOR i = k UNTIL imax DO
       M[k,i] = A[k,i];
    x[k] = b[k]};

FOR k = 1 UNTIL N DO
   {imax = MIN (k+m, N);
    FOR i = k+1 UNTIL imax DO
       {uik = M[k,i] / M[k,k];
        FOR j = i UNTIL imax DO
           M[i,j] = M[i,j] - uik * M[k,j];
        x[i] = x[i] - uik * x[k];
        M[k,i] = uik};
    x[k] = x[k] / M[k,k]};

FOR k = N STEP -1 UNTIL 1 DO
   {imax = MIN (k+m, N);
    FOR i = k+1 UNTIL imax DO
       x[k] = x[k] - M[k,i] * x[i]};
```

Fig. 1a. Symmetric band elimination

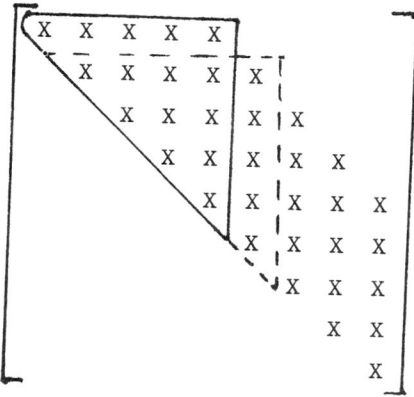

Fig. 1b. The window on the band of A advances at each step.

to ignore) is just that for the window, namely

$$S_{AS}(N,m) = 1/2\ (m + 1)\ (m + 2).$$

An obvious refinement of this algorithm is to save as much of the factorization in core as possible, but, when core storage is exhausted, to make room by moving those rows of U not needed for the next stage of elimination (i.e., not in the window) to auxiliary storage. In a certain sense, in-core band elimination on computers with large virtual memory has the same effect: When no real memory is available, the operating system moves the least recently used pages (i.e., rows of U) out to the swapping device (i.e., auxiliary storage), and then retrieves them as they are referenced during back-solution.

While auxiliary storage band elimination can be used to solve large band systems of linear equations on computers with limited core storage, it does have certain disadvantages. First, a large amount of auxiliary storage is required to save the factorization. Second, the added cost of transferring the factorization to and from auxiliary storage can not be neglected. While in principle this input/output can partially overlap the numerical computation, in practice the degree of such overlap is highly dependent on the machine, auxiliary storage device, and operating system in use. Third, retrieving the rows of U in reverse order requires the ability to read backward or random access auxiliary storage, an operation which is again highly dependent on the program environment.

III. MINIMAL STORAGE BAND ELIMINATION

The disadvantages associated with auxiliary storage band elimination are inherent in the use of auxiliary storage. In this section, we introduce a minimal storage band elimination algorithm for solving band systems of linear equations with limited core storage and NO auxiliary storage. Rather than trade input-output and auxiliary storage for a reduction in core storage, we trade additional arithmetic operations instead.[3] The basic idea behind the algorithm is quite simple. We discard most nonzero coefficients in the reduced triangular system as they are computed and regenerate them during back-solution; only enough information is retained to solve for a subset of the unknowns at each stage, thus reducing the size of the problem to be solved.

Observe that, in solving (S) using auxiliary storage band elimination, after the $(N - m)^{th}$ variable has been eliminated, the coefficients and right hand side of the resulting m x m system remain in core. Thus we can solve for the last m components of the solution without referencing auxiliary storage. Moreover, we can use these values to reduce the size of the problem to be solved. Writing (S) as a block system conforming to the N - m unknown variables x_1 and the m known variables x_2,

$$\begin{pmatrix} A_{11} & A_{12} \\ A_{12}^t & A_{22} \end{pmatrix} \begin{pmatrix} x_1 \\ x_2 \end{pmatrix} = \begin{pmatrix} b_1 \\ b_2 \end{pmatrix},$$

we see that the remaining unknowns x_1 satisfy the reduced system

$$A_{11} x_1 = b_1 - A_{12} x_2 \equiv \tilde{b}_1.$$

This suggests the following method for solving band systems with limited core storage and no auxiliary storage:

(1) Use band elimination to eliminate the first N - m variables, discarding the rows of U as they are computed (i.e., we store only the window).
(2) Solve the resulting dense positive definite system of m equations in the last m variables.
(3) Substitute these values into the original system to obtain a new system of N - m equations in the remaining N - m unknowns.
(4) Solve the new system by the same algorithm.[4]

---

[3] Advances in semiconductor technology have made the central processing unit (as well as attached processors such as array processors) relatively inexpensive compared to auxiliary storage devices. Thus, such an exchange is not unreasonable.

Clearly the storage required is the same as that for auxiliary storage band elimination, i.e.,

$$S(N,m) = 1/2 \ (m + 1)(m + 2);$$

but what is the increased cost? Letting $\theta(n,m)$ denote the work required, we have[5]

$$\theta(N,m) \cong \theta_B(N,m) + \theta(N - m,m)$$

$$\cong 1/2 \ Nm^2 + \theta(N - m,m) \ .$$

Therefore,

$$\theta(N,m) \cong 1/4 \ N^2 m,$$

i.e., the work has increased by a factor of $N/2m$. For our model problem, we have reduced the storage required from $\sim n^3$ to $\sim 1/2 \ n^2$, but the work has increased from $\sim 1/2 \ n^4$ to $\sim 1/4 \ n^5$. Fortunately, we can do much better.

A basic technique for speeding up algorithms is divide-and-conquer. Rather than reduce a problem to a slightly smaller subproblem at each stage, it is often more efficient to reduce it to TWO subproblems each of at most HALF the size. Thus, suppose we could solve for the middle m components of the solution. If we write (S) as a block system conforming to the first $\sim (N - m)/2$ variables x_1, the middle m variables x_2, and the last $\sim (N - m)/2$ variables x_3,

----

[4] Note that the coefficient matrix in the new system, being a principal submatrix of A, is again a symmetric positive definite band matrix with bandwidth (at most) m. Thus the procedure can be applied to the new system.

[5] For ease of exposition, we have assumed that the bandwidth does not decrease and that only m components are solved for at each stage; otherwise the work would be somewhat smaller.

$$\begin{pmatrix} A_{11} & A_{12} & 0 \\ A_{12}^t & A_{22} & A_{23} \\ 0 & A_{23}^t & A_{33} \end{pmatrix} \begin{pmatrix} x_1 \\ x_2 \\ x_3 \end{pmatrix} = \begin{pmatrix} b_1 \\ b_2 \\ b_3 \end{pmatrix}$$

then the remaining unknowns x_1 and x_3 satisfy two INDEPENDENT $\sim (N-m)/2 \times \sim (N-m)/2$ linear systems,

$$A_{11} x_1 = b_1 - A_{12} x_2 \equiv \tilde{b}_1$$

$$A_{33} x_3 = b_3 - A_{32}^t x_2 \equiv \tilde{b}_3.$$

Since the coefficient matrices of the two subproblems are again principal submatrices of A, they are symmetric positive definite band matrices with bandwidth (at most) m. Thus the algorithm can be applied recursively to each of the subproblems. However, to use this technique, we need a method for solving for the middle m components of the solution.

Recall that symmetric Gaussian elimination can be viewed as an elimination process. That is, each equation is used to eliminate the corresponding variable from the remaining equations, and the resulting triangular system is solved for the unknown variables. For band elimination, we observed that, when we eliminate the variables in forward order, no nonzero coefficients are created outside the band. Thus we need only store and operate on coefficients within the band. Of course, the same is true if we eliminate the variables in reverse order, since reversing the order of the variables and equations preserves the band structure. Moreover, since A is positive definite, any order of elimination is numerically stable [7].

This suggests another minimal storage band elimination method:

(1) Eliminate the first $\sim (N-m)/2$ unknowns in forward order, using a triangular window and discarding the rows of U.
(2) Eliminate the last $\sim (N-m)/2$ unknowns in reverse order,

again using a triangular window.[6]
(3) Solve the resulting dense positive definite system of m equations in the middle m unknowns.
(4) Use these values to split the problem into two independent subproblems.
(5) Apply the algorithm recursively to solve each subproblem.

The storage required is approximately twice that of our earlier method, since we must maintain the contents of both windows; in fact, precisely[7]

$$S_{MS}(N,m) = (m+1)^2$$

locations are required. Let $\theta_{MS}(N,m)$ denote the work required to solve a system of N equations with bandwidth m using this algorithm. The work to solve for the middle m unknowns is exactly the same as before so that[8]

$$\theta_{MS}(N,m) \cong \theta_B(N,m) + 2\,\theta_{MS}((N-m)/2, m)$$

$$\cong 1/2\,N\,m^2 + 2\,\theta_{MS}(N/2, m).$$

Thus

---

[6] Evans and Hatzopoulos [3] have used two-sided band elimination to solve centro-symmetric ($a_{ij} = a_{n-i+1,n-j+1}$) band systems of linear equations.

[7] Storing two complete windows would require $(m+1)(m+2)$ locations. However, when reverse elimination (Step (2)) begins, the last column of the forward window contains an unmodified column of A and need not be stored.

[8] Again, for ease of exposition, we have assumed that the bandwidth does not decrease.

$$\theta_{MS}(N,m) \cong 1/2 \ N \ m^2 \ \log_2 \ (2N/m).$$

While minimal storage band elimination avoids the problems associated with the use of auxiliary storage, it does have certain disadvantages. First, the work required has increased logarithmically, although this can be improved somewhat by reordering the subproblems at each stage to minimize bandwidth (see Section IV). Second, the method has no memory. We solve for one right hand side but do not save any of the information needed to solve for additional right hand sides (as in auxiliary storage band elimination). Third, the method is somewhat more complex than in-core or auxiliary storage band elimination.

IV. MINIMAL STORAGE BAND ELIMINATION FOR THE MODEL PROBLEM

In deriving the operation count for minimal storage band elimination, we did not make any additional assumptions about the induced subproblems. We merely observed that the coefficient matrices, being principal submatrices of A, were again symmetric and positive definite with bandwidth (at most) m. As a consequence, the decrease in storage engendered a logarithmic increase in work. However, if the matrix A has more structure, one would expect that the bandwidths of some subproblems could be reduced by reordering the variables and equations, thus reducing the total work required. The savings can be quite significant. We show in this section that the number of arithmetic operations needed to solve our model problem is approximately 5/3 that for band elimination.[9]

Consider minimal storage band elimination applied to a five-point problem on an nxn grid. During the first partial solution step, we solve for the variables on a horizontal grid line[10] which divides the grid into two ~(n/2)xn subgrids (see Figure 2a). Given these values, the problem splits into

----

[9]Similar results are easily obtained for more general finite difference and finite element approximations to self-adjoint elliptic partial differential equations. The key property is that the subproblems generated have a sufficiently regular structure that one can analyze the effect of reordering to minimize bandwidth.

independent five-point problems on each of the two subgrids. The optimum ordering for each subproblem (in terms of minimizing the bandwidth) is the column-by-column ordering for which the bandwidth is ~ n/2 [4]. During the second partial solution step (as applied to the optimally ordered subproblems), we solve for the v vertical grid lines[10] which further subdivide the grid (see Figure 2b). Each resulting subproblem is a five-point problem on an(~ n/2)x(~ n/2)grid. Thus we have reduced our problem to four structurally similar problems of approximately one-fourth the size which can now be solved in the same manner.[11]

```
o o o o o o o                    o o o o o o o
o o o o o o o                    o o o o o o o
o o o o o o o                    o o o o o o o
x x x x x x x      ----->
o o o o o o o                    o o o o o o o
o o o o o o o                    o o o o o o o
o o o o o o o                    o o o o o o o
```

Fig. 2a. The variables on a horizontal grid line subdivide the grid.

---

[10] When n is even, the middle m variables do not lie on a single grid-line; however, we could equally well solve for the m variables on either of the two central grid-lines.

[11] It is interesting to note that the order in which we solve for the variables is essentially the reverse of the nested dissection ordering proposed by George [4] for sparse elimination.

```
o o o x o o o          o o o    o o o
o o o x o o o          o o o    o o o
o o o x o o o          o o o    o o o
              ----->
o o o x o o o          o o o    o o o
o o o x o o o          o o o    o o o
o o o x o o o          o o o    o o o
```

Fig. 2b. The variables on a vertical grid line further subdivide the grid.

Let $\theta_{MS}(p)$ denote the number of arithmetic operations required to solve a five point problem on a p x p grid using optimally ordered minimal storage band elimination. From the preceding discussion, we have

$$\theta_{MS}(p) \cong \theta_B(p^2, p) + 2\theta_B(p^2/2, p/2) + 4\theta_{MS}(p/2)$$

$$\cong 1/2(p^2)(p)^2 + 2 \times 1/2(p/2)^2$$

$$+ 4\theta_{MS}(p/2) + 0(p^3)$$

$$\cong 4\theta_{MS} p/2 + 5/8 p^4 + \theta(p^3).$$

Therefore

$$\theta_{MS}(n) \cong 5/6 \, n^4 + 0(n^3)$$

so that the total work is approximately 5/3 that for band elimination. The total storage is just

$$S_{MS}(n) = (n+1)^2$$

versus $\sim n^3$ for band elimination.

During the execution of this algorithm, we eventually reach a value of p sufficiently small that the entire factorization of each pxp subproblem can be kept in core. In particular, if

$$p < n^{2/3},$$

then the storage required for band elimination satisfies

$$S_B(p^2,p) \cong (p^2)(p) = p^3 < (n^{2/3})^3 = n^2,$$

whereas we have assumed that the amount of storage available is at least $\sim n^2$. Thus we could switch to band elimination at this point. The switch would have very little effect on the total number of arithmetic operations since most of the work is done in the first few stages. None-the-less, the reduced book-keeping makes it a good idea in practice.

REFERENCES

1. Bunch, J.R., Analysis of sparse elimination, SIAM Journal on Numerical Analysis 11:847-873, 1974.

2. Eisenstat, S.E., Schultz, M.H., and Sherman, A.H., Minimal storage sparse elimination. To appear.

3. Evans, D.J. and Hatzopoulos, M., The solution of certain banded systems of linear equations using the folding algorithm, Computer Journal 19:184-187, 1976.

4. George, J.A., Nested dissection of regular a finite element mesh, SIAM Journal on Numerical Analysis 10:345-363, 1973.

5. Jennings, A and Tuff, A.D., A direct method for the solution of large sparse symmetric simultaneous equations, In J. K. Reid, Editor, Large Sparse Sets of Linear Equations, Academic Press, 1971.

6. Martin, R.S. and Wilkinson, J.H., Symmetric decomposition of positive definite band matrices, Numerische Mathematik 7:355-361, 1965.

7. Wilkinson, J.H., The Algebraic Eigenvalue Problem, Clarendon Press, 1965.

A LARGE MATHEMATICAL MODEL IMPLEMENTATION
ON THE STAR-100 COMPUTERS

E. Dick Giroux
Lawrence Livermore Laboratory, University of California

Abstract -- A large two-dimensional mathematical model has been programmed for the CDC STAR-100 computer using vector programming techniques. The program is currently running on the two STAR-100 computers and also on the four CDC 7600s at Lawrence Livermore Laboratory.

Key implementation methods are discussed with reference to the hardware characteristics that influenced the selection of those methods. Results of a problem run are shown along with some running times.

I. INTRODUCTION

CDC STAR-100 computers (1) have been in operation at Lawrence Livermore Laboratory (LLL) for about two years. One of the applications systems that has been implemented on these machines is a large two-dimensional mathematical model called HEMP (2). This program was also used as a key preacceptance program (for hardware checkout) and as one of the acceptance test benchmark programs. The program has been previously implemented at LLL on the IBM 7030 (STRETCH) and on the CDC 7600 machines (3).

This paper describes the mathematical model HEMP in general terms, discusses some of the implementation methods used, (4), gives performance comparisons of the STAR-100 vs. the CDC 7600, and the results of a problem run.

II. THE PROBLEM - THE HEMP MATHEMATICAL MODEL

Since the early days of digital computers, mathematical models have been used to simulate the deformation, motion and interaction of materials as they are subjected to force fields. Material properties, dimensions and configuration are described or "inputted" and the model proceeds to calculate the characteristics of the physical system at later times. These results are often correlated with physical experiments that are used to confirm and refine the calculational methods.

Although all physical things are three dimensional, in many cases they have symmetry in one direction. Therefore a model that follows the motion in two directions (i.e., two-dimensional) can be used to solve these problems. HEMP is a two-dimensional model that has the following characteristics:

1. Lagrange coordinate system.
2. Explicit finite difference scheme.
3. Elastic-plastic flow; Fracturing.
4. Multiple material modeling, including high explosive burn modeling.
5. Decoupled grid calculation (sliding).
6. Diverse boundary conditions.

The solution of the problems by the finite difference method requires that the materials be divided into arbitrarily spaced quadrilateral of the material called "zones". The intersection of these dividing lines at the zone corners are called "nodes".

These nodes are followed in space and time as they are acted upon by the parameters associated with the surrounding four zones. The position and velocities of the four nodes that surround each zone in turn affect the parameters associated with each zone.

III. THE METHODS - THE VECTOR IMPLEMENTATION

Vector codes require that large amounts of intermediate (temporary) data be saved as a problem is being solved (5). This can tax the memory capacity of a machine to a far greater extent than a similar serial implementation. For this reason, it is especially important that the main processes involved in solving the problem be separated so that each process has maximum memory space available to it. It is particularly desirable to separate the main "physics" calculation from the other functions.

The vector HEMP implementation consists of a group of nine programs (CONTROLLEES) that are run by an executive program (CONTROLLER) (6). The CONTROLLEES do tasks that can be conveniently separated and which require minimum communication with each other. This communication is done through the use of short alphanumeric messages that are sent and received by the CONTROLLER and CONTROLLEES. These messages are used for control purposes. The problem data is shared between the CONTROLLEES through large disk files. The principal controllee is the physics CONTROLLEE.

A. Spanning Machines

While the impetus for producing the Vector HEMP system of codes was the impending arrival of the STAR-100 computer, it was decided to create a program that could run from the same source "decks" on both the STARs and 7600s.

One reason for source deck compatibility was to have Vector HEMP debugged and running prior to the arrival of the STAR machines. Another reason was to allow the running of HEMP "production" problems on both types of machines, using a single source program.

The source programs for all CONTROLLEES were written in LRLTRAN (LLL's extended Fortran) (7) and (8). LRLTRAN has vector language extensions and a macro facility. The STAR-100 vector instructions are emulated on the CDC 7600 by compiler generated subroutine calls to a set of highly efficient assembly language coded routines. STACKLIB (9) and (10) is the name of the vector emulation library. BLIB (11) is the vectorized input-output library. There is a STAR-100 version of BLIB and a 7600 version of BLIB.

B. Vector Length vs. Execution Rate

Vector execution rates are a function of the item count of the vector operation and a fixed "start-up" time. Since start-up times tend to be relatively large, it is essential that the vectors be sufficiently long. Start-up time becomes negligible for vectors of lengths greater than about 1000 elements.

A "typical" HEMP problem will have from 30 to 250 nodes in each grid row or column. Because of the start-up time loss associated with short vectors, it would be prohibitively costly to treat each row or column as a separate vector. The two-dimensional grid is structured into vectors and the vectors are manipulated using various techniques.

C. Importance of Thorough Vectorization

Because of the wide disparity in the execution rates of the scalar operations vs. the vector operation on the STAR-100s, it is essential that virtually all of a mathematical model be vectorized. The STAR-100 runs about five times faster than the CDC-7600 when executing vector instructions. In serial mode however, (using LLL's "STAR" compiler) the STAR-100 runs about five times slower than the 7600. Table 1 shows the importance of thorough vectorization for optimal STAR-100 performance.

Table 1

A Comparison of STAR-100 vs. 7600 CPU Times with Various Percentages of Vectorization ("STAR" Compiler)

	7600 CPU Run Time	STAR-100 CPU Run Time
100% Vectorized	100 Min.	20 Min.
20% Scalar 80% Vectorized	20 Min. Portion 80 Min. Portion 100 Min. Total	100 Min. (Scalar) 16 Min. (Vector) 116 Min. Total
50% Scalar 50% Vectorized	50 Min. Portion 50 Min. Portion 100 Min. Total	250 Min. (Scalar) 10 Min. (Vector) 260 Min. Total
100% Scalar	100 Min.	500 Min (Scalar)

D. Vector Manipulation

A Vector is defined to be a contiguous array of data whose boundaries are specified by a structured descriptor word which specifies a data address and an item count. The data contained in a vector may be floating point, integer, bit, byte or character.

The ease with which one can manipulate data is the essential feature of vector programming. We can manipulate word vectors with such operations as:

1. Compress   -selects a subset of a vector under the control of a bit vector
2. Merge   -puts together two vectors under the control of a bit vector.

3. Compare   – generates bits in a bit vector as a result of comparing two vectors.
4. Transmit
   index list– collects into a contiguous result vector, discontiguous elements from another vector by using an index vector.
5. Transmit
   index destination – stores into discontiguous locations the contiguous elements of another vector by using an index vector.

E. Geometric Data Manipulation

The HEMP equations-of-motion require the calculation of a line integral at each node. This is represented by the dashed line shown connecting nodes I, II, III, and IV in Fig. 1. In addition, zonal data must be accessed at zones (1), (2), (3), and (4).

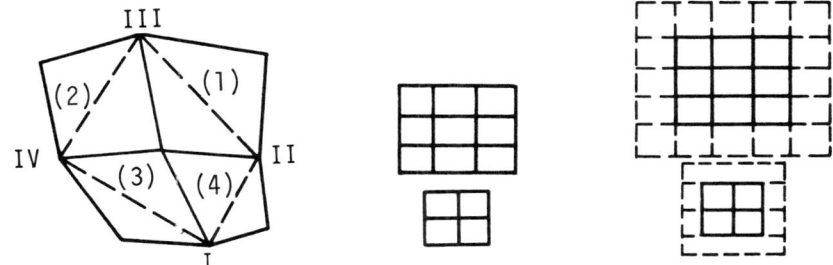

Fig. 1 HEMP acceleration   Fig. 2 A simple   Fig. 3 HEMP grid
        arms   HEMP grid   with phony
                                                           zones and nodes

The movement of the boundary points, while subject to various non-general conditions, are substantially calculated with the same equations (and therefore in the same vectors) as the interior grid points. For the purpose of describing the vector techniques used in doing some of the calculations, a tiny grid with a slide-line is shown in Fig. 2. In order that we may treat all nodes with the same equations to obtain a "tentative" acceleration, we expand the nodal vectors with a "geometric bit string." By geometric bit string, we mean a bit string whose bit pattern is dictated by the grid's shape and size. This expansion creates a vector that has vacant elements for the insertion of "phony node" values. The expanded grid is shown in Fig. 3. Through the use of compression, expansion, and controlled-store operations, the phony nodes

are assigned the values of the adjoining real boundary nodes.
The zonal quantities are expanded out in a similar manner.
Now we have vectors that includes phony nodes and phony zones.

Compression with appropriate geometric bit strings is
done to isolate the diagonal end points. The diagonal differences (which are zonal-centered quantities) are calculated.
These diagonal differences are compressed with another set of
geometric bit strings to produce nodal-centered values. These
are used to calculate the acceleration terms. New velocities
are calculated that are used to reposition the nodes.

Since acceleration terms are needed for the boundary calculations (including slide-lines), it is more efficient to
calculate these terms in one vector pass. For boundary
points, the position is only tentative and may be overriden by
subsequent calculations.

F. Decoupled Grid Calculations

The decoupled grid calculations (see Figs. 2 and 3) are
referred to as slide-line calculations.

Slide-line calculations are complex. They require that
nodes and zones on each side of the slide-line be associated
with nearby nodes and zones on the opposite side of the slide-line. Fig. 4 shows how zones must be mapped across a slide-line. This relationship can change from problem cycle to problem cycle. A search procedure is required to determine this
relationship. This was at first thought to be an inherently
serial process. We vectorized this procedure so that it is
done in a few iterations, through the use of cascading compare
and compress operations.

Fig. 4 Side-line mapping

An "ordering index" vector is calculated and saved from
cycle to cycle. This vector describes the relative nodal positions at that cycle. During each cycle, the ordering index
vectors are updated to reflect positional changes. All nodes
on one side of the line are compared with their previously
known solution points on the other side to determine if those
solutions are currently correct. The currently correct nodes
are compressed out of the vector. A trial ordering adjustment

is made with the reduced vector. If found to be satisfactory, these solutions are compressed out. This iterative procedure is continued until all solutions are found. The relative positions of the slide-line nodes change little from cycle to cycle. Ordinarily, only one to three iterations are required to update all the ordering index numbers. This process quickly cascades from full-length slide-line vectors to much shorter vectors. Although they are more involved, subsequent slide-line calculations that use these ordering numbers cascade in a similar manner.

Slide-line manipulation requires the building and use of dynamic bit strings. These conditional bit strings are used to compress a sequential index set that is used to fetch or store elements of data within the slide-line vectors. Slide-lines are relatively short, and we may have several slide-lines in a problem. Therefore, they are catenated so that all slide-lines can be calculated in one vector pass.

G. Material Properties Calculations - Equations-of-State Handling

Each problem can have associated with it a number of material property modeling equations-of-state. In practice, the same equation-of-state is associated with many contiguous zones. This enables us to:

1. select zones with like material properties,
2. arrange the zonal variables into material-related vectors,
3. calculate similar zones concurrently.

A particular zonal grid vector is composed of packed integer fields. One field is a group of numbers that is associated with a particular equation-of-state form. Another field is a material number within that form. The material number within the form is used as an index to access equations-of-state coefficients within that form. When the material properties are to be calculated within a problem cycle, this vector is unpacked (using vector operators) into a number of full-word vectors. A vector compare is done to determine which zones are associated with each equation-of-state form. The appropriate variables are then compressed out using the resulting bit string. The corresponding material within the form numbers is also compressed out. The form number is used to control a branch to the appropriate equation-of-state coding. The material number within the form number is used as an index to select the appropriate equation-of-state coefficients for the material. The program makes repeated passes through this procedure until all zonal material properties are calculated. The program is provided with a list of forms for a given problem.

H. Dynamic Calculation Method Selection

In general, a particular vector compare produces a different bit string each problem cycle. Calculational selection is done in vector programming through the use of vector compare operations and the utilization of the resulting bit vector to control the subsequent calculations. In a serial program this would be done by conditional branching. We use two methods of control logic. One method is the previously mentioned vector compare-compress-calculate-expand-and-store series of operations. There is overhead in doing the compressions and expansions in this method. A second method is to use full-length (uncompressed) vectors, and then use a bit string(s) to control the storing of the results. Here we are calculating many results that are going to be unused, and therefore wasted. Whether to use the compress-expand method or the controlled-store method depends on the density of the bit string and the amount of calculation on each side of the fork.

When the bit string is relatively sparse, it is generally more efficient to compress, calculate, expand, and store. When the bit string is relatively dense, it is generally more efficient to calculate the entire vector and use the controlled store. The method to use is determined through the use of an equation that has in it the vector lengths, the operation types, and the number of operations on each side of the fork (12).

I. Dynamic Operation Skipping

The issuance of one vector instruction produces a large number of results. This has introduced another time-saving flow-control technique that is not available in serial programming – operation skipping (12). Some of the HEMP equations contain terms that are not used in a particular problem. In serial programming, it is often more expensive to check a flag and possibly skip an operation each time through a long loop than to issue the unnecessary instruction(s). In vector programming, a scalar test may allow a sequence of vector instructions to be skipped, thereby saving hundreds or thousands of unrequired operations.

J. Descriptor-Data Tree Structures

Some index sets, bit strings, and other data sets are constructed at problem generation time; others are built dynamically during execution. Because of the wide divergence of HEMP problem sizes, shapes, and options, the use of fixed blocks of memory to store this data would be a waste of storage space. To conserve core, we pack this data in memory. We access this data through a series of linked descriptors or "tree structures" that point to the data. The top descriptor points to a vector of descriptors, each of which points to another vector of descriptors or data. Each descriptor tree eventually points to data.

K. Dynamic Temporary Vector Allocation

The evaluation of a typical vector arithmetic expression requires temporary vectors of the same length as the result vector. The length of result vectors in typical HEMP problems are 1500 to 10,000 elements long. As in serial programming, certain calculational results must be saved for later use. In serial programs, this does not present a memory management problem, since each saved result needs only one word of memory. In vector programming this is a serious problem. Each saved result is a vector that requires a large amount of memory. To alleviate this problem, we reuse the same dynamic vector space as much as possible. This procedure gives rise to a major vector allocation problem. This problem is alleviated through the use of a simple "saved vector" allocation scheme.

The base addresses of saved temporary word vectors are kept in a stack. Initially, the base addresses in a stack are in ascending order. The number of words between any two adjacent entries in a stack is the same (the length of the longest result vector needed). When a calculation needs a result vector, it takes the next entry (address) from a stack. When a result vector is no longer needed, the address is returned to the stack.

L. Multiple Vector Passes Per Problem Cycle

When discussing the equations, it was assumed that all vectors were full grid size. This was a simplistic view to make the discussion easier to understand. In actual practice, a problem may be calculated by making multiple passes through the equations. This is necessary because the 7600's and STAR-

100's do not have enough core memory available for the save-vectors to be the length of a large full grid vector. The number of passes through the equations is a function of the maximum size of a saved result vector and the size of a grid vector.

IV. THE RESULTS

HEMP was used as a key test program prior to the delivery of the STAR-100s. It was also used as part of the acceptance tests. Since that time (about two years) it has been used extensively in solving physics problems of various types. Problems vary in size from a few hundred to over 45,000 zones and in running time from a few minutes to several hours.

A. Calculational Speed

Most HEMP problems contain several materials, several slide-lines, and numerous external boundary condition constraints. Problems of normal size calculate on the STAR-100s at a CPU rate of about 25 nodes per millisecond (40 microseconds per node). The typical speed-up factor of a STAR-100 vector code calculation over the same problem run using the serial code on the 7600s is about 4 to 6 times. The vector code on the 7600s runs about 20% faster than the serial code on the same machine.

This speed-up factor has been important in a number of ways, one of which is the fact that we are able to do large problems on the STAR-100 that would have taken prohibitively long on the 7600 serial code, i.e., problems that would have taken from 15 to 20 hours using the 7600 serial code can now be done in 3 to 4 hours on the STAR-100s.

B. Problem Results

Fig. 5 shows computer generated configuration plots of a flat nosed projectile of tungsten striking a steel plate one inch thick. The projectile is one inch in diameter, four inches long, and traveling at a velocity of 5,000 feet per second. The figure has configuration plots at 0, 40 and 80 microseconds after the initial impact. As can be seen the projectile easily penetrated the one inch thick plate. Other calculations show that a four inch thick plate is able to stop the projectile. A two inch plate is also penetrated by the projectile. The four inch problem takes over two hours to run on the 7600 but only about 25 minutes to run on the STAR-100.

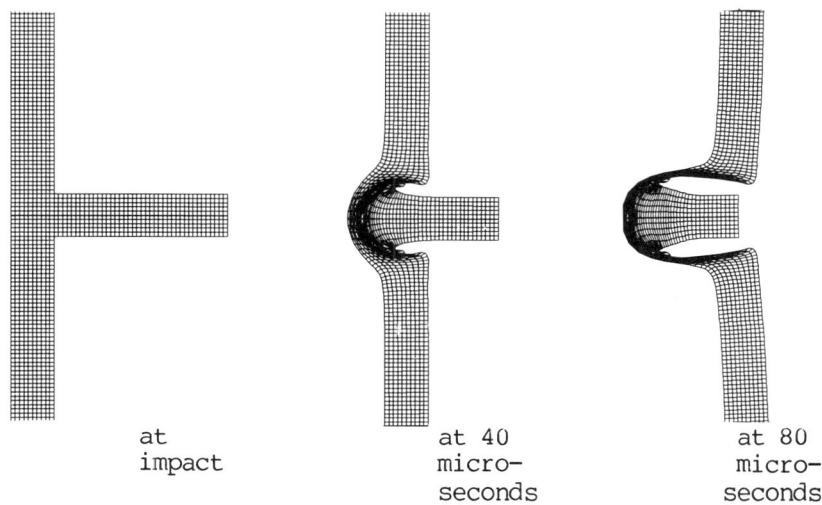

at	at 40	at 80
impact	micro-	micro-
	seconds	seconds

Figure 5 Tungsten Cylinder Striking Steel Plate

V. CONCLUSION

The hardware characteristics of the STAR-100 are such that a program must be thoroughly vectorized using long vectors and few scalar operations if it is to execute at a near optimum rate.

This thorough vectorization of the HEMP mathematical model for the STAR-100 computers at LLL has produced significant improvement in calculational ability over the 7600 scalar version of the mathematican model. We now run problems that were too large for, and/or would have taken prohibitive amounts of time on, the 7600 computers.

VI. ACKNOWLEDGEMENTS

This work was performed under the auspices of the U.S. Energy Research and Development Administration.

Many of the programming techniques used in the implementation of Vector HEMP were suggested by Jerry L. Owens. Valere J. Kransky and Owens participated in the early design work. Gary A. Long made major contributions including the design and implementations of the vector libraries. A key programmer in the entire HEMP developmental effort has been J. Alan Leibee.

VII. REFERENCES

(1) Control Data Corporation, "STAR-100 Computer System Hardware Reference Manual", (1971), 125 pp.

(2) Wilkins, M. L., "Calculation of Elastic-Plastic Flow", Lawrence Livermore Laboratory, UCRL-7322, Rev. 1 (Jan. 1969), 101 pp.

(3) Giroux, E. D., "HEMP Users Manual", Lawrence Livermore Laboratory, UCRL-51079, Rev. 1 (Dec. 1973), 206 pp.

(4) Kransky, V. J., Giroux, E. D. and Long, G. A., "Parallel Implementation of a Two-Dimensional Model", Lawrence Livermore Laboratory, UCRL-74894 (Aug. 1973), 9 pp.

(5) Litterst, R., et al., "Vector Programming Tools and Techniques", Lawrence Livermore Laboratory, UCIR-856 (Jan. 1975), 233 pp.

(6) Control Data Corporation, "Control Data STAR Computer System". Control Data Corporation, (1975), 400+ pp.

(7) Zwakenberg, R., "LRLTRAN Extensions", Lawrence Livermore Laboratory, UCID-30019 (July 1971), 17 pp.

(8) Zwakenberg, R., "LRLTRAN LANGUAGE Used with the CHAT and STAR Compilers", LTSS, Part III, Ch. 207 (Jul. 1973), 170 pp.

(9) McMahon, F. H., Sloan, L. J., Long, G. A., "STACKLIB - A Vector Function Library of Optimum Stack-Loops for the CDC 7600", Lawrence Livermore Laboratory, UCID 30083 (Nov. 1972), 90 pp.

(10) Long, G. A., and Owens, J. L., "Bit and Byte Vector Operations and an Introduction to STARTRAN", Lawrence Livermore Laboratory, UCID-30005 (April 1971), 58 pp.

(11) Long, G. A., "The BLIB76 Subroutine Library and Macro File CF76 Compatible with the BLIBSTAR Subroutine Library and Macro File CFSTAR", Lawrence Livermore Laboratory, UCID 30098, Rev. 1 (1975), 77 pp.

(12) Owens, J. L., "The Influence of Machine Organization on Algorithms", Lawrence Livermore Laboratory, UCRL-74795 (May 1973), 30 pp.

AN ANALYSIS OF THE RECURSIVE DOUBLING ALGORITHM

P. Dubois and G. Rodrigue
Lawrence Livermore Laboratory

I. VECTOR NOTATION

We will be using the vector notation developed in [6]. That is, if R_k is the set of k×k real matrices, then $v = [v_1, \ldots, v_m]^T$ is a vector of length m having elements in R_k and $v(i) = v_i$. If $C = (c_{ij})$, $i,j = 1, \ldots, n$ with $c_{ij} \in R_k$, then the vectors c_j for $j > 0$ denotes the j-th superdiagonal of C and c_{-j} for $j \geq 0$ denotes the j-th subdiagonal of C. The matrix C is then to be denoted as $C = (c_j)$, $-(n-1) \leq j \leq (n-1)$. We also adopt the notation $v = c$ for some $c \in R_k$ means $v(i) = c$ for all i.

II. THE RECURSIVE DOUBLING ALGORITHM

Let $A = (a_j)$, $-(n-1) \leq j \leq (n-1)$, such that $a_0(i)$ is the k×k identity matrix, and for some integer $\ell > 0$, $a_j = 0$, $j \neq -\ell$. We consider the problem (*) of solving the system of equations $Ax = r$. Now, $A = I - B$ where $I = nk \times nk$ identity matrix and $b_j = 0$, $j \neq -\ell$. We then get the following generalization of Stone's recursive doubling algorithm, [1]:

Theorem 1 Let $y_0 = r$ and for $i = 0, 1, 2, \ldots$ let $y_{i+1} = y_i + B^{2^i} y_i$. Then y_α is a solution of (*) for α such that $\alpha \geq \log_2(n/\ell)$.

Proof: It is easy to show that $y_i = (I + B + B^2 + \ldots + B^{2^i-1})y_0$. Since $B^\gamma = 0$ for $\gamma \geq n/\ell$, $(I-B)^{-1}r = \sum_{i=0}^{\gamma} B^i r$.   Q.E.D.

__Corollary 1__ Suppose for some integer $p \geq 0$ we have $a_{-\ell}(m) = 0$, $m = jp$, $j = 1, 2, \ldots$. If $y_0 = r$, let y_i be calculated as in Theorem 1. Then y_α is a solution (*) for α such that $\alpha \geq \log_2(\beta/\ell)$, $\beta = \min\{p,n\}$.

A. Stability

Although the algorithm of recursive doubling will terminate after a fixed number of steps, the algorithm is subject to computer overflow problems. This is evident from Theorem 1 where it is observed that the approximation to the solution (*) is calculated by matrix multiplications. To analyze this problem, we say that the algorithm of recursive doubling is __stable__ if there exists a constant $K > 0$ such that $||y_i|| \leq K$, $i = 0, 1, 2 \ldots$ and is said to be __weakly__ __stable__ if $||y_i|| \leq K2^i$, $i = 0, 1, 2, \ldots$.

__Theorem 2__ The algorithm of recursive doubling is i) stable if $||B|| < 1$, and ii) weakly stable if $||B|| = 1$.
 Proof: By **Theorem 1**,
$$||y_{i+1}|| \leq || \sum_{j=0}^{2^{i+1}-1} B^j || \ ||y_0||.$$
If $||B|| < 1$, $||y_{i+1}|| \leq ||y_0||/(1-||B||)$. If $||B|| = 1$, then $||y_{i+1}|| \leq 2^i ||y_0||$.   Q.E.D.

III. M-TERM LINEAR RECURRENCE RELATIONS

 Consider the general m-term linear recursive relation
(†) $P_m(i)q_{i-m} + P_{m-1}(i)q_{i-m-1} + \ldots + P_0(i)q_i = R(i)$ where $m \geq 1$ and $P_0(i)P_m(i) \neq 0$. Without loss of generality we assume $P_0(i) = 1$ for all i. We wish to compute a particular solution $\{q_i\}_{i=m}^\infty$ defined by the initial conditions $q_i = a_i$, $0 \leq i \leq m-1$. Now, the recurrence relation (†) is equivalent to the 1-term vector recurrence $\bar{r}_i = \bar{q}_i - G_i \bar{q}_{i-1}$, $i = m$, $m + 1, m + 2, \ldots$ where

$$G_i = \begin{bmatrix} -P_1(i) & \cdots & -P_m(i) \\ 1 & 0 & 0 \\ 0 & 1 & 0 \end{bmatrix};$$

$$\bar{q}_i = \begin{bmatrix} q_i \\ \vdots \\ q_{i-r+1} \end{bmatrix}, \; i \geq m-1 \; ; \; \bar{r}_i = \begin{bmatrix} R(i) \\ 0 \\ \vdots \\ 0 \end{bmatrix}, \; i \geq m.$$

It follows that the calculation of $\bar{q}_j$, $1 \leq j \leq M$, is equivalent to the solving the system (**) $Aq = r$ where

$$A = \begin{bmatrix} I & & 0 \\ -G_1 & \ddots & \\ 0 & -G_M & I \end{bmatrix}, \quad q = \begin{bmatrix} \bar{q}_{m-1} \\ \vdots \\ \bar{q}_M \end{bmatrix}$$

$$r = \begin{bmatrix} \bar{r}_{m-1} \\ \vdots \\ \bar{r}_M \end{bmatrix}, \quad \bar{r}_{m-1} = \begin{bmatrix} a_0 \\ a_1 \\ \vdots \\ a_{m-1} \end{bmatrix}$$

Notice that the system (**) is in the same form as (*) where in this case, $k = m$ and $\ell = 1$. Hence the recursive doubling algorithm of Theorem 1 can be applied to solve (**) and thus (†).

IV. TRIDIAGONAL LINEAR SYSTEMS

A. LU-Decomposition

Let $T = (t_j)$, $-(n-1) \leq j \leq (n-1)$, be a tridiagonal matrix, i.e., $t_j = 0$ for $j \neq -1, 0, 1$. In solving the system $Tx = k$ on a computer, one first calculates two matrices L and U such that (i) $LU = T$, (ii) L is a lower bidiagonal matrix with unit diagonal, (iii) U is an upper bidiagonal matrix. More specifically, $U = (u_j)$, $-(n-1) \leq j \leq (n-1)$, where $u_j = 0$ for $j \neq 0, 1$, $u_1 = t_1$, and

$$u_o(1) = t_o(1)$$

(4.1)
$$u_o(i) = t_o(i) - \left[t_{-1}(i-1)t_1(i-1)/u_o(i-1) \right],$$
$$2 \leq i \leq n,$$

and $L = (\lambda_j)$, $-(n-1) \leq j \leq (n-1)$, where $\lambda_0 = 1$ and $\lambda_{-1}(i) = t_{-1}(i)/u_o(i)$, $1 \leq i \leq n-1$. Note that once the vector u_o has been determined, the computation of λ_{-1} and hence the matrix L can be done easily in parallel. Thus, if an efficient parallel method for calculating (4.1) can be devised, the LU factorization of T is complete.

Following the technique of Stone [1], we first define

$$q_o = 1, \quad q_1 = t_o(1)$$

(4.2)
$$q_i = t_o(i) - t_{-1}(i-1)t_1(i-1)q_{i-2}, \quad 2 \leq i \leq n,$$

so that $u_o(i) = q_i/q_{i-1}$, $2 \leq i \leq n$. Hence, if a parallel method for calculating (4.2) can be developed, then the calculation (4.1) can be obtained immediately. Note that (4.2) is a 2-term linear recurrence relation so that the recursive doubling technique developed in sections III and IV can be used. In this case, we have for $2 \leq i \leq n$ that $R(i) = 0$, $P_1(i) = -t_o(i)$, and $P_2(i) = t_{-1}(i-1)t_1(i-1)$. Hence, the matrices G_i of section IV are given by

$$G_i = \begin{bmatrix} t_o(i) & -t_{-1}(i-1)t_1(i-1) \\ -1 & 0 \end{bmatrix}$$

1. *Stability*

By Theorem 2, weak stability of the recursive doubling algorithm as applied to the LU decomposition of a tridiagonal system will be assured if $||B||_\infty = \max ||G_i||_\infty \leq 1$. Since the ℓ_∞ matrix norm is the maximum absolute row sum, we see that weak stability is assured if $||B||_\infty = \max\{1, |t_o(j)| + |t_{-1}(j-1)t_1(j-1)|\} < 1$. Let $C = ||B||_\infty$ and $T' = C^{-1}T$. It is clear that a weakly stable recursive doubling can be used to generate $T' = L'U'$, the LU decomposition of T'. It then follows that $C L'U' = L'(CU') = T$ is the LU decomposition of T. That is, by using recursive doubling to generate the LU decomposition of the "scaled" matrix T', one can then obtain easily the LU decomposition of the original system T.

The recursive doubling algorithm for generating the LU decomposition was programmed in LRLTRAN ([2]), compiled with the FENIX compiler, and executed on a CDC-STAR-100 for the n×n system T defined by $t_o = 10$ and $t_1 = t_{-1} = -1$. The algorithm caused overflow for $n \geq 350$. The algorithm was then executed on the scaled system $C^{-1} T$ where $C = 12$ and no overflow was observed for n as high as 4000.

It must be added that possible underflow may still present problems in some cases, and that more numerical experimentation is required to see if difficulties occur on real problems. Presumably, if $||B^{2^i}||$ becomes small, then y_i is already "close" to the answer. But trouble could presumably occur if some elements are large while others are small.

B. Backward-Forward Substitution

Once the LU decomposition of T has been performed, the solution of the tridiagonal system Tx = k is a two step process. Letting y = Ux, we have Tx = LUx = Ly = k. The equation Ly = b is easily solved by recursive doubling as it is already in the prescribed form described in section II where in this case $\ell = 1$ and r = k. The system Ux = y is solved by the 1-term recurrence relation:

$$x_n = y_n/u_o(n) \quad , \quad x_i = y_i - x_{i-1}t_1(i+1)/u_o(i) \quad .$$

Thus, recursive doubling can again be used.

1. Stability

By Theorem 2, stability for recursive doubling will be assured if

$$\max \{|t_1(j+1)/u_o(j)|\} < 1 \text{ and } \max \{|t_{-1}(j)/u_o(j)|\} < 1 \enspace .$$

Since the $u_o(i)$ are precisely the pivot elements from Gauss Elimination, it can be shown (cf [4]) that the above inequalities will hold in the case when T is symmetric and diagonally dominant. We thus get:

Theorem 3 Let T be symmetric and diagonally dominant. Then recursive doubling applied to the backward and forward substitutions is stable.

2. Computational Aspects

Recursive doubling was executed on a CDC-STAR-100 to solve a tridiagonal system. It is known (cf. [3]) that the execution time should behave like $O(n \log_2 n)$. A STAR assembly language version of Gauss Elimination, on the other hand, has been shown in [3] to behave like $O(n)$. On executing both algorithms on the STAR it was found that recursive doubling was slower than Gauss Elimination for $n \leq 4000$. Apparently n has to be very large to produce the asymptotic behaviors described in [3].

V. OPERATOR SPLITTING

On solving time dependent parabolic partial differential equations by operator splitting techniques (cf [5]) one has to repeatedly solve triple diagonal systems of the form (i) $Rx = k$, $R = (r_j)$, $-(n-1) \leq j \leq (n-1)$, where $r_j = 0$ for $j \neq -1, 0, 1$, and (ii) $Sx = k$, $S = (s_j)$, $-(n-1) \leq j \leq (n-1)$, where $s_j = 0$ for $j \neq -\ell, 0, \ell$. For purposes of clarity, let us assume n is a perfect square and $\ell = \sqrt{n}$. Then, the system (i) has the additional property that $r_1(i) = r_{-1}(i) = 0$ for $i = \ell, 2\ell, 3\ell, \ldots$. Hence, on using recursive doubling for the backward-forward substitutions of the above systems the results of Corollary 1 hold. That is, the algorithm will terminate at step α where $\alpha \geq \frac{1}{2} \log_2 n$. Also, the systems described above are in general symmetric and diagonally dominant so that the stability results of Theorem 3 apply. That is, if the LU decomposition of the systems are calculated via some stable algorithm (this need not be by recursive doubling), then the forward and backward substitutions can be done by a stable recursive doubling algorithm. Run time (in microseconds) comparisons on the STAR for solving a system (i) described above are given in Table 1. The Gauss Elimination algorithm was coded in assembly language and recursive doubling was used in both the LU decomposition and the forward-back substitution.

TABLE 1

n	Gauss Elimination	Recursive Doubling
500	4235	4165
2000	16966	15264
4000	33978	31021

VI. REFERENCES

(1) Stone, H.S., "An Efficient Parallel Algorithm for the Solution of a Tridiagonal Linear System of Equations," JACM, Vol. 20, No. 1, January 1973.

(2) Martin, S., Solbeck, S., Zwakenberg, R., LRLTRAN Language Used with Chat.

(3) Lambiotte, J., Voigt, R., "The Solution of Tridiagonal Linear Systems on the CDC STAR-100 Computer," ICASE Report, July 1974.

(4) Wilkinson, J., "Error Analysis of Direct Methods of Matrix Inversion," JACM, 8, 281-230.

(5) Yanenko, N., The Method of Fractional Steps, Springer-Verlag, 1971.

(6) Madsen, N., Rodrigue, G., Karush, J., "Matrix Multiplication by Diagonals on a Vector/Parallel Processor," Info. Proc. Letters, Vol. 5, No. 2, June 1976, 41-45.

(7) Dubois, P., Rodrigue, G., "An Analysis of the Recursive Doubling Algorithm," Dec. 1976, LLL report, UCRL-79071.

(8) Heller, D., "A Determinant Theorem with Applications to Parallel Algorithms," Carnegie-Mellon Computer Science Report, March 1973.

(9) Sameh, A., Kuck, D., "A Parallel QR Algorithm for Symmetric Tridiagonal Matrices," Univ. of Illinois Computer Science Report, July 1975.

(10) Sameh, A., Kuck, D., "On Stable Parallel Linear System Solvers," Univ. of Illinois Computer Science Report, Feb. 1976.

ALGORITHM DESIGN FOR DIGITAL IMAGE CORRELATION
ON A PARALLEL PROCESSOR

David L. Ackerman
Topographic Division
U.S. Geological Survey

Digital image correlation pertains to image point matching on digital representations of continuous-tone photography. The correlation process is very time consuming due to the many arithmetic operations required to determine a correlation value. The number of arithmetics varies according to the method of correlation. Three methods are the linear correlation coefficient, covariance, and sums of absolute differences. Two techniques for image correlation are line correlation and area correlation. Line correlation involves searching along epipolar lines using a one-dimensional window of gray shades (pixels). Area correlation pertains to using a two-dimensional window of pixels to search for a match point either over an area or along a specific epipolar line. Epipolar lines are defined by the geometry of a stereoscopic pair of photographs. Correlation experiments using the above methods were performed at USAETL on a GAC S1000P STARAN.

The first step in algorithm design for STARAN is extracting the parallelism in the problem. The parallelism in digital image correlation consists of the many additions and multiplications which must be performed. The computations require the sum of the pixels in the window, the sum of the pixels in the search area covered by the window, and the sum of the products of the pixels in the window with the corresponding pixels in the search area. The analyst must determine the most efficient method for storing the pixels into the STARAN's arrays. If the pixels are not properly arranged, maximum parallelism will not be realized. The digitized image may be stored as it appears in the photograph, each scan line running horizontally across an array, one scan line per word. A second method is to store the scan lines vertically in array fields with one or more lines stacked vertically per field. The first method makes very inefficient use of the array space. For eight bit data (256 gray shades), scan lines of 32 pixel length would be the maximum line size that could be stored across one word of an array. If sign bits are included the length would be even less. Storing the image in this manner breaks up the array space in such a way that it cannot be used efficiently for computations. Storing the scan lines vertically in array fields makes maximum use of the parallelism. If the windows are small (16 x 16 pixels or less), one or more windows can be lined up with the corresponding patches in the search area. A minimum amount of array space is used. The vertical fields allow the analyst to take advantage of the computing technique called tree summing.

Data management in the arrays is extremely important. Not only must the algorithm arrange the data properly, but it must manipulate it properly. Digital image correlation involves a great deal of computational overlap. Each patch of n x n pixels in the search area will have many pixels in common with preceding and succeeding patches. The amount of overlap depends on the size of steps (in pixels) taken as the window moves through the search area. Ideally, the analyst should design his algorithm to take advantage of the computational overlap. In real life he may elect not to do this because the number of partial sums is large, the array space is limited and the coding necessary to store and retrieve the partial sums to or from control memory is bulky. In the area correlation experiments, the computational overlap was ignored due to the above reasons. The line correlation experiment did take advantage of the overlap. This was possible because more correlations could be performed in one array than in area correlation.

Both of the area and line correlations used tree summing to compute the sums of the pixels and their products. A tree sum in STARAN requires n additions to sum a field containing 2^n values. Another reason the line correlation test was able to use computational overlap was a technique called running tree sum. This tree sum creates the sum of all words within a summing modulus of 2^n of an array field up to and including the word of interest. In other words, each word position in the resultant array field will contain the sum of its contents and the contents of all word positions above it and within the selected modulus. These partial sums are the numbers that are saved for the overlap.

1. Ackerman, D.L., Crombie, M.A., Powers, M.L., "Image Correlation on a Parallel Processor," U.S. Army Engineer Topographic Laboratories, Fort Belvoir, VA 22060, ETL-0061, 1976.
2. Ackerman, D.L., "General Programming on a Parallel Processor, "U.S. Army Engineer Topographic Laboratories, Fort Belvoir, VA 22060, ETL-0062, 1976.
3. Radosevic, R.G., et.al., "Associative Array Processing for Topographic Data Reduction," Interim Report, U.S. Army Engineer Topographic Laboratories, Fort Belvoir, VA 22060, ETL-CR-74-1, AD-779 045, February 1974

ITERATIVE METHODS FOR ASYNCHRONOUS MULTIPROCESSORS

Gérard M. Baudet
Carnegie-Mellon University

In the implementation of most parallel algorithms, synchronization seems to be required to assure the communication between the processes, and to guarantee their correct executions. However, the main drawback of synchronization is that it degrades considerably the performance of the algorithms since it is very time consuming. The class of asynchronous iterative methods avoids this drawback; it includes iterations corresponding to parallel implementations in which the cooperating processes use a minimum of intercommunication and no synchronization. The Purely Asynchronous method (PA method), described in [1], is a typical asynchronous iterative method.

In [2], Chazan and Miranker introduced chaotic relaxation schemes requiring a condition which can only be satisfied by using repeated checking and some form of synchronization at each step of the iteration. Asynchronous iterative methods relax this condition and are more general than chaotic relaxation schemes. They further generalize to asynchronous iterative methods with memory to allow the use of different values of the same variable within the same computation. Using the notions of contracting and m-contracting operators, sufficient conditions (satisfied for a large class of operators) are given that guarantee the convergence of any asynchronous iterations and any asynchronous iterations with memory.

In the second part of [1], asynchronous iterative methods are evaluated from a computational point of view. General bounds on the efficiency of asynchronous iterations are first derived directly from the proof of the convergence theorem. Although these bounds are sharp for a parallel implementation of Jacobi's method, they are of little applicability since they require to know a priori the exact specification of each

---

This research was partly supported by the National Science Foundation under Grant MCS 75-222-55, the Office of Naval Research under Contract N00014-76-C-0370, NR 044-422 and a Research Grant from IRIA, Rocquencourt, France.

step of the iteration. Alternate bounds are then derived under additional conditions which are usually satisfied in practical applications. The bounds are compared with the results of a series of experiments conducted on C.mmp [4], and they are consistent with the actual measurements. These bounds can be largely improved by taking into account specific characteristics of the problem being solved: an analysis is presented in [1] for the <u>Asynchronous Newton's method</u> as defined in [3].

Several asynchronous iterative methods have been implemented to solve a large linear system of equations. They range from Jacobi's method, requiring a full synchronization of all the processes at each step of the iteration, to the PA method, which requires no synchronization at all. In between, the AJ and AGS methods are derived from the usual Jacobi's and Gauss-Seidel's methods, and they require the use of a critical section. Experimental results show a considerable advantage for the PA method: for a number of processes up to the number of processors available on C.mmp, the PA method exhibits full parallelism and has an almost optimal speed-up compared to Gauss-Seidel's method, the best sequential method experimented with. The AJ and AGS methods have a very similar behavior; with 6 processes, the overhead caused by the critical section implies that 38 percent of the time a process is waiting for entering the critical section. As is intuitively expected, Jacobi's method has the worst behavior of all the methods considered; with 6 processes, the overhead due to the synchronization of all the processes at each step of the iteration implies that 57 percent of the time a process is waiting for the other processes to finish their computations.

On the basis of these experimental results, and for the problem we have considered, there does not seem to be any alternatives: the PA method is obviously the most efficient one. In addition, another advantage of the PA method is that it is the easiest one to implement, and, spacewise, it is also the most efficient one.

REFERENCES

1. Baudet, G., Asynchronous iterative methods for multiprocessors, CMU Report, 1976. (To appear in <u>J. ACM</u>.)
2. Chazan, D., and Miranker, W., Chaotic relaxation, <u>Lin. Algebra Appl.</u> 2, pp. 199-222, 1969.
3. Kung, H. T., Synchronized and asynchronous parallel algorithms for multiprocessors, in Algorithms and Complexity: New Directions and Recent Results (J. F. Traub, Ed.), pp. 153-200, Academic Press, New York, 1976.
4. Wulf, W. A., and Bell, C. G., C.mmp - A multiminiprocessor, in Proc. AFIPS, 41, pp. 765-777, 1972.

EXPERIENCE WITH A VECTORIZED GENERAL CIRCULATION CLIMATE MODEL ON STAR-100

David B. Soll, Nadim R. Habra, Gary L. Russell
GTE Information Systems, Goddard Institute for Space Studies

This paper presents the experience gained from converting the Goddard Institute for Space Studies (GISS) general circulation climate model to run efficiently on a CDC STAR-100.

The particular model used was a coarse grid version of the nine layer GISS general circulation model[1] which in turn was derived from the three layer weather model developed by Arakawa and Mintz at U.C.L.A. This model performs a time integration of the "primitive equations" on a regular cylindrical grid with different time steps for each of the three principal sections: dynamics (winds, etc.), physics (transport equations), and radiation. The coarse grid consists of 24 meridians each of which contains 16 latitude points.

An important aspect of the conversion was that several scalar algorithms did not lend themselves to direct vectorization and had to be rewritten. A simulation of the vectorized code was conducted in scalar FORTRAN to test the validity of the reorganized logic and the modified algorithms. Two STAR vector languages were selected: (1) LRLTRAN[2] written at the Lawrence Livermore Laboratory (LLL), University of California, and (2) CDC's STAR FORTRAN[3], a standard program product. The dynamics section was coded in both languages, whereas the physics section was written only in STAR FORTRAN. This paper discusses primarily those two sections, as vectorization of the radiation section is not yet complete. Several runs of the model were made at three separate installations. At LLL, the LRLTRAN version of the dynamics was used, while the entire code in STAR FORTRAN was run at CDC's Data Center in Arden Hills, Minnesota. The timings for the original scalar code were measured on the 360/95 at GISS.

As seen in Table I, the speed improvement for one call

to the dynamics section is almost twice that obtained from one call to the physics section. This is because the dynamics algorithms lend themselves more readily to vectorization. A run of the model for 14 simulated days yielded a net speed-up factor of 10.23. While this figure includes several sources of overhead such as I/O and housekeeping, the effect of the slower physics is offset by the fact that the dynamics routines are called six times as often.

TABLE 1

Machine Comparisons

	360/95(GISS) secs.	STAR(CDC) secs.	95:STAR
Dynamics*	0.65	0.056	11.61:1
Physics*	0.41	0.070	5.85:1
14-day run	1472.31	143.92	10.23:1

*Timings are for a single call

Since we believe that a vector formulation is a more "natural" expression of the problem, it would seem that as vector machines become more prevalent, increasing numbers of algorithms will be written directly in vector form. Therefore, it is our opinion that vectorizers now have and will continue to have only limited utility. Thus, the greater part of the future effort in software development should be directed towards the vector languages themselves.

REFERENCES

1. Somerville, R.C.J., et al., "The GISS Model of the Global Atmosphere" - Journal of the Atmospheric Sciences, 31, No. 1 pp. 84-117 (1974).
2. Martin, J.T., Zwakenberg, R.G., and Solbeck, S.V., Livermore Time-Sharing System, Pt. III, ch. 207 - LTSS-207 (Ed. 4) - December 1974.
3. Control Data Corporation - FORTRAN Language Reference Manual - STAR-100 Computer System - No. 60386200 - 1976.

SOME LINEAR ALGEBRAIC ALGORITHMS
AND THEIR PERFORMANCE ON CRAY-1*

T. L. Jordan and Kirby Fong
Los Alamos Scientific Laboratory

ABSTRACT

This paper is concerned with the efficient implementation of various algorithms in linear algebra and their performance on CRAY-1. We will show that if familiar algorithms are implemented optimally on CRAY-1, that factors up to 3 can be gained in their performance relative to common implementations. The key to high performance is the order in which the loops of the normally triply nested DO loops are ordered. Basically, the difference in performance is due to the number of main memory references made and is relevant to other computers requiring two level stores to implement these algorithms. Several algorithms will be compared across various implementations. In addition to identifying performance levels for many direct methods, some timing comparisons will be made with other computers.

I. SUMMARY

1. Hardware and Performance Levels

A brief description of new hardware features that are somewhat unique to the CRAY-1 are first described, including vector registers and the so-called chaining properties of the CRAY-1. We then characterize three natural levels of performance achievable on CRAY-1 with an indication of where these performance levels can occur. These are:

    a. Scalar (S) performance will be the performance of code that is not vectorized or vectorizable and uses only A,

---

*This research was supported by the U.S. Energy Research and Development Administration.

B, S and T registers. Such codes are expected to execute about twice as fast as the CDC-7600.

    b. Vector or (V) performance is a performance level involving vector operations in which memory references are the limiting factor. We present a table that contains some dyadic and triadic operations with times for STACKLIB[1] on the CDC-7600, STAR and CRAY (estimates) in which memory is the limiting factor in performance. A performance ratio between the CRAY-1 and the CDC-7600 of roughly four or five seems reasonable for V level computations based on current timing data.

    c. Super vector (SV) performance is a performance level involving vector operations in which performance is limited by the availability of the functional units and/or vector registers. SV performance is available in algorithms where a considerable amount of arithmetic is done on a few operands so that the vector registers can serve as the primary memory. We expect this level to be at least twice that of the previously defined V performance. Matrix multiplication, polynomial evaluation of a vector and the solution of linear equations are some fundamental problems that can be performed at this level.

2. Matrix Multiplication and Polynomial Evaluation

To illustrate the principle involved we consider various ways of implementing matrix multiplications, we compare two common methods of implementation with one that is optimal for the CRAY-1.

    a. The first of the conventional approaches is an outer product method that uses a subroutine to compute Z=AX+Y where A is a scalar and X, Y and Z are vectors.

    b. The second of the conventional methods uses the classical inner product approach using a dot product subroutine.

    c. A method that is optimal for CRAY-1 multiplexes many inner products.

These methods are based on reorderings of the three DO loops needed to code the matrix multiplication. The orderings are defined and the required references to main memory are counted. We show that the times required by each of the 3 methods described by (a), (b) and (c) are proportional to values approximately 3, 2, and 1, respectively, and correlate with the memory activity.

---

[1] STACKLIB is a package of vector subroutines written by Lawrence Livermore Laboratory for the CDC-7600.

Incidentally, we also show that polynomial evaluation is another important calculation that can be performed at the SV speeds.

3. *Linear Equations*

The most common of the direct methods for solving various types of linear systems are described and analyzed for performance on the CRAY-1 in a manner similar to that described for matrix multiplication. The problems analyzed are:

a. The general linear system by elimination;
b. The general linear system by Gauss-Jordan;
c. The symmetric positive definite system by root-free Cholesky;
d. Matrix Inversion by Gauss-Jordan;
e. Tridiagonal systems;
f. Least squares systems by Householder transformations;
g. General banded systems;
h. Symmetric positive definite banded systems.

The implementation of the LU decomposition of a full linear system is discussed in considerable detail. Also the three approaches described for matrix multiplication are analyzed for this problem with corresponding performance obtained. In addition, we present times for this problem on the CDC-7600, CDC STAR-100 and the CRAY-1. Finally, coding complications necessary to achieve the optimal CRAY-1 performance are defined and their solution described.

Despite the fact that the Gauss-Jordan method for solving linear systems requires $O(1/2N^3)$ operations compared to $O(1/3N^3)$ required for Gaussian elimination, the Gauss-Jordan method may be more suitable for the CRAY-1. Factors that compensate for this extra arithmetic are a simpler overall logic and better performance for the average vector length. CRAY-1 is constrained to work with vectors less than 65 in length and its performance degrades with smaller N because of fixed start-up times. Since the average vector length is N for Gauss-Jordan and about 2/3 N for Gaussian elimination, the megaflop rate is always better for the former and substantially so for small N. Also, for smaller N, the N^2 term in the work polynomial is more important and is the same for both algorithms. Such $O(N^2)$ tasks as searching, scaling and swapping rows go at the slower V rates. The performance profiles of Gauss-Jordan may well be the more attractive for orders of most interest.

Two methods of implementing Gauss-Jordan to do matrix inversion are described. One will perform at V rates and the other at SV rates. The most elegant implementation of matrix inversion is with a single triply nested DO loop. However, this implementation allows only V speed. Nevertheless, if one breaks up the single triply nested DO loop into two triply nested DO loops, each with half the range, then SV rates are achieved for matrix inversion with Gauss-Jordan.

Symmetric positive definite linear systems are considerably easier to implement for optimal performance than the general linear system. In addition to the absence of a requirement to pivot and consequently no searching or swapping, the vectors that are subtracted from a given column in the reduction are uniform in length. Hence, this system can be solved at SV speeds.

There is a slight wrinkle to the Householder (HH) reduction which is used extensively in least squares problems and elsewhere. The characteristic approach of reducing a specific column completely by subtracting the appropriate multiple of the preceding columns works here as well. So this part of the work can be done at SV rates. However, half of the work done is in computing the multipliers of each of the preceding columns. This requires a dot product which will go at V speed. Hence, the total performance is expected to be the mean of SV and V performance.

Banded systems are troublesome if they are either too "fat" or too "thin." If they are too thin, e.g., tridiagonal systems, then the vectors are too short and performance is better in the scalar mode. If the bandwidth is large, say greater than 64, then there are complications due to the block logic required and greater fractionation of the vectors. The arithmetic can be performed at SV rates, but these complicating factors are more degrading than similar factors for the full linear system.

We review various representations of Gaussian elimination for solving the tridiagonal system of equations and observe that such a system is solvable at essentially S rates. However, it is not uncommon for problems in 2- and 3-dimensions to allow the solution of many diagonally dominant systems simultaneously. Times to solve up to 64 such tridiagonal systems simultaneously are presented.

The complete paper is available in report LA-6774.

NONLINEAR RECURRENCES AND PARALLEL COMPUTATION[*]

D. Stott Parker, Jr.
University of Illinois at Urbana-Champaign

I. INTRODUCTION

Although it is now well-known that the execution time of linear recurrences can be reduced significantly through the exploitation of parallelism, attempts to speed up nonlinear recurrences have failed except in special cases. If the mth-order recurrence problem

$$x_k = F(x_{k-1}, x_{k-2}, \ldots, x_{k-m}) \quad (1 \leq k \leq n)$$

is to be solved on a parallel machine, then only $O(\log n)$ steps are required when F is linear [2], while if F is nonlinear little has been discovered about solutions requiring less than the obvious $O(n)$ serial time. Kung [3] has studied the problem and has in fact proved that when F is a rational function of degree greater than one and algebraic methods are used, the recurrence can be sped up by at most a constant factor using parallelism. Thus the Newton-Raphson square root iteration

$$x_{n+1} = 1/2 \; (x_n + A/x_n) = (x_n^2 + Ax_n)/(2x_n)$$

being of degree two cannot be sped up significantly by algebraic transformations on x_n, forward substitution, etc.

This paper attempts to show solutions may lie in other approaches: Kung's theorem does not preclude the existence of nonalgebraic (transcendental) transforms which lead to speed-ups. For example, with the Newton-Raphson iteration above the (not useful, but illustrative) change of variables

$$y_k = \text{arccoth}(x_k / \sqrt{A})$$

---

[*]This work was supported in part by the National Science Foundation under Grant No. MCS73-07980 A03.

converts it to the trivial linear recurrence $y_{n+1} = 2y_n$.
Thus given $x_0 > \sqrt{A}$ the entire recurrence can be solved by:

(1) undergoing the change of variables
$$y_0 = \phi(x_0) = \text{arccoth}(x_0/\sqrt{A})$$
(2) rapidly computing $\{y_k | 1 \leq k \leq n\}$ in parallel
(3) finally computing $\{x_k = \phi^{-1}(y_k) | 1 \leq k \leq n\}$ in parallel.

We are naturally only going to compute these changes of variables to finite precision, as any computer would; this distinguishes the approach of *analytic* complexity here from that of *algebraic* complexity, under which ·transcendental functions cannot be evaluated. The change of variable approach costs us no loss of generality, assuming we plan to implement the resulting computational scheme on a real machine, and leads possibly to gains in time and stability. For example, given the computation x^k (x positive, k integral), an algebraic complexity theorist would have to assume the evaluation would take $O(\log k)$ steps -- engendering possibly $\log_2 k$ units of roundoff error -- while the analytic complexity theorist would compute it as $\exp(k \log(x))$ in essentially constant time and unit roundoff.

II. FIRST-ORDER NONLINEAR RECURRENCES

With the above approach in mind, we consider using the change of variables $y = \phi(x)$ to transform the first-order nonlinear recurrence $x_{n+1} = F(x_n)$ into $y_{n+1} = c \cdot y_n$ for some constant c. Since then $y_{n+1} = \phi \circ F \circ \phi^{-1}(y_n)$, the problem is to find a map ϕ which transforms F to a constant multiple map under conjugation. This problem has been solved in part by Levy and Lessman [4], who show how to construct explicit power series for ϕ^{-1} in terms of the derivatives of F at the attractive fixed point (stable point) in whose neighborhood the iteration takes place.

As an example, we give a new parallel algorithm for the *Arithmetic-Geometric Mean* (AGM) procedure. The AGM has been shown recently by Brent [1] to have useful computational properties; it is a simple iterative process developed by Gauss at the age of fourteen for computing the elliptic integral
$$K(m) = \int_0^{\pi/2} \frac{d\theta}{\sqrt{1 - m \sin^2\theta}}$$

and other special functions. The iteration consists of compounding the named means in tandem:

$$a_0 = \sqrt{1 - m} \qquad b_0 = 1$$
$$a_{k+1} = \sqrt{a_k b_k} \qquad b_{k+1} = (a_k + b_k)/2$$

with convergence to the fixed point $a_\infty = b_\infty = \pi/2K(m)$.

Now let $F(x) = [2\sqrt{x} / (1 + x)]$ and define for $k > 0$ $x_0 = \sqrt{1 - m}$ and $x_{k+1} = f(x_k)$. We then claim that

$$\pi/2K(m) \simeq \prod_{k=0}^{n} ((1 + x_k)/2)$$

with the quadratic convergence of the unaltered AGM algorithm, proof lying in the facts that $x_k = a_k/b_k$ and $(1 + x_k)/2 = b_{k+1}/b_k$. Note that the iteration function F has fixed point one ($F(1) = 1$) so we can compute, using [4] and ALTRAN, the change of variables

$$\phi(x) = \log(-(x - 1)/8 + (x - 1)^2/16 - 5(x - 1)^3/128 + \ldots)$$
$$= \log(1 + 2\sqrt{x} - (x - 1)^5/8192 [1 - 5/2(x - 1) + \ldots])$$
$$\phi^{-1}(y) = (1 - 2\exp(y))/(1 + 2\exp(y))^3 (1 - 4\exp(2y)$$
$$+ 16\exp(5y) - \ldots)$$

These lead to the linearized iteration $y_{n+1} = 2y_n$, and this AGM algorithm can then be implemented on a parallel machine exactly as indicated above with the Newton-Raphson square root algorithm. Unfortunately, convergence of ϕ here is terrible when m approaches one; finding closed form for ϕ would repair this problem.

III. PROBLEMS AND CONCLUSIONS

Briefly, there are several problems with this method. First, the iteration function F must be C^∞ at its fixed points and its behavior must be completely understood to compute the change of variables ϕ. It is clearly desirable to have fixed points independent of the data (like the modified AGM scheme above, and unlike Newton's method). Thus algorithms would have to be manipulated into "incremental" forms like

$$\text{Solution}(x_0) = \prod_k (1 + \psi(x_k)) \qquad [x_k = F(x_{k-1})]$$

where F's fixed-point is known in advance. The worst problem, however, is ensuring the convergence of the change of variables (Levy and Lessman guarantee only the analyticity of ϕ).

By way of conclusions we can say three things. First, generally speaking analytic complexity seems a more realistic measure for this type of problem than algebraic complexity, and future optimality/lower bound arguments should bear this in mind. Second, the change of variables approach, even if not advantageous speed-wise, may have nice stability properties due to its simplicity: all error is made in changes of variables and the final merging (if any) of the x-iterates. Lastly, the method is an approach, apparently with good potential, for generating new algorithms for parallel machines.

IV. REFERENCES

[1] Brent, R. P., "Fast Multiple-Precision Evaluation of Elementary Functions," J. ACM, Vol. 23, No. 2, pp. 242-251 (April 1976).

[2] Chen, S. C., and Kuck, D. J., "Time and Parallel Processor Bounds for Linear Recurrence Systems," IEEE Trans. Comput., Vol. C-24, No. 7, pp. 701-717 (July 1975).

[3] Kung, H. T., "New Algorithms and Lower Bounds ...," J. ACM, Vol. 23, No. 2, pp. 252-261 (April 1976).

[4] Levy, H., and Lessman, F., Finite Difference Equations, (esp. Ch. 5) London: Sir Isaac Pitman and Sons, Ltd., 1959.

MINIMAL PARALLELISM FOR COMPUTATIONS UNDER TIME CONSTRAINTS

Don Heller
Pennsylvania State University

If we demand that a computation use no more than t steps, where t is too small for a standard computer, then a parallel computer may be one way to meet the time constraint. We consider the problem of finding the minimal number of parallel processors needed to perform the computation within t steps. This is dual to the usual problem of finding the minimal time to perform the computation given a fixed set of processors. Study of minimal parallelism as a function of the computation and time constraint indicates sources of inefficiency, which can sometimes be eliminated by relaxing the constraint.

As an initial step toward understanding these problems in some detail, we consider computation of $A_N = a_1 \circ a_2 \circ \ldots \circ a_N$, where $\circ$ is associative and can be performed in one step. Not allowing operations other than $\circ$ and assuming instantaneous data communication between any pair of processors, the minimal number of parallel processors required to compute A_N in at most t steps (w(N,t)) is determined for $n = \lceil \log_2 N \rceil \le t \le N-1$. This generalizes an earlier result of Muraoka for the special case t = n, and provides a lower bound for more general problems under time constraints. By examining the entire range of feasible times we can see how w(N,t) varies as t varies, and give bounds on the optimal efficiency.

We first consider the optimal algorithms for A_N given P processors; these will require m(P,N) steps. w(N,t) is then found by minimizing P subject to the constraint $m(P,N) \le t$. Also of interest is L(P,t), the largest N such that A_N is computable in t steps using P processors. Reasoning by analogy between parallel algorithms and binary trees, leaves = operands and non-leaves = operations, we have L(P,0) = 1, L(P,s+1) = L(P,s) + min(P,L(P,s)). By definition $L(P,s-1) < N \le L(P,s)$ implies m(P,N) = s, and $m(P,N) \le t < m(P-1,N)$ implies w(N,t) = P, where $m(0,N) = \infty$ in the degenerate case. In closed form, with $p = \lceil \log_2 P \rceil$ and $n = \lceil \log_2 N \rceil$,

$$L(P,t) = 2^{\min(p,t)} + P \max(0, t-p),$$
$$m(P,N) = \min(p,n) + \max(0, \lceil (N-2^p)/P \rceil).$$

The second term of $m(P,N)$ represents the time in which the processors are working to full capacity and the first term represents those steps in which a set of partial results must be "fanned-in" to the final result.

Muraoka's result, to be generalized, is the formula $w(N,n) = \max(N - 2^{n-1}, \lceil (N - 2^{n-2})/2 \rceil)$. For $N \geq 2$, $n \leq t \leq N-1$, let $s = t - n$, and define $a = \lceil \log_2(s+2 + \lceil \log_2 s+2 \rceil) \rceil - 1$. Then

$$w(N,t) = \max\left(\left\lceil \frac{N - 2^{n-a}}{s + a} \right\rceil, \left\lceil \frac{N - 2^{n-a-1}}{s + a + 1} \right\rceil \right).$$

The proof is a somewhat tedious case analysis. With $K = w(N,t)$ and $k = \lceil \log_2 K \rceil$, we have

$$\left(\frac{K-1}{K}\right) t + \left(\frac{k+1}{K}\right) \leq m(K,N) \leq t,$$

so for large K the time constraint is just barely satisfied. One more processor might improve the time for A_N, and one less processor will definitely require more than t steps, but there are limits to the effect of these changes:

$$\left(\frac{K-1}{K+1}\right) t + \left(\frac{2k+1}{K+1}\right) \leq m(K+1,N) \leq m(K,N) \leq t,$$

$$t + 1 \leq m(K-1,N) \leq \left\lceil \frac{Kt-k}{K-1} \right\rceil \leq t + \left\lceil \frac{s + a + 1}{K - 1} \right\rceil.$$

Relaxing the time constraint by one step will decrease the processor requirements, with the greatest reduction when t is near n:

$$w(N,t+1) \leq w(N,t) \leq \left\lceil \frac{s + a + 1}{s + a} \, w(N,t+1) \right\rceil.$$

It is precisely those values of t near the minimal time n that lead to inefficient use of processors. With the efficiency measure $E(N,t) = (N-1)/(m(K,N)K)$, we have $E(N,t) \geq (s+a+2)/(2t)$ and $E(N,n+s) \to 0$ as $N \to \infty$ for a fixed integer $s \geq 0$. However, $t = \lfloor (1+c)n \rfloor$ for a constant $c > 0$ yields $E(N,t) \geq c/(2(1+c))$ and $E(N,t) \to c/(1+c)$ as $N \to \infty$. Thus a relative increase in time over the minimum implies a uniform nonzero lower bound on the optimal efficiency. While $w(N,\lfloor (1+c)n \rfloor)$ still grows unboundedly with N (it is $O(N/(\log N + \log\log N))$) it does so at a much slower rate than $w(N,n+s) = O(N)$, leading to the improved asymptotic efficiency.

REFERENCE

Muraoka, Y., Parallelism Exposure and Exploitation in Programs, Dissertation, Dept. of Computer Science, University of Illinois, Urbana-Champaign, 1971.

EFFECTIVENESS OF MULTI-MICROPROCESSOR NETWORKS
FOR SOLVING THE NONLINEAR POISSON EQUATION

Gerard G. L. Meyer
North Carolina State University

I. INTRODUCTION

The solution of the nonlinear Poisson equation

$$\nabla^2 \psi = f(\psi) \tag{1}$$

is an important step in the solution of turbulent flow problems. Equation (1) is solved by (i) discretizing the domain of integration, using a LxL mesh; (ii) discretizing the ∇^2 operator, using a five point formula; (iii) reducing the nonlinear Poisson equation to a sequence of k_2 linear equations using a relaxation technique and finally (iv) solving approximately the linear Poisson equations by using k_1 iterations of the successive over relaxation method (SOR).

Difficulties occur when LxL is large: the computational time to solve (1) on a general purpose computer is substantial and the cost of solving (1) is prohibitive. There exist two approaches to alleviate these drawbacks. The first one consists of using special purpose computing elements and the second one consists of using special purpose networks of general purpose computing elements.

Special purpose computing elements are efficient when the problem to be solved possesses an appropriate structure. The computations to be performed on the data must leave the structure of the data invariant. If this is not the case, the time necessary to realign and rearrange the data after each iteration may dominate the computational time and all the gain in efficiency due to the use of special devices is lost. An examination of the algorithm used to solve equation (1) shows that two different tasks must be performed on L^2 points: (i) the iteration of SOR and (ii) the computation of $f(\psi)$. It is therefore necessary to use at least two special devices D_1 and D_2, where D_1 performs the SOR iteration and D_2 evaluates $f(\psi)$. At each relaxation iteration, L^2 pieces of data must be sent from D_1 to D_2 and from D_2 to D_1 and the total computational time is bounded from below by a quantity proportional to the total number of points in the mesh.

Special purpose networks of general purpose computing elements do not suffer the disadvantages of special purposes elements for solving equation (1). Each general purpose computing element may perform both the SOR iteration and the evaluation of $f(\psi)$ and the amount of data to transfer between elements is greatly reduced. In this approach, the two most important design parameters are the connecting network, i.e., the connection assignment and the amount of memory associated with each computing element. The connecting network depends on the partitioning of the original problem. The partitioning in turn must satisfy three constraints: (i) a high degree of parallelism between the various segments of the problem must be achieved; (ii) the total number of connections in the network must be of the order of the number of computing elements in the network and finally (iii) the segmentation of the original problem must be achieved through a simple process. In this paper, we assume a partitioning of the problem into N segments, each containing approximately the same number of mesh points, such that every segment possesses at most two neighbors. The size of the memory associated with each computing elements depends on the size of the problem to be solved, the characteristics of the computing elements and the definition of the efficiency of the network.

The computational cost of a network of N elements, relative to a specific problem is defined to be $E(L;N) = C(L;N)T(L;N)$, where $C(L;N)$ is the cost of the network and $T(L;N)$ is the time necessary to solve the given problem on the network. Models of various complexity may be used for $C(L;N)$ and $T(L;N)$. In this paper, only the simplest model will be investigated.

II. HARDWARE COST

Assume that the cost of one computing element is P_1, where P_1 includes the cost of storing the program and the cost of the communication links with two other computing elements. Assume that the cost of storing one word of data is P_2. Then, if one neglects the inefficiencies in the data storage due to the partitioning of the problem, the cost of a network of N elements is

$$C(L;N) = \alpha_1(L)(1 + \alpha_2(L)N) \tag{2}$$

with

$$\alpha_1(L) = L^2 P_2 \tag{3}$$

$$\alpha_2(L) = P_1/\alpha_1(L). \tag{4}$$

III. COMPUTATIONAL TIME

Assume that the time necessary to process one mesh point is T_1 for the SOR iteration and T_3 for the evaluation of $f(\psi)$, assume that the time necessary to send or receive one data word is T_2 and assume that there is not simultaneous transmission of data and computation, then, if one neglects the possible conflicts of access to data channels between the computing elements and if one assumes a computational efficiency of one, the computational time necessary to solve (1) becomes

$$T(L;N) = \alpha_3(L)(1 + \alpha_4(L)/N) \tag{5}$$

with

$$\alpha_3(L) = 4LT_2 k_1 k_2 \tag{6}$$

$$\alpha_4(L) = (L^2 T_1 k_1 k_2 + L^2 T_3 k_2)/\alpha_3(L). \tag{7}$$

IV. COMPUTATIONAL COST

The computational cost of solving a problem on a L x L mesh with a network of N computing elements is

$$E(L;N) = C(L;N)T(L;N). \tag{8}$$

Using (2) and (5), the optimal number of elements N_{opt} may be obtained by setting $\partial E(L;N)/\partial N = 0$. Some algebraic manipulations show that, if it is assumed that $\alpha_5 L^2 \geq 1$, then,

$$N_{opt} = \alpha_5 L^{1.5} \tag{9}$$

with

$$\alpha_5 = ((P_2 T_1 k_1 + P_2 T_3)/(4P_1 T_2 k_1))^{0.5}. \tag{10}$$

The optimal amount of memory to associate with each computing element (in addition to the memory necessary to store the program) can now be deduced from (9):

$$M_{opt} = L^2/N_{opt} = L^{0.5}/\alpha_5. \qquad (11)$$

The computational cost corresponding to the optimal network, i.e., the network of N_{opt} computing elements is

$$E(L;N_{opt}) = \beta_1 L^2 + \beta_2 L^{2.5} + \beta_3 L^3 \qquad (12)$$

with

$$\beta_1 = P_1 T_1 k_1 k_2 + P_1 T_3 k_2 \qquad (13)$$

$$\beta_2 = 4k_2 (P_1 P_2 T_2 k_1 (T_1 k_1 + T_3))^{0.5} \qquad (14)$$

$$\beta_3 = 4 P_2 T_2 k_1 k_2. \qquad (15)$$

The computational cost of solving the problem on a network of only one computing element, i.e., with no parallelism is

$$E(L;1) = \beta_1 L^2 + \beta_5 L^4 \qquad (16)$$

with

$$\beta_5 = P_2 T_1 k_1 k_2 + P_2 T_3 k_2. \qquad (17)$$

We conclude that the use of one computing element results in a computational cost which grows like L^4 and that the use of an optimal number of computing elements results in a computational cost which grows like L^3. The advantages of using an optimal number of computing elements is now illustrated by an example.

V. EXAMPLE

Suppose that P_1 = 2000 \$, P_2 = 0.4 \$, $T_1 = T_2 = T_3$ = 10 µs, k_1 = 5, k_2 = 10 and L = 256. Then, the optimal number N_{opt} of computing elements is 32, and C(256;32) = 90214 \$, T(256;32) = 1.74 s, and E(256;32) = 156948 \$s. If we solve the same problem on a network of only one element, we obtain C(256;1) = 28,214 \$, T(256;1) = 39.3 s, and E(256;1) = 1,109,419 \$s. It follows that if we use an optimal network of 32 computing elements instead of a network of one element, we multiply the cost of the hardware by three, we divide the computational time by twenty-two and we divide the computational cost by seven.

III
System, Software, and Algorithm Performance

ANALYSIS OF APPLICATIONS PROGRAMS AND
SOFTWARE REQUIREMENTS FOR HIGH SPEED COMPUTERS

John M. Gary
University of Colorado at Boulder

Abstract

This paper describes workload statistics (tape mounts, data transmission for disk, microfilm written, etc.) for the NCAR CDC 7600. A simple comparison of the cost effectiveness of the CRAY, CYBER-175, and AP-120B machines is given. A summary of the vector oriented features of several proposed and actual languages (APL, ASC-FORTRAN, TRANQUIL, VECTRAN, CFD, etc.) is given.

I. INTRODUCTION

    We will attempt to illustrate some of the problems which arise in the application of high speed computers to problems in the physical sciences. We will illustrate these difficulties by looking at the problem of numerical weather prediction in particular, and computing in support of atmospheric science in general.
    We will rather arbitrarily split the function of a high speed computer into four parts.
    1. Algorithm solution ("number crunching").
    2. Debugging and code development.
    3. Data editing, display and file management.
    4. Data communications.
    Our attention will be focused on the attempt to speed up the first function, although we will have some comments on the last three. Until recently most progress has occurred as a result of a reduction in the clock time in the hardware. In the future most progress will probably result from parallel execution of algorithms. We may also see a reduction in the cost of computers in the CDC 7600 class, which could provide

an effective speedup, provided the problem does not require more than an hour or two on the CDC 7600.

All computing is subject to the problem of programmer productivity, and large modeling efforts are no exception. I suspect that programming costs exceed hardware costs even for large parallel machines. If the parallel machines are too difficult to program, it will still be impossible to make much progress on large models, even though the machine is capable of executing the models rapidly when carefully hand coded. We will discuss some of the basic factors in the design of a language for parallel machines, and illustrate the discussion with examples from existing or proposed languages.

II. An example of work load statistics.

In this section we will give some work load statistics derived from the NCAR[1] computing facility. These statistics were gathered in November 1976. At that time the CDC 7600 configuration contained 65K small core memory (SCM), 512K large core memory (LCM), 14 tape drives, 8-819 disk packs (300 × 10^6 bytes each) on two controllers, one microfilm recorder, two 1200 lpm printers, one 1200 cpm card reader, one 250 cpm card punch, and a front end computer to handle remote batch access. The operation is strictly batch, although the batch jobs may be entered from a remote slow speed terminal, and the output delivered to the terminal. Perhaps the most noteworthy aspect of these statistics is the amount of user data which is handled, both from tape and disk. Of course, these statistics might change in a time shared environment. However, much of the data is external, from aircraft, satellites, etc., and would have to be read and stored in any case. Tom Wright at NCAR made a count of the microfilm frames produced during a single day in January, 1977. Of these 30% were x-y graphs, 25% contour plots, 37% alphanumeric printer pages, and 8% miscellaneous. Perhaps fewer graphs would be drawn if they could be viewed interactively. The NCAR system contains a "virtual tape" feature which permits a user to stage a tape file onto a disk and then access the file from the disk. When there is no longer room on the disk some of these files are automatically "aged off" to physical tapes.

The table below provides an indication of the data rates for the NCAR 7600. The data shown is for the month of November, 1976. The load does vary somewhat from month to month. The numbers give only a rough indication of data rates, since there is some inaccuracy in the data collection. The data is for the CDC 7600 only.

---

[1] National Center for Atmospheric Research.

TABLE 1

NCAR 7600 data flow for November, 1976

Number of jobs run	27000
Total CPU time	390 hrs.
Total peripheral processor time	320 hrs.
Total CRU (computer resource units)	920000
Microfilm frames (35mm)	980000
Cards punched	370000
Pages printed	580000
Words read from the program library	0.67×10^9
Entries to program library	9700
Words read from user's disk area	0.32×10^9
Words written to user's disk area	0.06×10^9
Entries to user's disk area	19000
Words read from system library	1.5×10^9
Entries to system library	27000
Words read from physical tape	$10. \times 10^9$
Words written to physical tape	4.5×10^9
Physical tape mounts	10800
Words read from virtual tapes	$13. \times 10^9$
Words written to virtual tape	$11. \times 10^9$
Virtual tape entries	28000
Words read from card reader	0.03×10^9
Words written to printer	0.14×10^9
Words written to microfilm plotter	1.2×10^9
Words read from temporary user disk files	53×10^9
Words written to temporary user disk files	70×10^9

The statistics certainly depend on the system configuration, thus it is hard to decide exactly what they imply. However, it is clear from discussions at NCAR, LASL and LLL that data processing and file management is very important in a scientific computing center. In an atmospheric science computing center data handling may be a more important problem than parallel processing. Satellites can produce thousands of data tapes. The U. S. Weather Service uses two IBM/195 computers and several minicomputers to process satellite data. About 50% of the time on the 195 machines is used for the satellite data, about 35% of the 2 Megabyte memory is used and the ratio of wall clock to CPU time is 5:1 [41].

An indication of the distribution of jobs according to size is given below. The CPU time is measured on the CDC 7600 in seconds. The computing resource units (CRU) is a composite figure used for accounting which reflects CPU time, peripheral processor time, memory usage, etc. Note that 120×10^9 words transferred per month is a steady 550,000 characters per second assuming the computer is running for 600 hours wall clock time per month

TABLE 2

NCAR 7600 job distribution for November, 1976

Range of CPU times	Percentage of jobs in range		Percentage of CPU time used by jobs in range		Percentage of CRU used by jobs in range	
		Cumulative		Cumulative		Cumulative
t ≤ 5 sec	59.8%	59.8%	1.6%	1.6%	5.1%	5.1%
5 < t ≤ 30 sec	22.7	82.5	5.8	7.5	8.1	13.2
30 < t ≤ 60 sec	7.0	89.4	5.9	13.1	5.8	19.0
1 min < t ≤ 5 min	7.9	97.4	19.1	32.1	18.6	37.6
5 min < t ≤ 10 min	1.2	98.6	9.9	42.0	8.6	46.2
10 min < t ≤ 30 min	0.9	99.5	18.4	60.4	16.9	63.1
30 min < t	0.5	100.0	39.4	100.0	36.9	100.0

A. The Data Processing Load

We will briefly describe several problems taken from the NCAR computing center which require a large amount of externally generated data to be processed by the computer. A heavy load may still be imposed on the arithmetic unit, but the main aspect of the problem is the transmission, storage, and retrieval of a very large number of bits. This data processing may be more of a problem for the management of an atmospheric science computing center than the codes oriented toward arithmetic computation. We note that the NCAR computing center stores about 40000 tapes currently, that about 40000 tapes are mounted each month (real and virtual) that about 10^7 characters are transmitted for each tape mounted, and that the average record length on the tapes is 5000 characters. These numbers are not too accurate, but they provide some indication of the data flow from tapes. We will next list some of the projects which involve the transmission or storage of a large amount of data.

One requires the processing of radiation data taken by a satellite. This experiment will generate about 800 tapes full of data. The solution of an integral equation is required to obtain temperature fields. Another 1000 tapes containing radar data are processed each year. This data is first preprocessed by a mini-computer, which is the case for much of

the data which ends up on the central computer. Some of this
data is probably processed on the large machine because the
microfilm processor is on the large machine, but much of it
also requires a powerful arithmetic processor. It is difficult to estimate how much of this processing could be accomplished on a medium sized machine such as the Interdata 8/32,
perhaps a large fraction provided the machine had suitable
tape drives, disk capacity, and graphics capability.

Another project is the processing of solar data from a
satellite. This is estimated to require about 400 hours per
year of CPU time on the CDC 7600, will involve about 10^{11} bits
of data, and 200,000 frames of microfilm per year.

The aircraft facility processes about 500 tapes, writes
another 500 tapes, and uses about 700,000 computer resource
units (somewhat less than one month of machine time) per year.
This data processing requires about an equal amount of central
processing and peripheral processing time on the 7600. It
generates about 1.5E + 6 frames of microfilm per year.

It would be desirable to obtain a parameterization of
this work load. This would permit the construction of a model
to simulate the efficiency with which various computer systems
could process this data. In particular, such a simulation
might indicate if a distributed system containing less expensive machines is competitive with a large system. It might
also compare the effectiveness of mass store devices, such as
the Ampex Terabit memory or the IBM or CDC data cells, with a
distributed system. This parameterization might include the
frequency with which the data is used, what percentage of the
data is read on each run, how this required data is distributed through the file, how often the data must be updated,
how severely the access differs from sequential, and how much
arithmetic processing is required per unit of data accessed,
and in the case of random accessing, the size of the data
block required and the allowable response time. A major
factor in the evaluation of a data processing facility is the
reliability of the hardware-software combination and the ease
of usage. This would not show up in a simulation.

B. On the Design of Computing Systems to Support Scientific
Research

Programming large models is expensive and the difficulty
in programming is a major impediment to progress. Software
costs may exceed hardware costs even in computing centers
which use large machines such as CRAY-1 or the CDC 7600.
Therefore a considerable investment in programming aids can
be justified. This might be a modification of the Programmers
Workbench (PWB) [16]. This is a collection of software

on an interactive system, in this case a DEC PDP-11/45 or 11/70 under the UNIX operating system. It is intended for the development of code which will be run in production on a different, larger batch system. It provides the following features, among others.
1. Text editing source code.
2. Easy submission of jobs to the large batch system and the return of results for interrogation on the interactive system.
3. Automated documentation aids and a source code control system. This includes a method to keep a history of changes to the source code.
4. A file manager.

A system of this type would be very useful for modeling on large high speed machines. The system described by Dolotta [16] might be modified in order to be more effective for code development which involves long production runs as part of the code development process. Many of these codes are never really "developed", they are continually changing. Also they generate a great deal of output in the form of graphs and contour plots, and they may require a great amount of input. Such a system might include a method to easily interrogate on the interactive system the results of a run on the large machine. This might require a specialized file manager (on top of the usual one) and a mechanism to quickly display graphic information on a terminal. It should be possible to easily locate and display the output from a specified run. The system should assist the user in keeping an "audit trail" or history of numerical experiments as well as changes to the source code. It might be convenient to place graphical output on this history file. It should be possible to easily "age" this history file off the disk onto a tape. This file would be a partially automated "lab record book" for the numerical experimenter. Such a system should provide diagnostic tools such as the MNF or WATFIV compilers and the PFORT and DAVE static checkers. We shall have more to say about this later in connection with languages.

Since graphics data will have to be transmitted over phone lines, it may be important to develop methods to produce such graphics in a relatively compact form. This might also be useful if several hundred contour plots must be stored on a satellite computer for interrogation at an interactive graphics terminal. A graphics terminal system is in use at LLL using a large file store and high speed data links. An analysis of methods to transmit contour plots over phone lines is given by Adams and Gary [1]. A contour plot from a numerical weather prediction code on a 74 by 37 grid was used. This contained 65 contours with an average of 30 line segments per contour. To transmit the array values and then build the contour plot at the receiving end would require 27,380 bits if 10 bits are used for each array value. If the contour plots are generated on the sending computer and the line segments are transmitted in the usual manner, then about 25,000 bits are required. These segments can also be transmitted in a more compact manner which requires 9100 bits. These three methods all transmit the plot quite accurately, there is very little smoothing or distortion of the plot. A fourth method is the use of a bicubic spline to approximate the array values. The coefficients of the expansion are transmitted over the phone line. This requires only 4500 bits, however the array values must be reconstructed at the receiving end and the contour plot must also be constructed at the receiving end. Also the contour plot is smoothed which is sometimes not desirable.

I believe that such a PWB tailored to scientific modeling on large machines would repay its cost several times over, even if it is used in only a single large center. All centers have some of this software, but it has not been carried far enough in any center that I am familiar with.

A computing system for large scale scientific modeling could be a network containing nodes which satisfy the following four functions.

USER INTERFACE

Time shared machine
Remote batch entry
Printer and reader I/O
Electrostatic printer
Microfilm output
Permanent file system

MASS STORE DEVICE

FLOATING POINT COMPUTING

CPU, memory hierarchy, and local disk

DATA PROCESSING

General purpose computer
Tape drives
Local Disk

Each of these functions could be satisfied by a large machine such as the CDC 7600, Honeywell 6000 series, or large DEC 10 for the user interface and data processing, and the CRAY, STAR, ASC, or BSP (Burroughs) for the floating point computing. Instead of a network containing a few nodes, a large network consisting of less expensive nodes such as the DEC 11/70 or DEC 11/45, or PRIME computers could be used. A network node might be largely free standing, consisting of a DEC 11/70, an FPS AP-120B, and an Interdata 8-32 for example. Such a node would be capable of performing all four of the above functions. The use of such independent nodes might eliminate the need for the mass storage device and greatly reduce the data traffic on the network. The network might still be necessary for system availability and some local specialization within the nodes.

Such a system might incorporate a terminal with CRT, CPU, 128KB memory, small disk and 2400-4800 baud communication link for a single user. In the near future the cost of such a terminal might drop to $10,000-$15,000 and would permit local editing, compilation, and even execution for debugging of large models. The programmer's work bench could be implemented on such a single user machine.

A method to determine the optimal configuration for a computing system for a given institution probably awaits a better understanding of the computing load in such installations. When it is possible to parameterize the computing load, then it may be possible to model the behavior of various computer configurations for various problem loads and thereby select an optimum.

III. A COMPARISON OF COST EFFECTIVENESS

We have chosen three machines and will attempt to provide a very rough estimate of their cost effectiveness for large scientific codes. This is highly problem dependent so the numbers provide only a rough indication. We are not giving a precise comparison, but are simply raising some issues relevant to such a comparison. The numbers for the Floating Point Systems machine (FPS-AP-120B) are completely conjectural since we were unable to locate any benchmark figures for the large scientific codes that we are concerned with.

The first machine is the CRAY-1 [15]. Benchmark figures published by LASL indicate this machine to be about 2.5 times faster than the CDC 7600 when both are hand coded in assembly language [26]. A reasonable rate for the CDC 7600 when carefully hand coded is probably 10 million floating points operations per second (10 Mflop). A reasonable rate for Fortran on the CDC 7600 is perhaps 2-4 Mflop. If we assume that the ratio between the CRAY and the CDC 7600 is also 2.5 for Fortran codes, then the Fortran rate for Cray-1 is 5-10 Mflop. We will further assume that the rate for calculations involving only long vectors is the same on the CDC 7600 for both Fortran (using stacklib) and hand code, namely 10 Mflop. The ratio for handcoded vector codes between the two machines is 5:1 as estimated in the LASL report. This gives a vector code rate of 10 Mflop for the 7600 and 50 Mflop for the Cray.

The second machine shown in the table below is the CDC Cyber 175 (we were unable to obtain cost figures for the Cyber 176). We assume the Cyber 175 is one half as fast as the 7600, although it is probably a little faster. This configuration includes a 262K memory, 4-819 disk drives, a disk controller and the CPU.

The third machine is the Floating Point Systems array

TABLE 3

Cost effectiveness comparison

Cray	Cyber 175
10^6-64 bit memory 50 n.s. memory cycle \$4.00/word \$8.9 × 10^6 total cost 5-10 Mflop scalar 50 Mflop vector 0.6-1.2 $\frac{\text{flop}}{\$}$ scalar 5.6 $\frac{\text{flop}}{\$}$ vector	0.262 × 10^6 60 bit memory \$5.40/word \$4.4 × 10^6 total cost 1-2 Mflop scalar 0.2-0.5 $\frac{\text{flop}}{\$}$ scalar

AP-120B
0.256 × 10^6 38 bit memory 333 n.s. memory cycle \$0.35/word \$322,000 system cost 1-4 Mflop scalar 3-12 $\frac{\text{flop}}{\$}$

processor FPS-AP-120B [3]. This is an array processor so it must be attached to a host computer, in this case a mini computer such as the Interdata 8/32. The inclusion of this machine is certainly conjectural, since it is microcoded, has a relatively small control memory, has been used mainly as an array processor, and has no high level language. However, it can have up to 10^6 words of memory for data (38 bit floating point) with a 333 n.s. cycle at a cost of \$0.35 per word. This machine contains a pipelined floating point processor with a 167 n.s. clock which does an add in 2 clocks and a multiply in 3 clocks. It has two scratchpad memories of 32 words, each of which can be read and written on the same clock cycle. It has a control memory (64 bit word) to hold the microcode which can be up to 4K in size. In addition to the large data memory mentioned above it has another smaller "table" memory which can hold frequently used constants. There is a faster (167 n.s.) but more expensive (\$1.31/word) data memory available. The data memory does not appear to have the bandwidth to support pipelined vector operations at the clock rate since only one operand can be accessed every clock cycle, or every other clock cycle. Operations can be supported at the clock rate from the scratch pad memories, but this requires a high number of floating point operations per datum which is probably not attainable except in special cases. The vendor provides routines for vector add and multiply which run at a 1 Mflop rate from the data memory using the faster memory. We will assume that it is possible to write a highly optimized compiler for this machine which would run a scientific code at a 1-4 Mflop rate. The larger range in the speed reflects our lack of any reference to extensive benchmark experience for this machine. We assume a host computer similar to the Interdata 8/32 which might cost around $100,000. It is probably feasible to have a much less expensive host computer, use the AP-120B memory for program storage, and do all computing on the AP-120B. A controller is available which allows a disk or other high speed peripheral gear to be attached to the AP-120B instead of the host computer. Four 80 Mbyte disks would cost around $100,000. We include a 256K data memory which costs $92,000. The floating point unit costs $30,000. We ignore the software cost which is likely to be rather high. To make the system viable this cost would have to be distributed over many such systems. Our guess on the cost effectiveness of the FPS AP-120B is clearly highly conjectural. However, the possibilities offered by the use of less expensive, slower machines should certainly be included in any cost effectiveness study.

The following loop was used as a benchmark to estimate the speed of the AP-120B. It was coded in assembly language by the vendor. If startup and termination time is ignored, then this loop can be executed in 11 clocks/step with the slow memory and 7 clocks/step with the fast memory which yields a computational rate of 7.6 to 12 Mflop. It might be difficult to design a compiler to produce such a tight loop, but it should be possible.

```
      REAL U(64,64),W(64,64),T(64,64)
      I = 2
      DO 10 J = 2,63
10    T(I,J) = U(I,J) + C * (W(I,J+1) + W(I,J-1)) *
     (U(I,J+1) - U(I,J-1)) + D * (ABS(U(I+1,J) - U(I,J)) *
     (U(I+1,J) - U(I,J)) - ABS(U(I,J) - U(I-1,J)) *
     (U(I,J) - U(I-1,J)))
```

Thus our estimate of 1-4 Mflop for the overall speed of the AP-120B is probably conservative, especially since code optimization for this machine does not require long vectors. It does require very careful but conventional handling of loops and the effective use of the 64 scratch pad registers.

IV. LANGUAGES TO SUPPORT PARALLEL COMPUTING

The quality of the software certainly has a profound influence on the effectiveness of a computing system. Programming costs are high enough so that expensive "custom" software can be justified if it results in even a modest improvement in overall user productivity. If there are 50 programmers working full time on a system at $30,000 to $50,000 institutional cost and 200 scientist working 1/5 time programming at $50,000 each, then this is a programming cost of $3.5M to $4.5M per year. A diagnostic Fortran compiler, or a compiler for a special language, which cost $250,000 could be justified by a 2% productivity improvement over a three year period if the programming cost is $4M per year. We will describe a few languages which have been proposed for parallel computing, or have features which might be useful on a parallel machine. Some of these have been implemented. The proceedings of the 1975 SIGPLAN conference on languages for parallel machines contains several articles from which we have drawn information.

One approach to code generation on a parallel computer is the modification of a Fortran compiler so that it will recognize code segments which can be executed in parallel and generate code accordingly. The Fortran compiler for the Texas Instruments ASC machine is designed to do this [4]. At least one compiler for the Cray machine which will attempt to generate vector instructions from Fortran is under development. Workers at Massachusetts Computer Associates have published work on such a compiler [24]. Several people have expressed the opinion to the author, that it is very difficult for a Fortran compiler to generate good vector code for typical large production programs unless those programs are first rewritten by a human. Efficient vector operation seems to require structural changes in the algorithm which may be impossible for a compiler. On the other hand, work by Professor Kuck and his students seems to indicate that an automatic generation of vector code from "typical" Fortran could keep 8 to 16 processing elements busy in a network type parallel computer [30]. I believe this work ignores any problem with memory conflicts or the interconnection of the PE's. Of course, any such quantitative results are problem dependent. The approach of carefully **rewriting** the Fortran program, retaining the program in standard Fortran, then depending on a Fortran compiler to produce vector code, will probably work well in many cases, perhaps in most cases. However, the following code segment may not compile efficiently unless the compiler is very well written.

```
      DO 100 I = 1,N
        IF(X(I).LT.0.) GOTO 80
        T(I) = 1.                                              (1)
        GOTO 100
 80     T(I) = EXP(C*X(I))
100   CONTINUE
```

The CRAY, STAR and ILLIAC IV machines can all execute this code in parallel although vector code for both replacement statements must be executed for the full vector T(*). The execution of the replacement statement must be controlled in some way by a "bit" vector which is set by the Boolean expression.

To handle this type of problem it may be desirable to extend Fortran to include vector declarations and vector operations. If this is properly done it could result in a language which is more convenient than Fortran, even on a scaler computer. Examples of such an extension to Fortran are the compiler for the ASC machine, the LRLTRAN compiler in use at the Lawrence Livermore Laboratory, and IVTRAN for the ILLIAC-IV [4,24,52]. A rather complete proposal for such an extension has been made by Paul and Wilson and is called VECTRAN [44]. Another vector language is SL/1 by Basili and Knight [5]. It is specifically designed for the STAR and has a syntax reminiscent of PL/1. The CFD language is specifically designed for the ILLIAC-IV, as is GLYPNIR. Both of these languages have been implemented [12,33].

A. Vector Language Syntax and Compilation

Here we will be concerned with languages which allow significant operations on vectors and arrays. The best known of these languages, and the one with the richest set of operations, is APL [25]. The other languages that we will discuss have been specifically designed for efficient operation on one or another parallel machine although not all have been implemented. We are most interested in those language features which are important to efficient and convenient usage of parallel computers. Therefore we will largely ignore general questions of language design such as ease of structured programming, reliable subroutine parameter passing, existence of general data types, user defined data types and operations on these data types, etc. Some features which seem to be especially relevant to parallel computing are the following:

1. Are the elements in vector operands associated by conformability or by a vector iteration command (we will explain this below).

2. Can the user explicitly allocate the data to memory

to insure efficient access, if this is necessary? An example might be skewing in ILLIAC-IV. Another example might be allocation to bulk memory or disk. Can the user explicitly request access to rows, columns, diagonals, rectangular subarrays, etc.? [33].

3. How are vector conditional evaluations of the type in the code segment (1) expressed? This conditional evaluation can be done with vector operations in CFD, GLIPNIR, TRANQUIL, IVTRAN, and VECTRAN. In VECTRAN we can write [44]

```
REAL X(100),T(100)
RANGE /N/X,T
WHEN(X.LT.0.) T = EXP(C*X),OR T = 1.
```

Note that VECTRAN extends the elementary functions such as EXP to array arguments. With index sets this could be written [19]

```
INDEX I
I = 1..N
INDEXIF X(I) .LT. 0. THEN
    T(I) = EXP(C*X(I))
ELSE
    T(I) = 1.
ENDINDEXIF
```

4. Can the user explicitly call for vector operations? For example

```
REAL A(64),B(64)
A(*) = B(*)**2
```

would explicitly call for a vector calculation on a vector of length 64. The alternative would have the compiler "vectorize" normal Fortran code. Such a compiler would thus provide implicit vector operations. The ASC Fortran compiler will attempt such vectorization.

5. What type of vector operations are explicitly represented. In particular are the following included: summation (or the more general APL reduction), inner product, compress and expand (in the APL sense), and merge of two vectors according to a "bit" vector (in the manner of the CRAY computer). The VECTRAN and SP/1 languages have special vector operations such as inner product, compress, etc. LRLTRAN also has additional operators, some as dot delimited operators, some as subroutines. The ASC compiler has special operations implemented as subroutines.

6. Are there explicit features in the language which allow the user to control allocation of data to the disk? For example, the BUFFERIN/BUFFEROUT type of statements, or subroutine calls. Can the data be placed under a specified head group and can the angular position of the data on the disk be specified? Does the user have access to I/O channels

which can be used concurrently, or does the user have no control over the assignment of channels? A very high level language might allow the user to specify a "disk block" of data and also specify the manner in which the data is to be accessed. Then the compiler would set up the I/O commands required to buffer data for a "FOR...DISK" type of iteration command. Dan Anderson has implemented a preprocessor at NCAR which helps with the management of disk contained data [2].

7. How is vector temporary storage, required for the evaluation of vector expressions, assigned? Is the user allowed to set a maximum stack size for these temporaries?

8. Can the user define vector valued functions?

We will proceed to discuss the first two questions in more detail.

B. Vector Definition and Vector Operations

First we consider how vectors and vector operations are described in various languages. APL is certainly the most widely known vector language. APL is likely to be implemented as an interpreter largely because there are no explicit declarations in the language. A variable may be scalar at one point in a program and a vector at another. This requires execution time testing and will probably make the language too slow for large models. It has been pointed out that much of this testing can be eliminated by compile time program flow analysis [8]. Kolsky and Evans have considered the application of APL to large scientific problems [17,27]. Another disadvantage of APL is the lack of structured commands to control program flow. However APL has been modified in the APLGOL language to include structured branching and **repetition** commands such as

$$IF...THEN...ELSE...FI$$

and this language has been implemented on the HP3000 [28].

C. Conformable Versus Subscripted Vector Notation

Vector (or array) operations in APL are based on the concept of conformable arrays [25]. These are arrays with the same number of elements within each subscript range. Thus the arrays a_{ij} and b_{ij} below are conformable

a_{ij} where $-10 \leq i \leq 10$, $0 \leq j \leq 10$

b_{ij} where $0 \leq i \leq 20, 10 \leq j \leq 20$

whereas a_{ij} is not conformable with the following c_{ij} array

c_{ij} where $0 \leq i \leq 10$, $-10 \leq j \leq 10$

The APL representation of the following expression is a little indirect because the arrays U_{ij} and C_j are not conformable

```
FOR I := 1 TO 64 DO
    FOR J := 1 TO 63 DO
        W(I,J) := U(I,J) + C(J) * U(I,J+1);
```

An alternative method to define vector operations is by use of a vector iteration command. An example of this is taken from the TRANQUIL language proposed for the ILLIAC-IV by Kuck [10]. This language uses "index sets" to define subscript values which can then be used to create array operands within an arithmetic expression. Parallel or simultaneous evaluation of the expression over the index sets is obtained by use of the "FOR...SIM" command which is similar to the DO statement in Fortran, except that evaluation of the expressions within the scope of the "FOR...SIM" is done in parallel. For example consider

```
ISET ← [1,2,...,64];
JSET ← [1,2,...,63];
FOR(I,J) SIM(ISET, JSET)DO
    W[I,J] ← U[I,J] + C[J] * U[I,J+1];
```

The variable ISET is an index set defined to be those values between 1 and 64 with an increment of 2-1 = 1. Thus ISET consists of the integers ISET = $\{i | 1 \leq i \leq 64\}$. There is no need to have conformable arrays. In the expression C[J] * U[I,J+1] the operands are matched by use of the same index J in the operands. The index J generates a vector (or simultaneous) evaluation because its appearance in the FOR...SIM requires its simultaneous evaluation over the set of values defined by JSET.

The IVTRAN language, also designed for the ILLIAC-IV, has a similar "simultaneous" DO statement. For example

```
        DO 10 FORALL (I,J)/[1..64].C.[1..63]
            W(I,J) = U(I,J) + C(J) * U(I,J+1)
     10 CONTINUE
```

D. Indexed Array Expressions

In both TRANQUIL and IVTRAN the parallel or vector evaluation is obtained by an explicit command, the FOR...SIM or DO...FORALL. In TRANQUIL there is an explicit data type to indicate the subscript values over which the evaluation is to be done. We have proposed that the use of index sets could imply vector (i.e. simultaneous) evaluation [19]. For example

```
      REAL U(64,64),W(64,64),C(64)
      INDEX I,J
      I = 1..64
      J = 1..63
      W(I,J) = U(I,J) + C(J) * U(I,J+1)
```

Here the index set is a data type which carries a lower and upper bound for subscripts. Use of an index in an array subscript is then used to define the array elements over which the expression is to be evaluated. Each expression has an associated index list (a scalar expression has an empty index list). For example

```
         REAL U(64,64,2),W(64,64),V(64,64),C(64),D(64),S
         INDEX I,J,K
         INTEGER N
         I = 1..64
         J = I
         K = I
         N = 1
   10    U(I,J,N) = W(I,J) + C(I) * C(J)
   20    U(I,J,2) = C(I)
   30    V(I,J) = V(J,I) + V(I,I)
   40    S = +/V(I,J)
   50    D(I) = W(I,J) +/* C(J)
   60    U(I,J,1) = V(K,I) +/[K] * (C(I) + W(J,K))
```

In line 10 the index list of the expression C(I) *C(J) is (I,J), the expression evaluates to the direct product. The index list of the result of a product is the union of the index lists of the two operands. The order is not important. The index list of the array on the left of a replacement statement must contain the index list of the expression on the right but the two lists need not be equal. For example, the statement in line 20 is allowed, but C(I) = U(I,J,2) is not correct. In statement 30 we are doubling the diagonal of the matrix V and also taking the transpose. The **operator** +/ is a unary reduction or summation operator which sums out all the indices in the index list of its operand expression. The result is a scalar. To restrict the reduction to a specified index we can write C(I) = +/[J]V(I,J). The operation +/* is the inner product taken over all indices which are common to the two operand expressions. In line 50 this results in the index J being reduced out. In line 60 the index K is reduced out. The reduction operators provide a more concise notation than in TRANQUIL, otherwise the index driven operations are similar to those defined by the FOR...SIM.

E. Expressions Based on Conformable Vectors

The languages just described above are quite different from those which use conformable operands, such as APL, VECTRAN, and to some extent Fortran on the ASC computer. The APL programmer usually tries to avoid subscripted arrays. Instead the rich set of operators in APL is used. For example, consider the following finite difference expression on a one-dimensional mesh.

```
FOR I := 2 TO 63 DO
    U[I] := W[I] + DELT
            *(W[I-1]-2.*W[I]+W[I+1]) / DELX ↑ 2;
U[1] := GA(T); U[64] := GB(T)
```
With index subscripts this would be
```
I = 2..63
U(I) = W(I) + DELT
       * (W(I-1)-2.*W(I)+W(I+1)) / DELX ** 2
U(1) = GA(T); U(64) = GB(T)
```
In APL it could be written as below, assuming that U and W are vectors of dimension 64 and DELT, and T global variables

```
    ∇W←DXX V
[1]   WI←((-2↓V)-(2×(-1↓(1↓V))) + (2↓V)) / (DELX×DELX)
[2]   W←(GA(T)-W[1]),WI,(GB(T)-W[64])
    ∇
    U ← W + DELT×DXX(W)
```
Note that we have defined a vector valued function and used it to produce a more readable algorithm than the original ALGOL-like description. It is desirable to have functions with results of vector or array type available in the language. We have proposed a finite difference operator extension of FORTRAN which is designed for this type of algorithm [18].

I find that the requirement of conformable vector operands imposed by APL is sometimes inconvenient. Also, if subscripts are used, then APL can produce results which I find counter intuitive for a FORTRAN programmer. For example, if A and B are arrays of dimension (64,64), and

```
I ← ι64
J ← ι64
B ← .5×(A[I;J]-A[J;I])
```

then B is not the skew symmetric part of A, but is instead identically zero. Also, as we indicated earlier, the multiplication of arrays of different dimension is a little awkward when conformable operands are used, consider

```
FOR I = 1 TO N DO
    FOR J = 1 TO M DO
        U[I,J] = W[I,J] * C[J];
```

In APL this can be written, assuming U, W, and C are arrays of dimension (N,M) and (M), as follows using an outer product

$$U = W \times ((N\rho 1) \text{ o.} \times C)$$

The judgement, as to the comparative clarity of these two expressions, is highly subjective. The first is probably easier to compile efficiently.

F. The Definition of Subarrays

The ASC FORTRAN compiler, and VECTRAN allow the user to define subarrays and then perform operations over conformable subarrays within a FORTRAN setting. They do not provide the full set of APL operators, although they probably could. These all allow use of a "slice" (ALGOL68) or "crossection" as indicated below

```
REAL A(64,64),X(64)
X = A(5,*) + 2.*X
```

In ASC Fortran the SUBARRAY statement defines an array whose elements are taken from another array. For example

```
REAL A(7,2)
SUBARRAY S(5,2) AT A(3,1) BY (2,1)
```

Then S is a subarray of A with maximum subscript values 5 and 2. The subscripts start at 3 and 1 with increments 2 and 1. Thus

$$S(*,*) = \begin{vmatrix} A(3,1) & A(3,2) \\ A(5,1) & A(5,2) \end{vmatrix}$$

These languages are designed as extensions of FORTRAN and therefore store the elements in row order.

G. Memory Allocation

The CFD and IVTRAN languages are designed for the ILLIAC-IV and therefore must consider the mapping of array elements into memory. IVTRAN provides three methods to allocate array elements to the PE memories. The first is the skewing scheme proposed by Kuck, for example

```
REAL A(3,4) [(1),$(2)]
```

The "$" designates the "preferred" subscript. This means that the vector A(1,*) can be accessed into the PE's without setting up a vector in the index registers of the PE's. The storage is

PE_0	PE_1	PE_2	PE_3	PE_4	PE_5
$A_{1,1}$	$A_{1,2}$	$A_{1,3}$	$A_{1,4}$		
	$A_{2,1}$	$A_{2,2}$	$A_{2,3}$	$A_{2,3}$	
		$A_{3,1}$	$A_{3,2}$	$A_{3,3}$	$A_{3,4}$

The vector A(*,1) can also be obtained with one memory access, but less efficiently. The allocation for

REAL A(3,4) $[\$(1),(2)]$

would be

PE_0	PE_1	PE_2	PE_3	PE_4	PE_5
$A_{1,1}$	$A_{2,1}$	$A_{3,1}$			
	$A_{1,2}$	$A_{2,2}$	$A_{3,2}$		
		$A_{1,3}$	$A_{2,3}$	$A_{3,3}$	
			$A_{1,4}$	$A_{2,4}$	$A_{3,4}$

A "multiindex" can also be used. For example

REAL A(2,3) $[(1,1)]$

would yield the allocation

PE_0	PE_1	PE_2	PE_3	PE_4	PE_5
$A_{1,1}$	$A_{2,1}$	$A_{1,2}$	$A_{2,2}$	$A_{1,3}$	$A_{2,3}$

An "aligned" index can also be specified

REAL A(3,4) $[\#(1),\$(2)]$

which gives the allocation

PE_1	PE_2	PE_3	PE_4
$A_{1,1}$	$A_{1,2}$	$A_{1,3}$	$A_{1,4}$
$A_{2,1}$	$A_{2,2}$	$A_{2,3}$	$A_{2,4}$
$A_{3,1}$	$A_{3,2}$	$A_{3,3}$	$A_{3,4}$

CFD is a high level language which is tied more closely to the ILLIAC-IV than is IVTRAN. For example, the declaration

DIMENSION A(*,2,3),X(*),B(*,64)

yields the allocation

PE_0	PE_1	$\ldots$	PE_{63}
$C_{1,1,1}$	$C_{2,1,1}$		$C_{64,1,1}$
$C_{1,2,1}$	$C_{2,2,1}$		$C_{64,2,1}$
$\vdots$			
$C_{1,2,3}$	$C_{2,2,3}$		$C_{64,2,3}$

An expression is then of the form

    X(*)**2*(A(*+1,1,1)-A(*-1,1,1))/DELX

The subscripts *±1 produce an end-around shift through the PE's; that is, this subscript is evaluated module 64. Subscripts of the form IV(*) are allowed in the second position only, that is B(*,IV(*)). All vectors are of length 64 and must have a "*" in the first subscript position.

H. A Basic Set of Vector Operations

    These are operations that should be contained explicitly in a language, and that a machine would hopefully execute in parallel. The usual unary and binary operators should be extended to array operands, either in the conformable or index format (or both). These would include the arithmetic operations (+,-,/,*,**), relational, and logical operations on the usual data types. In addition the APL operators floor (minimum), ceiling (maximum), reduction (summation), reshape, size, take, drop, inner product, and outer product should be included. These could be provided in function format, although infix format seems to be superior.

    In addition the following operations could be included. These are similar to a suggestion made to the author by Dick McHugh of the CDC Boulder office. In the following we assume that B is a logical vector or array which is conformable with the real arrays V, W, and R. The first is a "mask" defined by

    IF B(I) THEN R[I] := V[I] ELSE R[I] := W[I] FI

The second is a "merge" given by

```
        LB := 1; KB := 1;
        FOR I := 1 TO N DO
           (IF B[I] THEN
               (R[I] := V[KB]; KB := KB+1)
            ELSE
               (R[I] := W[LB]; LB := LB+1))
```

The next is the APL compress

```
        KB := 1;
        FOR I := 1 TO N DO
          (IF B[I] THEN (R[KB] := V[I]; KB := KB+1))
```
The next is a "decompress"
```
        KB := 1;
        FOR I := 1 TO N DO
          (IF B[I] THEN (R[I] := V[KB]; KB := KB+1))
```
The last is essentially the APL expand (S is a scalar operand)
```
        KB := 1;
        FOR I := 1 TO N DO
          (IF B[I] THEN
              (R[I] := V[KB]; KB := KB+1)
           ELSE
              (R[I] := S)
```

In addition to these operations the "gather" and "scatter" memory accessing methods might be explicitly allowed within vector expressions. The CFD language and the STAR assembly language do allow something similar. The "gather" is defined by R[I] := W[K[I]] and the "scatter" by R[K[I]] := W[I]

V. ACKNOWLEDGEMENT

We are indebted to Stewart Patterson, director of the NCAR computing facility, for permission to use the NCAR statistics. These statistics were obtained under the direction of Paul Rotar, head of the systems group. We received valuable information at NCAR from Roy Jenne and Margaret Drake concerning data processing, and from Dan Anderson, Dick Sato, and Dave Williamson concerning large PDE models. At Los Alamos we used information from Tom Jordan, Bill Buzbee, Roger Lazarus, and several others. At Livermore Fred Fritsch, Dick Girouix, Lansing Sloan, Gerry Owens, and others were very helpful. We are also indebted to Dick McHugh of CDC-Boulder and James Sherfey and Wayne Martson of Floating Point Systems.

VI. REFERENCES

1. Adams, J., and Gary, J., "Compact representation of contour plots for phone line transmission", Comm ACM, V.17, No.6, pp.333-336, 1974.
2. Anderson, Dan, "FLOW: A Collection of routines for facilitating the programming of noncore-contained codes", unpublished manuscript, NCAR, Boulder, CO, 80302, 1976.

3. AP-120B Processor handbook, Floating point systems, Beaverton, OR, 97005, May 1976.
4. ASC Fortran Reference Manual, Texas Instruments, Nov., 1971.
5. Basili, V., and Knight, J., "A language design for vector machines", Proceedings of a conference on programming languages and compilers for parallel and vector machines, ACM(SIGPLAN), March 18-19, 1975, pp.39-44.
6. Batcher, K. E., "Sorting networks and their applications" Spring Joint Comp Conf. V.32, pp.307-314 (1968).
7. Batcher, K. E., "STARAN parallel processor system hardware" Fall Joint Comp Conf, V.43, p.405 (1974)
8. Bauer, A., and Sall, H., "Does APL really need run time checking", Software, V.4, pp.129-138, 1974.
9. Bhandarkar, D., "On the performance of magnetic bubble memories in computer systems" IEEE Trans Computers, V.24, pp.1125-1129 (1975).
10. Budnik, P., and Kuck, D., "A TRANQUIL programming manual", File no. 316, Computer Science Dept., Univ. of Illinois, Dec., 1969.
11. Budnik, P., and Kuck, D., "The organization and use of parallel memories" IEEE Trans Comp, V.20, pp.1566-1569 (1971).
12 CFD--a Fortran based language for Illiac IV, Version 2.0, Ames Research Center, NASA.
13. Chen, S., and Kuck, D., "Time and parallel processor bounds for linear recurrence systems" ibid pp.701-718.
14. Cody, W., "Desirable hardware characteristics for scientific computation", SIGNUM newsletter, V.6, No. 1, pp.16-31, Jan. 1971.
15. CRAY-1 Computer system reference manual, Bloomington, MN 55420.
16. Dolotta, T., and Mashey, J., "An introduction to the programmer's workbench", Proc. Second Int. Conf. on Software Engineering, Oct.1976.
17. Evans, D., "Problem formulation using array processing techniques", (see Basili and Knight) 1975.
18. Gary, J., "PDELAN: A mesh operator variant of FORTRAN, Rep. CU-CS-049-74, Univ. of Colorado, Boulder, CO 80302, 1974.
19. Gary, J., "A vector language for the solution of PDE problems", Rep. CU-CS-068-75, Comp. Sci. Dept., Univ. of Colorado, Boulder, CO 1976.
20. George, A., Poole, W., Voight, R., "Analysis of dissection algorithms for vector computers", ICASE Rep.76-17, submitted to Transactions on Mathematical Software, 1976.
21. Gold, D. E., and Kuck, D. J., "A model for masking rotational latency by dynamic disk allocation" Comm ACM, V.17, pp.278-288 (1974).

22. Hassitt, A., and Lyon, L., "An APL emulator on systems/ 370", IBM Systems Jour., V.15, No.4, pp.358-379, 1976.
23. Higbie, L., "Vector floating point data format" IEEE Trans. Comp, V.C-25, pp.25-32 (1976).
24. The IVTRAN manual, Massachusetts Computer Associates, Wakefield, MA 07880, Nov, 1973.
25. Katzan, H., "APL Programming and computer techniques", Van Nostrand, NY, 1970.
26. Keller, T., "CRAY-1 Evaluation", LASL Rep. LA-6456-MS, Los Alamos Scientific Lab, Los Alamos, NM 87545, Dec. 1976.
27. Kolsky, H., "Problem formulation using APL", IBM Sys. Jour, 8, pp.204-217, 1969.
28. Kolsky, H., "APLGOL: A structured programming language for APL", IBM symposium on programming methodology, Wildbad, Germany, Sept. 1974.
29. Kransky, V., Giroux, E. D., and Long, G., "Parallel implementation of a two-dimensional model", Proc. of the Sagamore Conf. on parallel processing, Aug. 1973.
30. Kuck, D., Muraoka, Y., Chen, S-C., "On the number of operations simultaneously executable in FORTRAN-like programs and their resulting speedup", IEEE Trans. on Comp. V.C-21, No.12 (1972).
31. Kuck, D., and Muraoka, Y., "Some thoughts", unpublished manuscript (1971).
32. Kuck, D., "A survey of parallel machine organization and programming", ACM Surveys, V.9, No.1, pp.29-60, 1977.
33. Layman, T., and Baer, D., "GLYPNIR reference manual", Illiac IV Document No. 263, Univ. of Illinois, Dec., 1972.
34. Lawrie, D., "Access and alignment of data in an array processor", IEEE Trans. Comp., V.C-24, No. 12, pp.1145-1155 (Dec., 1975).
35. Lazarus, R., "Sketch of a vectorized MCNG (Monte Carlo for Neutrons and Gammas", unpublished LASL manuscript, Los Alamos, NM 87544, 1976.
36. Melkanoff, M., Moszkowski, B., Lauterbach, C., "Implementation of MADCAP 6 on UCLA's 360/91 IMLAC system", Comp. Sci. Dept., UCLA, Los Angeles, CA 90024, May 1974.
37. Minter, C., "A machine design for efficient implementation of APL" Rep. 81, Comp. Sci. Dept., Yale Univ., New Haven, CT 06520, May 1976.
38. More, T., "Types and prototypes in a theory of arrays", IBM Cambridge Scientific Center, pp.320-2112, May 1976.
39. Morris, J., "A manual for the MODEL programming language", LASL manuscript, Los Alamos, NM 87544, July 1976.
40. Muraoka, Y., "Parallelism exposure and exploitation in programs", Ph.D.thesis, Dept. Comp. Sci., Univ. of Illinois, Urbana. (1971)

41. NOAA Technical Memorandum NESS 64, "Central processing and analysis of geostationary satellite data", NOAA, Washington, D.C., March, 1975.
42. Oliger, J., Wellck, R., Kasahara, A., Washington, W., "Description of NCAR Global circulation model", NCAR report, Boulder, CO 80302, May, 1970.
43. Orbits, D., and Calahan, D., "Data flow considerations in implementing a full matrix solver with backing store on the CRAY-1", Systems Eng. Lab., Univ. of Michigan, Ann Arbor, 48109, Sept 1976.
44. Paul, G., and Wilson, M. W., "The VECTRAN language" IBM Palo Alto Scientific Center, Rep. G32-3334, Aug. 1975.
45. Rudsinski, L., and Worlton, W., "Impact of scalar performance on vector and parallel processors", Los Alamos Rep. LA-UR-76-2656, LASL, Los Alamos, NM 87545.
46. Sloan, L. J., "An introduction to the triad subroutines", RDA-TR-035-DNA, R&D Associates, Santa Monica, CA, Sept. 1971.
47. Stone, H., "Dynamic memories with fast random and sequential access", IEEE Trans on Comp, V.C-24, pp.1167-1174 (1975).
48. Tuttle, P. G., "Implementation of selected eigenvalue algorithms on a vector computer", NPGD-TM-330, Babcock and Wilcox, Power Generation Group, Lynchburg, VA, 24505, July 1975.
49. Wells, M., and Morris, J., "The unified data structure capability in MADCAP-VI", Intl Jour Comp and Infor Sciences, V.1, No.3, pp.193-107, Sept 1972.
50. Williamson, D., and Washington, W., "On the importance of precision for short range forecasting and climate simulation", Jour. App. Meteorology, V.12, No.8, pp.1254-1258, Dec 1973.
51. Worlton, J., "Some estimates of the performance of STAR relative to the CDC 7600", unpublished report, LASL, Los Alamos, NM, Feb., 1974.
52. Zwakenburg, Z., Engle, J., Gotthoffer, D., and River, M., "Vector extensions to LRLTRAN" SIGPLAN proceed (see [5], Basili) pp.77-87.

APPENDIX 1.

The following statistics were developed by John Burk and Chuck Cole of the Lawrence Livermore Laboratory. Fred Fritsch was instrumental in obtaining them for this paper

TABLE 4

LLL Data Flow Statistics

Total Number of terminals	976
Number of RJE terminals	32
Number of TV display monitors	698
Available Storage capacity	
4-7600 online disk	1.6×10^{10} bits
2-STAR online disk	3.5×10^{10} bits
Mass storage (photostore, data cells)	2.0×10^{12} bits
Data rates	
Written to Data Cell per month	$3. \times 10^{10}$ bits/mo
Written to photostore per month	1.5×10^{11} bits/mo
Written to tape (by 4-7600's)	1×10^{12} bits/mo
Tape mounts per month (by 4-7600's)	10,000
Total information currently on photostore (including cells offline)	4.5×10^{12} bits

TABLE 5

LLL User Statistics

Number of users of OCTOPUS system

7600 System useage	Daytime	Night/Weekend
Average number logged on/machine	42	12
Average number of logons or "bye" to suffix/mach/hour	400	250
Average number of tasks executed/mach/hour	1600	500

The text editor is used an average of 457 times per day on each CDC 7600. The Fortran compilers an average of 237 times per day on each CDC 7600. These user statistics are highly variable.

Appendix 2.

TABLE 6

NCAR Software Development Costs in Salaries and Benefits

Type	FTE	% who program	% time in software development	Ave. S & B	Total Cost
Scientists	125	50	33	$33K	$ 681K
Support Scientists	55	90	50	25K	619K
Programmer	54	100	75	25K	1013K
Engineer	45	90	33	25K	334K
					$2645K

We are indebted to Dr. Stewart Patterson of NCAR for making these estimates available for this paper.

TABLE 3 - addendum

Cyber 176 cost

131K	SCM memory at $6.15/word
524K	LCM memory at $1.60/word
5.9×10^6	Total cost (CPU, memory, 4-819 disks and controller)

3	Mflop scalar
10	Mflop vector

0.5	flop/$ scalar
1.7	flop/$ vector

The CRAY configuration includes 8 disk drives and four controllers.

ALGORITHMS AND ARCHITECTURE

Paul Budnik, Jr.
System Development Corporation[1]
Joseph Oliger
Stanford University

We consider current trends in the construction of algorithms and the design of computing hardware with regard to their impact on certain large scale scientific computations.

Adequate calculations for many problems will only become feasible with envisioned supercomputers. The efficiency of representation of the solutions and needed data for these problems is very important and success depends on it. To date many of the algorithms have been highly regular and efficient implementations on the current vector and parallel architectures have often been rather obvious. However, the most efficient algorithms in terms of computational effort and data representation are often adaptive in nature since the complexity of the solutions often vary considerably over the problem domain.

We attempt to gain some historical insight into the development of parallel computing from several points of view. We look at parallelism in circuits for individual arithmetic operations and relate observations about these to the general mathematical theory of recursive ordinals. We describe where some current research fits in terms of this general mathematical theory. We contrast this general theoretical structure with what makes a useful tool, and finally, we venture some remarks about the future.

I. INTRODUCTION

The subject of high speed computing encompasses three broad problems: making existing computing structures faster, making computers faster by structuring them differently, and

___
[1] Supported in part by the Office of Naval Research under Contract N00014-75-C-1137

making computing faster by inventing better algorithms. The first question is primarily one of engineering and solid state physics. Our assumptions about the first area are that steady and significant progress will continue to be made for the immediately forseeable future and that the demand for performing large computations exceeds existing capabilities. In the past the demand for computing power has grown at a slightly greater rate than the supply and we can safely assume that there will be adequate demand for any practical cost effective schemes for enhancing computing power through the latter two approaches. It is these approaches that are the subject of this paper, areas which are likely to increase in importance in direct correlation with their success in providing cost effective enhancement in computing power.

Both of these approaches have been and are being pursued. Each approach has encountered its own set of difficulties. We now consider the conjectured utilization of parallel and vector machines for various problems.

The first highly structured parallel and pipeline machines were built with certain large problems in areas such as radar and seismic data processing in mind which, when solved using the algorithms of the day, had highly regular data structures which mapped onto the machines in an obvious way. Then: (1) the proponents of these machines went looking for other problems to put on them, and (2) others with large problems and needs for increased computing power turned to these machines. Many problems in fluid dynamics were obvious candidates, e.g., flow about various vehicles in aerodynamics and shipbuilding, atmospheric and ocean circulation problems, and problems in plasma physics stemming from nuclear fusion. Again, the classical algorithms yielded highly regular data structures. However, the implementation of algorithms for these problems immediately posed problems of dealing with irregular geometries. There were also problems which posed the difficulty of evaluating functions which depend on the solution and whose definitions and costs of evaluation are very different for various ranges of the solution. When the data was structured naturally for the remaining majority of the calculation this led to computations which had, figuratively, nearly infinite cost, but almost never happened. The forcing functions in meteorological calculations are an example of this last phenomenon (25). Language efforts early in the ILLIAC IV project recognized these geometry problems but they are still open. Mode bits on the ILLIAC IV and vector compress operations on the Texas Instruments ASC dealt with the branching problem but it is only distributed computing which naturally and effectively deals with the last problem cited above.

As indicated above, many unforseen difficulties have

arisen in the past. This pattern is repeating. Recently one
of us attended a talk about the Imsai proposal to construct
the hypercube, a four dimensional array of up to 10,000 microcomputers. At one point the lecturer explained why he felt
such a machine might be useful for many different problems.
He pointed out that it is certainly true that you can't construct a general compiler to map arbitrary sequential programs
onto such a machine. He then suggested that if you really
start thinking about any large problem you will most likely
begin to understand how to implement it on such a machine
efficiently. For an instant it was 10 years ago at the
University of Illinois and the machine in question was ILLIAC
IV.

There is an almost archetypal pattern of reactions to
the problems of highly parallel (or pipelined) computers. One
begins with an initial skeptical feeling that the class of
problems for which such a machine will be useful is likely to
be very narrow. Then, as one thinks about various problems at
a fairly general level, it becomes apparent that there is a
lot of exploitable parallelism in most big problems. This can
easily lead to the extreme optimism of our friend from Imsai
or that many of us felt almost a decade ago. Finally, one
actually constructs such a computer and trys to implement
various algorithms on it. Then the trouble begins.

It is not so much that one's observations about the
existence of exploitable parallelism are in error. It is
simply that it is an awful mess to get all the details right.
Of course this pattern of reaction is not solely limited to
the area of high speed computation. It is common to all human
endeavors when people have very big plans and very little
experience. It is a pattern that has characterized the construction and debugging of the hardware for high speed computation as well as the software. The psychological dimensions
of this pattern (14) are frequently more significant and more
fascinating than the technical dimensions. They are, however,
outside the scope of this paper and this conference. The
technical dimensions involve understanding the transformations that can be applied to an algorithm to make it
inherently more efficient, or make it conformable to a parallel
or pipelined architecture. These in turn involve understanding the topology of data interaction that is implicit in
the algorithm.

This sort of analysis did not begin with the current
generation of parallel and pipelined machines. Rather, the
techniques employed in the design of these machines are simply
extensions of techniques previously employed to make serial
machines faster. For example, the design of a carry look
ahead adder employs parallelism, redundant computations to
reduce delay, and a special logic circuit to select correctly

from the redundant subcomputations. Pipelining is at least as old as the first machine that could do memory accessing for one instruction while arithmetic computation was proceeding for an earlier instruction. Certainly all these ideas had much earlier antecedents. The current generation of high speed machines has extended these techniques from the bit and byte levels to the word and vector levels.

II. ALGORITHM DEVELOPMENT

We can easily identify three lines of algorithm development. Two of these have been a direct result of parallel and vector hardware, and the third is along traditional lines.
We now consider the two lines of algorithm development which sprang up with the advent of parallel machines. One was to reorganize traditional algorithms for parallel and vector machines. The other was to look for new, or revive discarded, algorithms which were generally inefficient for sequential calculations but which utilized the parallel structures effectively. Surveys of these efforts are given in the review paper of Miranker (23) and the bibliography of Poole and Voigt (27). There have been several impressive successes, and some of these developments have in fact influenced algorithms for sequential computation. Counter to this activity, and along more traditional lines of development, many adaptive algorithms which have instruction streams which are a function of the solution being computed, as it is being computed, have been developed. These algorithms attempt to minimize the number of arithmetic operations required to obtain an answer to given accuracy and/or the data required. It is usual that both of these objectives are attained simultaneously if the adaptive overhead does not get out of hand.
Adaptive algorithms are now the "state of the art" for most of the traditional one-dimensional problems of numerical analysis such as the initial value problem for ordinary differential equations (34), numerical quadrature (10, 21) and two-point boundary value problems (26). These algorithms are much more difficult to program and involve considerable overhead in the adaptive processes involved, but they are considerably more efficient and robust for most problems. Knowledgeable people use these methods regularly. Adaptive algorithms have also been developed for curve fitting (11, 31, 32) and integral equations (13). The study of these algorithms in the context of parallel computation has begun and, e.g., Rice (30), Lemme and Rice (20) have shown that a speedup factor of $M/\log m$ can be attained on an M-processor parallel machine with adaptive quadrature.
Most of this work has dealt with scalar problems—finding

a scalar or vector function of a single real variable over a given interval, or finding the integral of such a function. These are not the monster problems of continuum mechanics we mentioned earlier whose solutions are governed by partial differential equations. One exception is the recent work of Kahaner and Wells (15) on adaptive methods for multidimensional quadrature problems. Other workers have recently looked at adaptive methods for boundary-value problems for elliptic partial differential equations (2, 5).

Work has just begun on adaptive methods of this type for time dependent partial differential equations (3, 4, 22). Such methods seem especially well suited to problems which have generally smooth and uncomplicated solutions over most of their domains but which have locally violent behavior. Boundary layer phenomena is one such type of behavior, and it is probably most easily dealt with since its location is often known a priori and, though it may pose severe geometrical difficulties, these can be dealt with in an initial preprocessing phase. Other such behavior is exemplified by atmospheric fronts, tropical storms, oceanographic currents, and vortices which break off airfoils. These phenomena must be "tracked" in time and the mapping onto processors or assembly of vectors must be continually redone as the integrations progress. This imposes severe demands for sophisticated software. However, such methods are probably the only way that sufficient accuracy can be obtained for many of these problems in the foreseeable future. Furthermore, such methods will probably be most efficient for those problems with only locally complicated behavior as their scalar counterparts already are.

We now sketch such an algorithm, give some known properties, and discuss some of the accompanying difficulties. The basic philosophy is to equidistribute the local errors over the region of interest following deBoor (11). That is, there is an underlying attempt to divide the region into subregions in such a way that the error per computational interval is nearly constant. We will assume that the solution has a general behavior over most of the region which we can approximate sufficiently well by an underlying regular approximation. We will then refine on top of this underlying approximation. We will only attempt to approximately equidistribute the local errors for several reasons:

1) We don't want to have to restructure the computation too often. This is an effort to reduce the overhead.

2) We must be careful that local disturbances don't move out of the refined regions which are necessary for their accurate computation. If we do not accomplish this weak instabilities can result (6).

3) "Overkill" is often necessary to provide sufficient accuracy for "storms" to develop.

4) We will use "locally regular" approximations for computational ease and for theoretical reasons. We must be able to guarantee the stability of these techniques.

We will consider difference approximation of a partial differential equation

$$u_t = Pu \quad \text{on } \Omega \times [0,T]$$
$$u(x,0) = f(x) \quad \text{on } \Omega \tag{1}$$
$$Bu = g \quad \text{on } \partial\Omega$$

where $u(x,t)$ is a vector function, P and perhaps B are partial differential operators in the components of $x = (x_1,\ldots,x_n)$, and Ω is a bounded domain in R^n. We assume the problem to be well posed.

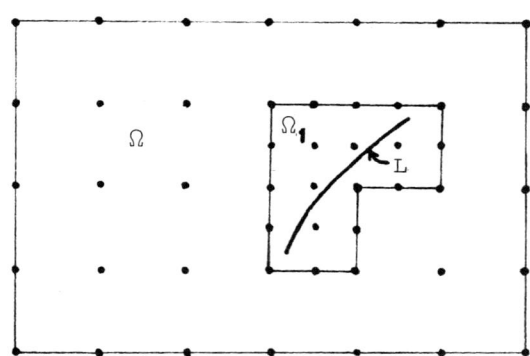

Assume that we can approximate (1) sufficiently well over $\Omega - \Omega_1$ with an explicit difference approximation.

$$v(t+k) = P_\Delta v(t) \quad \text{on } \Omega_\Delta \times [t | t = 0,k,2k,\ldots,T],$$
$$v(x,0) = f(x) \quad \text{on } \Omega_\Delta \tag{2}$$
$$B_\Delta v = g \quad \text{on } \partial\Omega_\Delta$$

where P_Δ and B_Δ are difference operators, and Ω_Δ and $\partial\Omega_\Delta$ are discretizations of Ω and $\partial\Omega$ with underlying discretization interval $h > 0$. We assume that this is stable and convergent. Assuming we have a steep gradient along the line L where the local errors violate our underlying error tolerance, we introduce a refinement Ω_1 about L such that the discretization interval $h_1 > 0$ in Ω_1 and discretization P_{Δ_1} yield local pointwise error in Ω_1 which is approximately the same as that satisfied in Ω. If (1) is a hyperbolic system, then this refinement can be introduced stably using the techniques discussed in Ciment (8) or Oliger (24). If (1) is parabolic obvious modifications of these techniques yield stable methods. If L "moves" as the solution evolves in time then Ω_1 must be "moved" along with it. This is done by periodically introducing the refinements to approximately equidistribute the local truncation error. Each time this is done the topology of the data structure changes--points have new neighbors. Let N be the total number of points required if the uniform algorithm P_Δ is used throughout with sufficiently small h to give desired accuracy. Let N_A be the total number of points needed to achieve this same accuracy with the adaptive approach. Let $\mu(M)$ denote the area or volume of a region M of R^n. Then it is shown by Bolstad and Oliger (4) using the methods of deBoor (11) and Pereyra and Sewell (26) that estimates of the form

$$\frac{N}{N_A} \approx \frac{\mu(\Omega)}{\mu(\Omega_1)}$$

can be attained where, as in our example, Ω_1 is generally the region where the solution is "complicated". The efficiencies in required data are clear for problems whose solutions are only complicated over small parts of the computational region. In one space dimension many problems yield $N/N_A \geq 10$, in two space dimensions N/N_A if often on the order of 100, and at least several hundred in three space dimensions. On top of these economies from the spacial discretization is another economy for the discretization in time. With such potential speed-ups we maintain that conventionally organized machines can compete with vector and parallel machines if regular algorithms are used on those machines for many problems.

The programming complications arising with these adaptive techniques are obvious. Since, at any given point $x_0 \in \Omega_{\Delta_j}$, the equation for $v(x_0,t+k)$ is a recurrence relation, and that it may only require information from a small number of points in the neighborhood of (x_0,t), it follows (see (16, 17, 37)) that the best orthogonal dissection of the computation in the x or t directions is the obvious choice--we distribute the computation of $v(x_j,t+k)$ as a function of the x_j over the processors, or align our vectors in this way. This distribution must be carried out each time we introduce a new region or delete an old one. Test calculations have been carried out by Bolstad (3) which indicate the practicality of these techniques. If the area of the regions where the solution is complicated are sufficiently small, the overhead expense is insignificant compared to the expense of the computation at the extra points required for a regular algorithm. Additionally, from another point of view, for very large computations the reduction in data size can make the difference between the possible and impossible because of the upper bound on the data that can be efficiently handled in any particular computational environment.

Sophisticated data structures and programming techniques are required for the implementation of these adaptive methods. The work of Kahaner and Wells (15) and of Bolstad (3) illustrate this well. In fact, Kahaner and Wells found it difficult to write a program which implemented their algorithm within the confines of the most commonly used languages and used the high level language Madcap implemented at Los Alamos Scientific Laboratory. This may become typical--the implementation of these complicated algorithms may often exceed what we are capable or willing to deal with operationally or psychologically within the framework of todays common computer languages.

It seems clear that we must be prepared to implement algorithms of this type on highly structured vector or parallel machines and, in fact, the success of these machines for many of the problems we mentioned will depend on this. The software demands of these algorithms are only barely met by what is presently available for sequential machines--and these demands will be much greater for the highly organized machines.

III. DOING SINGLE ADDS, MULTIPLIES AND EXPONENTIATIONS VERY FAST

We can gain some insight into the extreme difficulties involved in integrating complex algorithms with highly structured machines by considering the simplest sorts of problems. The techniques for highly structured computers evolved from techniques for serial computers as we observed earlier.

We begin with some observations on what sort of time versus logical complexity tradeoffs are theoretically possible for any computation. All actual computer programs can be thought of as computing a function from some finite range of possible inputs to a finite domain of possible outputs. Given the description of a computation in these terms there are a number of parameters that characterize the computation and that at least in theory can be determined. For logic with a particular delay, d, and fan in and fan out constraints, K, there is a minimum time in which the computation can be performed. A simple, but not necessarily greatest, lower bound can be derived which is only a function of the maximum number of bits B, that affect any output bit. This lower bound $\log_K(B)$ may be considerably smaller than the theoretical minima. But for simple functions like addition and even multiplication one can come fairly close to realizing these minima (35, 36). For more complex computations the amount of logic required for the minimum time computation can grow to astronomical dimensions. Any finite computation can be characterized by a series of time delay versus logical complexity tradeoffs, ranging from the minimum time realization to the minimum gate count realization. This series of optimal tradeoffs completely characterizes the range of practical possibilities for implementing the computation in question. There exist simple exhaustive algorithms that will theoretically compute these minimum tradeoffs. For all but the simplest cases exhaustive techniques are not practical.

Now we note that the above theoretical minimum time to perform addition, multiplication, or exponentiation is the same function of the number of bits in the operands. Yet, what is pragmatically possible is very different in each case. Addition and multiplication can both be realized in close to to theoretical minima for normal word sizes. However, much more logic is required for multiplication and this difference grows rapidly as the number of bits increase. The same logic can do either addition or subtraction in the same time. This is not the case for multiplication and division. One attempt we know of to implement an exponential function in hardware is the algorithm the SPS uses to compute sines and cosines. This uses two prestored tables 256 words long, requires two multiplies and an add, and only computes 16 bits of precision. And this algorithm is only good for sine and cosine and not for any of the many other exponential functions.

These three classes of arithmetic functions reside on the three lowest levels of a mathematical hierarchy which characterizes all possible topologies of data interaction in a recursive algorithm. We will now briefly describe this hierarchy and how it is related to some computer science concepts. We will then show how properties of this hierarchy allow us to interpret and extrapolate the above observations on simple arithmetic operations.

IV. PROGRAMMING LANGUAGES, THE RECURSIVE ORDINALS AND FUNCTIONS THAT GET VERY LARGE VERY QUICKLY

Consider the problem of defining computer languages in

which we can only write programs that halt. We know that one cannot construct such a language which has this property and in which all computer programs can be written. One can characterize any such language by the class of functions definable within it. A convenient way to define functions is to allow every program to have a single numeric value as input and a single numeric value as output when it halts. Again, there cannot exist a single language of this sort in which all recursive functions are definable, but there does exist a non-recursive hierarchy of such languages such that any function can be defined in one of the languages. These languages correspond directly to a mathematical hierarchy known as the recursive ordinals. These are ordinarily thought of in mathematics as being completed infinite structures. However, Kleene's proof (33) that every such ordinal has a recursive notation that effectively enumerates its structure is the key to interpreting this hierarchy as a theory of recursive iteration. The simplest infinite ordinal is the set of all integers. This can be represented by a Turing machine (TM) that enumerates the integers. We can think of a TM that has two kinds of outputs: integers, and the Gödel number of other TMs. Thus, we can represent infinite sets by the Gödel number of a TM that enumerates members of the set. We can require that the TM mark its outputs as being either the Gödel number of another TM or an integer. With these conventions the structure of any given recursive ordinal is completely described by some TM. The general theory of ordinal numbers in mathematics is a general theory of iteration in the sense that every known mathematical structure generally accepted as meaningful can be generated by iterating basic operations up to some ordinal (not necessarily a recursive ordinal).

There is a direct correspondence between the recursive ordinals and the hierarchy of programming languages mentioned above. For any such language there will be a recursive ordinal that characterizes the iteration schemes definable in this language. There are two related properties of these hierarchies which are of special interest to us. First, if the heirarchies are complete at each level than one can enumerate at a given level all the functions definable at all lower levels. At a given level it is possible to construct a function that grows more rapidly than any function defined at lower levels. The latter property is a direct consequence of the former since one can enumerate all functions and then generate a function whose nth output is the maximum of the first n outputs of the first n functions in the enumeration.

These maximal functions grow very rapidly and characterize the complexity of any given level of the hierarchy. Turning to our original examples with addition alone, the functions definable are quite simple. With addition and multiplication

the functions definable are the set of all polynomials. When
we add exponentiation virtually all of the well known mathematical functions are included. Yet we are still at only
the third tiny step in a hierarchy with no recursively definable limit.

V. WE KNOW A LOT ABOUT POLYNOMIALS

The increasing complexity as we move up this hierarchy
is directly reflected in how much we currently understand at
a given level. Addition is well in hand. Even networks for
doing the simultaneous addition of many numbers are fairly
straightforward. Circuitry for doing single multiplications
is also well understood. Much of the current research is
involved with understanding polynomials. The work here at
Illinois on parallelism in Fortran programs (18, 19) can be
regarded as looking at programs as a collection of polynomials and determining transformations that optimize their
suitability for parallel computation. This research has
established that most ordinary FORTRAN programs have a considerable amount of potentially exploitable parallelism and
that some have a great deal. People have in the past argued
that for theoretical reasons most programs could not effectively utilize parallel computers. Actual practical experience
with the current generation of such machines could well be
interpreted as providing theoretical evidence for such conclusions. Thus, it is very comforting to have reliable
quantitative measures of what sort of exploitable parallelism
does exist in ordinary programs. Looking at programs as a
system of polynomials is a general approach precisely because
most numerical programs can be interpreted as providing polynomial approximations to exponential functions.

Aside from the polynomial transformation approach there is
another dimension to understanding polynomials which is more
directly related to the problem of finding optimal logical circuits we discussed earlier. That is to find a particular
polynomial that optimally approximates some exponential function over a particular range in some given norm. Chebyshev
polynomials are one example of this sort of optimization.
Methods for computing optimal finite impulse response filters
are another example (28). Here, although we are still only
dealing with polynomials, the problem is much more complex
than the polynomial transformation problem and thus progress
tends to occur in a piecemeal fashion. Questions of this sort
can well turn out to be recursively unsolvable, as Hilbert's
tenth problem has turned out to be.

Hopefully, we have provided some perspective on why its
so difficult to get all the details correct. There does exist

a tremendous amount of exploitable parallelism in existing algorithms. Similarly, there are tremendous opportunities for designing more efficient algorithms. Although significant advances on both fronts have been made in the last ten years, our understanding of anything beyond polynomials is quite primitive. Further, our understanding of polynomial transformations is still at the theoretical level for machines with parallelism on the order of ILLIAC IV. To some degree this is inevitable. The step up in complexity from polynomials to exponential functions is gigantic. It is much greater than the increase in complexity in going from single arithmetic operations to polynomials--a step which is rather complex.

VI. USEFUL TOOLS

Probably the most widely heralded improvement in algorithm efficiency in the recent past has been the FFT. Rabiner and Rader in their introduction to one of the IEEE reprint series (29) make the following observation:

The publication of the Cooley-Tukey paper was not the first discovery of the exploitable structure of the DFT. It was, however, the first such publication to be widely noticed. One reason why the Cooley-Tukey paper was important, while the paper by I. J. Good a decade earlier was largely ignored (in spite of having described an essentially equivalent algorithm), was that by April 1965, a number of people were already involved in the use of computers to process waveforms.

What makes a good tool, be it algorithm or machine, of practical utility is not deep insight or broad generality but rather how well it meshes with a complex cultural system. We heartily concur that what made the algorithm that was ignored in the fifties so valuable in the sixties was the existence of machines capable of doing digital signal processing and people who wanted to use the machines for that purpose.

In the field of architecture an example of a useful tool is the Floating Point Systems machine AP 120. It is a commercial success, at least in part, because no original ideas were employed in its design and construction. The basic architecture was modeled after the Culler-Harrison machine, the CHI. One of the authors had the unfortunate experience of programming that machine and he finds it easy to understand why there are only two such machines in existence. There were many original ideas employed in the CHI's design. The AP 120 has a modest level of parallelism, a two stage pipelined adder, and a three stage multiplier. In addition, it has a large number of index and data registers with flexible data paths between registers and arithmetic units. A macro instruction allows one to do index arithmetic and register transfers in the same instruction in which an add and multiply are started. Thus, one has some chance of utilizing much of the potential arithmetic power in tightly coded inner loops. Add to this the existence of off the shelf interfaces to a variety of conventional host computers, and the software to execute array operations in the AP as subroutine calls in a FORTRAN program in the host. As a historical note, it is interesting to note that it was once proposed that ILLIAC IV be integrated into the Burroughs 6700 compilers in this fashion. This was the Cockroach proposal. To complete the ways in which the AP is well integrated into a cultural system we note that it is cheap, under $50K and that the company has at least one very good salesman whose presentation one of us has attended.

The general theory of recursive ordinals and the FFT algorithm lie at opposite ends of a spectrum that runs from the most general possible theory to an extremely useful tool. Research should be conducted simultaneously all along the spectrum. It is terribly important to have some understanding of where in the spectrum any particular piece of research lies and of the immense practical difficulties that can crop up in converting a brilliant idea or theory into a useful tool.

VII. THOUGHTS ABOUT THE FUTURE

We will center our discussion about the future on two old ideas. One of these is an almost universally valid observation and the other is an idea whose time is perhaps about to come. The first can be vaguely characterized as the need to isolate complexity. The adaptive algorithms for PDEs do this by selecting in real time those regions where the interaction is most complex. By using less complexity where possible, efficiency is greatly improved. Similarly, it is well known that, in optimizing a program, it is usually a small percentage of the code which accounts for the vast majority of execution time and one generally need only optimize the inner loops if they are properly chosen. In designing a code which requires a good deal more memory than is available in primary storage one tries to partition it into segments with a high degree of inter-segment calculation or complexity and small amount of intra-segment complexity. Although these examples may seem diverse they all deal with the need to isolate complexity. Looking back at our hierarchy of recursive ordinals we can relate this necessity to how complex things become as the size of a problem grows.

The idea whose time is perhaps about to come goes back at least as far as 1960 and the notion of a fixed plus variable computer (12). Computers have been proposed and built employing related ideas (1, 9, 12).

Cheap LSI circuits have the potential to radically alter the nature of scientific programming. They open the possibility of hardware systems of complexity comparable to that of large software systems. At some point in the future the construction of specialized hardware may be the most cost effective way to solve many programming problems. It should be possible to design a set of basic building block ICs that, in an abstract sense, have the same place in hardware design that high level language statements have in software design. The problem of constructing specialized hardware for a particular task could then become comparable to writing a program in a high level language. If the basic building block ICs are manufactured in large enough quantities their cost becomes negligible in comparison with the system design cost. Highly "pipelined" real time computing processes like signal processing are ideal first candidates for such an approach. Their structure is especially amenable to such an a approach and the timing constraints of real time processing makes such an approach particularly desirable. One can add processing capability without worrying about overloading some central computer.

VIII. REFERENCES

1. Arbuckle, W. L., and R. C. Mattson, "Macro modularity: a design concept to end computer generation gaps," Computer Design, pp. 69-73, August 1970.
2. Babuska, I., W. Reinboldt, and C. Mesztenyi, "Self-adaptive refinements in the finite element method," Comp. Sci. Tech. Rpt. TR-375, Univ. of Maryland, College Park, Maryland, 1975.
3. Bolstad, J., Stanford Ph.D. thesis, to appear.
4. Bolstad, J. and J. Oliger, "Adaptive methods for time dependent partial differential equations," to appear.
5. Brandt, A., "Multi-level adaptive solutions to boundary-value problems," to appear in Math. Comp.
6. Browning, G., H.-O. Kreiss, and J. Oliger, "Mesh refinement," Math. Comp., vol. 27, pp. 29-39, 1973.
7. Budnik, P. P., "Techniques for parallel computer design," Univ. of Illinois, Dept. of Comp. Sci., Rpt. UIUCDSC-R-75-763, 1975.
8. Ciment, M., "Stable matching of difference schemes," SIAM J. Numer. Anal., vol. 9, pp. 695-701, 1972.
9. Clark, W. A., et al., "Macro modular computer systems," Proc. SJCC, pp. 335-401, 1967.

10. DeBoor, C., "CADRE: an algorithm for numerical quadrature," <u>Mathematical Software</u>, J.R. Rice, ed., Academic Press, N.Y., pp. 417-449, 1971.
11. DeBoor, C., "Good approximation by splines with variable knots. II." Conference on the Numerical Solution of Differential Equations, Lecture notes in Mathematics, vol. 363, Springer-Verlag, Berlin-Heidelberg-New York, pp. 12-20, 1973.
12. Estrin, G., "Organization of computer systems--the fixed plus variable structure computer," Proc. WJCC, pp. 33-40, 1960.
13. Hanson, R. L. and J. L. Phillips, "An adaptive method for solving linear Fredholm integral equations of the first kind," Numer. Math., vol. 24, pp. 291-307, 1975.
14. Jung, C. G., <u>The Portable Jung</u>, Joseph Campbell, ed., The Viking Press, New York, pp. 222-229, 1971.
15. Kahaner, D. K. and M. B. Wells, "An algorithm for N-dimensional adaptive quadrature using advanced programming techniques," Los Alamos Scientific Laboratory, Rpt. LA-UR76-2310, Los Alamos, New Mexico, 1976.
16. Karp, R. M., R. E. Miller, and S. Winograd, "The organization of computations for uniform recurrence equations, JACM, vol. 14, p. 563-590, 1967.
17. Kogge, P. M., "Parallel solution of recurrence problems," IBM J. Res. Develop., pp. 138-148, March 1974.
18. Kuck, D. J., et al., "Measurements of parallelism in ordinary FORTRAN programs," Computer Magazine, pp. 37-46, January 1974.
19. Kuck, D. J., Y. Muraoka, and S. C. Chen, "On the number of operations simultaneously executable in FORTRAN-like programs and their resulting speed-up," IEEE Trans. on Comp., vol. C-21, pp. 1293-1310, 1972.
20. Lemme, J. M. and J. R. Rice, "Speedup in parallel algorithms for adaptive quadrature," Comp. Sci. Dept. Tech. Rpt. 192, Purdue Univ., West Lafayette, Indiana, 1976.
21. Lyness, J. N., "SQUANK (Simpson quadrature used adaptively-noise killed)," Algorithm 379, Comm. ACM, vol. 13, pp. 260-263, 1970.
22. Miller, K. and R. Miller, "Finite element methods with moving nodes," to appear in SIAM J. Numer. Anal.
23. Miranker, W. L., "A survey of parallelism in numerical analysis," SIAM Rev., vol. 13, pp. 524-597, 1971.
24. Oliger, J., "Hybrid difference methods for the initial boundary-value problem for hyperbolic equations," Math. Comp., vol. 30, pp. 724-738, 1976.
25. Oliger, J. E., R. E. Wellck, A. Kasahara, and W. Washington, "Description of the NCAR global circulation model," NCAR Tech. Note STR-56, National Center for

Atmospheric Research, Boulder, Colorado, 1970.
26. Pereyra, V. and E. G. Sewell, "Mesh selection for discrete solution of boundary problems in ordinary differential equations," Numer. Math., vol. 23, pp. 261-268, 1975.
27. Poole, Jr., W. G. and R. G. Voigt, "Numerical algorithms for parallel and vector computers: an annotated bibliography," Computing Reviews, vol. 15, pp. 379-388, 1974.
28. Rabiner, L. R. and B. Gold, <u>Theory and Application of Digital Signal Processing</u>, Prentice Hall, Englewood Cliffs, New Jersey, Chap. 3, 1975.
29. Rabiner, L. R. and C. M. Rader, eds. <u>Digital Signal Processing</u>, IEEE Press, New York, 1972.
30. Rice, J. R., "Adaptive quadrature: convergence of parallel and sequential algorithms," Bull. Amer. Math. Soc., vol. 80, pp. 1250-1254, 1974.
31. Rice, J. R., "Algorithm-ADAPT, adaptive smooth curve fitting," Comp. Sci. Dept. Tech. Rpt. 166, Purdue University, West Lafayette, Indiana, 1975.
32. Rice, J. R., "Adaptive Approximations, to appear in J. Approx. Thy.
33. Rogers, H., <u>Theory of Recursive Functions and Effective Computability</u>, McGraw-Hill, New York, pp. 205-213, 1967.
34. Shampine, L. F., H. A. Watts, and S. M. Davenport, "Solving nonstiff ordinary differential equations--the state of the art," SIAM Rev., vol. 18, pp. 376-411, 1976.
35. Winograd, S., "On the time required to perform addition," J. ACM, vol. 12, pp. 277-285, 1965.
36. Winograd, S., "On the time required to perform multiplication," J. ACM, vol. 14, pp. 793-802, 1967.
37. Winograd, S., "On the speed gained in parallel methods," IBM Research Rpt. RC4670, Yorktown Heights, N.Y., 1974.

THE COSTS OF PROCESSING POWER:
THE PROCESS, THE PROGRAMMER, AND THE PROCESSOR

David W. Hogan, John C. Jensen and Merrill Cornish
Texas Instruments Incorporated

I. SUMMARY

Many current large-scale programs cannot run efficiently on any known high performance machine because programmers ignore the realities of their systems. Efficiency is the synergistic product of the algorithm, its implementation, its compilation, and its execution. A program's execution time is controlled as much by the programmer's coding as by the machine's clock.

Programs written today are limiting the processors and processing of tomorrow:
- Today's programming techniques almost guarantee that tomorrow's large-scale programs either will not have the processing power they need or will have to pay too much for what they do get;
- Today's programmers are binding tomorrow's management by writing programs whose efficient execution leaves no choice in the selection of future processors; and
- Today's management is, in turn, binding tomorrow's machine designers by insisting that new machines run old, highly machine dependent programs well.

The effective migration of programs through the generation of machines requires:
- Algorithms must be chosen and programs written with generic parallel implementation always in mind; and
- Programs must be written to be machine independent with machine dependent optimizations left strictly to the compiler.

II. INTRODUCTION

Texas Instruments Advanced Scientific Computer, the ASC, has undergone ten years of design, development and now application to large-scale computation problems. We have been its hardware designers, compiler writers, operating system builders, and even its applications programmers. We are both the inflictor and the inflictee—and we are learning from both sides.

No one has seen or can foresee one machine that's power can be continually increased with time. To increase processing power, we must move from machine to machine. Migrating along the path of increasing processing power is simply the nature of things. Unfortunately, our benchmarking is showing us that most programs and programmers are ill prepared for the trip. With this migration comes tramatic conversions, herein lies the problem.

III. THE SOURCE OF THE PROBLEM

There are only two ways to increase processing power: increase the processing speed or increase the processing parallelism. Modern high performance machines are loosely referred to as "high-speed" machines. If the power of these machines were in their absolute speed, then *all* programs could take equal advantage of it. However, these machines get only part of their power from a high clock rate. They get as much and possibly more power from their numerous processing optimizations.

The principle optimization now evolving is the exploitation of general parallelism and not just vectors or arrays. Even single instruction stream machines exploit parallelism through multiple pipeline levels (IBM 370/195, ASC) as well as multiple functional units (CDC 6600/7600, ASC). A program will take advantage of this power only to the extent that it exhibits the optimized characteristics.

ASC benchmarks are showing us that current large-scale scientific processing is being done in a scalar world where high performance means high speed logic. At the same time, we can see that the available large-scale processors can deliver high performance only to programs that show certain forms of parallelism. This fundamental mismatch will plague us in the future unless we get to the source of the problem: the source code. Repeatedly we find that programmers are using algorithms, implementations, and constructs that prevent their programs from ever making effective use of the ASC *or of any known high performance processor*.

We have all heard programmers discuss how the available processors limit their programs. What is really happening is their programming style is inhibiting modern systems (processor-compiler pairs) from applying their full power. The power is in fact available to the programmer; but it is unused. The source of the problem is deep rooted and stems from the scalar mentality which has evolved over the last 20 years.

IV. WHAT IS THE PROBLEM?

This problem is actually a set of problems all with the same effect; each imposes unnecessary inefficiencies on the systems. Some major examples are listed below:
- Choosing serial algorithms over available parallel algorithms (using recursion rather than iteration).
- Using needlessly elaborate and convoluted control structure.
- Using coding techniques that hide implicit program parallelism (subroutine call as the body of a loop).
- Hiding general program information from the compiler (obscuring program data structure through COMMON and EQUIVALENCE).
- Embedding architecture dependent optimizations in the program source:
  - Unrolling loops to take advantage of instruction buffering (CDC's in-stack loops)
  - Contorting arrays to fit memory buffering (IBM's caching
  - Using library calls for ordinary operations (7600's STACKLIB)

Many of the above problems can be avoided if the programmer had no cause for machine dependent code, that is, appropriate compiler optimizations were invoked automatically by the source code. However, the compilers must have manuevering room if they are to optimally map the source code to the processor. When the programmer linearizes subscripts, unrolls loops, uses IF constructs when Fortran intrinsics are called for (MAX...), or any one of thousands of explicit coding techniques; it intrudes on the compiler's maneuvering room and will not yield optimal code on any but the current machine. It is the programmer's responsibility to tell the compiler *what* is to be done and let the compiler determine *how* to do it.

V. WHY IS THE PROBLEM?

   The problem exists for many reasons and they all amount to the people involved—system designer, programmer and manager—ignoring the operational realities of the system.

   A. Mismatching Machine Application and Compiler

   A design integrated through hardware and software and suited to the application will result in a well matched system (the STAR was designed to support APL but is used to execute Fortran). The full power of the machine must be available through the applications programming language or else contorted and machine dependent coding practices will result to circumvent the mismatch. Most current machines were designed so that full power is available only to assembly language programmers. To exclude a processor feature needed by the application language is to overlook a potential processor optimization and may provoke the programmer to try "tricks" of his own in the source. (Almost all languages, but almost no machines allow multidimensional array access.)

   B. Ignoring Conceptual Efficiency

   Restricting the job to mere correctness is not adequate. A larger responsibility for program efficiency must be undertaken by all elements of the system. The programmer must work at the algorithm efficiency and the compiler should   help   by noting inefficient program constructs. The manager should be concerned   with decerning ineffective programs (vs. inadequate processors) with efficiency control checks in addition to traditional correctness and scheduling checks during development.

   C. Ignoring Inevitable Upgrades

   A short term management strategy for long term programs will not be cost effective in the long run. Machine dependent optimizations may quickly solve the immediate problem; but in the long run, they will result in a larger conversion cost and larger upgrades than absolutely necessary.

VI. THE PREAMBLE TO THE FUTURE

A real life case history might enforce these points. A well-known research group bought Machine-X some years ago when it was one of the biggest available. They modified their programs to take full advantage of this machine's architecture. Programs originally written in Fortran are now effectively written in "X-tran". The internal structure of their programs faithfully reflects the internal structure of their machine. They brag that they get more power from their machine than anyone—including the vendor—thought possible. They are right. They do. But now they need more power. They want to buy a faster version of Machine-X, but there is none. They now have two unattractive choices. They may buy Machine-Y that is several times more powerful than they need to overcome the inefficiencies of code dependent solely on Machine-X. Or, they may convert all of the X-tran programs back into their original Fortran.

From this example there are three major issues that point to problems in the future. The short term management practices of today are leading to high cost and under-utilized machines.

A. Consequences of Short Term Planning

Machine dependent optimizations woven into the fabric of a program for short term gains are seldom of benefit to new, different machines and may actually be detrimental. Speakers at the Spring COMPCON 77 supercomputer session uniformly lamented the problem of moving existing (assembly) code to the STAR and ILLIAC. The Navy's computer evaluation office (ADPESO) is taking a pragmatic approach to the problem. Rather than standardizing the languages, they are assembling a set of standard conversion aids. Conversion is simply seen as a fact of life—another of the costs incurred in buying a new machine. What conversion there is, should be recognized as a liability charged against existing software methodology rather than the architecture of a new machine.

B. Under-Powered Programs

If a program is pushing the limits of processing power, then its inefficient use of a machine cannot be compensated by getting a bigger machine. These programs cannot be satisfied by even the biggest machines because of the power they waste with mismatched machine dependent optimizations.

C. Architectural Misdirection by Customer Procurement

Management recognizes that the existing software is a huge investment that must be preserved. This attitude is alright by itself. However, this existing software is typically machine-dependent and can only be preserved by a new machine as much like the old one as possible. Management will sometimes find that preserving their machine-dependent software leave no choice in new computers.

Designs that emphasize the preservation of old machine dependencies will naturally lead to a preservation of old machine architectures. Improvements may be gained in this way—maybe even dramatic ones. But in the long run, such inbred designs are a dead end. At the extreme, this trend can lead to future hardware that is "perfect" for executing programs that are 10-15 years out of date.

Captain Grace Hooper offers the example of IBM System/370 computers running in IBM 7090 emulation mode, running in IBM 1401 emulation mode, running programs written 15 years ago. She refers to this as "inefficiency squared". There is no advantage to running ineffective programs efficiently.

VII. WHAT CAN WE DO TO SAVE OURSELVES?

The computing power of the future will be bought with a different coin than in the past. This new coin will, in part, go to paying for better program design. Attention must shift from producing architectures with exotic look-ahead and buffering schemes to producing algorithms coded in a generic parallel fashion. The compiler's responsibility is then to map this code to the featured processor optimization. The hardware designers' responsibility is to present to the compiler a tractable mapping technique.

Management must be concerned with purchasing the processor-compiler *pair*. Management must then follow through requiring coding in a truly machine independent fashion. This independence gives management freedom to migrate to new machines as required. It also gives the designer the maneuvering room needed to advance the architectural state-of-the-art and gives the user the power needed. Certainly, machine dependent optimizations are necessary to do the job, but they should be an investment in increased compiler optimization. Lacking appropriate compiler support, management must understand that an investment in architecture dependent code is going to limit their options for more power in the future and indirectly determine architectural advancements.

A programmer who deliberately exploits the parallelism available in the algorithm and clearly expresses that parallelism to the compiler will find that the program improves with age, like a good wine. As new hardware becomes available, the program will automatically move up to the new machine. By contrast, many programs now in use will age something like dead fish.

MATCHING MACHINES AND PROBLEMS[1]

J. E. Wirsching[2] and T. Kishi
Lawrence Livermore Laboratory, University of California

Five research projects related to enhancement of computational efficiency are discussed. Problems of parallelism and concurrency are reviewed and conversion of applications to high-speed computers with these characteristics is delineated. Programming methodology is assessed with respect to these applications. The critical issues of parallelism are then exposed and conclusions are drawn.

I. INTRODUCTION

When the Lawrence Livermore Laboratory was organized in 1952 to develop nuclear weapons, the need for high-speed computers was immediately recognized. Since that time the computational facilities of the Laboratory have grown into a multi-million dollar complex of high-speed computers, control systems, archival storage systems, peripheral equipment, and a network of remote job-entry and terminal consoles (1).

The process today is quite different from that of 20 years ago. At that time, raw numbers were fed into computers and raw numbers came out. Now most of the computational power of the facility is used to give the computing process a "mobility" that it did not have before. We foresee this trend increasing particularly in the areas of result presentation and information retrieval.

There has been a continual inquiry into clearly different ways to do problems, from both the type of machine used and

---

[1] Work performed under the auspices of the U.S. Energy Research and Development Administration, contract No. W-7405-Eng-48.

[2] J. E. Wirsching was formerly employed at LLL and is now an independant consultant.

the programming approach. During the past several years, five research projects of note have investigated some of these problems. The common objective of these projects was to find new, more cost-effective approaches to LLL problems.

II. LLL COMPUTER RESEARCH PROJECTS

With the advent of highly parallel and highly concurrent computing systems, it became clear that certain classes of problem-solving methods used at LLL were not compatible with these architectures. Therefore, if we were to use these systems at their best level, we must either find new methods or adapt old ones. If this were not possible, we would have to research computer architectures that might serve better. The research has not always been conclusive, and further investigations will need to follow the investigations described below.

A. The ILLIAC IV

The ILLIAC IV[1] and its predecessors had been considered by LLL during their emergence, and as the ILLIAC IV came closer to realization the Laboratory became more involved in its development. Under contract with ARPA, we investigated the desirability of using the system for the TENSOR code (2), a two-dimensional shock hydrodynamics code used in the study of cratering. The TENSOR code was chosen because it used a solution method that appeared to be quite compatible with an array processor. The objective of the project was to prove the feasibility and speed of the ILLIAC IV for such a code.

The TENSOR code could have been more readily reconfigured if the maximum length of any array had been restricted to less than 64 and if the boundary condition had been reduced to a simple form. Constrained by the primary requirement of reconfiguring an existing production code, the development of effective parallel-processing methods for the ILLIAC IV computer system has been exceedingly difficult. It could not have been accomplished by a simple translation of the existing FORTRAN code to a comparable language for the ILLIAC IV. The task has only been accomplished by reformulating and reexamining the basic finite-difference equations.

---

[1] Mention of a company or product name does not imply approval or recommendation of the product by the University of California or the U.S. Energy Research and Development Administration to the exclusion of others that may be suitable.

The objectives of the contract with ARPA could have been more easily accomplished if an appropriate higher-level language could have been used rather than the lowest level of programming, machine language. Our experience has shown that a task of this magnitude cannot be accomplished easily unless:

- One restructures the data to fit the constraints of the array-processor memory even if the new data structure is not compatible with the existing-code.

- A higher-level language can be used in developing algorithms and data-array structures for efficient parallel processing.

- The operating system and supporting software are well defined and operational.

In addition, the TENSOR code would be an inadequate research tool without:

- Provision for additional memory or the inclusion of an extended core storage to augment memory

- Additional software support and equipment to process the vast amount of data generated.

Unfortunately, we have not been able to completely check the entire TENSOR code (3). However, we have developed the proper algorithms for parallel processing the TENSOR code and contributed substantially to the effective treatment of boundary calculations for both the array and vector processors.

B. Culler Harrison, Inc., Array Processor

A number of special-purpose signal-array processors are currently available to provide high arithmetic performance, especially for the fast Fourier transform (FFT), which is necessary in signal processing. We investigated this processor to determine if its special architecture could be used for LLL applications. In particular, we chose the Culler Harrison, Inc., (CHI) AP signal processor (4) because it provided the following features:

- An available, operational system
- High arithmetic performance
- Microprogramming
- Up to seven concurrent functions
- Relatively low cost

In the CHI signal system, the AP array arithmetic processor (X-AP) operates concurrently with the CHI host computer, the MP-32 Macroprocessor, which acts as a driver to the AP. For higher processing rates, multiple AP's may be driven by the MP-32.

There are two disadvantages to the existing signal system: both the AP and the MP-32 are difficult to microprogram because the microinstruction format is complex, and the function-box concept does not allow latitude in design studies. Thus, we abandoned the function-box concept and began a series of studies with the AP as a bonafide central-processing unit. Our efforts centered on three areas:

- Rewriting the code-generation phase of the LLL CHAT compiler to produce simulated language macros
- Writing a simulator and studying benchmark programs
- Investigating the appropriateness of the word size (32 bits)

The sample programs were written in the simulation language and executed in the target machine. The same programs were also compiled with CHAT and executed on the CDC 7600. The answers from both executions agreed. Parameters were further studied by: (1) varing the memory cycle, (2) changing the branch-instruction times, (3) allowing or disallowing concurrency among the several units, and (4) changing the arithmetic speeds. The results of the experiments shown in Table 1 are tabulated in Tables 2 and 3.

The results from this phase of the investigation indicate that:

- By programming X-AP in a macrolanguage, we can achieve performance within 3% of an optimized microcode.
- Compiled programs resulting in macrosequence can approach 1/2 the speed of hand-coded programs.
- Programmable random-access memory (RAM) is generally too small to hold programs of any significance.
- Continual loading and unloading of microcode would swamp RAM and degrade performance drastically.
- Word size of 32 bits for scientific data is marginal at best.

Encouraged by the simulation studies, we initiated a design study with Culler Harrison, Inc., to see if the X-AP could indeed serve as the nucleus of a special-purpose processor, provided that a fast, large, random-access memory could be integrated into the system.

The initial design studies have been completed and the results are available (5). We have found that the X-AP can be integrated into a special-purpose, high-performance/

TABLE 1

Experiment Parameters

Experiment No.	Parameters
1	Normal CHI* execution times
2	Three times normal memory-cycle time
3	Thirty times normal memory-cycle time
4	No overlap in address arithmetic
5	Two times normal arithmetic time
6	One-half normal branch time

*Culler Harrison, Inc.

TABLE 2

*Clock Values for Experiment Parameters**

CHI Instructions	Experiment No.					
	1	2	3	4	5	6
Memory references	3	9	30	3		
Floating divide	20				40	20
Random number	6				12	6
Fix/float MPY	4				8	4
Floating add	2				6	3
Square root	25				50	25
Jump	4	10	4			2
Index pad	1					
Index data pad	0			1	0	
Fall-thru-jump	1					
Register swap	0			1	0	
Absolute value	1				2	1
Convert fix to FLT	3				6	3
Convert FLT to fix	4				8	4
Shift	1					
Fix add	1					

*Blank spaces in this table are equivalent to the first integer to the left of that space.

TABLE 3

Ratio of Running Times of CHI to CDC 7600

Codes	Experiment No.					
	1	2	3	4	5	6
Monte Carlo						
Collision						
Fortran	2.3	3.5	7.5	2.8	3.4	2.2
Handcode	3.3	5.0	10.8	4.0	4.9	3.2
Tracking						
Fortran	3.7	4.7	10.0	5.1	6.2	3.6
E.O.S.						
Table value	2.7	3.9	8.5	3.8	4.5	2.7
Polynomial	4.6	4.9	4.5	6.5	8.7	4.4
1-D Hydro	3.6	5.1	10.0	4.6	6.0	3.4

low-cost computer system that can process macroinstruction sequences to within a few percent of microinstruction speeds. From simulation studies, macroinstruction sequences can achieve up to 1/3 the performance of an equivalent CDC 7600 program. The macrosequence can be readily generated by a modified LRLTRAN (6) compiler. The performance:price ratio is far superior to any commercially available medium-to-large-scale computer system.

C. Burroughs D-Machine

Burroughs' low-cost, general-purpose microprogrammable building block (7) called the "interpreter" or "D-Machine", provides a convenient way to investigate new computer design.

In the first phase of this investigation, a compiler that would accept LRLTRAN source statements was written for the D-Machine-based system. In the second phase, code activity analysis of the problem was used together with fine-tuning techniques to improve execution efficiency. The results of the study are shown in Table 4. Instruction-usage analysis showed that approximately 18% of the total instructions

TABLE 4

Monte Carlo Tuning Results

Experiment No.	Experiment	Time (sec)	Instructions, in millions
	ALGOL versions		
1	Untuned single standard, D-Machine	1010	8.67
2	Untuned single D-Machine; floating-point hardware	450	8.67
3	Two untuned D-Machines; floating-point hardware on one, negative log of random number on other	316	*
4	Tuned LOG and EXP, one D-Machine; floating-point hardware	239	3.84
5	Tuned LOG and EXP, first-pass tuning of problem, one D-Machine with floating-point hardware	197	2.99
6	Tuned LOG and EXP, second-pass tuning of problem, one D-Machine with floating-point hardware	142	1.78
7	Tuned LOG and EXP, third-pass tuning of problem, one D-Machine with floating-point hardware	98	0.96
8	Tuned LOG and EXP, fourth-pass tuning of problem, one D-Machine with floating-point hardware	78	0.60
	LRLTRAN/ALGOL versions		
9	Untuned single standard D-Machine	1120	*
10	Untuned (with floating-point hardware)	585	*

*Not counted

executed were numerical evaluations. Adding a floating-point unit to the system more than doubled performance.

Since the existing D-Machine-based system includes multiple D-Machines, we tried a simple experiment using two processors on a single problem. Timing analysis showed that if one D-Machine without floating-point hardware continuously generated the negative log of a random number, it would always have the value ready before another D-Machine (with floating-point hardware) executing the remainder of the program needed a new result. This experiment resulted in a 30% reduction in execution time (see experiment No. 3 as compared to No. 2 in Table 4).

The fine-tuning process consists of identifying frequently executed areas in the original ALGOL program. These areas are then replaced by special operators hand-coded in microcode. The analysis feature of the emulator provides an automatic means of identifying those areas of code that are most advantageous to microcode. Increased performance can be traced primarily to two sources: the instruction fetch and interpretive section of the emulation is avoided, and the hardware unit can be treated as the top position of the evaluation stack. This technique avoided a large number of loads and stores in the floating-point unit that are performed as normal instructions in the emulator.

In summary (8), we have found that microprogramming sequences can be fine tuned to a great advantage, and this feature coupled with a floating-point unit reduces the raw microprocessor time by over a factor of ten. In addition, multiprocessing was shown to be feasible.

D. Particle Pusher for STAR-100

Historically, plasma-physics codes have evolved from small grids and simple physics to larger and larger grids with more complex physics. In the process, little attention has been given to the computational procedure, because up to now it has been quite adequate. However, with the advent of highly parallel "vector" type computers such as the ILLIAC IV, STAR, and ASC, a new problem has arisen: The computational procedure currently in use cannot be easily or efficiently adapted to this class of machines. We intend to describe here a method that may be efficient for "vector" solution of plasma and particle-in-cell codes.

The problem that occupies a great portion of the "particle pusher" type of code is basically a table look-up in which the values to be retrieved are essentially randomly located in the table. To a serial computer this is no drawback, but to a vector computer such a look-up is highly inefficient. Although table look-up has been hardwarized on the STAR, this does not ensure high speed.

The answer to the problem is to develop, if possible, a way of efficiently creating contiguous vectors out of random processes (9). The method described here attempts to do this.

Looking at the computational process, we note that the list of particles we started with is maintained in the computer memory in their original order, even though the particles wander around through the physical grid. However, after a number of time steps, the relationship between a particle's position in the list and its position in the physical grid is lost. This has suggested the thought (by perhaps many persons) that the particle list be rearranged at each cycle. This rearrangement, however, appears to be a monumental task, because there may be hundreds of thousands of particles to deal with.

However, continuing a little deeper we find that there are two more facts that may be of value: A particle will not skip entirely over a neighboring cell in one time step, and the order in which the particles are kept within each cell is inconsequential. These points suggest the possibility of treating much less of the grid when dealing with a particular cell. To make this clear we have chosen the RHO-update portion of a two-dimensional "particle-pusher" code.

The problem here is that charges accumulate at the grid points. Thus, if any success is to be gained in vectorizing the process, all of the particles in each cell must be made into a contiguous vector. Consider Fig. 1, which depicts the cells in the interior of a doubly periodic grid of size $M \times N$. For simplification, this grid can be thought of as having a single index k, which is derived by numbering from some corner and proceeding row by row in a linear fashion. Thus, a linear transformation of the m,n indices can be made to the k index by use of the formula $k = m + (n - 1)M$. To avoid further confusion let us take $M = N = 32$ (see Fig. 2).

From a previous constraint given above, we know that, after the particles have been moved to new positions during a time step, the only cells from which a particle can enter cell k are those shown in Fig. 2. Thus, if we start with the particle set ordered by cells, we need only concern ourselves with 9 out of the 1024 cells when reordering the particle set of a cell. Let's step through the process:

1. Starting with an ordered set of particles and a vector of 1024 addresses that point to the beginning of each subvector, the particles are moved to their new positions using the regular equations of motion. This is a straight-forward vector operation on all particles.

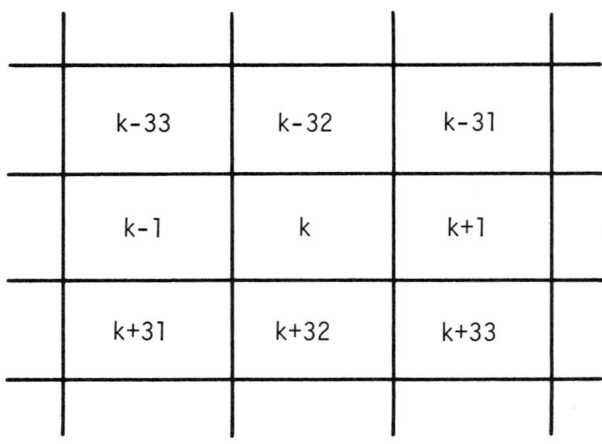

m-1, n-1	m, n-1	m+1, n-1
m-1, n	m, n	m+1, n
m-1, n+1	m, n+1	m+1, n+1

Fig. 1. Grid notation, N × M matrix.

k-33	k-32	k-31
k-1	k	k+1
k+31	k+32	k+33

Fig. 2. Grid notation linearized to k (square grid, 32 × 32).

2. A vector K is created that is the set of linear indices of cells in which the particles now reside.

3. The code proceeds now, from cell to cell and using the address vector, collects into contiguous vectors those nine K vectors associated with the cell being treated, as well as the vectors containing the particle variables.

4. The cell number presently being treated is compared with the K vector just produced, and a control-bit vector is formed with binary ones where the comparison is equal (all the particles in that cell).

5. This control vector is then used to compress the other collected contiguous vectors, reducing the set to just those in the cell being treated. These compressed vectors are then appended to the lists of previously derived vectors.

6. A population count is made of the "ones" in the K vector; this count tells exactly how many particles are now in that cell. This value is appended to a vector of such counts and is used to derive the addresses of the new particle vectors from a partial sum on the list.

7. When this process is completed for all cells in turn, we have the particles all rearranged and a set of addresses to each individual cell.

8. At this point the RHO update of the problem consists of summing the weights assigned to the particles of a cell, which are now contiguous vectors, and forming vectors of 1024 such sums. These can then be manipulated in vector fashion in any manner desired and added to RHO (a contiguous vector of 1024 values) and restored.

A hidden but important advantage (for the vector machine) of this method shows up in the memory allocation of the information during the process. We note that this problem can now be treated in much the same way as a hydrodynamics code with respect to the grid: as one proceeds, only three rows of the grid are required in the memory at a time (with some trivial exceptions at corners).

This analysis points out the necessity of completely rethinking the physics and logic of an application when faced with "vector" architectures. In this case as in most others, the program must be completely rewritten from scratch. Even sections that appear to have remained the same must be rewritten because the data structure has changed.

E. Problems of Converting Serial Code to Parallel

In this investigation, a relatively simple two-dimensional diffusion code has been used to show the difficulties in transferring a code from a conventional serial computer to a vector processing machine.

In this case, the original program was written in LRLTRAN (a version of FORTRAN) for the CDC 7600, and the target machine for translation was the CDC STAR-100. In addition to this translation, we took an intermediate step by translating the code to STACKLIB[1] (set of callable macroroutines that provide vector-processing capabilities under LRLTRAN). The STACKLIB version can be compiled into object code for either the 7600 or the STAR-100. Therefore, both the original LRLTRAN version and the STACKLIB version have been timed. Timing figures were derived for various subsections of the code by different programming techniques. These are given in Table 5.

The code uses a two-dimensional alternating-direction-implicit method of solution in which the grid is traversed in both coordinate directions in separate sweeps. The grid size chosen for this study is 42 × 82, which is quite realistic. To attain the best parallelism possible during the implicit part of the procedure, the grid must be handled a column at a time in the column direction and a row at a time in the other. For those computations that are not implicit, the entire grid can be treated as a single vector.

---

[1] F. H. McMahon, L. J. Sloan, and G. Long, Lawrence Livermore Laboratory, private communication.

TABLE 5

Diffusion-Code Timings (msec/cycle) and Megaflops Rates

Code section	Programming versions				
	CDC 7600		CDC STAR-100		
	LRLTRAN	STACKLIB	With IVTRANS	With QVTIND	Implicit part of R serial
Coupling constants & boundary conditions	46.0	50.0	5.7	5.7	5.7
Z-sweep	15.1	6.9	5.9	5.9	5.9
R-sweep	16.6	7.6	6.2	6.2	133.0
Data transposes			22.6	16.1	
Totals	77.7	65.4	40.4	33.9	143.6
Megaflops rates	2.35	2.80	4.53	5.40	1.28

To reach maximum efficiency on the STAR-100, the vectors must be located in consecutive or contiguous addresses in the memory. Therefore, in this code several of the two-dimensional matrices of values must be transposed during the implicit part of the code at a time between the column-wise and row-wise computations. Programming methods to perform the transposition are explained in a subsequent section.

The procedure to convert the code can then be summarized as follows:

1. Search for the implicit recursions and separate them from the explicit part of the code.

2. Transform the explicit two-dimensional DO loops into one-dimensional vector operations.

3. Transform the implicit two-dimensional DO loops into one-dimensional DO loops that operate on columns or rows as vectors (this process eliminates only the inner loop of the nest).

4. Develop a procedure of transposing the data matrices to attain contiguous vectors with respect to both indices j and k.

5. Put these parts together as outlined above.

6. Restructure all dimension statements to reflect these conversions.

Data-matrix transposition is required only for those machines in which the vector-processing efficiency depends on contiguity of the values in a vector with respect to the linear addressing scheme of the computer memory. Since the STAR-100 has a hardwarized 8 × 8 matrix transpose, it may appear offhand to be ideal for this task. However, this 8 × 8 transpose is found to be quite slow compared to readily available alternatives. Three other basic methods have been devised, each of which is efficient for particular cases. The first method, called IVTRANS, uses the hardware instruction MERGE to accomplish the transform. It is most effective when the matrix to be transformed has long rows and short columns. The second method, called ICTRANS, uses the COMPRESS instruction and is most effective when the rows are short and the columns are long. The third method, called QVTIND, uses the TRANSMIT INDEXED LIST instruction and is best for large, more or less square matrices.

During the analysis, we found that the transposes consumed a substantial amount of time compared to the total. This prompted us to further analyze the actual size of the effect. A third STAR-100 timing analysis was made by splitting the R-sweep implicit part out of the vectorized

part of the code. In this case the implicit part was run as
a serial piece of coding, which eliminated the need for
transposes.

This version was timed, showing an excessive amount of
time used in the serial part of the code. In theory this
part of the code could be hand programmed to run nearly as
fast as the 7600, which would make this method very competitive with the code using the QVTIND transpose. However, for
particle considerations a compiled code must be used as the
point of reference, and one may then conclude that the transpose is worth using for this code, even though it requires
extra programming work.

Referring again to Table 5, we see that in general the
STAR-100 is about twice as fast as the 7600. More importantly, timing can vary widely for various algorithms and
coding methods. This variation implies that considerable
analysis is required to achieve efficient code conversions to
the STAR-100 or for that matter to any highly parallel computer and that the work involved is not trivial.

III. SUMMARY OF RESULTS

The objectives of the five experiments described in
Section II are quite varied. However, a number of generic
concepts can be derived from them. Three basic findings are:

- If any of the systems studied are to be used for
  general-purpose computation, they must be capable of
  operating efficiently using high-level languages.

- Certain special system functions and nonparallelizable
  applications can be programmed for the microprogrammable and concurrent architectures, substantially
  improving cost effectiveness.

- Converting problems for efficient execution on the new
  class of "highly parallel" machines requires an almost
  complete reanalysis and rewrite of the program.

One of the most critical issues of today's computer
technology is the cost of programming and program maintenance.
Hardware is becoming a smaller and smaller fraction of the
overall cost. The main problem lies in "portability" of
programs from one machine to another and from one generation
of machines to the next. This has been solved to a great
extent by the use of high-level languages, although complete
portability has never been attained. In spite of this, the
universal trend is toward the use of high-level languages, as
distinct from assembly languages or microprogamming, with new
emphasis on "structured" languages.

It would be foolhardy to oppose this trend. We must therefore approach <u>all</u> computing machines from the standpoint of high-level languages. The only exeception to this rule lies in high-payoff situations, where two factors are in favor of the exception: the function or application is executed universally and very frequently, and the function is not cost effective on the general-purpose computer it is presently being executed on.

Many computer installations are composed of a single general-purpose computer to do all of the work of that installation. In most of these cases certain functions are known to be inefficient, but little can be done. Where installations contain more lattitude, a spectrum of machines can be netted together to perform a spectrum of job classes. In this case, each job class can be more efficiently done on a particular appropriate computer. Examples of these job classes are text editing and nonvectorizable application programs such as Monte Carlo or particle-in-cell codes.

The latter class of codes is appropriate in discussing the use of new architectural classes of computers, classes sometimes generally spoken of as "highly parallel." Because these computers gain their speed by operating on vectors, they will operate inefficiently on a problem that cannot be vectorized. However, as we have seen, some ingenuity in re-structuring problems may prove fruitful in moving the problem into the vector architectures.

We find that moving to these machines generally requires a complete rethinking of the physics and a rewriting of the entire code. This may cause side effects, such as the need to rewrite input generators, editing and data-presentation routines, and programs that use selected output as a basis for further analyses.

In these cases we are also plagued by the conclusions of our first finding: high-level language must be used. Since there is a significant architectural change, the high-level language must also be changed. Considerable work is being done to provide an easy transition through extensions to the languages. This does not help the average user who has a working code and does not want to reprogram. He expects the "portability" to be built-in. This is also being feverishly worked on in the form of "vectorizing" compilers that will (presumably) automatically convert a standard program to a vectorized version. This work has met with some success but it is only superficial at this time. It will only forstall the ultimate need to rework the complete application.

IV. THE CRITICAL ISSUES OF PARALLELISM

The issue of parallelism is central to all of the projects mentioned in Section III. At this point we shall identify the critical parameters involved. Four basic questions can be asked:

1. How much parallelism and concurrency is there in application programs?

Assuming that there is some:

2. Can the average programmer find the parallelism and concurrency? If so:

3. Can the parallelism be expressed by the programmer through the use of a high-level language?

We must also ask:

4. Are present hardware structures a good match for the parallelism and concurrency in applications?

The class of applications being treated in this paper deal almost exclusively with modeling of the real world and as such are totally parallel and concurrent. However, in the process of making the real-world environment into a discrete model that can be "computed," extraneous controls not found in nature are introduced. These consist of spatial and temporal constraints that are oriented to the mathematical solution method, as well as controls that are introduced by the nature of the computational procedure itself.

We have such things as boundary conditions, computation of elapsed model time, constraints because of explicit versus implicit solution methods (precedence), conditional procedures (nonuniformity of computation over entire grid), counting the number of spatial divisions in the grid, etc. In spite of these constraints, a great deal of parallelism and concurrency is easily found, and in fact is the generic principle of the computing machine; i.e. many sequences of instructions are executed repeatedly. If this were not so, computing machines would not exist. Thus, we can conclude that applications are indeed highly parallel and concurrent but that controls introduced in modeling restrict this parallelism.

Our next question is: Can the programmer find this parallelism and concurrency? Obviously the answer is "yes." Although conventional computing machines are serial in their execution, parallelism is reflected by program "loops" that are repeatedly executed. However, not <u>all</u> of the parallelism and concurrency is discovered, because the structure of the uniprocessor has made it unnecessary to do so. We conclude that the programmer can find the parallelism, but for computer architectures different from the uniprocessor he must look for more parallelism. Incorporating more parallelism will almost always affect data structure.

Our next question deals with language. First, we have just concluded that not all natural parallelism and concurrency is discovered in uniprocessor programs. Thus, we must ask if the additional parallelism is implicit in those programs. To the best of our knowledge it is not, or if it is, so complexly that it is impractical to search for. From this we conclude that a line-by-line translation of a uniprocessor program to a highly parallel architecture will lack full parallelism.

The second issue of the language question is the extension of a known language (or development of a new one) to allow full expression of all parallelism *and* concurrency. (Up to now we have not pursued the ability to employ concurrency, but, as will become apparent in answering the next question, concurrency is of utmost importance.) There seems to be no reason whatsoever that languages cannot contain constructs to express parallelism and concurrency; the literature is full of such work. However, this does not mean that programs will automatically be written to capture maximum parallelism. Even some programs written for uniprocessors either do not take advantage of proper looping or include extraneous work within loops. Capturing the most parallelism is a problem of education and simply requires time. We conclude that languages can be developed to treat parallelism and concurrency but that it will be a matter of time before programmers become completely familiar with the constructs. Program writing will still be an art that allows abuse of resources.

Our last question deals with the efficiency of applying parallel architectures. Here is where we must separate the two forms of simultaneity — parallelism and concurrency. Parallelism is simultaneous execution of like things; concurrency, of unlike things.

The "highly parallel" architectures of today have been constrained to deal almost exclusively with parallelism as defined above and, with few exceptions, have ignored or been forced to ignore concurrency. This is a result of the memory-processor organization. Without going into great detail, the crux of the argument is simply this: within some limits, a scalar operation takes as much time as a vector or parallel operation. If a computation consists of short vector operations and many scalar operations (as introduced by modeling), the advantage of parallelism may be lost. This problem can be alleviated by executing the scalar and vector operations concurrently. Present architectures cannot do this because they cannot effectively provide the necessary data streams to both parts of this processing system simultaneously.

A second and equally serious problem is the computation involved in conditional statements that divide a data base into two parts — each requiring a different subsequence of operations. This problem has to do with the ordered structure of the memory and the lock-step or temporarily conditioned arithmetic unit. The solution for this problem is much more severe than that for the previous problem. Here we must either be able to select random vectors with full-memory bandwidth or we must be able to execute concurrent processes in the arithmetic section.

Because none of the present-day "parallel" architectures solve these problems with any degree of effectiveness, we must conclude, in answer to our fourth question, that present hardware structures are not a very good match to the application. This of course feeds back into our third question about effective high-level languages that may or may not be developed independently from the hardware.

Given time, the architecture will improve and the languages along with it. The ultimate goal is a computer that hides or overlaps all of the extraneous control introduced by modeling. Machines of the future must pay more attention to concurrency (10,11) and not just parallelism.

V. REFERENCES

1. *Octopus Computer Network*, Lawrence Livermore Laboratory, Rept. UCRL-74338, November (1972).
2. T. Cherry and V. Kransky, *Two-Dimensional Stress Induced Adiabatic Flow*, Lawrence Livermore Laboratory, Rept. UCID-30013, Parts 1, 2 and 3 (1971).
3. T. Kishi, *Final Report of the Tensor/ILLIAC IV Project*, ARPA Order 1839, October (1973).
4. *TMA8-AP-90 Reference Manual*, Culler Harrison, Inc., Goleta, California, Rept. 29204 (1974).
5. Culler Harrison, Inc., *CHI and LLL, Design Study of the CHI-X, A Special Purpose Computer System, Final Report*, Lawrence Livermore Laboratory, Rept. UCRL-13658 (1975).
6. J. T. Martin, R. Zwakenberg, and S. Solbeck, *LRLTRAN Language as Implemented on the CHAT and STAR Compilers*, Lawrence Livermore Laboratory, Rept. LTSS-207 (1974).
7. *Technical Summary of the Interpreter-Based System*, Burroughs Corporation, Paoll, Pennsylvania, Rept. TR 71-1 (1971).

8. *Burroughs Interpreter-Based System Study*, performed for Lawrence Livermore Laboratory, December (1975).
9. T. Kishi and T. Rudy, *Star Trek*, Lawrence Livermore Laboratory, Rept. UCRL-76268 (1974).
10. J. E. Wirsching, "Computer of the 1980's, Is it a Network of Microcomputers?", *IEEE 1975 Fall*, digest of papers, p. 23.
11. C. G. Bell and W. A. Wulf, "C. mmp - A Multi-Processor," *AFIPS Conference Proceedings* (AFIPS Press, Montvale, New Jersey, 1972), vol. 41, part II (1972), pp. 765-778.

NOTICE

"This report was prepared as an account of work sponsored by the United States Government. Neither the United States nor the United States Energy Research & Development Administration, nor any of their employees, nor any of their contractors, subcontractors, or their employees, makes any warranty, express or implied, or assumes any legal liability or responsibility for the accuracy, completeness or usefulness of any information, apparatus, product or process disclosed, or represents that its use would not infringe privately-owned rights."

TO VECTORIZE OR TO "VECTORIZE": THAT IS THE QUESTION

R. N. Remund and K. A. Taggart
Los Alamos Scientific Laboratory

Large computer codes can benefit from vectorization in two ways. The first is an increase in running speed and the second is more transparent and orderly code structure. However, not all operations in a large code are vectorizable in the usual sense. We have found that one can expand the scope of vectorization on both the CDC 7600 and CDC STAR-100. The characteristics and performance of a representative set of vector subroutines for the CDC 7600 are presented. These subroutines allow for a broader definition of vector operations, and a single coding example serves as an indication that this broader concept of vectorization can also be extended to the STAR-100. It is likely that other (and future) large-scale scientific computers will provide similar opportunities for non-obvious exploitation of the basic vector concept.

I. INTRODUCTION

In the vector approach to computation, single valued (scalar) operations are applied successively to the elements of one dimensional argument arrays (i.e., multi-dimensional vectors) to produce a result array (or a single result in the case of functions such as dot product). In programming terms such operations are represented by:

```
      DO 10 I = 1, N
   10 R(I) = F(A1(I), A2(I),...,AK(I))
```

where one or more of the A-arrays <u>may</u> be R(I); and

```
      R = 0
      DO 10 I = 1, N
   10 R = F(A1(I), A2(I),...,AK(I), R)
```

respectively.

In actual practice one or the other of two generalizations of such operations is required. In the first generalization, the assignment statement is performed for only a predetermined subset of the values of I. In the preceding DO-loops this is accomplished by making execution of the assignment statement conditional on the state of the Ith element of a control-vector array, ICV. Thus, the assignment is prefixed with either IF(ICV(I)) or IF(.NOT.ICV(I)) as required.

In the second generalization, the order of selection of elements in the result and/or argument arrays depends on a predetermined index-vector array, IXV(I), such that $1 \leq IXV(I) \leq M$ for $1 \leq I \leq N$, and with IXV(I) = IXV(J) for one or more $J \neq I$ specifically allowed. In the preceding DO loops this is accomplished by replacing some or all occurrences of I in the assignment statement with IXV(I). Such random accessing (or more appropriately, non-sequential accessing) of arguments and/or results is inherently foreign to the usual concept of vector operations.

Currently three computers provide hardware implementations (and the appropriate related architecture) for vector operations. The Control Data STAR-100 and the Texas Instruments ASC both provide a very large set of operations while the Cray Research CRAY-1 provides a basic (but well chosen) set of operations.

It was not generally recognized that the Control Data 7600 was also well adapted to vectorized programming until McMahon, Sloan, and Long at Lawrence Livermore Laboratory (1) developed a package of routines (STACKLIB) to emulate the vector functions of the STAR-100. In general, codes organized to exploit these functions ran up to twice as fast as their "scalar" counterparts. For some codes such a performance gain could be obtained by specialized assembly-language programming of inner-loop computations. However, such coding is not only very poorly adapted to evolutionary development, but also is generally useless for other applications.

Furthermore, many codes (for example, large hydrodynamics codes) have no single inner-loop which accounts for a large fraction of computational time; but, rather, the time spent is evenly distributed throughout the code. Hence, the vector-oriented approach on the 7600 is generally more useful and cost effective. Vectorization also produces a more transparent, more flexible, and more compact set of code. A strategic overview of these matters is presented in a 1973 paper by Feustel, Jensen and McMahon (2). We agree with their viewpoint except as it relates to the universal superiority of implementing control-vectors as bit strings.

These results were known in 1973 when the authors began to develop a new large scale, coupled hydro-heat flow code at the Los Alamos Scientific Laboratory. Also, machines with vector hardware were soon to be available. Consequently, we decided to organize the code in a "vector" manner. We did not directly apply the STACKLIB vector subroutine package for two reasons.

1. The routines were coded to interface with a compiler whose calling conventions were incompatible with ours.

2. The control-vector implementation was that of STAR (i.e., as bit strings) and we felt this was not the most effective approach for the 7600.

The first point could have been overcome, but the second was deciding. Since then Livermore's system has been installed at LASL and at least one code has been implemented very successfully using STACKLIB. However, the control-vector implementation based on STAR does generally impose a greater time penalty than ours (refer to III. B).

Originally, it was expected that a later version of our code would run on the STAR-100, so we spent some time looking for efficient ways to implement critical algorithms on that machine. We did discover an efficient but somewhat indirect solution to one very important computational process for which the built-in STAR vector operations are not really satisfactory. This result is described in IV.

II. IMPLEMENTATION APPROACH ON THE 7600

There are two major differences between our approach and that used in existing vector computers. First, we emphasize the use of multi-operation functions (with and without control and/or index vectors). For example:

```
      DO 10 I = 1, N
   10 R(I) = A(I) * B(I) + C(I) * D(I)
```

Second, we chose to represent control-vectors and index-vectors in precisely the same way: as arrays of indexes with one index per word.

A. Multi-Operation Considerations

If result-production rates near the theoretical maximum are to be achieved on the 7600, calculations must be highly interleaved <u>and</u> overhead instructions minimized. The use of multi-operation vector functions facilitates this by:

1. providing flexibility in scheduling the issuance of instructions;

2. eliminating redundant store and re-fetch of intermediate results; and

3. amortizing loop startup and control overhead over more calculations.

It also simplifies the programmer's task since storing two results per loop execution (versus four or more) is both the practical limit imposed by the number of registers available, and sufficient to permit perfect (or near-perfect) scheduling of instruction execution. Also, with only two results per cycle the startup overhead is reduced.

It is worth noting that the CRAY-1 computer has hardware features which make possible multi-operation vector computations, whereas other existing vector machines do not. This is a capability which should be required in any future vector computer.

B. Control-Vector Considerations

On the 7600, bit string control-vectors must be effectively converted to the associated sequence of indexes during execution of "controlled" vector operations. While this can be done reasonably efficiently, it is still more expensive than accessing an array of pre-computed indexes. While memory traffic (and hence, the potential for bank conflicts) is increased by our method, interference effects are negligible in practice (refer to III. B).

Storing control-vectors as index arrays rather than bit strings appears very wasteful of storage on a computer with 60-bit words. However, we have found that in our code (typical of <u>one</u> important class of applications) the actual amount of memory involved is trivial. We have never needed more than three such arrays of length $N + 1$ at a time, and $N \leq 500$ is the limit for problems solvable in an acceptable amount of machine time. We have found that it is <u>generally</u> practical to store only one result per loop-execution for controlled vector functions. For $R = A + B$, this results in a (worst-case) 83% reduction in the result storage rate as compared to the corresponding sequential function (see III. B). However, for four-argument operations (e.g., R = A*B + C*D) the worst-case penalty falls below 30%. Thus, the use of multi-operation functions is important where a large amount of controlled computations are required.

C. Index-Vector Considerations

While control and index-vectors have the same form in our implementation, the same is not true of the routines which employ them in the case where the output array may also be one of the inputs. While this is rarely the case, there is one very important exception in our code (and in others like it):

```
      DO 10 I = 1, N
   10 R(IXV(I)) = R(IXV(I)) + A(I) * B(I)
```

where IXV(I) is known to be nonzero for all I. In this case, each value of R must be stored before the next one is fetched, or the fetch must be omitted when IXV(I + 1) = IXV(I).

By coding the loop both ways, we found that the second method was never more costly than the first, and faster when the indexes were equal. But since we do several of these computations for each instance of IXV, we also coded a routine which interleaves two distinct instances of the calculation in a single loop. Unfortunately, "several" is not necessarily an even number so we need the other version as well.

III. EXAMPLES ON THE 7600

The following seven vector calculations are typical of those implemented for the CDC 7600:

$$R(I) = A(I) + B(I) \qquad (1)$$

$$R(I) = A(I)*B(I) \qquad (2)$$

$$R(I) = A(I)*B(K) + C(I) \qquad (3)$$

$$R(I) = A(I)*B(I) + C(I)*D(I) \qquad (4)$$

$$R(ICV(I)) = A(ICV(I))*B(ICV(I)) + C(ICV(I))*D(ICV(I)) \qquad (5)$$

$$R(IXV(I)) = R(IXV(I)) + A(I)*B(I) \qquad (6)$$

$$R(I) = R(I) + A(I)*B(IXV(I)) \qquad (7)$$

In examples 1 through 4, 6, and 7, I takes on values from 1 through N. In example 5, I takes on values 1,2,... until ICV(I) = 0. Examples 6 and 7 involve the use of index-vectors (as defined in section I), and thus are extensions of the basic vector concept.

The number of results stored per DO-loop execution for the associated routines is, respectively: 4, 2, 2, 2, 1, 1 and 2. All DO-loop implementations are "perfect" (in the sense that instructions are issued as fast as theoretically possible) except for routine 4 in which one machine cycle is wasted. Also in routine 5, three instructions are needed to control the loop rather than the customary two. This is characteristic of our approach to implementation of all "controlled" vector operations. It is necessitated by the fact that for optimum scheduling, one must retain three successive values of ICV during each loop execution.

A. Routine Validation and Performance Analysis

There are three important questions to be answered for each vector routine:

1. Is it valid (i.e., does it get the correct results in all permissible cases)?

2. Does its main loop execute at the expected rate?

3. How sensitive is its performance to memory bank conflicts?

We have developed a simple but general test-tool which provides the answers to these questions with a minimum of effort.

The test-tool validates the optimized routine by comparing the answers it produces for a given set of inputs to those produced by an equivalent FORTRAN version for vector lengths in the range 1-10. We do not generally test for zero vector lengths as our routines are coded to expect $N \geq 1$. We chose to omit a test for N = 0 since it is better performed at a higher computational level.

If the results compare identically, the test-tool performs a timing analysis of the optimized routine using vectors of length 100. Arguments are selected randomly from a set of 50 vectors in one of two ways:

1. All arguments including the result are unique.

2. All input arguments are unique, but not necessarily the result.

Three hundred samples are timed at each of the 32 possible relative displacements of the orgins of the vectors. (The high-speed memory of the 7600 is 32-way interleaved.) The execution time in machine cycles is determined for each case, and summary statistics are printed out.

TABLE 1

*Total Machine Cycles for Randomly Selected Sets of Argument-Vectors of Length 100 at Various Displacements**

Operation: Displacement	R = A*B + C			R = A*B + C*D		
	Max	Min	Average	Max	Min	Average
Case 1:	result-vector distinct from input-vectors					
0	3256	2767	2817	4516	3989	4006
3	2266	1022	1194	2667	1213	1412
8	2844	1031	1447	4011	1228	2170
11	2368	1022	1184	2615	1213	1434
16	3260	1480	1929	4456	2031	2898
19	2005	1022	1184	2397	1213	1406
24	2844	1031	1462	4000	1228	2230
31	2202	1022	1220	2563	1213	1432
Case 2:	result-vector not necessarily distinct from input-vectors					
0	3221	2756	2816	4661	3997	4003
3	2042	1022	1196	2907	1220	1424
8	2840	1031	1501	4011	1235	2216
11	1991	1022	1179	2493	1220	1392
16	3176	1480	1939	4011	2038	2893
19	2068	1022	1200	2710	1220	1458
24	2840	1031	1487	3997	1235	2244
31	1934	1022	1208	2391	1220	1433

*Based on 300 sets chosen at random from a population of 50 vectors origined 4*32 + d words apart, where d is termed the displacement.

B. Performance Results

Performance results for two of the example vector

routines are shown in Table 1. The times shown include the cycles required by the transfers to and from the routines, but not those required by the instructions which prepare registers prior to the call. As might be expected, even displacements are to be avoided. It is less intuitively obvious, but the general result of our tests, that any odd displacement is satisfactory. Additionally, it does not appear to matter whether or not the result argument is permitted to be one of the inputs.

Table 2 summarizes the results of our timing analysis for the seven example routines.

TABLE 2

Machine Cycles per Result Stored for Randomly Selected Argument-Vectors of Length 100 at Odd Displacements

		Limit (1)	Min	Avg (2)	Ratios A/M	A/L
$R = A + B$		6	6.82	8.14	1.19	1.36
$R = A*B$		6	6.55	7.68	1.17	1.28
$R = A*B + C$		9.5	10.22	11.95	1.17	1.26
$R = A*B + C*D$		11.5	12.13	14.29	1.18	1.24
$R_c = A_c*B_c + C_c*D_c$	(3)	15	15.60	18.30	1.17	1.22
$R_x = R_x + A*B$	(4)	17	17.89	19.16	1.07	1.13
$R = R + A*B_x$	(4)	10.5	11.83	14.18	1.20	1.35

(1) The number of cycles per result required by the main loop given no memory conflicts.
(2) Averaged over all cases and all odd displacements.
(3) ICV(I) = I for I = 1, N.
(4) IXV(I) chosen randomly in the range 1,100.

From this it can be seen that the actual performance of optimum vector routines should be expected to average 15 to 35 percent less than the theoretical performance. It is also apparent that a vector length of 100 is sufficient to amortize the calling and startup overhead to at most 9 percent of the theoretical rate except for example 1. In this case, the startup time is fairly long because the main loop is 4-way interleaved.

Finally, the advantage of multi-argument operations is clear. To accomplish R = A*B + C is 32 percent more expensive when routines 1 and 2 are used than when routine 3 is used. To accomplish R = A*B + C*D is 64 percent more expensive when routines 1 and 2 are used than when routine 4 is used.

It is also worth noting that the "controlled" version of R = A*B + C*D is only 28 percent more expensive than the uncontrolled version when ICV(I) = I for I = 1, N (the worst case). This compares favorably with the bit-vector implementation in STACKLIB, which is stated as increasing execution times by about 100 percent (2).

C. A Further Extension of the Vector Concept

We have implemented two routines which further generalize the vector concept by producing multiple result arrays. These routines were rewritten in assembly language because they consumed a sizeable fraction of the overall running time of the code. The most straightforward of these routines accomplishes:

```
      DO 10 I = 1, N
      J(I) = X(I)
      Z1 = X(I) - J(I)
      Z2 = Y(I) - AINT(Y(I))
      W1(I) = 0.25*Z1*Z2
      W2(I) = 0.25*Z2
      W4(I) = 0.25*Z3
      W5(I) = 0.25
    5 W3(I) = W2(I) - W1(I)
      W6(I) = 0.25 - W4(I)
      W7(I) = W4(I) - W1(I)
      W8(I) = 0.25 - W2(I)
   10 W9(I) = W6(I) - W3(I).
```

Where X and Y are input vectors and J, W1,...,W9 are result vectors. AINT(Q) is the integer portion of Q in floating point.

The assembly-language version of this routine is broken into two loops, the break occurring just before statement number 5. It runs 4.5 times faster than the FORTRAN version and generates results at a rate of one every 4.25 machine cycles. In the case of this routine, we can optimize the relative placements of the vectors involved so that the theoretical rate is actually attained.

IV. AN EXAMPLE ON THE STAR-100

The example presented here demonstrates that at least one nonsequential-access operation for which there is no STAR-100 hardware implementation can be "vectorized" effectively (in the generalized sense of the term). Specifically we have devised a method for computing

$$R(IXV(I)) = R(IXV(I)) + C(I)$$

for $I = 1$, N with $1 \leq IXV(I) \leq M \leq \sim 200$. This is example 6 of section III, with $\bar{A}(I)*\bar{B}(I)$ replaced by $C(I)$ by use of the built-in vector capability of STAR.

Our method uses some large subset of the 256 registers of the STAR-100 as a fast random access memory, and involves the construction of a string of instructions by means of vector operations alone. These instructions are then streamed through the central processor to accomplish the desired computation. This approach is based on recognition of two basic facts of STAR-100 architecture. First, scalar operations involving random access to central memory are very much slower than on the 7600. Second, it is possible to load scalar instructions four times faster than it is possible to execute them. By using the registers as a random access memory and streaming instructions to the CPU at near the maximum rate, it is possible to perform scalar arithmetic at the maximum machine rate of 2 cycles per operation subject only to register reservation conflicts.

A. General Approach

Our basic idea is to place $R(1)$ through $R(M)$ in registers R_1 through R_M, initialize two registers for use in block moving C-array values from memory to registers k at a time, and then repeat the following sequence of operations p times, where $k*p = N$:
   Block transfer $C(I)$ through $C(I+k-1)$ to registers C_1-C_k
   $R_{IXV(I)} = R_{IXV(I)} + C_1$
   $\vdots$
   $R_{IXV(I+k-1)} = R_{IXV(I+k-1)} + C_k$
   $I = I+k$ (i.e., advance the C-array access point)
Each of these operations corresponds to a single half-word instruction (3). Thus k should be even, and the block transfer and address-increment instructions placed together. The key to use of this procedure is an efficient method for producing a sequence of computer words with the required operational structure.

B. Constructing the Instruction Stream

Construction of the instruction stream requires the availability of three constants. The first is a word containing the instructions 7D C0 C1 0 and 63 C0 K0 C0, where 7D and 63 are the (hexadecimal) codes for the swap and add-address instructions. C0 denotes a register containing k in the leftmost 16 bits and (initially) the address of C(1) in the rightmost 48 bits. K0 denotes a register containing the integer k, and C1 denotes the first of k consecutive registers into which values of C(I) are brought (C1 must be an even numbered register).

The second "constant" consists of p consecutive copies of a block of k 32-bit words of the form

0 7	8 15	16 23	24 31
00	C1	R0	R0
...			
00	Ck	R0	R0

where C1 is as previously defined, Ck denotes the register whose number is k-1 greater than that of C1, and R0 denotes the register whose number is one less than the first of the M consecutive registers assigned to R(1) through R(M).

The final "constant" is a bit-string (STAR control vector) consisting of p consecutive copies of the binary pattern consisting of a 1 followed by $k/2$ zeroes. This control vector is used in the final merging step of the construction process.

Assuming the existence of the index-vector IXV(I), consisting of 32-bit integers, the desired sequence of instructions is constructed by executing four vector operations. First the 89 instruction is used to (integer) multiply each value of IXV(I) by (hexadecimal) 101, storing the result as an N-word vector of 32-bit integers, J1(I). Next, the 80 instruction is used to (integer) add the (N-word) second "constant" vector to J1(I) to produce J2(I). This vector contains the registers associated with R(IXV(I)) in the positions required by the 62 (scalar add-normalized) instruction.

Third, the 9B instruction is used to pack a (hexadecimal) 62 into the leftmost 16 bits of each J2(I) to produce J3(I). Finally the BD instruction is used to merge (using the 64-bit-operand option) the first constant with the J3(I) vector under control of the bit string specified by the third "constant." The result of the fourth step is the required instruction string, and is stored into a location (e.g., the body of a subroutine) from which it can be executed.

The execution-time overhead for the string construction process is 5 cycles per ultimate result, excluding vector startup which will be significant unless N is 500 or more (4,5). The execution time for the string itself is 5 cycles per result assuming k = 40. In most applications, the string will be executed several times for different R, C vector pairs so the construction time can be amortized down to one or fewer cycles per result.

V. CONCLUSIONS

Our conclusion is, hopefully, obvious: the basic concept of vectorization is sufficiently powerful to warrant considerable generalization. In particular, one should not be intimidated by vector hardware into concluding that new algorithms are required when all that may be needed is "vectorization." Furthermore, generalized vectorization is not only an effective means of exploiting certain hardware features but also a sound programming methodology.

VI. REFERENCES

(1) McMahon, F. H., Sloan, L. J., and Long, G. A., "STACKLIB - A Vector Function Library of Optimum Stack-Loops for the CDC 7600," Lawrence Livermore Laboratory, LTSS-510.
(2) Feustel, E. A., Jensen, C. A., and McMahon, F. H., "Future Trends in Computer Hardware," Lawrence Livermore Laboratory, UCRL-74761, May 1973.
(3) Hardware Reference Manual, Control Data, STAR-100 Computer System, Publication No. 60256000.
(4) Preliminary Execution Tuning Manual, Control Data STAR-100 Computer System, Publication No. 60440600.
(5) Nelson, Harry L., "STAR Timing Tables," Lawrence Livermore Laboratory, internal document.

THE EFFECT OF COMPUTER ARCHITECTURE
ON ALGORITHM DECOMPOSITION AND PERFORMANCE

Robert W. Hon and D. Raj Reddy
Carnegie-Mellon University

INTRODUCTION

There are many problems in image processing and signal processing which require processing powers in the range of 10^8 to 10^{10} instructions per second. Cost-effective solutions to these problems require some form of functional specialization in the computer architecture. The processor-memory-switch structure of the functionally specialized system, in turn, affects algorithm decomposition and overall performance. Depending on the design choices, different aspects of the system become the main bottlenecks. In this paper we examine the effects of processor speed, memory access time, bandwidth, and capacity on algorithm decomposition and system performance.

SYSTEMS

To study the effect of architecture on performance, we have chosen three systems currently under development at Carnegie-Mellon University: C.mmp, a multi-mini processor computer; Cm*, a network of microprocessors; and HARP, a high-speed uniprocessor.

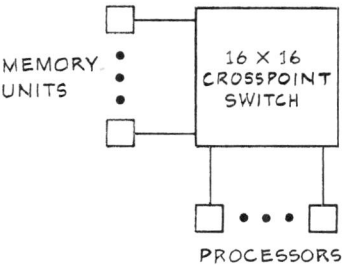

C.mmp

C.mmp [Wulf and Bell, 1972] is 16 minicomputers (PDP 11/20s, /40s, /40Es), each connected to one port of a 16×16 crosspoint switch. A megaword of memory is distributed at the other 16 positions. Each machine may access any word of memory at a cost of .5 - 1 microsecond plus the switching overhead of .25 microsecond, assuming no contention. Instruction execution time for each of the 16 processors is about 2 microseconds.

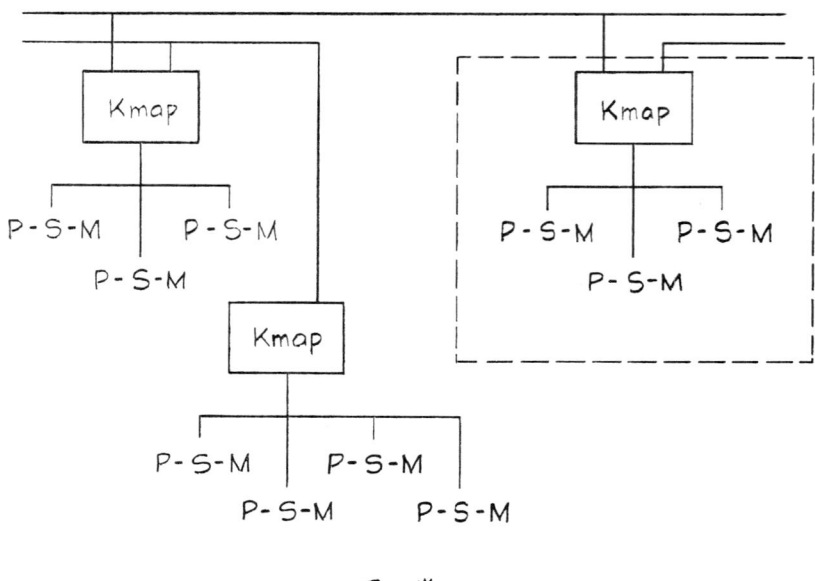

Cm*

Cm* [Swan et al., 1976] is a multi computer module machine where each computer module consists of 1 microprocessor (LSI 11) and its memory. One to fourteen computer modules are connected together in a structure called a cluster. Theoretically hundreds of microprocessors may be connected in a Cm* configuration, currently systems of several clusters of 8 to 12 processors each seem reasonable. Each microprocessor can execute an instruction in 5 - 10 microseconds but there are three types of memory accesses available. The first type is to each LSI 11's local memory (2 - 3 microsecond); second, any processor can access the memory of any other processor in the same cluster at a cost of 5 - 7 microseconds; lastly a processor may access the memory of a processor in another cluster in about 20 microseconds. It is important to note that a processor sees only a virtual address space, it has no knowledge of where a particular virtual address will map into the physical address space. The mapping may, in fact, change dynamically with program execution.

HARP [Kriz et al., 1975] is a high speed pipelined processing element designed to be connected to one port of a double ported buffer memory. The other port is connected to the UNIBUS of a PDP 11. Internal to HARP are 64 instruction registers and 64 data registers; any piece of data located in a data register may be operated on in the basic instruction cycle time of 30 ns. Blocks of from one to sixty-four data or instruction words may be transferred between the registers and the buffer memory at the rate of one word every 20 ns plus 200 ns per block transferred. The buffer memory must be filled from the PDP 11 memory at UNIBUS rates (.5 - 1 microsecond per word).

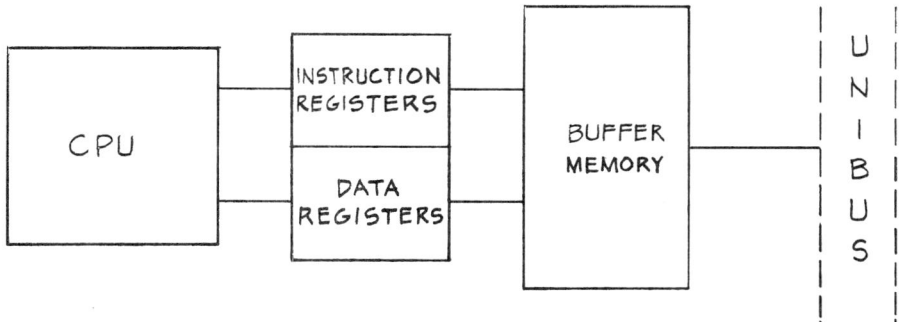

ALGORITHMS

The algorithms chosen for study come from current research in image understanding systems. A typical picture is represented by a rectangular array of picture elements (pixels). Each pixel is a small integer (8 bits in our case) representing a gray scale value or, for color images, the intensity of a primary color. A number of low level operations are useful in image understanding, among them are edge detection, smoothing, hole filling, thinning, histogram formation and thresholding. All operate on the original matrix of pixels and preprocess it so that higher level operators like object identifiers may be invoked.

Edge detection produces an outline drawing from the original gray scale picture. Frequently this is accomplished by assigning a gray scale value to a pixel in the outline picture on the basis of the gradient in a small neighborhood around the corresponding pixel in the original picture. If the gradient around the point is large a boundary may be indicated and a large gray scale value is assigned to the pixel. On the other hand if there is only a slight difference in the neighborhood around the point a small (or even zero) gray scale value is assigned to the pixel. The Sobel operator [Duda and Hart, 1973] is an example of a gradient operator for a 3×3 window.

```
a b c
d e f
g h i
```

The gradient at pixel e is defined as

$$|(a+2b+c)-(g+2h+i)| + |(a+2d+g)-(c+2f+i)|$$

This process is repeated for every pixel in the picture and produces a new picture where only fairly well defined changes in the original are shown. The outline drawing may be further enhanced by the application of thresholding techniques described below.

Smoothing, hole filling and thinning reduce noise and help to separate regions. These three operations are similar in nature and may be implemented by the use of a local neighborhood operator [Kruse, 1973]. Several coefficients arranged in a rectangular matrix (e.g., 3×3) are used as weighting factors for the pixels surrounding a particular element in the picture.

coefficients			pixel window		
c_{00}	c_{01}	c_{02}	e_{ij}	$e_{i,j+1}$	$e_{i,j+2}$
c_{10}	c_{11}	c_{12}	$e_{i+1,j}$	$e_{..}$	$e_{i+1,j+2}$
c_{20}	c_{21}	c_{22}	$e_{i+2,j}$	$e_{..}$	$e_{i+2,j+2}$

Each coefficient c_{kl} is multiplied by the pixel in the corresponding position and the results summed to produce a new gray scale value for the pixel in the center of the matrix. Thus, if e_{ab} denotes the pixel at a,b in the picture:

$$e'_{i+1,j+1} = c_{k,l} e_{i+k,j+1} \quad k=0,1,2 \quad l=0,1,2$$

A 3×3 matrix with a coefficient of zero in the center and 1/8 everywhere else will eliminate isolated dots (nonzero pixels) in blank areas of the picture as well as fill in isolated, blank picture elements. Note that the Sobel operator is a specific case of the local neighborhood operator.

Histogram formation and thresholding [Ohlander, 1975] help to differentiate regions which are similar in some respect from the rest of the picture. Histogramming involves keeping track of the frequency of occurrence of each gray scale value; thus for eight bit pixels 256 such frequencies (simple counters) must be maintained. If "histog" is a zero origin vector representing the histogram and pixel[i,j] is the gray scale value of the pixel at i,j then the program fragment

histog[pixel[i,j]]←histog[pixel[i,j]]+1

will update the histogram to include the pixel at i,j. The histogram may provide useful guidelines for separating regions of the picture, for instance, a large number of pixels may have gray scale values between 100 and 150. This peak in the histogram might indicate a distinct area of the picture such as the sky. Subsequent filtering (thresholding) on the basis of the limits provided by the histogram may isolate the region of interest. A typical program sequence to perform the thresholding operator for an m by n picture is:

```
FOR i TO m DO
   BEGIN FOR j TO n DO
      BEGIN IF (pixel[i,j] < lowlim) OR (pixel[i,j] > highlim)
         THEN pixel[i,j]←0 ELSE pixel[i,j]←1
      END
   END
```

By appropriate use of thresholding regions may be isolated from the picture or subtracted from it; a new histogram may then be determined for the picture and further separations performed.

An algorithm used in research at the University of Maryland [Willet, 1976] was also studied. It is composed of several of the previously described algorithms (edge detection, histogram formation, thresholding) and is referred to as EHT for the remainder of this paper. In EHT a gradient is calculated by summing the gray scale values in 4 2X2 arrays labeled TOP, BOTTOM, RIGHT, LEFT surrounding a given point in the image.

```
        a b
      c d e f
      g h i j
        k l
```

For this cross shaped window TOP is given by a+b+d+e, RIGHT by e+f+i+j, etc. The gradient at d, which must be stored, is the maximum of ($|$TOP-BOTTOM$|$, $|$LEFT-RIGHT$|$). These results are used to form a histogram of the gradients of the picture. Once this is accomplished the area under the histogram is integrated and the value below which 80% of the gradients lie is found. Each gradient is compared to this 80% value; if the gradient is less, a zero replaces the corresponding pixel in the original picture. Simultaneously with this thresholding operation the remaining pixels are averaged. A second thresholding operation is performed using this average as a low limit, all pixels which are less than the average are replaced by zero.

While some of the algorithms involve very simple computations, they must be applied to a large amount of data. A black and white picture of roughly the same resolution as a TV screen represents about 300,000 pixels and requires 300 kilobytes of storage. In many of the primitive image understanding operations each pixel must be examined at least once and some computation performed, additionally an intermediate result may be generated and stored. Since the volume of data is so large, careful decomposition and implementation of an algorithm can result in substantial savings.

DECOMPOSITION OF ALGORITHMS

The efficient implementation of an algorithm on a particular machine is largely shaped by the architecture of that machine. Relatively subtle changes in architecture can affect extensive changes in the performance of the algorithm. Each of the algorithms detailed above differs from the others in the ways it may be effectively decomposed for various architectures. For example edge detection typically involves a number of mathematical operations but usually can be organized to effectively utilize a parallel architecture. Histogramming is unique in that a single copy of the data structure must be continually updated. Since 300,000 pixels must be placed in 256 buckets the memory contention problems in a parallel architecture are formidable. This section explores the ways that algorithms must be reorganized as the architecture of the machine changes.

Lack of space prevents a detailed examination of all the algorithms here so we have singled out EHT since it combines several of the important low level operators. The following table summarizes performance of the various systems before and after the algorithm was reorganized. As a benchmark the edge detection and histogram formation portions of EHT were coded for a PDP 11/40. This code was translated for C.mmp (assuming 16 processors) and HARP without restructuring the algorithm; those times are shown in the first row. The second row shows the speed ups achieved when the algorithms were reorganized to take advantage of the hardware capabilities. All times are the number of microseconds required per pixel.

	PDP 11/40	C.mmp	HARP
original	80.5	11.5	7.8
reorganized	----	5.2	2.0

No execution times for Cm* are shown but it is expected to perform very much like C.mmp when one process is assigned to one microprocessor (in a 16 microprocessor system). Other processing configurations are possible with Cm* which may lead to efficient processing for different classes of algorithms. We will now discuss some principles that we have formulated based on our analyses.

As processor speed increases relative to memory speed it becomes necessary to reorganize the algorithm so that the number of data references made is minimized. For a machine like C.mmp where instruction execution and data references take about the same amount of time, an attempt to minimize the total number of instructions executed and data references should be made. As the processor speed increases a larger proportion of the total time is spent in referencing data. This term soon dominates the total execution time and must be reduced in order to obtain significant speed ups. For example, on a PDP 11/40 the EHT algorithm was implemented by taking two passes through the data: the first pass calculated and stored the sums for each 2×2 array, the second pass found the gradient and updated the histogram. HARP is capable of executing PDP 11-like instructions at about 50 times the speed of a PDP 11/40. However, coding EHT for HARP in the same fashion as for a PDP 11/40 resulted in only a tenfold speed increase. The algorithm was recoded (see appendix) to take only one pass through the data so that the number of memory references could be decreased. This resulted in an execution speed about 40 times faster than the PDP 11. The penalty was increased complexity in the code and more instructions being executed.

As the capacity of the primary memory decreases the algorithm should be decomposed to minimize the number of page faults between primary and secondary memory. This implies avoiding multiple passes through the data which increase the frequency of secondary memory accesses. It is desirable to execute as many instructions as possible on the data in primary memory before bringing in a new page. In spite of this if little computation is involved an algorithm which makes efficient use of the data in primary memory will still run slowly since the processor is forced to wait more often for data to be brought in from mass storage. A decrease in the bandwidth of the primary/secondary memory link or an increase in the secondary memory access time will necessitate the same type of reorganization. Since more time is required to fill a buffer in primary memory the algorithm must do all the computing that it can before initiating another transfer to or from secondary memory. Careful decomposition of the algorithms to be implemented on a machine may permit the use of slower secondary memories and lower bandwidth channels between primary and secondary memory.

Multiprocessors may not provide an effective means of increasing the execution speed of certain computationally expensive algorithms. The algorithm under examination may not lend itself to decomposition for a multiprocessing environment. Examples are problems that involve one or more critical sections of code of uneven length or involve the need to update a common data base (e.g., the same copy of a histogram). In these cases synchronization can introduce significant overhead and the time lost by processes waiting for the same memory location may be large. Here a uniprocessor which is N times as fast is likely to be preferable to an N process parallel system. Conversely, algorithms which allow favorable scheduling of processes and/or the data to be partitioned into independent chunks often can run N times as fast given N processes. The extra synchronization overhead is small compared to the increase in number of instructions executed per second; such is the case with the EHT algorithm examined in this paper. The algorithm was decomposed so that each process had a copy of the inner loop code and 256 memory locations for a local histogram. Since each process compiles a histogram only for its slice of the picture contention problems are eliminated. Extra overhead is incurred by the necessity of summing the individual histograms to obtain the overall histogram--fortunately this cost remains fixed regardless of the size of the picture processed. Slightly more memory is required to store the independent copies of the inner loops and the individual histograms but this too is independent of the size of the picture being processed.

Loosely couple multiprocessors can perform well with algorithms which allow the data flow to be pipelined; a large, randomly accessed data base requires a more tightly coupled multiprocessor. In loosely coupled multiprocessor networks each processor has a relatively small amount of local memory associated with it; data can be passed between processors, but more slowly than a processor can move data within its local memory. Such networks are particularly attractive because of their low cost per MIP. Algorithms can take advantage of this computing power if the data can be operated on in a pipelined fashion, with each process completing its task and passing the data to the next. Algorithms which require random access to a large data base run more efficiently on a tightly coupled multiprocessor where any process can reference any memory location for the same cost. On such algorithms the extra overhead of passing many small messages (packets of data) limits the performance of a loosely coupled network.

In summary, it is clear that each different processor architecture demands careful consideration and restructuring of the algorithms. Maximum performance from an algorithm can only be obtained when it has been coded with a particular machine architecture in mind. Effective decomposition of algorithms is dependent on the programmer knowing the hardware capabilities and coding his algorithm to take advantage of the machine's strengths.

PERFORMANCE ANALYSIS

In this section the effect on performance of changing one parameter of the computer architecture (e.g., instruction execution time, capacity of primary memory) is examined while the other parameters remain constant. It is assumed that instruction memory (e.g., writeable microstore) and data memory are distinct and possibly of different speeds; thus their characteristics may be varied independently. "Primary memory" refers to the semiconductor or core memory in which non-local data currently being processed is stored. "Secondary memory" is mass storage, usually disk or drum, which has a slow access time compared to the primary memory. Execution time is used as a measure of performance throughout.

One general principle emerges from our study: _As the characteristics of one component of the machine improve performance improves until some other component becomes the bottleneck in the system._

An infinitely fast processor does not reduce the execution time for the algorithm to zero. Even if the uniprocessor's microinstruction execution time is zero, the overall performance of the system is still limited by the number of data accesses that must be made. Since data access time is essentially wasted as far as the processor is concerned ideally one would hope to keep data access time at a very low percentage of the processor's total execution time. This becomes more difficult as the speed of the processor increases relative to the speed of the memory. A similar effect is noted if the primary memory access time goes to zero, namely performance is still limited by the number of microinstructions which must be executed. Performance is eventually limited by the slower of the two components; increasing the processor speed and the memory speed may upgrade the system's performance until bandwidth limitations become the dominating factor.

As the bandwidth of the primary/secondary memory link decreases the performance of the system is limited by the number of accesses made to secondary memory. Serious bottlenecks can arise if the processor requires data faster than the primary to secondary memory link can supply it. Given that the processor, primary memory, and secondary memory all are infinitely fast, a system using one disk channel with a one megabyte bandwidth still can only attain a one megapixel per second throughput.

Performance is bound by the speed of primary memory as the number of high speed registers approaches zero. The time spent doing bookkeeping operations increases dramatically as control counters, etc. are moved to locations in primary memory. In image analysis operations many tight loops are encountered; the lack of a high speed register to store a loop count means that the processor must make two extra data accesses. The cost of those extra accesses may equal the cost of manipulating the actual picture data. This problem is related to the one above since we are faced with a bandwidth/access time limitation between the high speed registers and the slower primary memory. Similar performance problems arise as the number of index registers decreases. Frequently image analysis algorithms require the retrieval of data from several places in the pixel array. For these applications having a sufficient number of index registers can preclude inefficient address calculations. A shortage of registers becomes even more of a handicap when the processor can execute instructions much faster than it can access primary memory. In the case of HARP a reference to memory outside of its high speed registers requires the same amount of time as executing about seven instructions--for inner loops which are only about 15 instructions long the increase is intolerable.

The cost of accessing secondary memory dominates the performance of the system as the capacity of primary memory is diminished. This is an extension of the principle for high speed registers just discussed. There is seldom enough primary memory to keep the entire image in it at one time; satisfactory performance may be attained if sufficiently large buffers can be kept in primary memory and data can be obtained from secondary memory quickly enough to keep at least one buffer full. As the size of the primary memory shrinks the system performance will become bound by the access time of secondary memory. Even if the bandwidth of the primary/secondary link is infinite the system can only run as fast as data can be transferred from the disk.

CONCLUSIONS

In order to minimize the cost-performance ratio the machine architecture must be carefully chosen for the class of algorithms of interest. Ultra-fast processors may not produce the expected execution times if the algorithm requires many accesses to data. Tradeoffs must be made between primary memory speed and capacity--if the memory is too small time is wasted in paging, while a large chunk of idle memory represents dollars that could have been applied to increase computing power. Even if the primary memory is well matched to the speed of the processor, insufficient bandwidth between mass storage and primary memory may cause the processor to wait as buffers are refilled. The architecture must be designed so that the performance of each component matches that of the others--any that are vastly inferior will degrade performance while while superior elements only waste capabilities by sitting idle.

Once the hardware has been chosen the algorithms must be designed to take full advantage of the machine architecture's features and strengths. While multiprocessing can be a cost-effective way to obtain many MIPS it may be that the algorithms to be implemented cannot be decomposed to take advantage of those MIPS. The serialization of the data stream at one point in the algorithm may limit the overall performance of the system, in spite of the computing power available.

In this paper we have examined several architectures and algorithms and tried to derive some basic principles regarding their relationships. Although many more algorithms and architectures should be examined before one can formulate general principles such as those given in the above sections, we believe that they are applicable to a wide variety of algorithms and architectures.

REFERENCES

R. O. Duda and P. E. Hart (1973), __Pattern Classification and Scene Analysis__, Wiley, NY.
S. Kriz, S. Saunders, S. Rubin (1975), "HARP", unpublished report, Carnegie-Mellon Univ., Pittsburgh, PA.
B. Kruse (1973), "A Parallel Picture Processing Machine", IEEE Trans. Computers, vol. C-22, no. 12, December 1973.
R. B. Ohlander (1975), "Analysis of Natural Scenes", dissertation, Dept. of Comp. Sci., Carnegie-Mellon Univ.
R. J. Swan, S. H. Fuller, D. P. Siewiorek (1976), "The Structure and Architecture of Cm*: a Modular, Multi-Microprocessor", Comp. Sci. Res. Rev. 75-76, Carnegie-Mellon Univ.
T. Willet (1976), "Algorithms and Hardware Technology for Image Recognition", Tech. Rep., Comp. Sci. Dept., Univ. MD.
W. A. Wulf and C. G. Bell (1972), "C.mmp - a Multi-Mini-Processor", Proc. FJCC 1972, 765-777.

APPENDIX

The code below is a sample from the inner loop code used on the PDP 11/40 during the first pass through the data. The image is treated as a vector of pixels; a row is LEN pixels long. R4 and R5 (Rn refers to a PDP 11 register) are initialized to the first pixel in the first two and the first pixel in the second row, respectively. R3 contains a pointer to where the sum for the 2×2 array is to be stored. R1 contains a pointer to the first pixel in the image (i.e., first pixel in the first row--the upper lefthand corner). R0 is used to accumulate the sum. The algorithm scans along the image from the upper lefthand corner, accessing two new pixels, adding them to the last two it used, and storing /the sum. Thus data from two different rows is examined each time to loop is executed.

```
CONT:   MOVE    R4,R0           ;sum is accumulated in R0
        ADD     R5,R0           ;add up pixels from last loop
        MOVB    1(R1),R4        ;pick up first new pixel
        BIT     #377,R4
        MOVB    LEN+1(R1),R5    ;pick up last new pixel
        BIT     #377,R5
        ADD     R4,R0           ;add in new pixels
        ADD     R5,R0
        MOVB    R0,(R3)+        ;store sum
        INC     R1              ;inc source pointer
        DEC     R2              ;subtract 1 from loop count
        BGT     CONT            ;test and loop
```

The second pass through the data is handled in a similar fashion; the algorithm slides a window through the sums, picking up the four relevant ones (TOP, BOTTOM, LEFT, RIGHT) and calculating the gradient. Clearly, a number of accesses are made to data memory (which is the same as instruction memory for the PDP 11). The number of data references is far outweighed by the number of instructions executed, thus best performance is obtained when a minimum number of instructions and data references are made.

HARP, which executes instructions in 30 ns (vs. 2 microseconds for the PDP 11), requires about 360 ns to complete the instruction portion of the loop shown above. Yet the loop above makes three references to data memory which takes about 3 microseconds at Unibus transfer rates (assuming 1 microsecond memory). Restructuring the algorithm to be one-pass reduces the number of data references from 8.2 to 2.3. Although the resulting algorithm was more complex, the overall performance improved by a factor of 3.9.

A SOFTWARE TECHNIQUE FOR REDUCING THE ROUTING TIME ON A
PARALLEL COMPUTER WITH A FIXED INTERCONNECTION NETWORK

H. T. Kung
Carnegie-Mellon University

D. Stevenson
Institute for Advanced Computation

I. INTRODUCTION

This paper considers the problem of executing an arbitrarily given parallel algorithm on an array computer with a fixed interconnection network. A general technique is given for reducing the routing time without changing the algorithm and the network.

The technique relies on finding a suitable mapping which maps the algorithm organization onto the memory organization. Using this mapping the algorithm can be executed with the minimum number of routing steps. The mapping problem is defined formally in the next section.

II. THE MAPPING PROBLEM

A. Interconnection Network on Memories

We assume that there are n memory modules $M_0,\ldots,M_{n-1}$, which are connected by an interconnection network. The network is defined by a set of interconnection functions, each a bijection on $\{0,\ldots,n-1\}$. When the routing instruction associated with interconnection function C is executed, data is sent from M_i to $M_{C(i)}$, for all the "active" memories M_i which are specified by some masking scheme.

Let P be any partial function mapping the set $\{0,\ldots,n-1\}$ into itself. By performing the <u>transfer P</u> we mean moving data from M_i to $M_{P(i)}$ for all i to which P assigns values. Let D(P) be the minimum number of <u>routing steps</u> (i.e., executions of routing instructions) needed to perform the transfer P. D(P) is defined to be infinity if the transfer P cannot be

---

The first author is supported in part by the National Science Foundation under Grant MCS 75-222-55 and the Office of Naval Research under Contract N00014-76-C-0370, NR 044-422.

achieved by the network. Therefore, associated with each interconnection network there is a <u>distance function</u> D defined on the set of all partial functions.

B. Parallel Algorithm on Memories

Consider a parallel algorithm using n memories, $m_0, \ldots, m_{n-1}$. During the execution of the algorithm, it is usually necessary to transfer data among memories m_i. Assume that the transfers take place at r different time instances and they are transfers P_j, $0 \le j \le r-1$, where P_j are some partial functions mapping $\{0, \ldots, n-1\}$ into itself. That is, for each $0 \le j \le r-1$, the jth transfer sends data from m_i to $m_{P_j(i)}$ for all i to which P_j assigns values.

C. Mapping an Algorithm onto a Network

Suppose we want to execute an algorithm with transfers P_j, $0 \le j \le r-1$, on a network with a distance function D. For the execution we must map the "logical" memories $m_0, \ldots, m_{n-1}$ onto the "physical" memories $M_0, \ldots, M_{n-1}$. The usual approach has been to map m_i to M_i for all i. Then the number of routing steps needed to execute the algorithm on the network is

$$\sum_{j=0}^{r-1} D(P_j).$$

Suppose that m_i is mapped to $M_{F(i)}$ for all i, where F is some bijection on $\{0, \ldots, n-1\}$. Then the jth transfer of the algorithm sends data from M_i to $M_{(FP_jF^{-1})(i)}$. This implies that with respect to the mapping F the number of routing steps needed to execute the algorithm on the network is

$$R(F) = \sum_{j=0}^{r-1} D(FP_jF^{-1}).$$

Let I be the identity function. Then $R(I) = \sum_{j=0}^{r-1} D(P_j)$, which is the number of routing steps needed in the usual approach. We are interested in finding F such that $R(F) < R(I)$ or proving that the usual approach is in fact optimal. More generally, we want to find F which minimizes $R(F)$. The problem can be stated more precisely as follows:

Given D and $\{P_0, P_1, \ldots, P_{r-1}\}$

find a bijection $F: \{0,\ldots,n-1\} \to \{0,\ldots,n-1\}$ such that

$$R(F) = \sum_{j=0}^{r-1} D(FP_j F^{-1})$$

is minimized.

We call this problem <u>the mapping problem</u>. If F minimizes R over all the bijections, F is said to be an <u>optimal mapping</u>. Informally, the mapping problem is the problem of mapping the m_i onto the M_i so that the transfers needed by the algorithm can be performed most efficiently on the network (see Fig. 1). Hence the mapping problem deals with the interface between the algorithm and memory organizations, and it arises whenever a given algorithm is to be executed on memories with a fixed interconnection network.

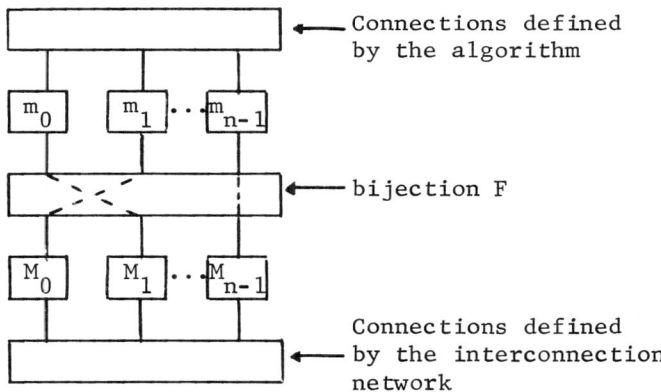

Fig. 1. The mapping problem is to find a bijection F so that the algorithm can be performed most efficiently on the network.

III. ALGORITHMS USING SINGLE TRANSFERS

In this section we consider algorithms where only one transfer P on the memories $m_0,\ldots,m_{n-1}$ is needed, i.e., $P_0 = \ldots = P_{r-1} = P$. We shall show that this type of algorithm can always be executed efficiently, even on the simplest network, namely, the <u>linearly connected network</u>. (The interconnection functions for the linearly connected network are C_+ and C_- defined by $C_+(i) = i+1 \bmod n$ and $C_-(i) = i-1 \bmod n$.)

Theorem 1.

For any injective partial function P, there exists a bijection F such that with respect to the mapping F the transfer P on the m_i can be performed in at most four routing steps on the linearly connected network.

Proof

Suppose that P is a bijection. Then P corresponds to a collection of cycles. For example, for the perfect shuffle permutation on $\{0,\ldots,15\}$ (see, e.g., Stone (7)), the cycles are given as follows:

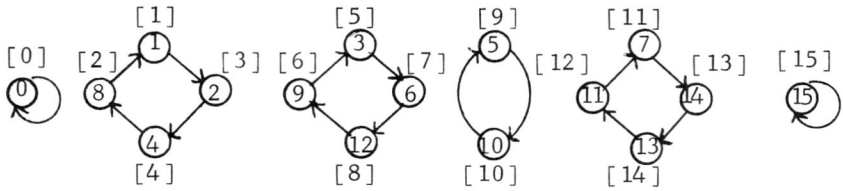

The numbers inside the square brackets are obtained by numbering the cycles one by one and by using the breadth-first numbering for each individual cycle. Observe that using this numbering scheme the numbers at any two adjacent nodes differ at most by two. Define F(i) to be the number given to node i. Then with the mapping F the m_i are mapped onto the linearly connected metwork such that for any i m_i is at most two elements away from $m_{P(i)}$ in either of the two directions. Hence the transfer P can be performed in at most two routing steps in each direction. (For the perfect shuffle example, we have F(3) = 5, F(6) = 7., etc., and the m_i are mapped onto the network as shown in Fig. 2.)

Suppose that P is not a bijection. Then P corresponds to a collection of cycles and linear lists. We number the cycles and lists one by one by using the breadth-first numbering for each of them. All the results still hold for this numbering. ∎

The proof of Theorem 1 is instructive in the sense that it shows that the mapping problem corresponds to a graph numbering problem. This correspondence can be made very general to cover cases where we have more than one transfer to be performed on a general network. The resulting graph numbering problems will be generalizations to the well known bandwidth or profile reduction problems encountered in sparse matrix computations. In the next section, a mapping problem will be dealt with by using bandwidth reduction algorithms.

Corollary 1

For any injective partial function P, there exists a bijection F such that with respect to the mapping F an algorithm with $P_0 = \ldots = P_{r-1} = P$ can be executed in at most $4r$ routing steps on the linearly connected network. (Note that if F is taken to be I as in the usual approach, the number of routing steps can be as large as $\frac{1}{2} nr$.)

A. Matrix Transposition

Let A be a $2^r \times 2^r$ matrix, stored in row major order in the memories m_i. Stone (7) has shown that the matrix transpose of A (i.e., A stored in column major order) can be obtained by performing r shuffles on the m_i. Suppose now that we have the linearly connected network. The straightforward method would take $O(2^r)$ steps to transpose A. By Corollary 1, we can transpose A in $4r$ steps, provided that the elements of A are stored according to the mapping F. To illustrate the idea, consider the case when $r = 2$. The storage arrangements of A and the realization of the transposition of A, with respect to the F defined in the proof of Theorem 1, are shown in Fig. 3. Note that each shuffle takes four routing steps, and after two shuffles a memory which originally had a_{ij} will have a_{ji}.

M_i	$m_{F^{-1}(i)}$
M_0	m_0
M_1	m_1
M_2	m_8
M_3	m_2
M_4	m_4
M_5	m_3
M_6	m_9
M_7	m_6
M_8	m_{12}
M_9	m_5
M_{10}	m_{10}
M_{11}	m_7
M_{12}	m_{11}
M_{13}	m_{14}
M_{14}	m_{13}
M_{15}	m_{15}

Fig. 2. The mapping for the perfect shuffle permutation.

B. Polynomial Evaluation

The parallel polynomial evaluation algorithm considered by Stone (7) requires a sequence of shuffles on the masks. Again by Corollary 1 these shuffles can be done efficiently on the linearly connected network, provided that the coefficients of the polynomial are stored according to the mapping F.

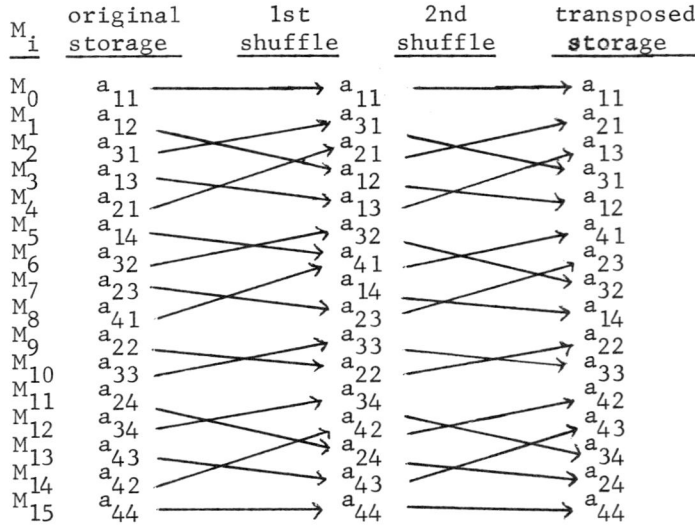

Fig. 3. The storage arrangements and the realization of the transposition of A with respect to the mapping F defined in the proof of Theorem 1.

IV. ALGORITHMS USING DIFFERENT TRANSFERS

This section deals with algorithms where different transfers are needed. A mapping which minimizes the time to perform one transfer is in general not suitable for minimizing the time to perform another transfer. Hence, it is usually difficult to solve the mapping problem for an algorithm which uses different transfers. In the following, we study three examples.

A. The Bitonic Sort on a Mesh-Connected Network

Batcher's bitonic sort algorithm (1) on $n = 2^r$ elements requires r different transfers $P_0, \ldots, P_{r-1}$, where the transfer P_j matches the m_i whose indices differ by the jth bit in their binary representation. Moreover, for $0 \leq j \leq r-1$ the transfer P_j is performed $r-j$ times during the execution of the algorithm.

Suppose that we want to perform the bitonic sort on a mesh-connected network such as the ILLIAC IV network. Thompson and Kung (8, Section 8) discovered that with respect to a certain mapping the bitonic sort is optimal in time within a small constant factor. Here we shall just describe the basic idea used in finding the mapping. The reader is referred to (8) for more discussions.

Consider the problem of mapping the 16-element bitonic sort algorithm on a 4×4 ILLIAC-IV-like network. Suppose that the m_i are mapped onto the array in row major order (Fig. 4), i.e., $F = I$. Then $D(P_0) = 2$, $D(P_1) = 4$, $D(P_2) = 2$ and $D(P_3) = 4$. This implies that

$$R(I) = \sum_{j=0}^{3} (4-j)D(P_j) = 4\cdot 2 + 3\cdot 4 + 2\cdot 2 + 1\cdot 4 = 28.$$

```
m₀ — m₁ — m₂ — m₃
 |    |    |    |
m₄ — m₅ — m₆ — m₇
 |    |    |    |
m₈ — m₉ — m₁₀— m₁₁
 |    |    |    |
m₁₂— m₁₃— m₁₄— m₁₅
```

Fig. 4. Row major order

Since the transfer P_1 is more expensive than the transfer P_2, and P_1 is performed one more time than P_2, the row major order mapping can be improved by simply interchanging the 1st and the 2nd bits of the indices of all m_i. After doing so, the m_i are mapped onto the array as shown in Fig. 5. Let the mapping be F_s. Then it can be seen easily that

$$R(F_s) = 4 \cdot 2 + 3 \cdot 2 + 2 \cdot 4 + 1 \cdot 4 = 26,$$

which is smaller than $R(I)$ as we expected. The general idea therefore is to make the transfer P_j less expensive than the transfer P_{j+1} for all $0 \le j < r-1$, in view of the fact that P_j is performed more often than P_{j+1}. This idea has led to a mapping called "shuffled row major order". With respect to this mapping, the bitonic sort takes only $O(\sqrt{n})$ routing steps on the ILLIAC-IV-like network, rather than $O(\sqrt{n} \log n)$ steps which are needed if F is taken to be I.

```
m₀ — m₁ — m₄ — m₅
 |    |    |    |
m₂ — m₃ — m₆ — m₇
 |    |    |    |
m₈ — m₉ — m₁₀— m₁₃
 |    |    |    |
m₁₀— m₁₁— m₁₄— m₁₅
```

Fig. 5. Shuffled row major order

This example shows that considerations on the mapping problem may lead to large improvements in algorithm speed.

B. The Fast Fourier Transform on the Linearly Connected Network

The fast Fourier transform (FFT) algorithm (3) on 2^r elements requires the same transfers as the bitonic sort algorithm does. But the FFT algorithm performs each transfer exactly once (see Pease (5) and Stevens (6)). The transfers are illustrated in Fig. 6 for the case r = 3. Suppose that we want to perform the FFT on the linearly connected network. Note that if F = I, then

$$R(I) = \sum D(P_j) = \sum 2 \cdot 2^j$$
$$= 2(2^r - 1).$$

(In fact $R(F) = 2(2^r-1)$ for any F which is defined by a permutation on the bits of the binary representation of indices.) Observe that the output at each m_i depends on the inputs at all m_i, $0 \leq i \leq n-1$. To achieve this on the linearly connected network, at least 2^r-1 routing steps are needed. Hence $R(F) \geq 2^r-1$ for any F. Therefore the identity map is optimal within a factor of two.

The purpose of this example is to show that the usual approach of choosing F to be I may be optimal or close to optimal. But even in this case it is still of interest and challenging to prove the optimality of the identity map.

C. Simulating the Shuffle and Exchange Functions with Linearly Connected Network

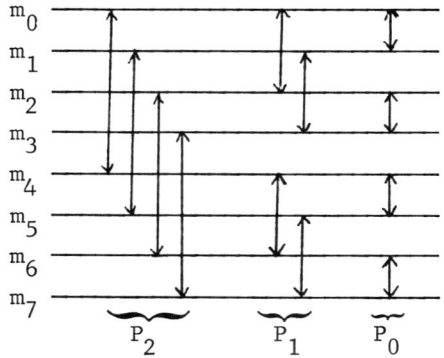

Fig. 6. The FFT transfers

We want to use the linearly connected network to simulate both the shuffle (S) and exchange (E) functions, which are needed in many applications (see, e.g., Lang and Stone (4)). It is easy to check that if we use the identity map then

$$R(I) = D(S) + D(E)$$
$$= 2(\frac{n}{2}-1) + 2$$
$$= n.$$

As in the proof of Theorem 1, S and E correspond to two graphs. We superpose the two graphs and consider the resulting graph. Such a graph for the case n = 16 is shown in Fig. 7. Suppose that the graph has been numbered by $0,1,\ldots,n-1$, and has bandwidth B. Then with respect to the F defined by the numbering on the graph, $R(F) \leq 4B$. Therefore, if we can find a numbering which gives $B < n/4$ then we have found a mapping F which is better than the identity map. This

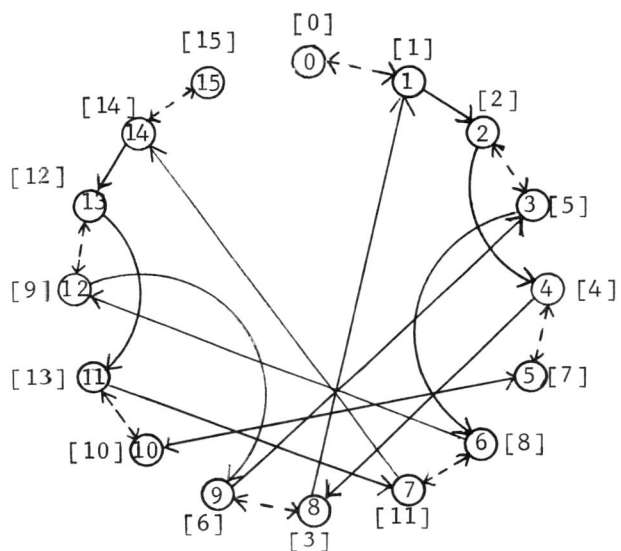

Fig. 7. The graph resulting from superposing the S and E graphs, where ——— and ---- are S and E edges, respectively. The numbers in [ ] are obtained by a bandwidth reduction algorithm.

motivated us to use bandwidth reduction algorithms (see, e.g., (2)) to number the graph. This approach has brought us some nontrivial mappings which are better than the identity mapping. For example, a numbering is obtained for the graph in Fig. 7. With respect to the mapping F defined by this numbering, an S transfer followed by an E transfer can be done in 12 steps, rather than 16 steps. Examples of results for n up to 1024 are given in Table 1. The table shows that using mappings obtained by bandwidth reduction algorithms reduces the routing time significantly.

By this example, we wish to illustrate that the mapping problem can be solved approximately by bandwidth reduction algorithms. This example also shows that when one network is used to simulate another one the simulation time may depend on the mapping function.

TABLE 1

The number of routing steps
needed to simulate an S transfer
followed by an E transfer on the
linearly connected network

n	Using the identity map	Using mappings obtained by bandwidth reduction algorithms
8	8	8
16	16	12
32	32	24
64	64	48
128	128	88
256	256	172
512	512	324
1024	1024	624

V. CONCLUDING REMARKS

From the examples of this paper, we observe that by mapping an algorithm properly onto a network, the time to execute the algorithm on the network can sometimes be reduced significantly. We believe that this mapping problem deserves serious consideration, since its solution give a very cheap way of speeding up computation; all it involves is essentially a renaming of the memory modules. Further research is needed to find good techniques for solving the mapping problem for algorithms which use more than one transfer. We expect that they will be generalizations of the techniques now used in sparse matrix computations. This paper is a preliminary report of our research on this subject. Further results will be appearing in the future.

VI. REFERENCES

1. Batcher, K. W., "Sorting Networks and Their Applications," 1968 Spring Joint Computer Conf., AFIPS Proc., Vol. 32, Washington, D.C. Thompson, pp. 307-314, 1968.
2. Chvátalová, J., Dewdney, A. K., Gibbs, N. E., and Korfhage, R. R., "The Bandwidth Problem for Graphs - A Collection of Recent Results," Report, The Dept. of Computer Science, Univ. of Western Ontario, London, Ontario, Canada, Sept. 1975.
3. Cooky, J. W., and Tukey, J. W., "An Algorithm for the Machine Calculation of Complex Fourier Series," Math. Comp.

Vol. 19, pp. 297-301, April 1965.
4. Lang, T., and Stone, H. S., "A Shuffle-Exchange Network with Simplified Control," IEEE Trans. Computers, Vol. C-25, pp. 55-65, Jan. 1976.
5. Pease, M. C., "An Adaptation of the Fast Fourier Transform for Parallel Processing," J.ACM, Vol. 15, pp. 252-264, April 1968.
6. Stevens, J. E., "A Fast Fourier Transform Subroutine for ILLIAC IV," CAC Document No. 17, Univ. of Illinois at Urbana-Champaign, Oct. 1971.
7. Stone, H. S., "Parallel Processing with the Perfect Shuffle," IEEE Trans. Computers, Vol. C-20, pp. 153-161, Feb. 1971.
8. Thompson, C. D., and Kung, H. T., "Sorting on a Mesh-Connected Parallel Computer," Proc. of the Eighth Annual ACM Symp. on Theory of Computing, pp. 58-64, May 1976. A revised version to appear in C.ACM, April 1977.

PREPAGING AND APPLICATIONS TO THE STAR-100 COMPUTER

Kishor S. Trivedi
Duke University

I. INTRODUCTION

The Control Data Corporation (CDC) STAR (STring ARray) computer is a high performance vector machine capable of performing up to 100 million operations per second. Although the size of the main memory is limited to either 1/2 million or 1 million 64-bit words, the use of a virtual memory capability allows a virtual address space size of 4 trillon 64-bit words. The virtual memory is implemented by means of a paging mechanism. The system provides two page sizes, 512 (small) and 65,536 (large) words, respectively.

Because of a very high speed cpu, the system is highly I/O-bound for many problems [1],[2]. Since the paging device is a disk, the use of the large page size can reduce the I/O time considerably. Since the total number of large page frames is either 8 or 16, the use of a large page dictates a very small degree of multiprogramming. The second technique to improve the performance is to increase the size of the main memory [3],[4]. This allows a larger page allotment per program thus reducing the paging I/O. However, due to the small size of the main memory available on the STAR, thrashing can occur even with a very small degree of multiprogramming [3], [5]. Such an I/O limited and memory limited situation forces very low degrees of multiprogramming. Currently, many jobs are constrained to run in a monoprogramming mode. This, coupled with a demand paging environment, implies no cpu-I/O overlap whatsoever. In such an environment, one possible way to introduce the cpu-I/O overlap (and hence improve the throughput) is to use prepaging. Prepaging allows the overlap between the execution and I/O of the same job. Therefore, we expect it to improve the throughput, particularly for low degrees of multiprogramming. For further discussion on the usefulness of prepaging see [6],[7],[8],[9].
Note that the best that we can hope to do with prepaging is

The work reported here was performed under NASA Contract No. NAS1-14101 while the author was in residence at ICASE, NASA Langley Research Center, Hampton, VA 23665 either completely mask the I/O time or completely mask the cpu time, whichever is less.

The STAR system provides a feature known as ADVISE which allows prepaging. In Section 2, we describe our efforts to exploit this feature. We have developed a subroutine FPRQST which can be called by a FORTRAN programmer to request the operating system either to prepage or free a page. We also illustrate the use of this subroutine in a program carrying out a matrix multiplication. When we attempted to test our programs on the system, we found that the ADVISE feature does not work in the current version of the operating system. Hopefully, in a future version of the operating system, this feature will be debugged and the experiments of Section 2 may be carried out.

In Section 3, we do a timing analysis of the matrix multiplication routine with and without prepaging and using both the small and the large pages. We expect that the I/O time can be reduced by an order of magnitude by switching to large pages. It should also be clear that prepaging has a potential of cutting the total execution time in half for a balanced program.

In the current STAR system a global LRU paging algorithm is used [10],[11]. If prepaging is allowed in a multiprogramming mode, then a program can very rapidly steal pages away from other programs. This may imply an improvement in the performance of that program but the overall system performance can suffer. Even in a monoprogramming environment (or using a local replacement algorithm) a user can destroy his own performance if uncontrolled prepaging is permitted. In Section 4, we discuss how prepaging can be controlled.

II. PREPAGING ON STAR

A program can issue an ADVISE message to the operating system of an anticipated need for virtual space in an attempt to avoid a page fault or to advise the system of pages no longer to be used by this program. The ADVISE can be issued for at most one large page and at most eight consecutive small pages at a time [12].

Based on this feature, we have developed a routine FPRQST which can be called by a FORTRAN programmer, as follows:

CALL FPRQST (OUT, PGSIZE, PGCNT, VBA)

OUT is a logical variable indicating the direction of transfer, i.e., OUT = .FALSE. if a page is to be fetched and OUT = .TRUE. if a page is to be freed. PGSIZE is a bit variable such that PGSIZE = B'0' for small pages and B'1' for large pages. PGCNT is a 4-bit vector giving the number of pages to to be transferred. VBA is a 64-bit descriptor such that the rightmost 48-bits denote the virtual bit address of the first page to be transferred. The details of FPRQST routine are given in [21]. We now demostrate the use of the routine in a program that multiplies the matrices A and B storing the result in C. The matrices A, B and C are N by L, L by R, and N by R, respectively. The matrices are assumed to be stored columnwise, as in STAR FORTRAN [13]. Let $A = (a_1, a_2, \ldots, a_L)$, $B = (b_1, b_2, \ldots, b_R)$ and $C = (c_1, c_2, \ldots, c_R)$, where a_i denotes i th column of A. The algorithm we use forms the successive columns of C using the formula,

$$c_j = \sum_{k=1}^{L} b_{kj} a_k .$$

The corresponding program in STAR FORTRAN can be written as follows.

```
         DO    100    J = 1, R
            DO    10    K = 1, L
               C(1,J;N) = C(1,J;N)+B(K,J)*A(1,K;N)
10          CONTINUE
100      CONTINUE
```

Note that the notation A(i,j;n) denotes a vector considting of n contiguous array elements with the first element being A(i,j).

During the j th execution of the major loop, the program operates on the j th columns of both B and C and the whole array A. After the j th execution, the j th columns of B and C can be discarded from the main memory and the j+1 st columns of B and C can be brought in. However, the data transfer can only be done in the units of a page size (assumed to be equal to Z words). Let us assume that max (N,L,R) ≤ Z. Let DWS(j) denote the data working set of the program during the j th loop, and let P(x) denote the pages containing the subarray x. Then after a little thought, we arrive at the following expression for DWS.

$$DWS(1) = P(A) \cup P(b_1) \cup P(c_1)$$

$$DWS(j+1) = DWS(j) \quad \text{if } \left\lfloor \frac{jL}{Z} \right\rfloor = \left\lfloor \frac{(j-1)L}{Z} \right\rfloor \text{ and } \left\lfloor \frac{jN}{Z} \right\rfloor = \left\lfloor \frac{(j-1)N}{Z} \right\rfloor$$

$$= DWS(j) - P(b_j) \cup P(b_{j+1}) \quad \text{if } \left\lfloor \frac{jL}{Z} \right\rfloor > \left\lfloor \frac{(j-1)L}{Z} \right\rfloor$$

$$= DWS(j) - P(c_j) \cup P(c_{j+1}) \quad \text{if } \left\lfloor \frac{jN}{Z} \right\rfloor > \left\lfloor \frac{(j-1)N}{Z} \right\rfloor$$

$$= DWS(j) - P(b_j) - P(c_j) \cup P(b_{j+1}) \cup P(c_{j+1})$$

$$\text{if } \left\lfloor \frac{jL}{Z} \right\rfloor > \left\lfloor \frac{(j-1)L}{Z} \right\rfloor \text{ and } \left\lfloor \frac{jN}{Z} \right\rfloor > \left\lfloor \frac{(j-1)N}{Z} \right\rfloor.$$

The size of the DWS is constant and is equal to $\left\lceil \frac{N*L}{Z} \right\rceil + 2$ pages.
The above analysis suggests that we insert the code to prepage the first page of both B and C, and all the pages of A just before the J-loop. Between the statements labelled 10 and 100, we can insert the code to free and prepage one page each of B and C, conditionally. However, this procedure does not allow much overlap between the computation and the page transfer. To allow the desired overlap we assume that the program is allotted 2M (M = 1,2,...) page frames more than required to accommodate its DWS. If both N and L divide Z then M=1 is adequate. Otherwise a larger value of M is desirable to achieve enough overlap. Finally to make sure that the three arrays are aligned on a page boundary, each of them should be declared separately in COMMON. With these modifications, the program appears as follows:

    prepage the first page of both B and C

    prepage the whole array A

    prepage the pages numbered 2,..., M+1 of both B and C

    DO   100   J = 1, R

        DO   10   K = 1, L

        C(1,J;N) = C(1,J;N) + B(K,J)*A(1,K;N)

10   CONTINUE

    IF (J*N/Z .EQ. (J-1)*N/Z) GO TO 50

    free the page numbered J*N/Z of the array C

    IF ((J*N/Z+M+1) .GT. $\lceil N*R/Z \rceil$) GO TO 50

    prepage the page numbered (J*N/Z+M+1) of the array C

50   IF (J*L/Z .EQ. (J-1)*L/Z) GO TO 100

60   free the page numbered J*L/Z of the array B

    IF ((J*L/Z+M+1) .GT. $\lceil L*R/Z \rceil$) GO TO 100

prepage the page numbered (J*L/Z+M+1) of the array B

100 CONTINUE.

We will now show how to code the calls for prepaging and freeing using the FPRQST subroutine. We will only do this for the statement labelled 60; others can be translated similarly. This can be done by replacing the statement 60 by the following statement sequence.

ASSIGN DB, B(1, J; Z)

CALL FPRQST (.TRUE., PGSIZE, B'0001', DB)

Note that DB is assumed to be declared as a descriptor to the array B.

Unfortunately, the ADVISE feature does not work in the current version of the STAR operating system. Therefore, we could not test these programs and could not measure the performance improvement obtained by prepaging. Instead, we carry out a timing analysis of the two programs in the next section.

III. THE TIMING ANALYSIS

Let T_z denote the average time to fetch (or push) a page. Let T_d and T_p denote the total times to execute the matrix multiplication program of the previous section with demand paging and prepaging, respectively. We will assume that it takes zero time to push a page that is not modified. Similarly, it takes zero time to fetch a page that is uninitialized. Under demand paging, with a page allotment $\geq$ the size of the DWS $\left(=\left\lceil\frac{N*L}{Z}\right\rceil + 2\right)$, we need to fetch $\left\lceil\frac{N*L}{Z}\right\rceil$ pages of B and we need to push $\left\lceil\frac{N*R}{Z}\right\rceil$ pages of C. Let us denote the cpu time spent in a single iteration of the major loop by T_e. Then

$$T_d = \left(\left\lceil\frac{N*L}{Z}\right\rceil + \left\lceil\frac{L*R}{Z}\right\rceil + \left\lceil\frac{N*R}{Z}\right\rceil\right)T_z + RT_e.$$

Note that T_d is a lower bound which assumes a perfect sequence of replacement as in Belady's MIN algorithm [14].

For prepaging, we assume a page allotment $=\left\lceil\frac{N*L}{Z}\right\rceil + 4$. Since the total number of large pageframes available for data is either 7 or 15 in the STAR system, the largest matrices which we can handle are given by $\left\lceil\frac{N*L}{Z}\right\rceil= 3$ or 12. Since, for a large page, Z = 65,536, fairly large matrices are considered. To simplify the analysis, we assume that L divides N, and both R and N divide Z. Further let N = xL. After a little thought, an upperbound to T_p is easily found to be

$$T_p = \left(\frac{N*L}{Z} + 1\right) T_Z + \left(\frac{R*L}{Z} - 2\right) \max\left[\frac{ZT_e}{L}, (x+1)T_Z\right]$$
$$+ 2 \max\left[\frac{ZT_e}{L}, xT_Z\right] + T_Z.$$

An expression for T_e is derived as follows. During each iteration of the inner loop, one vector multiply (of length N) and one vector addition (of length N) are carried out. The times for these two are given by 159 + N and 71 + $\frac{N}{2}$ in machine cycles of 40 ns each [15].

$$T_e = ((159 + N) L + (71 + \frac{1}{2}N)L)*40*10^{-6} \text{ ms}$$
$$= (60N*L + .92*10^4 L) * 10^{-6} \text{ ms}.$$

The CDC model 819 disk drive is used as paging device. To simplify our analysis, we assume that the three matrices are stored on separate disk drives, and that each matrix is stored sequentially cylinder by cylinder. Then the average time to fetch a page can be expressed as

$$T_Z = T_{seek} + T_{latency} + T_{transfer} = N_{seek} * D_{seek} + \frac{1}{2} D_R + \frac{Z}{R}$$

where

D_{seek} is the time to move the disk head between the adjacent cylinders

N_{seek} is the average seek distance

D_R is the disk rotation time

R is the transfer rate in bits per millisecond.

For the 819 disk, D_{seek} = 15 ms., D_R = 33 ms., and R = 38 * 10^3 bits per ms [16]. N_{seek} is difficult to estimate in general; however, the assumptions made on data layout and the fact the program is running in a monoprogramming environment make reasonable estimates possible. The capacity of an 819 cylinder is very close to the size of a large page.

Therefore, $N_{seek} = 1$ for $Z = 65,536$. Also $N_{seek} \simeq \frac{1}{129}$ for the small pages.

Therefore, for
$$Z = 65,536 = 2^{16}, \quad T_Z = 15 + 16.5 + \frac{2^{16}*64}{38*10^3} \simeq 140 \text{ ms.},$$
and for
$$Z = 512 = 2^9, \quad T_Z = \frac{15}{129} + 16.5 + \frac{2^9*64}{38*10^3} \simeq 30 \text{ ms.}$$

As an example, let $L = 32$, $N = R = 1024$. Using small pages and demand paging, the total execution time is given by

T_d(small page) $\simeq 67,520$, similarly T_p(small page) $\simeq 65,280$ ms.

In this case, we see that a small percentage reduction in the total time is obtained due to prepaging. The reason for this behaviour is that the program is very highly I/O bound. In fact the total I/O time is 65,280 ms., and the total computation time is 2240 ms. The best that can be done by prepaging is to mask all the computation time.

Now for the same problem size, let us use a large page. In this case, T_d(large page) = 4760 ms. We see that more than order of magnitude reduction in the total time is obtained by switching to a large page. Also, T_p(large page) = 2660 ms. Thus, keeping the large page size and using prepaging further obtains a 45% reduction in the total execution time. In this case, we see that the total I/O time is 2520 ms. and the total computation time is 2240 ms. The best that can be done by prepaging is to mask all the computation time. Our prepaging scheme performs very close to the ideal prepaging scheme in this case. It is easy to see that for a nearly balanced program close to 50% reduction in the total execution time can be accrued due to prepaging. However, for a highly imbalanced program, relatively small percentage improvement can be expected. If the program is heavily I/O bound then the use of the large page size can improve the performance by an order of magnitude.

The following table gives the total execution time for different problem sizes with and without prepaging (assuming $Z = 65,536$).

N	L	R	T_d (ms.)	T_p (ms.)
1024	32	1024	4760	2660
1024	64	1024	7000	4900
512	512	512	11920	11080
512	32	512	3160	2520

IV. CONTROLLED PREPAGING

In the current version of the STAR operating system, a global LRU algorithm is used for the page replacement decision. Furthermore, an ADVISE to bring in a page is allowed to increase the page allotment of a program at the expense of some other program. In such an environment, a programmer interested in optimizing his own performance can quickly force out all the other programs from the main memory. With this type of environment, prepaging can only be recommended in a monoprogramming application. Even in a monoprogramming environment (or in multiprogramming environment with a local replacement algorithm) a naive user can fill up valuable space with almost useless pages thus destroying his own performance. The paging algorithm should guard against such possibilities as far as possible.

The first requirement of controlled prepaging is, then, that the user spaces be isolated from each other so as to implement a local paging algorithm in each individual space. Such a situation is desirable even in a demand paging environment [4], [11], [17]. However, if we require a total isolation of the user spaces from each other then we are constrained to the use of a fixed-memory paging algorithm. Since a program's memory requirements are expected to change during its execution, a variable-memory paging algorithm can potentially perform better than a fixed-memory algorithm. To resolve this issue, we allow the user space allocation to vary dynamically, however, the variation is not controlled by the user but is controlled by the system. The space allocation may be based on the performance of a program in the last interval of measurement. For further details see [11], [18], [19], [20]. With this approach, over short time intervals the space allocation can be assumed to be constant and a fixed-memory paging algorithm can be utilized.

In order to prevent a user from misusing the memory space allotted to him we impose the following requirements. When a user expresses the desire to prepage a page, this is not taken as a command but as an advice to the operating system. The operating system may execute it immediately, may defer it or even ignore it. Thus not only a user cannot steal a page away from other user by issuing a prepage request, but he cannot steal a page away from his own space unless the operating system permits it. The system does not allow a prepaged page to be brought in if this requires the replacement of a useful page. Similarly, when a program issues a request to free a page the empty space thus created remains in the space allotment of the program. Thus the space for prepaging is provided by the programmer himself. We assume that when a programmer issues a prepage request he is reasonably certain of the use of that page. Therefore, to avoid an extra page fetch, we require that a prepaged page cannot be replaced until after its first use. The procedure outlined so far is likely to deadlock as follows. Initially when all the space allocated to a program is empty, a programmer can issue repeated prepaging requests filling up the entire space. If, before using any of these pages, he requires (or page faults) another page then a deadlock will occur. To avoid the deadlock, we allow the prepaged pages to fill up at most a fraction $0 \le b < 1$ of the allocated space.

Let N denote the program's address space and let S_t denote the memory state at time t. Let c be the page allotment. The memory state S_t is divided into four disjoint sets: D_t denotes that set of pages which have been declared dead (or free), N_t denotes the set of pages which have been prepaged but not yet set up in the main memory, P_t denotes the set of pages which have been prepaged and set up in memory but not yet used, and $U_t = S_t - P_t - D_t - N_t$ denotes the rest of the pages which have been used at least once. Let $R_A(S,q,x)$ denote the page replaced by the paging algorithm A given that the memory state is S, the control state is q and the page x is to be brought into the main memory. The control state q imposes an ordering on the memory state S to help make the replacement decision. We assume that the ADVISE given by the programmer is either PRE(x) or FREE(x) for some $x \in N$. If we denote the reference string of the program by $r_1,\ldots r_t,\ldots$ then $r_t \in N$ or r_t = PRE(x) for $x \in N$ or r_t = FREE(x) for $x \in N$. Based on a demand paging algorithm A, we now define a prepaging algorithm FPA.

<u>FPA</u>:

[Step 1]   IF $r_{t+1} = x \in N$ THEN

    DO;

       [a]   IF $x \in N_t$ THEN

          DO;

          /* THIS IS ALMOST LIKE A PAGE FAULT.

             THE PROGRAM HAS TO BE SUSPENDED

             UNTIL THE REQUIRED PAGE IS SET-UP

             IN THE MAIN MEMORY, AFTER WHICH */

             $U_{t+1} = U_t + x$; $N_{t+1} = N_t - x$ and RETURN;

          END;

[b]   IF $x \in P_t$ THEN /* SUCCESS */
      DO;
          $P_{t+1} = P_t - x;$
          $U_{t+1} = U_t + x$ and RETURN;
      END;
[c]   IF $x \in U_t$ THEN /* SUCCESS */ RETURN;
[d]   IF $x \notin S_t$ THEN /* PAGE FAULT */
          IF $|S_t| < c$ THEN
              $U_{t+1} = U_t + x;$
                          ELSE DO;
              $U_{t+1} = U_t + x - R_{FA}(U_t \cup D_t, q, x)$ and RETURN; END;
      END;

[Step 2] IF $r_{t+1} = \text{FREE}(x)$ THEN DO;
          IF $x \in U_t$ THEN DO;
              $U_{t+1} = U_t - x;$ $D_{t+1} = D_t + x;$ and RETURN; END;
          IF $x \in P_t$ THEN DO;
              $P_{t+1} = P_t - x;$ $D_{t+1} = D_t + x;$ and RETURN; END;
          IF $x \in N_t$ THEN DO;
              $N_{t+1} = N_t - x;$ $D_{t+1} = D_t + x;$ and RETURN; END;
          END;

[Step 3] IF $r_{t+1} = \text{PRE}(x)$ THEN
          DO;
              IF $|S_t - D_t| < c$ and $|P_t \cup N_t| < b * c$ and $x \notin S_t$
              THEN
                  $N_{t+1} = N_t + x;$

              /* INSTRUCTIONS TO FETCH THE PAGE ARE
              ISSUED NOW. LATER, WHEN THE PAGE IS SET UP
              IN THE MAIN MEMORY IT WILL BE INTRODUCED INTO
              THE SET P_t AND TAKEN OUT OF THE SET N_t

BY SOME OTHER MODULE OF THE OPERATING SYSTEM */
IF $|S_t| = c$ THEN

$$D_{t+1} = D_t - y \text{ FOR SOME } y \in D_t;$$

END;

END FPA;

where

$$R_{FA}(U_t \cup D_t, q, x) \begin{cases} = y \text{ for some } y \in D_t, \text{ if } D_t \neq \phi \\ = R_A(U_t, q, x) \text{ otherwise.} \end{cases}$$

V. CONCLUSION

Many programs operating on large arrays are I/O-bound in the STAR system, and because of the relatively small memory, are forced to run in a monoprogramming environment. It is shown that the use of large pages for these arrays can reduce the I/O time by more than an order of magnitude and thus make it more balanced. Monoprogramming and demand paging imply that no cpu-I/O overlap is achieved. The use of prepaging introduces the overlap and thus reduces the total execution time of the program. If the program is balanced then a substantial reduction in the total execution time is shown to be achieved by prepaging.

The STAR system provides a feature known as ADVISE which supports prepaging. However, this feature does not work at present. The results of this paper will, hopefully, serve as an impetus to debug the feature. Even when this feature starts functioning, we can only recommend prepaging for a monoprogramming environment. We also provide a suggestion for a controlled prepaging algorithm which can be usefully implemented in a multiprogramming environment.

VI. ACKNOWLEDGEMENT

I would like to thank John Knight and Robert Voigt for helpful suggestions during the course of this work.

VII. REFERENCES

1. Knight, J. C.; Poole, W. G.; and Voigt, R. G.: "System Balance Analysis for Vector Computers," Proc. ACM Annual Conference, October 1975, pp. 163-168.
2. Lynch, W. C.: "How to Stuff an Array Processor," Third Texas Conference on Computing Systems, Nov. 1974.

3. Denning, P. J.: "Thrashing: Its Causes and Prevention," Proc. AFIPS SJCC 33 (1968), pp. 915-922.
4. Denning, P. J.: "Virtual Memory," Computing Surveys 2, 3 (Sept. 1970), pp. 153-189.
5. Brandwajn, A.: "A Model of a Time Sharing Virtual Memory System Solved Using Equivalence and Decomposition Methods." Acta Informatica 4, pp. 11-47.
6. Joseph, M.: "An Analysis of Paging and Program Behaviour," The Computer Journal 13, 1 (Feb. 1970), pp. 48-54.
7. Trivedi, K. S.: "Prepaging and Applications to Structured Array Problems," Ph.D. Thesis, University of Illinois, Urbana, June 1974.
8. Trivedi, K. S.: "Prepaging and Applications to Array Algorithms, "IEEE Transactions on Computers, Vol. C-25, No. 9, Sept. 1976, pp. 915-921.
9. Trivedi, K. S.: "On the Paging Performance of Array Algorithms," to appear in IEEE Transactions on Computers.
10. Control Data Corporation STAR-100 Hardware Reference Manual, St. Paul, Minn.
11. Knight, J. C.: "Scheduling Central Resources on the CDC STAR 100," ICASE Report, NASA Langley Research Center, Hampton, Virginia, August 1973.
12. Control Data Corporation STAR-100 Operating System Reference Manual, Sunnyvale, California.
13. Control Data Corporation STAR-100 FORTRAN Language Reference Manual, Sunnyvale, California.
14. Belady, L. A.: "A Study of Replacement Algorithms for a Virtual Storage Computer." IBM Systems Journal 5, 2(1966), pp. 78-101.
15. Control Data Corporation STAR-100 Preliminary Instruction Execution Timing Manual, Arden Hills, MN.
16. Control Data Corporation STAR-100 Peripheral Stations, Revision B, Arden Hills, Minn.
17. Denning, P. J.: "The Working Set Model of Program Behavior," CACM 11 5 (1968), pp. 323-333.
18. Chu, W. W. and Opderbeck, H.: "The Page Fault Frequency Replacement Algorithm," Proc. AFIPS FJCC, 1972, pp. 597-609
19. Denning, P. J.: "On Modelling Program Behavior," Proc. AFIPS SJCC, 1972.
20. Denning, P. J. and Schwartz, S. C.: "Properties of the Working Set Model," CACM 15, 3 (Mar. 1972), pp. 191-198.
21. Trivedi, K. S.: "Prepaging and Applications to the STAR-100 Computer," ICASE Report, NASA Langley Research Center, Hampton, Virginia, August 1976.

APPLICATION OF THE VECTORIZER FOR EFFECTIVE
USE OF HIGH-SPEED COMPUTERS

John M. Levesque
R&D Associates

"Vectorization" is a new style of programming which generates optimal code when used in the development of programs for the "new" generation of computers. With the advent of Vectorization, a corresponding analysis must be performed to determine if existing programs can be translated easily into vector instructions, and how much effort will be required to modify the existing code and make it optimal. This analysis and restructuring process is fairly complex when one considers the requirements which must be satisfied before a particular sequence of code is recognized as being vectorizable.

A recent development by Massachusetts Computer Associates of Wakefield, Massachusetts, is the software package called the "Vectorizer", an outgrowth of an ILLIAC IV research project. This package accepts standard FORTRAN, performs analysis on the DO loops and supplies diagnostics to the user pertaining to the vectorizability of the DO loops. Also, where appropriate, the Vectorizer will generate vector syntax to take advantage of the vector processing capabilities of various machines.

The Vectorizer program performs two basic operations: analysis and code generation. In performing the analysis, the Vectorizer analyzes FORTRAN instruction sequences for possible translation into a vector or array syntax. This phase is independent of the computer the program will run on. During code generation, translation into the vector or array syntax is performed. This phase is extremely machine independent since it must consider peculiar characteristics of the hardware when generating code to utilize a computer's vector capability.

In summary, the Vectorizer program accomplishes the following four steps in vectorizing a FORTRAN code: (1) syntax check, (2) vector analysis and diagnostics, (3) generation of vector sequences, (4) allocation of temporaries necessary when translating into vector syntax. The advantage of using the Vectorizer procedures are that they: (1)

enable the programmer to use standard FORTRAN, (2) recognize vector operations and let the programmer know where vector operations are not possible, (3) enable programs to remain transportable, since they are written in FORTRAN.

It is important that FORTRAN programs be restructured to facilitate recognition of "vector" or "parallel" instructions by the Vectorizer. While the Vectorizer has significant capability for translating FORTRAN DO loops, programmers must understand how to use diagnostics supplied by the analysis phase to assist the vectorizer in producing efficient vector code.

Vectorization, with the use of the Vectorizer, is a unique approach which reduces the amount of programming effort in developing programs which attain significant increases in computational rates on vector or parallel computers. The Vectorizer has been used successfully to generate optimal code for the CDC 7600 and the CRAY 1.

REFERENCES

1. "Review of Case Level II ILLIAC IV Program," R&D Associates, Marina del Rey, CA, RDA-TR-3800-006, Jan. 1975.
2. "Preliminary Results of a Comparative Analysis of ILLIAC IV Languages," papers given at 1975 Sagamore Computer Conference.
3. "Use of ILLIAC IV Disk Memory (14DM)," R&D Associates, Marina del Rey, CA, RDA-TR-3800-007, Sept. 1975.
4. "Investigation of a CFD Translation for CDC 7600," R&D Associates, Marina del Rey, CA, RDA-TR-8000-001, Jan. 1975.
5. "An Efficient CFD Translator for the CDC 7600," R&D Associates, Marina del Rey, CA, RDA-TR-0800-001, Oct. 1975.
6. "Optimal Utilization of Supercomputers, Vol. 1, The Control Data 7600," R&D Associates, Marina del Rey, CA, April 1976.
7. "A High-Speed Software Vector Processing Subroutine Library for the Control Data Corporation 7600," R&D Associates, Marina del Rey, CA, RDA-TR-3400-001, September 1976.
8. "Description and Use of RDALIB," R&D Associates, Marina del Rey, CA, October 1976.
9. "Optimal Utilization of Supercomputers, Vol. 2, The ILLIAC IV," R&D Associates, Marina del Rey, CA, RDA-TR-102701-002, February 1977.
10. "Optimal Utilization of Supercomputers, Vol. 3, The CRAY 1," R&D Associates, Marina del Rey, CA (in prep.).

11. "Description and Use of the Vectorizer," R&D Associates, Marina del Rey, CA, March 1977.
12. "Proceedings of a Conference on Programming Languages and Compilers for Parallel and Vector Machines," ACM SIGPLAN Notices, Vol. 10, No. 3, March 1975.
13. "Control Data's Vector Computer," paper presented at VIM Conference, R&D Associates, Marina del Rey, CA, Oct. 1976.

THE IMPACT OF SCALAR PERFORMANCE ON VECTOR AND PARALLEL PROCESSORS

L. Rudsinski and J. Worlton

During the execution of any given problem, production codes will have substantial interaction with the operating system, if for no other reason than to perform I/O. We have found at LASL that a typical production program spends 5-15% of its compute time in the operating system during its execution. Operating systems are sequential by nature, so even in the most idealistic case where all the algorithms in a code are parallel, scalar mode is inescapable. Thus, when considering the usage of a vector or parallel computer, we must assume a nontrivial amount of computational work will be done in scalar mode. These observations are consistent with Amdahl's findings (1) that, under the best conditions, 15-30% of the compute time will be spent in scalar mode. This paper will address the question of how important this scalar component is with respect to overall performance.

Figure 1 shows the performance bounds for three different ratios of scalar performance in the machines being compared. The values on the ordinate are the ratio of the performance of the scalar-vector machine to the existing scalar machine. The first scale indicates that both machines perform scalar operations equally well. Note that even for an infinitely fast vector processor, the performance gain from 50% vector work is at most a factor of two; the performance gain from 75% vector work is at most a factor of four; etc. This limitation on the performance gain is entirely due to the scalar work that remains after the time to complete the vector work is set to zero.

The second scale in Figure 1 illustrates the situation where the scalar speed of the scalar-vector computer is significantly slower than that of the existing machine. In particular, this ordinate displays the case where the scalar mode of the new machine is one fourth that of the existing machine. Note that we must have 75% vector results just to "catch up" with the performance of the existing scalar machine. Because we are also assuming infinite vector speed, in a real machine with these scalar characteristics vector results will have to be somewhat higher than 75% to "break even." This illustrates the severe penalty of incorporating a slow scalar processor into a scalar-vector architecture.

The third scale in Figure 1 shows the effect of speeding up the scalar processor in a scalar-vector architecture by a factor of two. Clearly, the effect of scalar performance on scalar-vector architecture is profound.

Scalar mode plays a critical role in almost any meaningful calculation. It is so important that if the scalar performance of new supercomputers cannot at least compete with the scalar mode of existing computers, the new machines probably do not warrant further consideration for procurement by users of such machines. On the other hand, if the scalar performance of the new machines is significantly faster than existing machines, then the programs that qualify can be moved directly to these machines with minimal effort and an immediate increase in throughput will be realized. This then allows a gradual modification of these code to exploit both parallelism in algorithms and the new hardware.

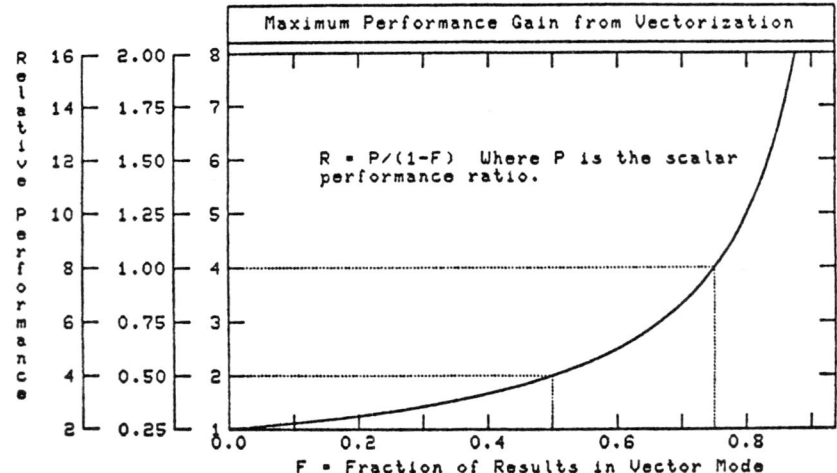

Figure 1.

1. Amdahl, Gene M., "Validity of the single-processor approach to achieving large-scale computing requirements," <u>Computer Design</u>, Vol. 6, No. 12, December 1967, pp. 39, 40.

PERFORMANCE BOUNDS IN PARALLEL PROCESSOR ORGANIZATIONS

Ruby Bei-Loh Lee
Stanford University

This paper considers the bounds on the performance improvement of a p-parallel processor over a uniprocessor, for a given computation. We are particularly interested in the speedup obtained, and show conditions under which this has an upper bound of p/ln p.

I. A MODEL OF COMPUTATION EXECUTION ON A P-PARALLEL PROCESSOR

A *computation* is a sequence of steps. At each step, a finite number (from 1 to p^*) of instructions may be simultaneously executed. p^* is said to represent the *logical parallelism* inherent in the computation.

A *p-parallel processor* is a computer organization with p identical processors, each of which is capable of executing one instruction (not necessarily the same type of instruction) per time-unit. Any number of processors (from 1 to p) may execute simultaneously in a time-unit. p is said to represent the *physical parallelism* available in the computer organization. Let $\{q_i, 1 \leq i \leq p\}$ be the probability that i parallel processors are used in a time-unit, $q_1 + q_2 + \ldots + q_p = 1$.

The *execution* of a computation on a p-parallel processor consists of a mapping from steps in the computation to time-units in the computer organization. If $p \geq p^*$, the number of time-units taken for execution is equal to the number of steps originally present in the computation, and the given computation is said to be executing at *maximum speed*. For the purposes of this paper, we may assume that $p = p^*$. The results for $p > p^*$ and $p < p^*$ are available in [1].

II. UPPER BOUND FOR SPEEDUP

Let T_p be the number of time-units taken by a p-parallel processor to execute a given computation. Then the *speedup* of the p-parallel processor over the uniprocessor (or 1-parallel processor) for the same computation is defined to be $S_p = T_1/T_p$.

It is clear that $1 \leq S_p \leq p$. However, the machine's potential maximum execution bandwidth of p instructions per time-unit is rarely obtained in practice. What order of speedup may then be expected?

First, suppose the distribution $\{q_i, 1 \leq i \leq p\}$ is not known. Let us assume, as usual, for mathematical tractability, that $q_1 = q_2 = \ldots = q_p$. Let H_p denote the pth harmonic number, $H_p = 1 + 1/2 + 1/3 + \ldots + 1/p$. Let ln p denote the natural logarithm of p. We know that $H_p = \ln p + \gamma + O(1)$, where $\gamma = 0.57721\ldots$, called "Euler's constant". So, $H_p > \ln p$. Also as $p \to \infty$, $H_p \to \ln p$, so that we may use ln p as an approximation to H_p, for large p.

Theorem 1: If $q_1 = q_2 = \ldots = q_p$ then $S_p = p/H_p < p/\ln p$

Proof: $S_p = \dfrac{T_1}{T_p} = \dfrac{T_1}{T_1 \cdot \sum\limits_{1 \leq i \leq p}(q_i/i)} = \dfrac{p}{\sum\limits_{1 \leq i \leq p}(1/i)} = \dfrac{p}{H_p} < \dfrac{p}{\ln p}$

Now, suppose we generalise to allow an arbitrary distribution $\{q_i, 1 \leq i \leq p\}$. When will the speedup still be bounded from above by p/H_p? The following theorem gives a necessary and sufficient condition for this to be true:

Theorem 2: $S_p \leq \dfrac{p}{H_p} < \dfrac{p}{\ln p}$ iff $\sum\limits_{1 \leq i \leq p} \dfrac{(q_i - 1/p)}{i} \geq 0$

We note that it is not necessary to know the exact values for all the $\{q_i, 1 \leq i \leq p\}$ in order to use Theorem 2. For example, if we know that the probability that a smaller number of processors is used in a time-unit is greater than or equal to the probability that a larger number of processors is used, so that $q_1 \geq q_2 \geq \ldots \geq q_p$, then the condition in Theorem 2 is satisfied and $S_p < p/\ln p$. Generalizing this, we can show [1] that Theorem 2 is satisfied if there exists k such that $q_i \geq 1/p$, for $1 \leq i \leq k$, and $q_i < 1/p$, for $k+1 \leq i \leq p$.

In order to see if Theorem 2 is satisfied in practice, we compare our result with the empirical speedups tabulated in [2]. The eighty-six programs examined were summarized into seven categories, according to the type of computation involved. These are the data points plotted in Fig. 1, where the average over the seven categories is also shown. Only two categories, involving matrix computations, exceed the p/ln p bound. The majority of the programs, about 80%, have speedups less than p/ln p, and the average over all the empirically derived speedups is O(p/ln p).

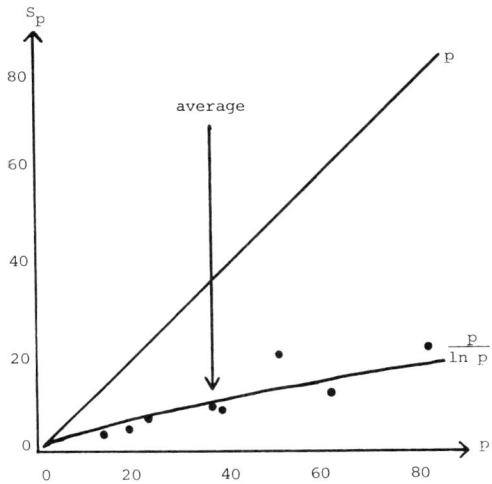

Fig. 1: Speedup versus number of processors

III. SOME RELATED PERFORMANCE MEASURES

Let the *efficiency* of the p-parallel processor be defined as $E_p = S_p/p$, and the *space-time product* as $ST_p = p \cdot T_p$. When Theorem 2 is satisfied, then $T_p \geq (T_1 \cdot \ln p)/p$, $S_p \leq p/\ln p$, $E_p \leq 1/\ln p$ and $ST_p \geq T_1 \cdot \ln p$. Otherwise, $T_p \geq T_1/p$, $S_p \leq p$, $E_p \leq 1$ and $ST_p \geq T_1$. Further discussion is available in [1].

IV. REFERENCES

1. Lee, R.B.L., "Performance Bounds for Parallel Processors", Stanford University DSL Technical Report No. 125, Nov. 1976.
2. Kuck, D., et al, "Measurements of Parallelism in Ordinary Fortran Programs", 1973 Sagamore Computer Conference on Parallel Processing.

AUTOMATIC ERROR ANALYSIS FOR SERIAL AND PARALLEL ALGORITHMS[*]

John Larson
University of Illinois at Urbana-Champaign

Abstract

Using Bauer's approach [1] to relative error propagation in numerical algorithms, methods are presented for performing various error analyses on serial and parallel algorithms. These analyses include: forward analysis, backward analysis, and B-analysis. A forward analysis determines relative error bounds in the computed solution. A backward analysis determines bounds on input perturbations such that the computed solution satisfies the perturbed problem. Finally, a B-analysis determines bounds on input and output perturbations such that the computed solution is near the exact solution of the perturbed problem. Additionally, conditions are specified for when a backward analysis is not possible. This inability reflects the high standard imposed by backward analysis, and shows the need for the B-analysis, which may always be done.

I. SUMMARY

A serial or parallel algorithm may be represented by a directed graph with arcs from operands to results. The graph contains r nodes, of which n are input nodes, ξ_i, and m are output nodes, η_j, where $\eta_j = f_j(\xi_i)$. Each node, assumed to be non-zero, is subject to local relative error (LRE) from representation or floating point computation. The effects of LRE's give rise to a total relative error (TRE) in each node. The relationship between LRE's and TRE's can be stated in the equation: $t = \bar{A}d + \bar{B}g$, where t is a vector of TRE's in output nodes; d and g are vectors of LRE's in data nodes and

---

[*] This work was supported in part by the National Science Foundation under Grant No. MCS75-21758.

computational nodes. $\bar{A}$ and $\bar{B}$ are matrices of partial relative derivatives which specify the effects of LRE's in data nodes and computational nodes on the output node values. A complete description of the generation of this system is given in Larson, Sameh [2].

A forward analysis finds a bound, p, on $||t||$, which, from the above equation, is $||\bar{A}|| + ||\bar{B}||$, since $||d|| \leq 1$, and $||g|| \leq 1$. Alternatively, one may obtain relative error bounds for each output by taking norms of the corresponding rows of $\bar{A}$ and $\bar{B}$. Thus, the computed outputs, $\bar{\eta}_j$, satisfy $\bar{\eta}_j = (1 + \pi_j \varepsilon) \eta_j$, where $|\pi_j| \leq ||\bar{a}_j|| + ||\bar{b}_j|| \leq p$, and ε is the unit roundoff. The quantity $||\bar{A}||$ is the condition of the problem, and $||\bar{B}||$ is the condition of the algorithm.

A backward analysis measures the stability of the algorithm, and here involves comparing two polytopes in R^m: $\bar{A}C_n$ and $\bar{B}C_{r-n}$, where C_k is the unit cube in R^k using the ∞-norm. $\bar{A}C_n$ is the set of all output TRE vectors assuming exact computation (g = 0 and d ε C_n), and $\bar{B}C_{r-n}$ is the set of all output TRE vectors assuming exact data (d = 0 and g ε C_{r-n}). The relative error bound is that expansion factor, θ, such that $\bar{B}C_{r-n} \subseteq \bar{A} \theta C_n$, i.e., $\bar{A} \theta C_n$ just covers $\bar{B}C_{r-n}$. Thus, any computed solution can be obtained by computing exactly with data $\xi_i(1 + \delta_i \varepsilon)$, where $|\delta_i| \leq \theta$; i.e., $\bar{\eta}_j = f_j(\xi_i(1 + \delta_i \varepsilon))$. This covering is not possible if rank $(\bar{A}) < m$.

The B-analysis ("Beidseitige," Panzer [4]) is an alternative stability measurement (Stewart [5]), and allows an additional perturbation in the output. Here, t = $(\hat{t} + \bar{A}d) + \bar{B}g$, where $\hat{t}$ is a LRE vector injected into the outputs. An input and output relative error bound, θ, is found such that $BC_{r-n} \subseteq \dot{A} \theta C_{n+m}$, where $\dot{A} = [I_m, \bar{A}]$, and $(\hat{t}, d) \varepsilon C_{n+m}$. Thus, any computed output, $\bar{\eta}_j$, is within a factor $(1 + \hat{\tau}_j \varepsilon)$ of the exact solution of the problem with data $\xi_i(1 + \delta_i \varepsilon)$, where $|\hat{\tau}_j| \leq \theta$, and $|\delta_i| \leq \theta$; i.e., $\bar{\eta}_j = (1 + \hat{\tau}_j \varepsilon) f_j(\xi_i(1 + \delta_i \varepsilon))$. This covering is always possible since rank $(\dot{A}) = m$.

The technique for B-analysis (and backward analysis) requires knowledge of a particular TRE vector, $\bar{B}g^*$, corresponding to a "worst" set of LRE's, g*. The expansion factor, θ, is governed by this vector, which is a vertex of $\overline{BC}_{r-n}$ of maximal relative distance from $\dot{AC}_{n+m}$. A method used by Miller [3] to obtain an approximate θ is employed to obtain the direction in which $\overline{B}g*$ lies. A projection method is then used to obtain an approximate $\overline{B}g*$. Experimental results indicate that the approximation is very good.

II. REFERENCES

[1] Bauer, F. L., "Computational Graphs and Rounding Error," SIAM J. N. A., Vol. 11, No. 1, pp. 87-96, March 1974.
[2] Larson, J., and Sameh, A., "Efficient Calculation of the Effects of Roundoff Errors," submitted to TOMS.
[3] Miller, Webb, "Software for Roundoff Analysis," TOMS, Vol. 1, No. 2, pp. 108-128, June 1975.
[4] Panzer, Karl, "Gutartigkeit von Rechenprozessen," Technische Universität München, Fachbereich Mathematik, Interner Bericht, Sept. 1974.
[5] Stewart, G. W., Introduction to Matrix Computations, Academic Press, New York, 1973.

SOME NUMERICAL EFFECTS OF A
FORTRAN VECTORIZING COMPILER ON A
TEXAS INSTRUMENTS ADVANCED SCIENTIFIC COMPUTER

Myron Ginsberg
Southern Methodist University

The Texas Instruments' Advanced Scientific Computer (ASC) has a FORTRAN optimizing compiler to utilize the vectorizing capabilities of its pipelined central processor. This paper describes the preliminary findings of a current investigation to assess the influences of both the vectorizing compiler and the pipeline architecture on the numerical behavior of scientific computations implemented in FORTRAN. The project focuses attention on the design, testing, and observation of a set of FORTRAN experiments dealing with relatively elementary sequences of floating-point arithmetic operations likely to be encountered in many large computational problems. Typical test cases involve the effects and monitoring of roundoff error propagation, compile-time versus run-time arithmetic, and vectorization of a variety of floating-point summation techniques. Brief descriptions of a few of these experiments are given below along with information about the computational environment in which the study was conducted. Detailed numerical results are presented in report CS7701, available from the author.

Since the numerical results are somewhat dependent on the specific model of ASC and/or the compiler used, it is important to note the specific environment in which the experiments were executed. A 1-pipe ASC (serial number 6) was used with the FORTRAN NX compiler. This compiler permits several levels of optimization. Each experiment was run under each of the following three options: Level I - minimal optimization with no attempt at re-ordering instructions; Level J - local re-ordering of source logic and of object code to minimize delays in the pipeline; Level K - full optimization (vectorization) on source code (where no vector hazard is detected) along with the re-ordering of Level J. Experiments are currently also being run using the FORTRAN FX compiler which provides fast compilation and no optimization.

One set of experiments deals with the behavior of individual floating-point arithmetic operations. As on the IBM 360 and 370 series, the ASC defines a single precision floating-point number using a 32-bit word in base 16 format with a six hexadecimal digit mantissa. However, during the course of the investigation, it was found that, unlike the IBM system which uses a single hex guard digit with single precision quantities, the ASC carries along eight hex guard digits through the pipeline for single precision addition and subtraction operations. Other experiments indicate that keeping intermediate single precision results in the pipeline at certain critical points in a sequence of calculations permits some of the eight guard digits to influence the six hex mantissa digits retained in resultants of single precision operations. This phenomenon implies what later experiments have verified - namely, that the creation of vector temporary storage for single precision floating-point calculations can influence the effect of the extra eight guard digits in sequences of intermediate calculations and can then lead to differences of numerical output dependent on how such storage is used.

Another group of experiments involves various techniques for accumulating a sum of floating-point numbers. This problem is important because floating-point summations and inner product calculations frequently occur in large-scale scientific computation. In one sequence of tests, twenty sets of 2048 and 4096 floating-point random numbers in the range (0,1) are summed to determine how the accumulated round-off error is affected at several levels of vectorization. Results were compared with outputs obtained in higher precision. It was observed that for recursive summing the absolute error for the fully vectorized result was on the order of 1000 times smaller than that in similar experiments run on an IBM 360/75. Unvectorized versions were not as accurate but did have the same order of magnitude of absolute error as on the IBM systems. Adding the numbers in ascending order (which tends to reduce round-off errors), although producing a smaller absolute error for the unvectorized versions than for the descending unvectorized versions, was still not as accurate as the ascending vectorized version. These results are consistent with the way vector temporary space is allocated by the compiler generated code.

Additional experiments are being conducted using floating-point random numbers covering the entire range of the machine and applying additional software techniques to improve the accuracy of double precision floating-point summation and inner product calculations. It is hoped that these and other tests will assist in characterizing the behavior of large-scale scientific computations on the ASC.

COMPUTERS IN CHEMISTRY: THE AMERICAN CHEMICAL SOCIETY
AND THE
NATIONAL RESOURCE FOR COMPUTATION IN CHEMISTRY

Peter Lykos
Illinois Institute of Technology

I. INTRODUCTION

The technical papers in this "Symposium on High Speed Computer and Algorithm Organization" display clearly that the evolution of information processing technology is leaving the age of general purpose serial processors and is entering the age of specialized, adaptive and highly concurrent devices. An inherent throttle limiting progress in this regard is the lack of an effective two-way channel of communication between the computer user/supporter on the one hand and the computer designer/vendor on the other. Hitherto the truism "what the manufacturer makes, the user takes" has been operating. The example of the Chemistry Establishment and the current national survey of users of large scale scientific computers (1) suggest that at long last the users are beginning to self-organize in order that their computer needs for their real-world problems may be better responded to by computer designers.

II. RANGE OF COMPUTER USE IN CHEMISTRY

A. Current Major Areas of Computer Use in Chemistry

    Real time data logging and experiment control;
    Simulation and modelling of complex chemical systems both static and dynamic;
    Design of synthesis of complex organic molecules;
    Chemical analysis including all types of spectroscopies-especially signal processing; and
    Literature and data information storage and retrieval
        which are leading to:
    Application of artificial intelligence to chemical problem solving;
    Graphic, oral and tactile input/output capability at the

man/machine interface;
Fewer restrictions on use of analytic functions through more facile use of numeric methods;
Fewer restrictions on use of complicated closed form analytic functions through symbol manipulation;
Improved blending of theory and experiment; and
Greater opportunities for phenomenology.

B. Three Specific Examples

1. Chemists think about physical systems in terms of molecular structure. Wilson has augmented the 3-D graphic molecular image with a ball connected to touch-sensitive winches such that the chemist can experience real-time tactile communication with any selected atomic nucleus in the molecule thusly represented. Here is a case where a scientist conceived of a computer application, designed a corresponding algorithm, assessed the speed and storage constraints and designed a corresponding special purpose computer to meet the design specification. Thus was born Touchy-Feely I.(2)

2. The liquid state of matter is the most important and least well understood (i.e., most highly empiricized). A critical point here is how many molecules need to be involved in order that an average over their molecular properties will lead to reliable predictions of bulk properties. Happily the answer seems to be a few hundred in some cases. Rahman and Stillinger (3) first demonstrated the viability of so-called Molecular Dynamics applied to a model of the most complex and important liquid of all - water.

3. Synthesis of complex organic molecules is an important part of chemistry and is amenable to a high degree of systematization. The combination of graph theory, artificial intelligence and a relatively small number of chemical facts seems to constitute a doable approach, via the computer, to the design of such syntheses.(4)

III. AMERICAN CHEMICAL SOCIETY (ACS) COMPUTER-BASED SERVICE AND ACTIVITIES

The ACS is 100 years old, has 110,000 members, and has a long history of effective and modern service to its members and to society as a whole.(5) Only two relevant ACS activities are described here.

A. ACS Chemical Abstracts Service (ACS)

ACS Chemical Abstracts Service (CAS), an operating subsidiary of the ACS, is a $25,000,000 per year operation. It examines 14,000 different primary journals published in 125 nations, patent reports from 26 countries, monographs, books, conference proceedings, government research reports and university theses, all of which generate more than 1,500,000 items per year in 50 languages, and of which about 25% contain information of interest to chemists. CAS produces about 1,500 abstracts per day in machinable form including appropriate code for retrieval. The process includes use of an algorithm for taking a computer graphics terminal image of a molecular structure and incorporating it, with redundancy checking, into the basic CAS File. A steady stream of corresponding computer readable material is distributed via magnetic tapes. They are listed in the 1977 brochure "Information Tools" published by Chemical Abstracts Service.

In addition CAS has designed and is using the Chemical Registry System whereby a unique identification number is assigned to every known compound indexed to a supporting file. Over 3,000,000 substances have been registered and the number increases at the rate of 300,000 per year.

B. Division of Computers in Chemistry (COMP)

The ACS Division of Computers in Chemistry (COMP) came into being in April, 1974, with several objectives including (a) to serve as a forum for computational chemists and (b) to serve as an interface between Chemistry and Computer Science and Engineering. COMP's 20 national symposia conducted thus far have included "Program Certification and Transportability", "Computer Networking and Chemistry", and "Algorithms for Chemical Computation". The next symposium will be held in Montreal on 1 June 77 with The theme "Minicomputers and Large-Scale Computation." In order to improve the chemistry/computer technology interface COMP is in the process of affiliating with the American Federation of Information Processing Societies (AFIPS).

IV. THE NIH-EPA CHEMICAL INFORMATION SYSTEM (CIS)

The sharing of published data constitutes the most obvious and least politically sensitive example of resource sharing through computer networking. A grass-roots coopera-

tive effort (6) is a good example of what chemists can do in
this regard. Fourteen data bases and application programs
are now part of CIS, and seventeen different organizations in
six countries have committed manpower and/or monies toward
the expansion and maintenance of CIS.

V. THE NATIONAL RESOURCE FOR COMPUTATION IN CHEMISTRY (NRCC)

Ever since September 1951, when a group of quantum chemists met at Shelter Island in Long Island, there has been a growing organized interest in and concern about the role of computers in chemistry. In May 1970, the then recently formed National Academy of Sciences-National Research Council Committee on Computers in Chemistry organized a Conference on Computational Support of Theoretical Chemistry. The proceedings of that conference, distributed nationwide as a National Academy of Sciences report, carried a detailed description and recommendation for creation of a National Resource for Computation in Chemistry. The proceedings of that conference also included (a) a comprehensive article on the ARPANet emphasizing both the feasibility and relevance of computer networking, (b) a description of a corresponding European effort already in operation (CECAM) and (c) a list of concerns about the impact of such discipline-oriented centers on university computer centers.

Both the Energy Research and Development Administration and the National Science Foundation became interested in the concept of an NRCC. In 1976, December, three ERDA laboratories, Argonne, Brookhaven and Lawrence Berkeley, submitted proposals to become the NRCC site and it is expected that within one year Phase 1 of the NRCC will be started.

Indeed, as was revealed at a recent National Oceanic and Atmospheric Administration (NOAA)-sponsored briefing of cognizant federal agencies by computer vendors, even the scattered federal laboratories may not be able to tap the potential of computer technology because the vendors are no longer willing to invest large sums in research and development for a high risk market. Scientific computers 100 times more powerful than the CDC 7600 may be technologically feasible by 1980, but a more coherent and organized analysis and demonstration of need will be required by OMB and the U.S. Congress before funding to realize that potential will be made available. The NRCC, and other similar discipline-oriented grassroots demonstrations of relevancy and need, can play an important role in bridging the gap.

VI. THE QUANTUM CHEMISTRY PROGRAM EXCHANGE (QCPE)

QCPE was created many years ago at Indiana University and was initially operated with some federal support as a minimum-level program exchange. QCPE became self-supporting via an NSF grant in the early seventies. QCPE has hundreds of members from all over the world. In addition to exchanging programs, QCPE serves as a communication network via its newsletter and other publications. As an indication of the trend toward complexity of programs used by chemists, a recent analysis of the 16 programs requested most often during 1976 (from the QCPE program library of about 300 programs) showed that they were complex major systems. The most popular of them is Gaussian 70 (QCPE #236) developed by John Pople and collaborators, a program that consists of over 13,000 symbolic cards.

VII. CONCLUSION

The large and developing structure within the chemistry community vis à vis computer applications in chemistry facilitates dialog between chemists and computer designer/vendors. The computer industry will flourish in direct proportion to the extent it is responsive to the needs of computer users/supporters.

VIII. REFERENCES

1. Lykos, P., and White, John, "An assessment of Future Computer System Features Needed for Large Scale Calculations" NCA2-OR320-701; A Joint Research Interchange Between NASA Ames Research Center and the Illinois Institute of Technology, 1976.
2. Wilson, K., "Multiprocessor Molecular Mechanics", chapt. in "Computer Networking and Chemistry". Am.Chem.Soc., Washington, D.C., 1975.
3. Rahman, A., and Stillinger, F., J. Chem. Physics 55, 3336 (1971).
4. For example see "The Discovery of Organic Synthesis Routes by Machine" (Topics in Current Chemistry, Vol. 41 (1973), Springer-Verlag).
5. Annual Report for 1976, ACS in Chem. and Eng. News, 4 April 77, Vol. 55, No. 14, pp. 37-60.
6. Heller, S. R., Milne, G. W. A., and Feldmann, R. J., "A Computer-Based Chemical Information System" in Science, 195, pp. 253-259, 21 Jan. 77.

Referees

ACKERMAN, D. L.
AVIŽIENIS, A.
BAER, J.-L.
BASKETT, F.
BUDNIK, P. P.
BUZBEE, B.
CANTARELLA, R.
CHANG, D.
CHEN, S.-C.
DAVIDSON, E.
DAVIS, E. W., JR.
EMRATH, P. A.
FLYNN, M. J.
GAJSKI, D. D.
GARY, J. M.
GEAR, C. W.
GOLUB, G. H.
HEIMERDINGER, W.
HELLER, D.
HINER, F. P., III
IRWIN, M. J.
JORDAN, T. L., JR.
KELLER, R. M.
KISHI, T.
KOCH, H. S.
KUCK, D. J.
KUNG, H. T.

LANG, T.
LAWRIE, D. H.
LEASURE, B.
LEVESQUE, J. M.
LOSQ, J.
LIU, C. L.
MARUYAMA, K.
MICKUNAS, M. D.
MILLER, R. E.
MIRANKER, W. L.
MOLER, C.
OGUS, R. C.
OLIGER, J.
ORTEGA, J.
PADUA, D.
PARKER, D. S., JR.
REDDY, D. R.
SAMEH, A. H.
STEVENSON, D.
STONE, H. S.
TAGGART, K. A.
TOWLE, R.
VOIGT, R.
WEN, K. Y.
WIRSCHING, J. E.
WOLFE, M.
ZWANKEBURG, R.